DRAW for COMIC BOOKS

Learn and earn in your spare time... at HOME!!

HUNDREDS OF NEW COMIC BOOKS ON SALE HAVE CREATED A TERRIFIC DEMAND FOR ARTISTS! NOW, A COMIC ILLUSTRATION COURSE HAS BEEN PERSONALLY PREPARED BY PROFESSIONAL COMIC BOOK ARTISTS! --TO ENABLE YOU TO BECOME A PROFESSIONAL COMIC BOOK ARTIST YOURSELF! NORMAN MAURER AND JOE KUBERT, THE MEN WHO PRODUCED THE WORLD'S FIRST 3-D COMIC BOOK, WILL TEACH YOU TO DRAW FOR COMIC BOOKS!

HI - I'M JOE KUBERT. IN THESE ART LESSONS, I'LL SHOW HOW TO DRAW STRAIGHT STYLE OR ADVENTURE COMICS! NORMAN AND I WILL GIVE YOU HUNDREDS OF IMPORTANT PROFESSIONAL TIPS -- THINGS THAT WE'VE LEARNED DURING THE 30 YEARS WE'VE BEEN IN THE COMIC BOOK BUSINESS!

I'M NORMAN MAURER. MY SECTION OF THE ART LESSONS WILL SHOW HOW TO DRAW COMIC STYLE OR HUMOROUS COMICS! OUR LESSONS WILL ALSO TELL YOU HOW TO WRITE, LETTER AND COLOR FOR COMIC BOOKS. YOU CAN LEARN BY PRACTICING AS LITTLE AS 15 MINUTES A DAY -- IN YOUR OWN HOME!

TALENT IS NOT NECESSARY! THE DESIRE TO DRAW IS IMPORTANT!! THIS COMIC BOOK ILLUSTRATORS INSTRUCTION COURSE GIVES YOU ALL THE INSIDE SECRETS! SIMPLE LESSONS MAKE LEARNING A JOY! EASY TO UNDERSTAND AS A COMIC BOOK ITSELF! NEW, NOVEL TEACHING TECHNIQUE MAY ENABLE YOU TO DRAW REAL COMIC-TYPE FIGURES IN A MATTER OF MINUTES! ENROLLMENT LIMITED! ACT NOW!

mail this TODAY!

GET COMPLETE FIRST LESSON FOR ONLY $1.00 ! ON OUR MONEY-BACK GUARANTEE or ASK FOR FREE INFORMATION!

TO: SCHOLART INSTITUTE
P.O. BOX 787, DEPT. T-354
BEVERLY HILLS, CALIFORNIA

☐ I AM ANXIOUS TO START IMMEDIATELY. RUSH LESSON #1 TO ME. ENCLOSED, FIND $1.00 IN CASH, CHECK OR MONEY ORDER. MONEY RETURNED IN 10 DAYS IF I'M NOT COMPLETELY SATISFIED!

☐ SEND FREE INFORMATION ON COMIC BOOK ILLUSTRATORS INSTRUCTION COURSE. I ASSUME NO OBLIGATION!

NAME _____
STREET _____
CITY _____
ZONE _____ STATE _____

ORDER BY MAIL SPECIALS

SORRY, WE CANNOT SHIP ORDERS FOR LESS THAN $1.00

50 BIKE DECALS. A terrific assortment of big, colorful decals to dress up your bike, models, luggage, etc. All different — every one a real beauty. Special bargain offer — worth over $2.00. Easy to Apply!
Order No. BD50 $1.00

250 MAGIC TRICKS. Shows you how to amaze & mystify your friends! These magic tricks are amazing — sensational — absolutely fabulous! Every trick fully explained! You can easily do every trick! Nothing Else to Buy!
Order No. MT250 50¢

300 CRAZY SIGNS. Printed on gummed labels . . . to decorate your books, etc. These zany signs & slogans will give you and your friends lots of laughs! They're strictly "nutty" . . . & a real bargain, too. Send for them today!
Order No. CS300 $1.00

500 ASSORTED PENNANTS— Includes all the top BASEBALL teams, FOOTBALL teams—and all the popular COLLEGES . . . printed on gummed label "stickons" that you paste on anywhere. Big bargain offer — only $1.00 for complete set.
Order No. GL350 $1.00

COMIC FELT PATCHES. Grab bag assortment of brilliant, color comic designs printed fine quality felt that you use on your T-Shirt, Jacket, Sweat Shirt, etc. A real bargain offer.
Order No. FP11 $1.00

1001 THINGS THAT YOU CAN GET FREE

500 KRAZY STAMPS Seal letters with a laugh! These are really wild! You get over 500 assorted funny sayings on gummed label stamps that you stick on envelopes, book covers, packages, etc. And what a bargain!
Order No. ST500 $1.00

This List Tells You Where To Send For Free Samples, Books, Foreign Stamps & Coins, Etc. Imagine! They're yours for the asking—hundreds of $$$ worth of free offers and giveaway items by writing to different manufacturers, associations, government agencies, etc. This list tells you where to write for the FREE ITEMS—such as Free Gifts, Free Product Samples, Informative Books, Maps, Show Tickets, Foreign Stamps & Coins, Toys, Films, Posters, etc.

Complete List For Only 50¢
Order #TF1000
SPECIAL-3 LISTS FOR ONLY $1.00

400 CRAZY LABELS. They're wild! You get over 400 assorted zany slogans & funny sayings printed on gummed label "stickons". They're strictly nutty. Terrific for dressing up your letters, school book covers, etc.
Order No. KL400 $1.00

DOLLAR BARGAINS • P.O. BOX 1225-NC • NEWARK 1, N.J.
SORRY, WE CANNOT SHIP ORDERS FOR LESS THAN $1.00

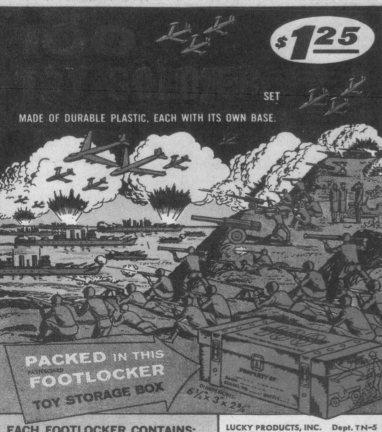

$1.25 SET

MADE OF DURABLE PLASTIC, EACH WITH ITS OWN BASE.

PACKED IN THIS FOOTLOCKER TOY STORAGE BOX
DIMENSIONS 6¼ x 3 x 2½

EACH FOOTLOCKER CONTAINS:

4 Tanks	8 Machinegunners	4 Bombers
4 Jeeps	8 Sharpshooters	4 Trucks
4 Battleships	8 Infantrymen	8 Jet Planes
4 Cruisers	8 Officers	8 Cannon
4 Sailors	8 Waves	4 Bazookamen
4 Riflemen	8 Wacs	4 Marksmen

LUCKY PRODUCTS, INC. Dept. TN-5
BOX 536
WESTBURY, L.I., N.Y.
NO C.O.D.'s
HERE'S MY $1.25!
Rush the TOY SOLDIER SET TO ME!
Name
Address
City _____ State _____ Zip

An Amazing Invention—"Magic Art Reproducer"

DRAW ANY PERSON IN ONE MINUTE

NO LESSONS! NO TALENT

You Can Draw Your Family Friends, Anything From REAL LIFE— Like An Artist.. Even if You CAN'T DRAW A Straight Line!

Anyone can Draw With This Amazing New Invention— Instantly!

De Luxe Model Complete for only $1.98

—With extra high power, extra clear and sharp "reproducer" units.

A New Hobby Gives You A Brand New Interest!
Yes, anyone from 5 to 80 can draw or sketch or paint anything now . . . the very first time you use the "Magic Art Reproducer" like a professional artist—no matter how "hopeless" you think you are! An unlimited variety and amount of drawings can be made. Art is admired and respected by everyone. Most hobbies are expensive, but drawing costs very little, just some inexpensive paper, pencils, crayons, or paint. No costly upkeep, nothing to wear out, no parts to replace. It automatically reproduces anything you want to draw on any sheet of paper. Then easily and quickly follow the lines of the "picture image" with your pencil . . . and you have an accurate original drawing that anyone would think an artist had done. No guesswork, no judging sizes and shapes! Reproduces black and white and actual colors for paintings.

Also makes drawing larger or smaller as you wish.
Anyone can use it on any desk, table, board, etc.—indoors or outdoors! Light and compact to be taken wherever you wish. No other lessons or practice or talent needed! You'll be proud to frame your original drawings for a more distinctive touch to your home. Give them to friends as gifts that are "different," appreciated.

Have fun! Be popular! Everyone will ask you to draw them. You'll be in demand! After a short time, you may find you can draw well without the "Magic Art Reproducer" because you have developed a "knack" and feeling artists have—which may lead to a good paying art career.

ALSO EXCELLENT FOR EVERY OTHER TYPE OF DRAWING AND HOBBY!

Create Your Own Design for All Hobbies! Reproduce on anything!
Copy all cartoons, comics.
Outdoor Scene landscapes, buildings
Copy photos, portraits of family, friends, etc.
Still life, vases, bowls of fruit, lamps, furniture, all objects.
Copy blueprints, plans.

FREE! "How to Easily Draw Artists' Models" This valuable illustrated guide is yours free with order of "Magic Art Reproducer." Packed with pictures showing all the basic poses of artists' models with simple instruction for beginners of art. Includes guidance on anatomy, techniques and figure in action.

SEND NO MONEY! Free 10-Day Trial!
Just send name and address. Pay postman on delivery $1.98 plus postage. Or send only $1.98 with order and we pay postage. You must be convinced that you can draw anything like an artist, or return merchandise after 10-day trial and your money will be refunded.

NORTON PRODUCTS Dept. 548, 296 Broadway New York 7, N.Y.
© Nat'l Comics Pub., Inc., 1961

FREE 10-DAY TRIAL COUPON
NORTON PRODUCTS, Dept. 548
296 Broadway, New York 7, N. Y.
Rush my "Magic Art Reproducer" plus FREE illustrated guide "How to Easily Draw Artists' Models." I will pay postman on delivery only $1.98 plus postage. I must be convinced that I can draw anything like an artist, or I can return merchandise after 10-day trial and get my money back.
Name
Address
City & Zone _____ State _____
☐ Check here if you wish to save postage by sending only $1 with coupon. Same Money Back Guarantee!

SUPERHEROES!

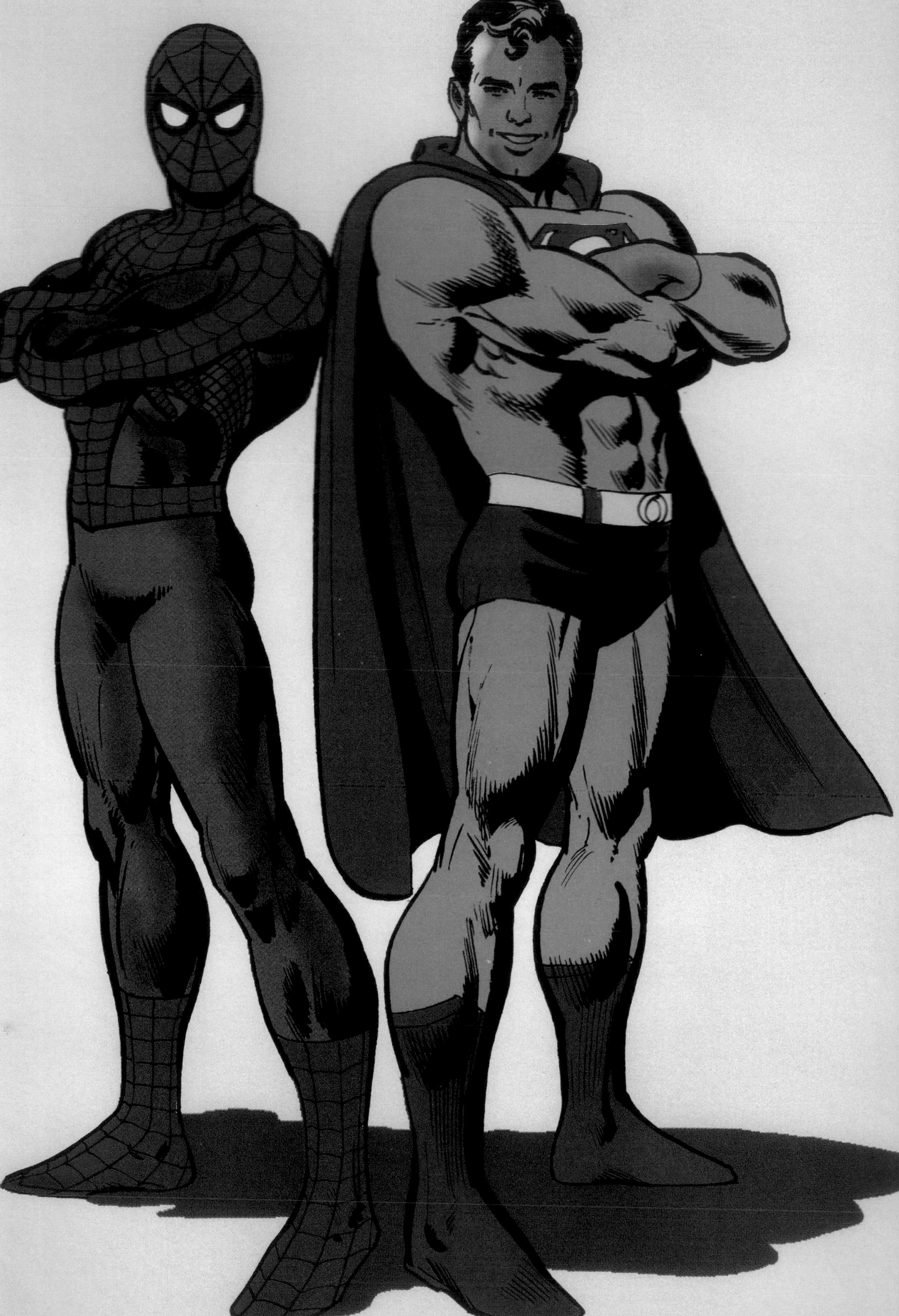

SUPERHEROES!

CAPES, COWLS, AND THE CREATION OF COMIC BOOK CULTURE

Laurence Maslon

Based on a documentary film by

Michael Kantor

A production of Ghost Light Films

CROWN
ARCHETYPE
NEW YORK

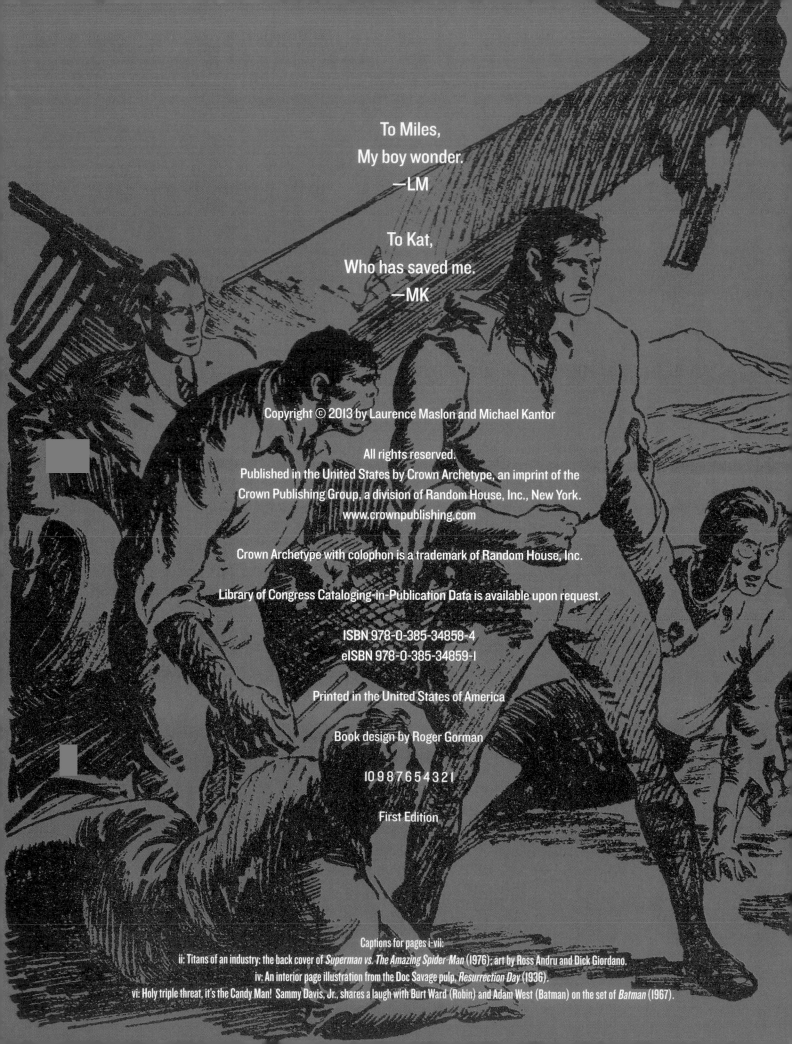

To Miles,
My boy wonder.
—LM

To Kat,
Who has saved me.
—MK

Copyright © 2013 by Laurence Maslon and Michael Kantor

All rights reserved.
Published in the United States by Crown Archetype, an imprint of the
Crown Publishing Group, a division of Random House, Inc., New York.
www.crownpublishing.com

Crown Archetype with colophon is a trademark of Random House, Inc.

Library of Congress Cataloging-in-Publication Data is available upon request.

ISBN 978-0-385-34858-4
eISBN 978-0-385-34859-1

Printed in the United States of America

Book design by Roger Gorman

10 9 8 7 6 5 4 3 2 1

First Edition

Captions for pages i–vii:
ii: Titans of an industry: the back cover of *Superman vs. The Amazing Spider-Man* (1976); art by Ross Andru and Dick Giordano.
iv: An interior page illustration from the Doc Savage pulp, *Resurrection Day* (1936).
vi: Holy triple threat, it's the Candy Man! Sammy Davis, Jr., shares a laugh with Burt Ward (Robin) and Adam West (Batman) on the set of *Batman* (1967).

CONTENTS

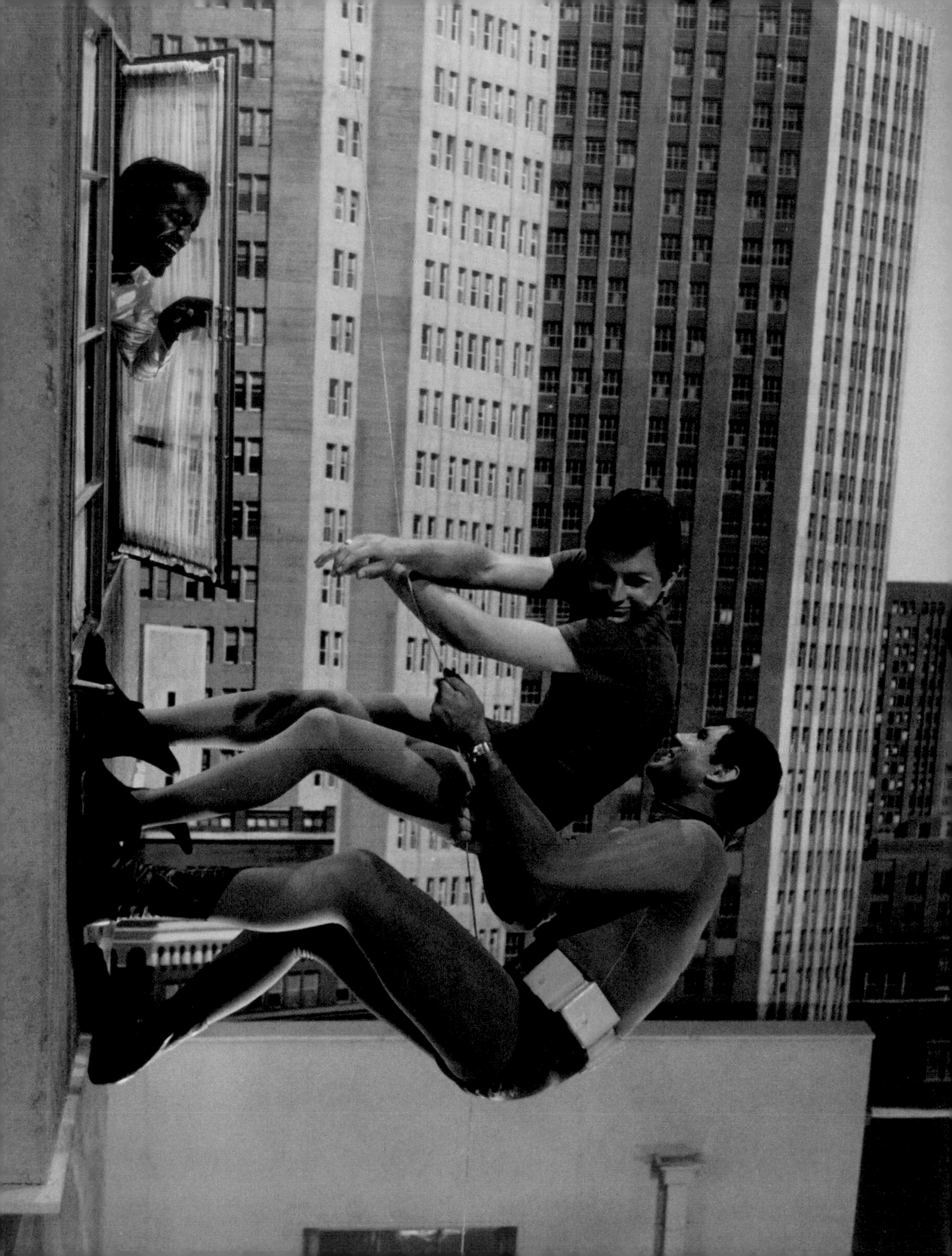

INTRODUCTION

WRITER'S WROSTRUM

Hey there, apostles of adventure!

Everyone has a favorite superhero, whether you first fell in love with Tobey Maguire's Peter Parker or Steve Ditko's original version—no matter how you got there, it's a good bet that your first encounter with a superhero made your heart soar a little higher, your life a little more colorful, your dreams a little bolder. It could be that you were still in your p.j.s one Saturday morning and glimpsed your first superhero on TV, or maybe he burst forth in full Dolby Surround sound in the darkened hush of a multiplex. Or it could be that you're one of those young upstarts who are digging your superheroes on those new-fangled devices, zooming from panel to panel by swiping your fingers across a screen.

But if you've picked up a copy of this book, the odds are good that you've also picked up a comic book at some point in your life. And you probably remember the first time a four-color superhero comic book caught your eye. Maybe it was on a spinning rack on the counter of your friendly neighborhood candy store; maybe it was lent to you by a pal in the bunk above yours at summer camp. Perhaps your mom bought it for you in the supermarket or perhaps you stumbled into a local comic book shop and gasped at the wide array of do-gooders and crime-fighters spread out on shelves against the wall. Still—it's hard to believe that superheroes have only been a part of the American culture for three-quarters of a century.

This companion volume complements our three-hour PBS documentary series, *Superheroes: A Never-Ending Battle*. Most of the time, that battle is between the forces of good and the purveyors of evil. But the battle extends into the conflict between art vs. commerce, expression vs. repression, tradition vs. progress. This book allows us a little more room to investigate and explore the legends of the superheroes and their astonishing cultural impact.

Some caveats: if you're a comic book fan, we can guarantee right up front that one of your favorite characters or titles or storylines hasn't made it into the book. Unlike the comic book universe, space and scope are not infinite here—but if it makes you feel any better, a lot of our favorites were "cancelled," too. Also, the dating of actual comic books is complicated—the cover date on any given comic book is not an accurate representation of when the comic met the public. For bizarre reasons of distribution and accounting, a cover date may register anywhere from two to four months ahead of when readers could buy the issue. When it is important for historical context to explain when a comic book hit the stands, we do so; at other times, we refer to the "official" cover date.

The backbone of both the documentary series and the companion volume are the more than fifty interviews conducted with the best and brightest pioneers in the field of the comic book industry. That said, we have to give an honorary super-team membership card to four extraordinary gentlemen: Joe Simon, Jerry Robinson, Joe Kubert, and Carmine Infantino. Sad to say, they each passed away between the time of their interviews and the completion of this project. It is doubtful that any one of them courted posterity when they got into the embryonic comic book business, but they have certainly earned the respect and admiration of millions of American since.

So, turn the page—we've got thrills, chills, and spills awaiting you! The world of superheroes is full of constantly shifting dynamics (and dynamic duos!), but here's one thing we can promise you: After reading and watching *Superheroes: A Never-Ending Battle*, no mom will ever dare to throw out her kid's comic book collection again!

Onward and upward!

(Literate) Larry Maslon

(Movie-Man) Michael Kantor

1938-1954

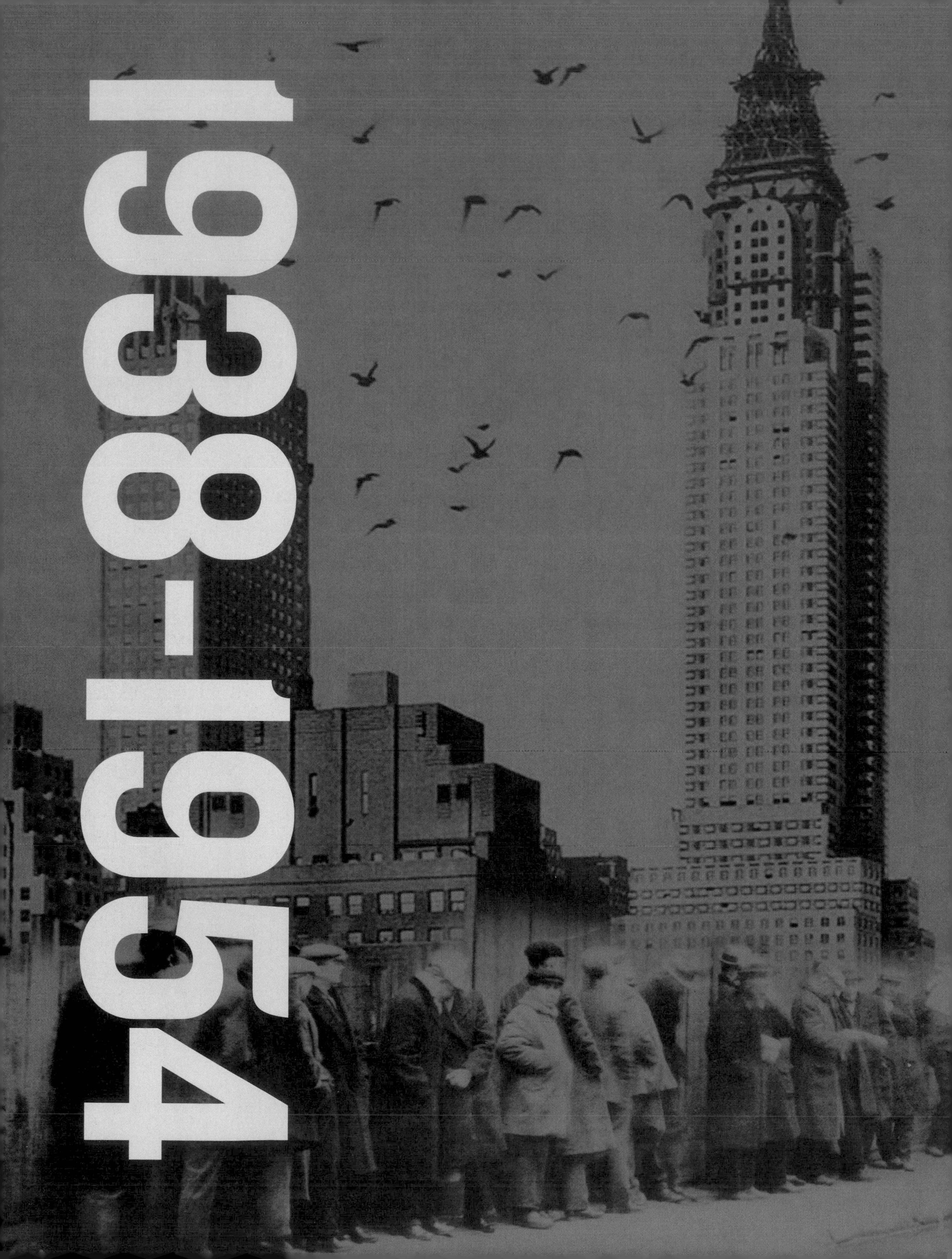

Part One

TRUTH ★ JUSTICE
AND THE AMERICAN WAY

I n the middle of the Great Depression, everything in America seemed rendered in black and white. It was a drab, colorless world, one with stark contrasts. You were either lucky to have a job or, like one-quarter of the workforce, you went begging for one. You were either one of the privileged few, or you were scrambling simply to survive.

Opportunity was also painted with a brush dipped in India ink. Your family could either afford to send you to college, or they couldn't. If you were sent to an influential Ivy League school, you were one of the accepted crowd or you were an outsider, restricted from the inner circle because of your background. If you were a woman, you stayed at home or, if necessary, you got a job. If you were lucky enough to find one, you earned half of a man's salary. In the South, if you were white, you got to vote and move freely in society; if you were black, neither option was available to you.

Harsh reality came in monochrome. Men wore dark suits and white shirts; women wore dresses in a narrow color range from blue to brown. City apartments were painted in dark green or dull cream, and crammed with heavy, dark mahogany furniture. Newspapers were printed in black and white, and so were the interior pages of all books and magazines. Theater programs had none of the spectacular hues to be seen on stage. Photographs were black and white. Movies, which had only recently begun to speak, came in only one variety.

There were exceptions, of course, little flashes of color to catch the eye. Postage stamps had the faint tint of pink or green. Your mother's kitchen might have a red-and-blue canister of Calumet Baking Powder, or a box of Quaker White Oats. If your dad sent you to the corner candy store or newsstand to buy his pack of Lucky Strikes, with its red bull's-eye, you might be tempted by the colorful wrapper of a Baby Ruth or the label on a Coca-Cola bottle. The magazine covers that peeked over the racks—the *Saturday Evening Post* or *Modern Screen* or, if you were an urban kid, *The New Yorker*—enticed the buyer with splashes of color.

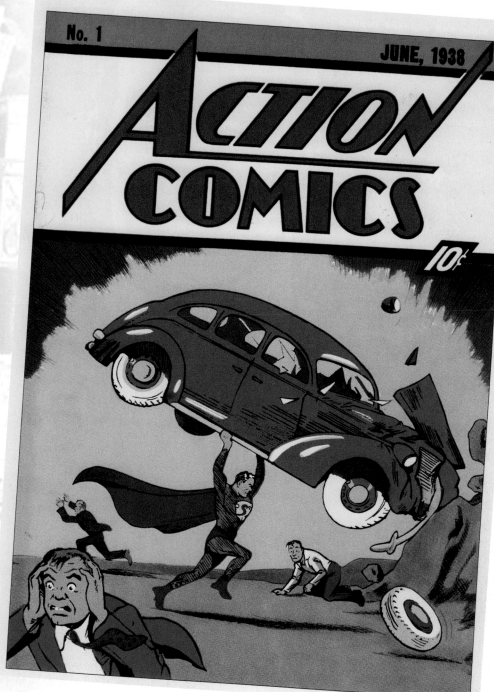

No. 1 JUNE, 1938

ACTION COMICS

10¢

OVERLEAF: A breadline in New York City, 1932. OPPOSITE: A comic book brightens a Depression childhood in the Bronx. LEFT: The milestone that started it all, *Action Comics* #1, 1938.

So, imagine going to that corner drugstore or newsstand for your dad's cigarettes or your own candy bar in the middle of April 1938. The dozen different black-and-white newspapers are filled with news about Germany's annexation of Austria and the Chicago Blackhawks winning the Stanley Cup. Somewhere on that drugstore counter is a spinning rack of ten-cent comic magazines; they were occasionally diverting, but usually filled with reprints from the comic strip pages. This week, there is something different, the debut of a new title: *Action Comics* #1.

On its blazing full-color cover, a well-muscled man in blue leotards with a flowing red cape is hoisting a green car over his head—the entire green car! And when did you ever see a green car? This impossible strongman has an "S" on his chest, but otherwise is completely unidentified on the cover—and certainly there is no warning that he was coming your way. On the bottom left-hand corner of the cover, a man is running toward you, eyes bugging out, head in hands, completely traumatized. This poor fellow has never seen anything like this red-and-blue phenomenon before.

No one had.

It was the beginning of an explosion that would color American culture for decades to come.

If you wanted to indulge in a rainbow explosion of color, however, you had only one option—the Sunday Funnies. If you pried the pages away from your father or your older brother, you could dive headfirst into the adventures of various detectives, spacemen, errant children, hillbillies, strangely proportioned sailors, and a host of other colorful characters. Every major paper across the country had a Sunday section in color, perhaps as a fantastical reward for kids who had to be on their best behavior in church that morning. Yet, the Funnies were meant to be shared with the family; they were never meant to be collected or saved as a child's private property.

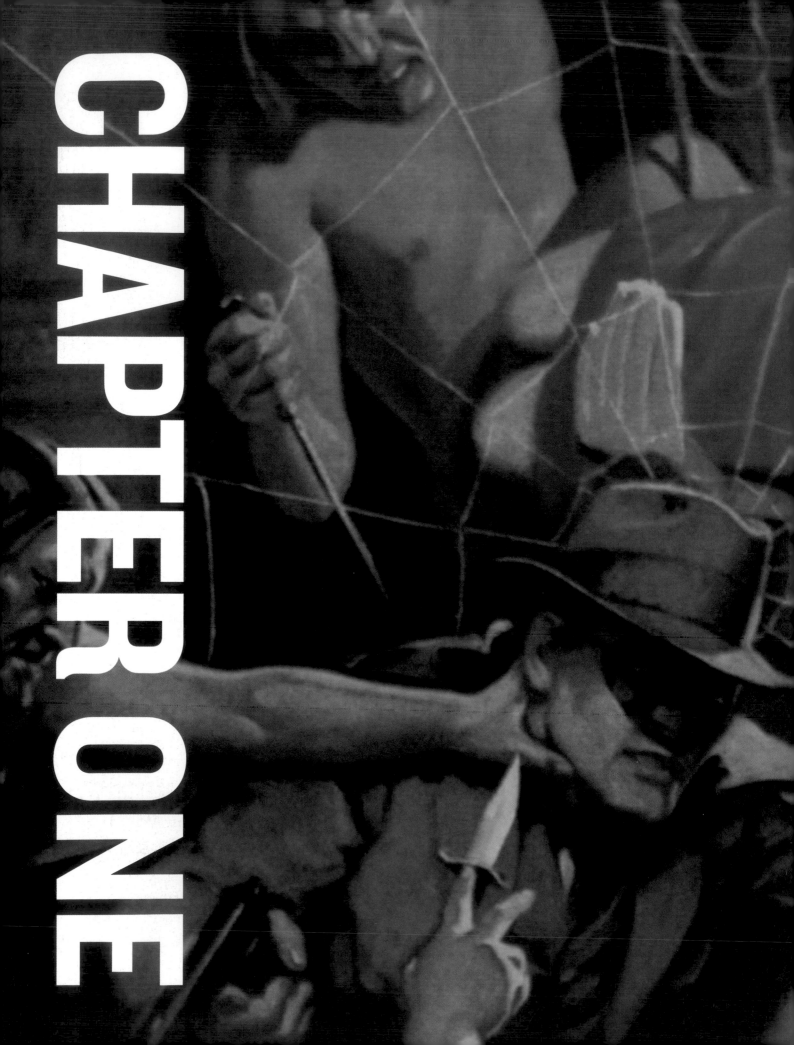

CHAPTER ONE

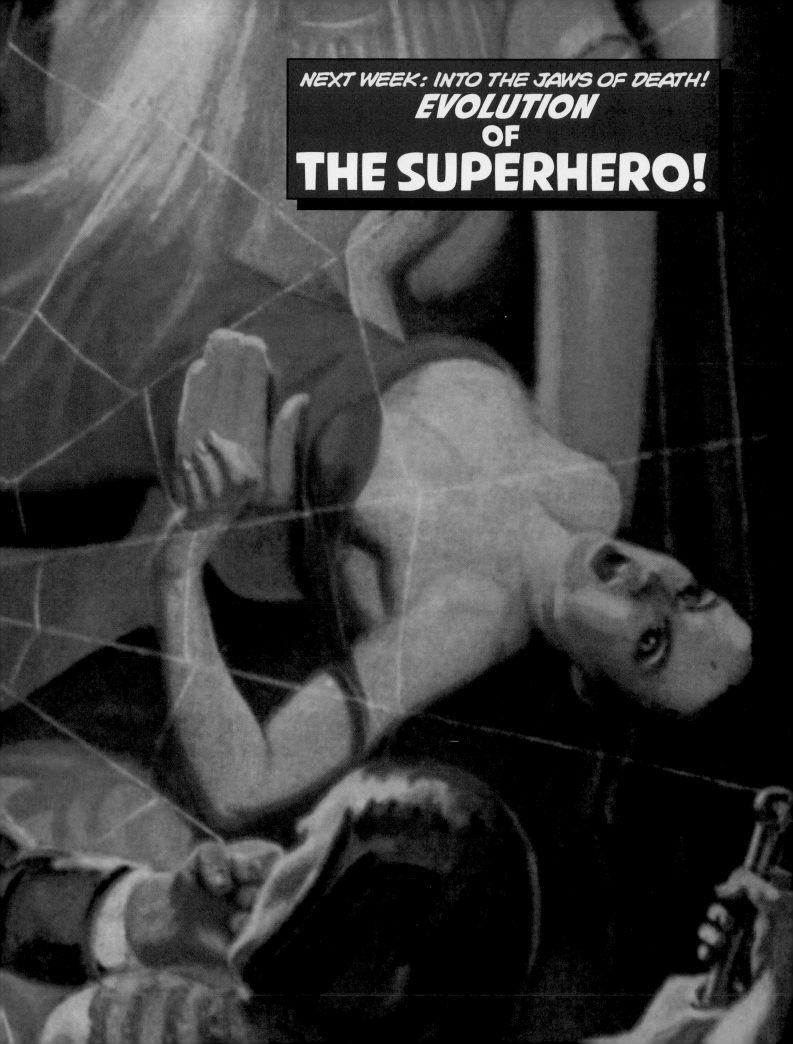

NEXT WEEK: INTO THE JAWS OF DEATH!
EVOLUTION OF THE SUPERHERO!

IN THE BEGINNING
The Comic Strips

here were two kinds of superstars on the funny pages: the colorful characters whose names were emblazoned at the top of the strip, and their creators, whose names were slugged next to them, in bold letters nearly as large.

Comic strips had become an American institution a few years into the 20th century. The early efforts varied in size, format, and quality, exemplified by Winsor McCay's *Little Nemo in Slumberland*, with its idiosyncratic look and exotic appeal. The comic strips were always packaged into a discrete section, popularly known as the "funny papers," or the Funnies. The early Funnies were exactly that—humorous digressions into American life, usually rendered through the antics of misbehaved children, gently embattled families, mismatched friends, or communities thrown into conflict by a variety of implacable or goofy characters. They were a gentle funhouse mirror of American life, and soon evolved from reflecting the American way of life to becoming an indelible part of it. As the popularity of the Funnies grew, so did the money to be made from them: cartoonists routinely submitted their work to national syndicates, who edited, refined, and packaged the strips, then "leased" them to papers around the country. By 1927, the forty million newspapers circulated daily across the nation contained more than two thousand different syndicated features: the vast preponderance of these features was comic strips.

In an age when radio was just beginning to extend its vast empire of the air, the daily newspaper strip was a powerful way of connecting with readers, young and old, and not just connecting with them on a visceral level, but on a *serial* level. The appeal of continuity cannot be overestimated; comic strips hooked readers on a daily basis in an unprecedented way. Aside from the most absurdist strips, or one-panel features, most comic strips developed some kind of narrative thread by the mid 1920s; the phrase "to be continued" supposedly was coined in 1903 for a comic strip. Newspapers quickly caught on to this benign addiction; the best-endowed papers leased the popular strips from the most powerful syndicates, such as the Chicago Tribune-New York News Syndicate and United Feature Syndicate. Woe betide the young fan of *Popeye* or *Blondie* whose father's politics veered to the liberal *New York Herald Tribune*; their escapades were only syndicated in the *Journal American*, a Hearst newspaper with conservative political values.

By the mid 1920s, a new kind of feature was added to the daily paper, an innovation whose power exploded exponentially every Sunday in the full-color sections: the adventure strip. Adventure strips were far more serious in nature and followed some sort of dashing hero (and often his cohorts) who used both might and main, as well as wits, to escape various hazards and perils. Perhaps these strips were inspired by the various real-life heroes, such as Charles Lindbergh, Babe Ruth, and Jack Dempsey, whose exploits were being celebrated in the front and back pages of the newspaper. Perhaps they were the logical extension of the taste for heroic fiction that emerged after the war, such as Edgar Rice Burroughs' *Tarzan of the Apes* or Johnston McCulley's serial "The Curse of Capistrano," which featured the swashbuckling Zorro. Perhaps readers had simply gotten weary of the pranks and silliness of most comic strips. It hardly mattered—the stage was set in 1924 when Harold Gray's Little Orphan Annie found herself in harm's way for the first (but not last) time, and Roy Crane's bumptious feature *Wash Tubbs* introduced a soldier of fortune named Captain Easy who quickly hijacked the strip and, by the end of the 1920s, commandeered the Sunday spread.

OVERLEAF: Pulp hero the Spider. OPPOSITE: Popeye and his wiffle hen. TOP: One of Sunday's greatest spacemen, Buck Rogers (1930). BOTTOM: Lee Falk's *The Phantom*, 1937.

In a seemingly impossible coincidence (although maybe not so improbable in a comic strip), two groundbreaking adventure strips debuted on the same day, January 7, 1929. *Buck Rogers*, a crudely drawn space opera, was repurposed from the pulp fiction adventures about a World War I veteran who was caught in suspended animation and awakened in the 25th century. Although the outer-space antics of Buck and company were to be widely imitated, the more influential strip that landed on the kitchen table with a thump on that cold Monday was *Tarzan*, consummately drawn by Hal Foster who, after a brief respite in 1930, continued with the strip until 1937. Transplanting the resourceful Ape Man from his fictional roots to the graphically exciting world of the comic strip proved to be a natural transition and set a high-water mark for the genre.

In 1934, two other cornerstones of adventure strips appeared. Alex Raymond achieved one of the most astonishing trifectas in comics history when, within two weeks in January, he debuted three separate narrative comic features: the spy strip *Secret Agent X-9* (scripted by, of all people, Dashiell Hammett); *Jungle Jim*, who buckled his swash, unsurprisingly, in the jungle; and perhaps the most ambitious of all strips, *Flash Gordon*, about a rugged blond adventurer who must endure the ultimate alienation effect when he's sent to the planet Mongo to fend off the imperialist mischief of Ming the Merciless. For fans of more down-to-earth adventures there was the ultimate soldier-of-fortune narrative, *Terry and the Pirates*. Created by artist Milton Caniff

THE LANCERS
ARE CAUGHT UNAWARES
FLAME RIFLES TURN THEIR
CAMP INTO AN INFERNO --FLASH AND
DALE ALONE REMAIN ALIVE TO RE-
SIST CAPTURE !----

NEXT WEEK: THE NET CLOSES !

RIGHT: Alex Raymond was perhaps the most admired of cartoonists. LEFT: In this panel of Flash Gordon (and his girlfriend Dale Arden), c.1934–35, one can easily trace the embryonic superheroics of the comics medium.

gangland warfare) showed that crime fighting could pay as well. Perhaps more effective than the strip's relentless, razor-nosed, eponymous detective were the dozens of bizarre, disfigured villains he pursued in the strip, each with an outward manifestation of some corrupt and criminal soul. Other popular and influential strips at the time were *The Phantom* (1936), the first adventurer to kick around in tights and a mask (which magically erased his pupils), and, of course, *Popeye*, who debuted as a featured character in another strip in the late 1920s. The rough-and-tumble sailorman played more as comedy than adventure, but certainly captured young readers' attentions with his feats of super strength (originally derived by rubbing himself with a magic hen!).

The men who created these vibrant characters (often in collaboration with clever editors) were usually trained artists who had attended prestigious art schools; several even had college degrees. They also had a brush or two in the magazine and advertising illustration worlds which, in an age before color photography in magazines, was a respected and lucrative profession. Devoting your entire life to conceiving, drawing, and inking comic strips (which, essentially, was the job description) was not exactly the stuff of their childhood dreams. In fact, Hal Foster took on the *Tarzan* assignment as a stop-gap in his advertising career; he eventually became intrigued enough with comics to return to *Tarzan* and to create the medieval adventures of Prince Valiant, which were rendered in some of the

and drawn in a unique and influential graphic style, the series chronicled a band of heroes across the Eastern Hemisphere.

Tarzan, Flash Gordon, and *Terry and the Pirates* offered comic strip art at its most sophisticated, but Chester Gould's often coarse renditions of violent gunplay in *Dick Tracy* (which debuted in 1931 at the height of America's internecine most handsome and intricate panoramas in comic strip history. Comic strip creators such as Foster, Raymond, Caniff, and Gould became personalities in their own right, featured prominently in newspaper articles, advertisements, and newsreels.

"Alex Raymond had always been an idol of mine," remembers comic book artist Joe Kubert. One day in the late 1930s, Kubert and a high-school chum called Raymond out of the blue and asked if they could interview him for the high school newspaper. Raymond invited them up to his tree-lined estate in tony Stamford, Connecticut:

His valet answered the door. I mean, this was a dream for us. And he leads us to Raymond's studio. Now, I'm coming from Brooklyn, from East New York. And we were just struck dumb by what we saw. In the middle of the studio is this big Great Dane lying on an oval rug. Raymond's got one full wall, all glass where you could see out into the woods. Books lining all the other walls. Shelves of all the stuff that he's done. He must have had all kinds of deadlines on work that he was doing, but he took out three or four hours. We just talked and talked and talked and he answered all our questions with the utmost of kindness. We were so nervous we didn't even sit down.

With lucrative syndicate contracts, endorsements, licensing, and so on, artists such as Raymond could become millionaires smack in the middle of the Depression. And the characters they created grew to have lives of their own; first in the hearts of young and old throughout the country, then on the radio, where many of them appeared in their own highly rated programs, in animated cartoons that often added to their legendary mythos (this is where Popeye traded in his magic hen for some spinach), and even in early movie serials. These daily adventurers had the power to infiltrate the national consciousness on the most popular level—and a mighty power it was, too.

However modest the roots of the comic strip, and whatever aversions these illustrators might have had to the daily grind, they eventually understood and embraced the creative freedom of the comics. As Alex Raymond put it: "I decided that comic art is an art form in itself. It reflects life and times more accurately and is more artistic than magazine illustration, since it is entirely creative. An illustrator works with cameras and models; a comic artist begins with a white sheet of paper and dreams up the whole business—he is playwright, director, editor, and artist at once."

ARTNERS OF **B**
A Smashing Novel

Popular Codes – Stories – F

The Shadow; the pulp incarnation with automatics blazing, 1936.

"CRIME DOES NOT PAY!"
The Bloody Pulps

I n many ways, the modern superhero owes his lineage to a strange interlude between a venerable tradition of heroic fiction and the new technology of the radio.

The appeal of adventure heroes in serialized fiction became obvious as early as 1844, when Alexandre Dumas released the escapades of his Three Musketeers and D'Artagnan in consecutive newspaper installments. Sherlock Holmes appeared before the British public in various magazine publications long before his adventures were collected in various hardcover anthologies. In America, the taste for quickly disposable adventure tales, pitched largely to a young, male audience, found an enduring repository in *Argosy* magazine, a cheaply printed monthly omnibus of tales. By 1896 *Argosy* had morphed into a successful format; it was joined by *The All-Story* in 1905, and, between the two publications (in their various incarnations), memorable characters such as Tarzan, John Carter of Mars, She-Who-Must-Be-Obeyed, and Zorro were given a launching pad to meet the American public.

These repositories of popular fiction could be found every month on every newsstand; each magazine cost the reader only one thin dime, which accounted for the cheap, pulpy paper on which they were printed. The "pulps," as they were popularly called, diversified after World War I, reaching out to selected readers enticed by, say, science fiction in *Amazing Stories*; horror stories in *Weird Tales* (which raised the curtain on Conan the Barbarian); aviation tales in *Flying Aces*; detective stories in *Detective Story*; or even more appealing detective stories in *Spicy Detective Stories*. In the decades before the advent of the paperback novel, these pulps filled an impressive niche for the reading public; in its heyday of the mid 1930s, the publisher Street and Smith Publications, one of the leaders in the field, sold millions of copies of various titles per month.

At the beginning of the Depression, Street and Smith would make an unprecedented commercial decision, one that would bring the world of heroic adventures to its widest audience yet. The publishers were based in New York City, the media capital of the world, so it seemed only natural for them to turn to the radio studio in order to promote their product. In an early example of synergy, the *Detective Story Hour,* a series of mystery dramas designed to promote the anthology detective magazine, debuted in the summer of 1930. Most radio shows needed some kind of host to organize the proceedings for listeners, so *Detective Story Hour* had a mysterious emcee, known only as the Shadow. If Street and Smith expected their penumbral host to sell magazines, the Shadow's haunting laugh was on them: listeners begged for a new magazine that featured the Shadow, while *Detective Story's* press run dwindled.

To their credit, the pulp publishers responded reasonably quickly to the demand, and the following spring, one of the greatest characters in popular culture emerged in his very own magazine.

> "Night—flattened high on the wall, a motionless batlike shadow. Slowly, the shadow begins moving its huge wings outspread in spectre-like form. Suddenly, the staccato cracking of mobster guns, but high above, in the cool night air rings a peal of laughter. The triumph laugh of the Master of Darkness—the Shadow! Thus does the Shadow go forth to battle crime—to vanquish his foes of the underworld and make justice triumph! Crime does not pay! The Shadow knows!"

The Shadow's adventures were ground out by a hearty soul named Walter B. Gibson, who was also an accomplished magician. Some of that magic was sorely needed, as "Maxwell Grant"—Gibson's *de rigueur* pseudonym—was responsible for two entire Shadow novels a month, an assignment that required approximately 140,000 words. Luckily, Gibson, who would write 282 of the Shadow's 325 pulp appearances, adjusted himself to the task with ingenuity: he placed a series of Remington typewriters in various rooms around his country house, just so he could type a sentence or two whenever the mood struck. Whether or not there was a typewriter in the bathroom is lost to history.

The pulp version of the Shadow proved to be enormously resilient, popular, and yet endearingly hard to know; perhaps that's why he was also referred to as the "Master of Darkness." Clad in

LEFT: The publishers of *Spicy Detective* would later form Detective Comics. RIGHT: Mystery solved: that's Orson Welles, who voiced the Shadow briefly in the late 1930s.

a black slouch hat with a billowing red-lined cloak, the Shadow would dispense justice to evil-doers without so much as judge or jury: "He battles crime with thrills and chills and smoking automatics," read one concise advertisement. He had a secret identity, which was constantly shifting; apparently a World War I flying ace named Kent Allard; when he was in New York City, the Shadow also bartered for the identity of Lamont Cranston, a wealthy playboy. Frequently, as a master of disguise, he took on a range of other personalities. The Shadow also used a variety of "operatives" and worked within the boundaries of the law when it suited him. He had an arsenal of weapons, including an early autogyro, a grappling hook, suction cups, and a mysterious ring that hypnotized interlopers. Although he took the occasional jaunt to the Far East (which seemed to hold the monopoly on both international mischief-makers and the go-to destination for the acquisition of super powers), the Shadow toiled within the warehouses, docks, opium dens, and art deco skyscrapers of Manhattan. With his beaky face, swarthy brow, and magnetic eyes, the Shadow was hardly an All-American ideal, in any event.

The Shadow became a breakout character for Street and Smith; by 1937, they yanked the anonymous host of the radio broadcast and created a new program, tailor-made to fit their pulp character. The Shadow's sepulchral voice now emanated from the Mutual Broadcast Network in his own weekly series (initially impersonated by none other than Orson Welles) which became a mainstay of radio drama for two decades. On the airwaves, the Shadow was given some new, mutually exclusive powers from his print counterpart. He now had the ability to "cloud men's minds so that they could not see him"; a regular girlfriend named Margo Lane; and the more regular identity of Lamont Cranston, a "wealthy young man about town." And if his maniacal laugh was still present in both media, the Shadow refrained from blowing evildoers away on the radio. If fans of the Shadow were confused by the difference, they didn't show it: both the pulp magazine and the radio show maintained their relative dominance of the field into the early 1940s. And if this tale of two Shadows was the first example of conflicting narratives for a hero in both print and media, it certainly wouldn't be the last.

The Shadow's popularity spawned a variety of imitators, includ-

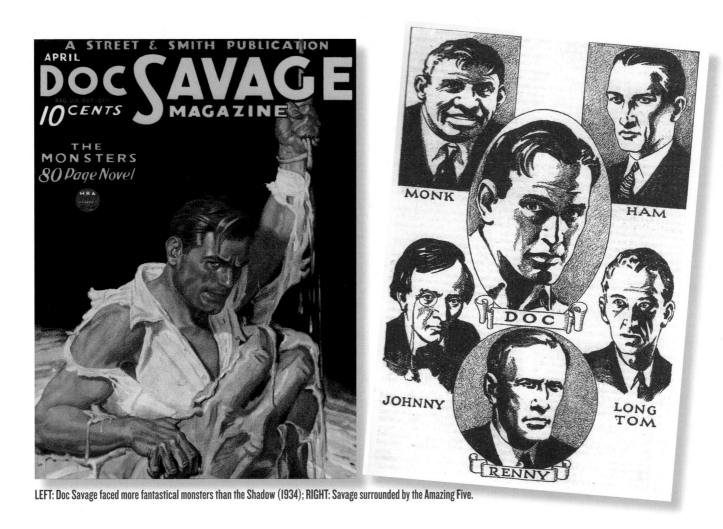

LEFT: Doc Savage faced more fantastical monsters than the Shadow (1934); RIGHT: Savage surrounded by the Amazing Five.

ing the Phantom Detective, another playboy-turned-vigilante. But his significant "other" was an equally indelible character who glistened as brilliantly in the sunlight as the Shadow flourished in the drapes of darkness. Street and Smith sought another marketable title and ordered up an adventurer in the soldier-of-fortune mode. They brought in Lester Dent, a gifted pulp writer with a fondness for gadgets, to refine the idea; and in March 1933, Doc Savage, the Man of Bronze, hit the stands.

If the Shadow played into the complicated scenarios of American vigilantism, Doc Savage was the American dream taken to an almost absurdly exponential degree. Clark Savage Jr. was heir to a mysterious fortune, derived from an unending supply of gold in the jungles of South America. He was raised to be perfect in almost every way; his six-foot-eight frame was covered with a bronze skin "deeply tanned by many tropical suns"; his muscles, developed by a daily routine of calisthenics, were "coiled like pythons." There was no physical feat beyond him, yet he was no clod-like muscleman; his daily regimen included mental logistics of calculus and he spoke two dozen languages. Doc carried an endless supply of gadgets, bombs, and miniature devices in his

oft-ripped shirt or in his utility belt. He even had surgical skills of such magnitude that he could operate on the brains of captured criminals and turn them back to the path of the straight and narrow. He was no shadowy gunman, either; Doc Savage made his headquarters in the center of Manhattan on the 86th floor of the world's tallest building (clearly, the Empire State Building, implied but never named). Anyone who was in trouble knew where to find him; often trouble came directly to Doc and his companions—and did so 181 times, once a month, over the next two decades.

Like most pulp scribes, Lester Dent had a house name imposed on his work—Kenneth Robeson—just in case he couldn't make his onerous deadlines. However, like Walter Gibson, he was devoted to his creation and kept at it for years without a replacement. (His trick for banging out the stories was different than Gibson's: Dent simply stopped mid-sentence when he took a break and picked right back up.) Dent also consolidated the idea of a team of adventurers that had proven effective since the serial escapades of the Three Musketeers. Doc was nearly always accompanied (sometimes claustrophobically so) by his Amazing

A bat? A spider? Those would make pretty good inspirations for masked heroes. Two pulps from the late 1930s.

Five, a band of spiritual brothers who each brought something necessary to the swashbuckling table: one was an ingenious chemist, one a master electrician, another a Harvard-educated lawyer (to negotiate Doc's lease at the Empire State Building, one supposes). Nearly two hundred adventures gives a writer a good deal of narrative breadth; Dent added many original aspects to Doc's mythos, including an impenetrable Fortress of Solitude in the frigid wastelands of the Arctic, where the Man of Bronze would occasionally retreat to better prepare for the battle on behalf of mankind.

It's not hard to discern the pulps' popularity. In addition to their inexpensive price point, they were reliable serial installments of hard-boiled adventures. The Shadow's violent and imperious escapades were the escapist complement to the explosion of gangland violence in the mid 1920s that continued into the 1930s; the Shadow was born into the same generation that deployed the Thompson submachine gun to such lethal effect, and his exploits overlapped with the imprisonment of Al Capone and the shooting of John Dillinger. As for Doc Savage's appeal, his "biographer" Philip Jose Farmer put it aptly: "The average [Depression-era] citizen was feeling frustrated, anxiety-ridden, and diminished. But for ten cents, he/she could be a superman/woman in brain and body. The man who picked up a *Doc Savage* could become for an hour the wealthiest man in the world. . . . Moreover, Doc could take his reader away from his grim world into the most exotic of places around the world."

Although there were actually some skilled graphic illustrations within the pulps, they obviously appealed first to the reader, or at least to one who didn't mind the overbaked, often redundant prose. The real visual enticement of the pulps was their imaginative, colorful covers, which had to condense a hundred pages of action into one spectacular image. Also impressive were the punchy idiosyncratic logos that splashed across the top of the magazine; given the way pulps were shelved on the newsstand, a logo had to be as recognizable as the character. *The Shadow* and *Doc Savage* had huge circulation numbers and inspired a host of imitators who would, in turn, be imitated in the comic book pages. There was the Spider, Master of

LEFT: The ruthless Avenger dispensed justice as a late addition to the pulp genre (1939). RIGHT: Resonant archetype from 1936: the nocturnal swinger in a black cape.

Men, who embossed his criminal prey with a red spider on their foreheads, as well as the Black Bat, a blind district attorney who dressed up in a mask and bat wings to tackle predators. Their successors seem pretty obvious, but there was also the Avenger, probably the most imaginative of second-line pulp heroes, a millionaire who was so traumatized by his family's murder that his hair and skin turned chalk white. He was able to mold his anesthetized face into a variety of disguises, a neat trick if ever there was one.

Still, lording over their progeny were the Master of Darkness and the Man of Bronze. The sheer number of their respective exploits was unprecedented—it was the first time since Sherlock Holmes that a popular heroic character could assemble both an extended biography as well as an apocrypha. Like many comic strip characters before them, they found success of sorts in other media: comic books, films, merchandise. Their fortunes in popular media were complementary: the Shadow had a major radio show, while Doc's never got out of the starting blocks. Likewise, *Doc Savage* had an astonishing revival in paperback reprints back in 1964, while *The Shadow* reprints didn't really catch on with a new generation. Still, both heroes cast long shadows, as it were. Doc Savage, born out of the action tradition, was, indeed, the modern superman, a paragon of clean living and ethical philanthropy, who stood proudly in the sunlight of America's metropolis to right wrongs. The Shadow, showcased in a detective magazine, was more of a morally ambivalent, nocturnal do-gooder, who haunted the darker corridors of the American character and the urban landscape. The chiseled metallic adventurer and the caped paladin of darkness would be the twin lodestars of the pulp fiction universe.

"ALL IN COLOR FOR A DIME"
The Early Days of Comic Books

The comic book has been with us so long and seems like such an ideal package of art and adventure that it's hard to imagine what a long struggle there was for it to discover its perfect form.

Popular comic strips had been anthologized in various book forms as far back as the beginning of the 20th century, but these were usually one-off experiments used for promotional purposes. By all accounts, the first real stab at a comic

book came out right before the Depression hit. George T. Delacorte Jr., chief of the Dell Publishing Company, exploited the popularity of the tabloid-sized Sunday funny papers by putting out a magazine called, understandably, *The Funnies*. It featured original cartoon material, one feature per page, in a publication the same size as the Sunday tabloid paper; it cost a dime and was published every week. This first attempt at a comic book wasn't a success, however. *The Funnies* lasted only six months, a victim perhaps of too much new stuff, too soon, and too different at a time when everyone was hunkering down, exploring their options as the Depression grew.

The next attempt at a comic book came in 1933, the brainchild of Harry Wildernberg, who ran a concern out of New York called Eastern Color Printing. As a way of helping commercial companies to promote their products, he came up with *Funnies on Parade*, a giveaway item that reprinted a bunch of minor comic strips in color. To the surprise of Wildernberg and his colleague, M.C. (Charles) Gaines, their print run went clean. Although distributors were skeptical that kids would buy reprints of strips they had already read (and presumably discarded), Eastern Color moved forward by putting out a book of strips called *Famous Funnies* #1 in 1934, and charging a dime a copy. It took a while to get off the ground, but within a few months, Eastern was making a nice profit with its 68-page funny books.

Part of the genius of *Famous Funnies* was Eastern's way of repurposing strips so that they would fit within a smaller format— half a tabloid page, turned sideways, and stapled in the middle. It is still, more or less, the dimensional format of comic books that is used today. George Delacorte was impressed enough to take another bite at the apple; in 1936 he turned to Gaines, now allied with the McClure Newspaper Syndicate, to use his color printing presses to put out a new set of comic books. Dell's *Popular Comics* upped the ante by licensing previously published Sunday pages featuring more high-profile characters such as Dick Tracy. It wasn't long before the syndicates realized they might do better by putting out their own comic reprints, rather than leasing them to Delacorte or anyone else. And so, by the beginning of 1937, eager readers with ten cents to spare could catch up on the adventures of Popeye and Flash Gordon in *King Comics*; Li'l Abner and Hal Foster's Tarzan in *Tip Top Comics* (published by United Feature Syndicate, which owned the characters); or Little Orphan Annie and Dick Tracy, reclaimed by the Chicago Tribune–New York News Syndicate in *Super Comics*.

Even with all this activity, there was still a piece or two missing from the puzzle: the comics were reprints and mostly featured humor strips. Combining this new visual medium with the slam-bang storytelling of the popular pulp adventure magazine would be the final, game-changing element. The quixotic visionary of this evolutionary step was a former US Calvary officer named Major Malcolm Wheeler-Nicholson. Wheeler-Nicholson had written tales of blood-and-thunder derring-do for various pulps, but his innovation was to come up with a series of more adventure-oriented comic books inspired by the pulp genres, but with original

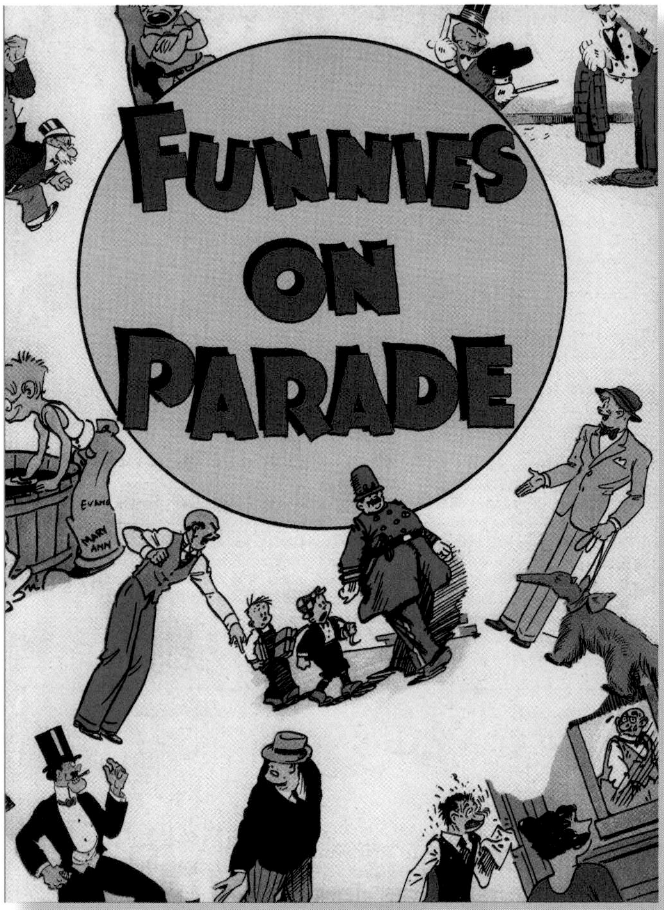
FUNNIES ON PARADE

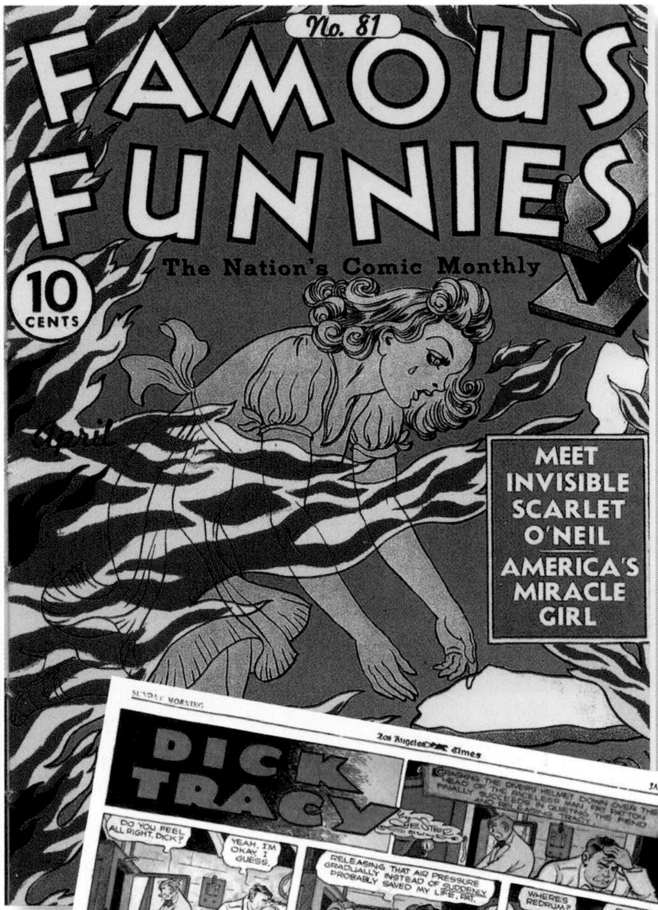
No. 81
FAMOUS FUNNIES
The Nation's Comic Monthly
10 CENTS
April
MEET INVISIBLE SCARLET O'NEIL
AMERICA'S MIRACLE GIRL

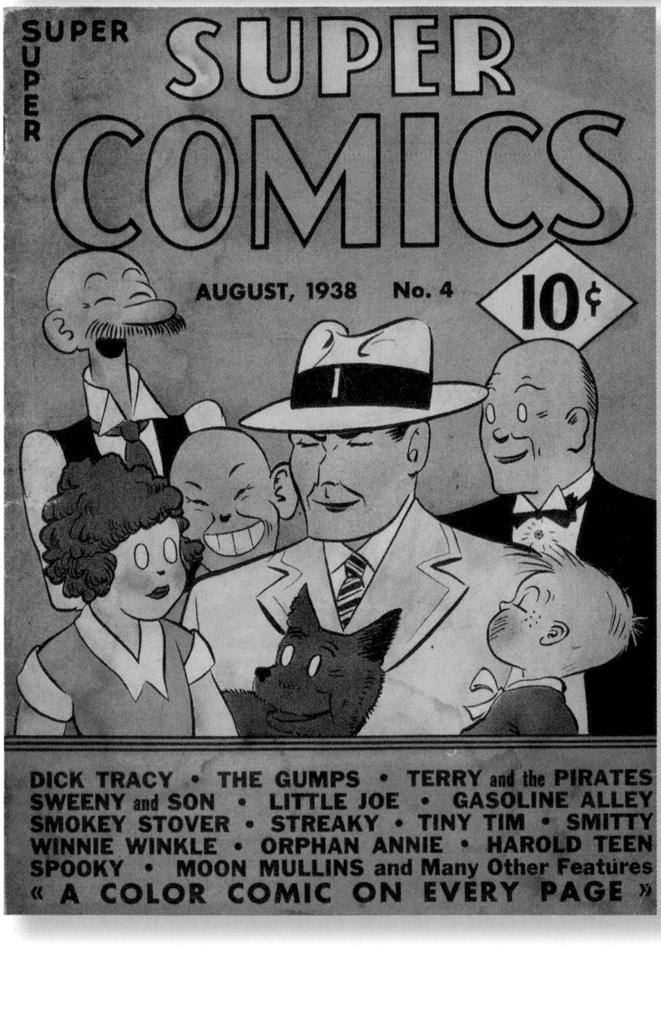
SUPER SUPER SUPER COMICS
AUGUST, 1938 No. 4
10¢
DICK TRACY • THE GUMPS • TERRY and the PIRATES
SWEENY and SON • LITTLE JOE • GASOLINE ALLEY
SMOKEY STOVER • STREAKY • TINY TIM • SMITTY
WINNIE WINKLE • ORPHAN ANNIE • HAROLD TEEN
SPOOKY • MOON MULLINS and Many Other Features
« A COLOR COMIC ON EVERY PAGE »

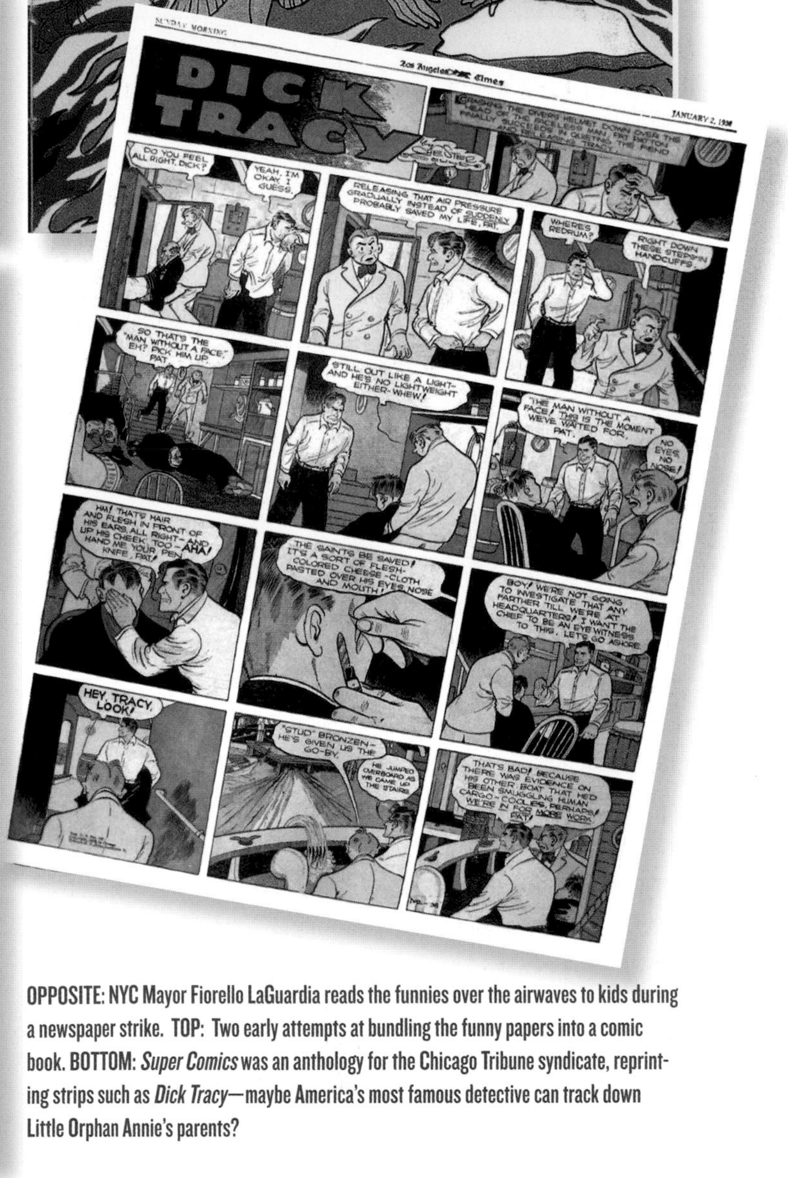
SUNDAY MORNING
DICK TRACY
JANUARY 2, 1938
DO YOU FEEL ALL RIGHT, DICK?
YEAH, I'M OKAY, I GUESS.
RELEASING THAT AIR PRESSURE GRADUALLY INSTEAD OF SUDDENLY PROBABLY SAVED MY LIFE, PAT.
WHERE'S REDRUM?
RIGHT DOWN THESE STEPS'IN HANDCUFFS.
SO THAT'S THE "MAN WITHOUT A FACE," EH? PICK HIM UP, PAT.
STILL OUT LIKE A LIGHT-AND HE'S NO LIGHTWEIGHT EITHER-WHEW!
"THE MAN WITHOUT A FACE!" THIS IS THE MOMENT WE'VE WAITED FOR, PAT.
NO EYES, NO NOSE!
HM! THAT'S HAIR AND FLESH IN FRONT OF HIS EARS, ALL RIGHT-AND UP HIS CHEEK, TOO-AHA! HAND ME YOUR PEN KNIFE, PAT!
THE SAINTS BE SAVED! IT'S A SORT OF FLESH-COLORED CHEESE-CLOTH PASTED OVER HIS EYES, NOSE AND MOUTH!
BOY! WE'RE NOT GOING TO INVESTIGATE THAT ANY FARTHER TILL WE'RE AT HEADQUARTERS! I WANT THE CHIEF TO BE AN EYE WITNESS TO THIS. LET'S GO ASHORE.
HEY, TRACY, LOOK!
"STUD" BRONZEN-HE'S GIVEN US THE GO-BY.
HE JUMPED OVERBOARD AS WE CAME UP THE STAIRS.
THAT'S BAD! BECAUSE THERE WAS EVIDENCE ON HIS OTHER BOAT THAT HE'D BEEN SMUGGLING HUMAN CARGO-COOLIES, PERHAPS! WE'RE IN FOR MORE WORK, PAT!

OPPOSITE: NYC Mayor Fiorello LaGuardia reads the funnies over the airwaves to kids during a newspaper strike. TOP: Two early attempts at bundling the funny papers into a comic book. BOTTOM: *Super Comics* was an anthology for the Chicago Tribune syndicate, reprinting strips such as *Dick Tracy*—maybe America's most famous detective can track down Little Orphan Annie's parents?

The magazine that started the adventure comic book industry: *Detective Comics*, cover date March 1937. OPPOSITE: Editor George Taylor (a predecessor of Perry White) summons Clark Kent (*Action Comics* #5).

MARCH, 1937

Detective COMICS

BRAND NEW! ACTION-PACKED STORIES IN COLOR!

stories. His first, under-capitalized, venture was *New Fun Comics* in 1935, which featured a more mature collection of original strips, albeit in black and white and in a tabloid size. The Major managed to turn out six issues of *New Fun* before it went bust—and he was only able to make it that far by paying younger, inexperienced artists and writers six dollars per page (one of the lowest rates offered) for their derivative detectives and daredevils.

Wheeler-Nicholson might have vanished from history, along with the entire concept of comic book superheroes, had he not persevered after the failure of *New Fun* and sought out additional funding from Independent News Company, a magazine publisher and distributor. The company was created in 1932 by Harry Donenfeld and Jack Liebowitz, both children of Eastern European Jewish immigrants who grew up in New York's rough-and-tumble Lower East Side. They made an unlikely, if complementary and formidable, team. Donenfeld was a gregarious risk-taker with connections to the mob; Liebowitz was a socially conscious bookkeeper with an abacus for a brain and a sense of restraint. Donenfeld had built his business with a series of "Spicy" pulp magazines (*Spicy Detective Stories, Spicy Western Stories*, and so on); near-pornography, or at the very least near-pornography grafted onto detective and western stories. Under the crusading banner of the newly elected mayor of New York City, Fiorello La Guardia, local moralists took a dim view of Donenfeld's brand of publishing appearing on the city's newsstands and in its candy stores. In order to turn the tide and, in some measure, to inoculate their distribution business against any kind of boycott on the shelves, the Independent News Company began to explore the lucrative, and seemingly innocent, world of comic books. Major Nicholson-Wheeler's failed experiments offered Independent News a slightly dilapidated room on the ground floor.

Independent News put up the funding for Nicholson-Wheeler's next two ventures, *More Fun Comics* and *New Comics*, under the condition that the publications come out in color and in the newer,

more compact size. *New Comics* transformed into *New Adventure*, filled with various new adventure stories—again, featuring the usual swashbucklers, big-game hunters, and G-men. As 1936 came to a close, Wheeler-Nicholson became convinced that the comic books could succeed by becoming more like the pulps; e.g., longer stories for more mature readers set in various genres. With the backing of Donenfeld and Liebowitz, he launched *Detective Comics*, which would have been the first detective comic book to hit the market at Christmastime 1936, had the Major been able to cough up enough money to pay the printing bills. (It was beaten to the bare-knuckled punch by *Detective Picture Stories*, published at the end of the year.)

The Major finally found the money to pay the printers, and, in early 1937 (cover date March), *Detective Comics* #1 finally hit the stands. Like most comic books—indeed like nearly all comic books over the next decade—it was an omnibus of different stories varying from four to eight to thirteen pages each in length, in this case featuring an anthology of detective and mystery-oriented types. Even though Wheeler-Nicholson had written a story or two for the book, the premiere issue of *Detective Comics* was also his last; the Major had defaulted on some of his payments, so Donenfeld bought him out to settle his debts. Donenfeld and Liebowitz also subsumed the name of the comic book's title as the larger banner for their new showcase imprint: Detective Comics, Inc.

Would the Major have held out longer if he knew what was beyond the horizon? It's doubtful—he was seriously in debt and, as much as he knew about life in the army, he knew practically nothing about the New York publishing racket and its various snares and stratagems. Donenfeld and Liebowitz also probably had very little prescience about what lay in store. All they knew was that they had acquired a couple of good platforms with which to launch a potential profitable business—their life raft to get them out of the sinkhole of dubious pornography. As to what kind of stories would unfurl out of the comic books they now owned— that was for other, more imaginative, folks to decide.

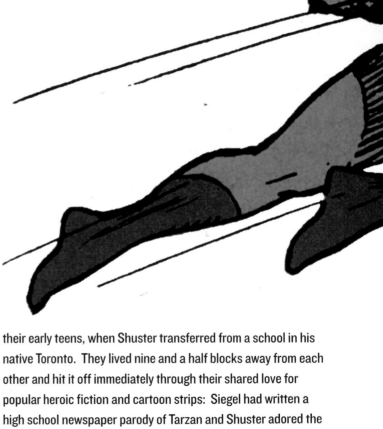

"DESTINED TO RESHAPE THE DESTINY OF A WORLD!"
Siegel and Shuster

Jerry Siegel and Joe Shuster met the way hundreds of kids had done before and, because of the dreams they shared, the way millions of kids would bond ever after.

Siegel and Shuster were paradigms of "geek culture" decades before the term was invented—a term invented largely because of their greatest creation. They were both teenagers, working through their adolescence in a Jewish section of Cleveland. Neither boy ran with the popular crowd; although the bespectacled Jerry loved writing and literature, he wasn't particularly assiduous as a student, and would have to attend summer school. He wasn't an athlete and couldn't compete for the girls. Joe Shuster was slight and small; a loner by nature, he loved to draw and covered butcher paper and wallpaper with sketches from his own imagination.

Jerry and Joe grew up on the fringes of poverty, made even more precarious by the advent of the Depression. There wasn't much money to spend on indulgences; Shuster lived in an apartment, Siegel in a small house. Their fathers were, as was typical for Jewish breadwinners, in the tailoring business and their families had to make do with what little was brought home. The boys spent lonely evenings among uncommunicative families; during the day at school, surrounded by their more ebullient classmates, they were probably even lonelier. Poor Siegel had it even worse; in 1932, when he was eleven, his father died suddenly, either shot during a robbery at his tailor shop, or dropping dead from the shock—newspaper accounts are unclear.

Siegel and Shuster met at Glenville High for the first time in their early teens, when Shuster transferred from a school in his native Toronto. They lived nine and a half blocks away from each other and hit it off immediately through their shared love for popular heroic fiction and cartoon strips: Siegel had written a high school newspaper parody of Tarzan and Shuster adored the cartoon shorts featuring the antics of Popeye. The adventures of silent film star Douglas Fairbanks was a particular favorite of both boys; his derring-do in various features where he played Zorro or D'Artagnan were always pulled off with the grinning panache of unerring confidence—something neither boy had much of.

Siegel was the more entrepreneurial of the two and, like many high schoolers, their friendship was formed when Siegel opened up his more sophisticated fantasy world to his friend. Siegel, enamored with space adventure pulps, produced his own in-house science fiction fan magazine, *Cosmic Stories*, on the school's

crude mimeograph machines and wrote all of the articles himself, using a raft of pseudonyms. He had a grand vision for its national dissemination, beginning with mail subscriptions; he even acquired some fans in the bargain. Had Jerry Siegel grown up in the Internet age, he'd be the first on his block to have a science fiction blog. As it was, he quickly enlisted his new pal to do some illustrations for a second fanzine, *Science Fiction*, and they were up, up, and away.

For the January 1933 issue of their fanzine, Jerry had the idea of a longer story, about a mad scientist who endows a homeless man with incredible strength and the ability to read minds. Joe illustrated the frontpiece. The "superman" becomes corrupt and

the story concludes in a welter of ethically confused endings. They decided to revise their character, now known as the Superman, into a plainclothes hero, and showcased him in a larger illustrated story—an early comic book. Later that year, Siegel, who had the courage of his restrictions, mailed it out to an embryonic comic book publisher, but it was rejected. Shuster was so deflated by the bad news that he destroyed nearly all of the artwork.

Perhaps the idea was too overblown and underbaked at the same time. There was even a crisis of faith on Siegel's part when he tried enlisting a professional cartoonist, the fellow who drew Buck Rogers, to re-imagine Superman on the printed page, but nothing came of it. In the meantime, the boys graduated from high school but kept in touch, tossing one idea after another back and forth, filching different elements of popular culture and stitching them together, like dime-store Dr. Frankensteins: there were strips about robots and G-men and two-fisted soldiers of fortune and far-off planets. It was all in good fun when one was supplying the kids in high school with such yarns but, by 1934, Siegel and Shuster were working odd jobs and living in their parents' homes.

Then, one sweltering summer night in 1934, according to a 1978 interview, Siegel was tossing and turning in his attic bedroom, "when all of a sudden, it hits me. I conceive of a character like Samson, Hercules, and all the strong men I ever heard of rolled into one, only more so." Working furiously through the night, Siegel jotted down a scenario on scraps of paper. As soon as the sun came up, he jogged over to Shuster's folks' apartment and laid out the idea; a superman, only this time, an unalloyed hero—and with a colorful costume out of Flash Gordon or the circus, just to prove he meant business.

Such a magnificent creation deserved only the best showcase—right next to every kids'

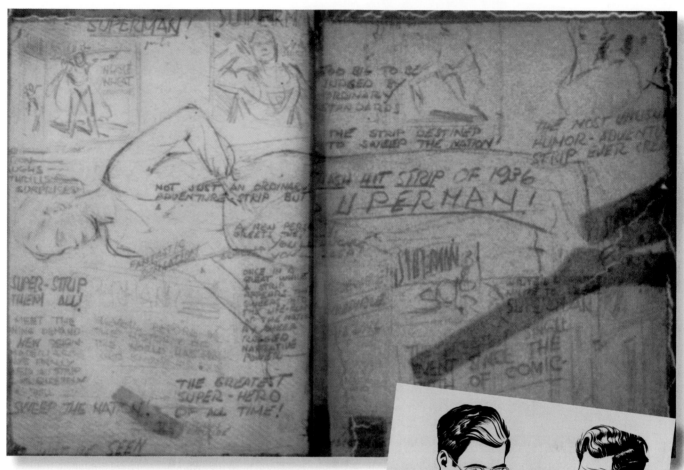

OPPOSITE: Early science fiction fanzines edited and written by Jerry Siegel; Joe Shuster provided the double-page spread. ABOVE: Joe Shuster's seminal sketchbooks for the Superman character. RIGHT: Two pals who would change popular culture, drawn by Shuster himself (1942).

corn flakes at the morning breakfast table. Shuster began to send out *Superman* to every comic strip syndicate he could think of. Siegel and Shuster were met with rejection after rejection from 1935 through 1937. "Too ridiculous." "Come back when you're better." The Bell Syndicate supposedly wrote back: "We are in the market only for strips likely to have the most extraordinary appeal and we do not feel that *Superman* gets into that category." M.C. Gaines at the McClure Syndicate, considered a kind of visionary of the comic book form, offered no encouragement either.

While *Superman* may have been the top of the line in the Siegel and Shuster portfolio, it was not their only creation. Although the high-toned comic strip syndicates weren't interested in their work, the early comic books were happy enough to fill their pages with heroes and adventurers created by two avid kids right out of high school. Before he went bust, Major Wheeler-Nicholson hired them to create some back-up features for his various *Fun* titles, including *Dr. Occult,* probably comics' first supernatural hero, and a series of G-men escapades. The Major sent them his usual stinting fee of six dollars per page. Still, Siegel and Shuster were being published (admittedly under awkward *noms-de-plume*). Toiling away in

Cleveland, nourished by tuna fish sandwiches prepared by their mothers, the boys were living the dream. The tarnish on that dream, however, was still the stacks of Bristol board submissions of *Superman* that lay collecting dust in syndicate filing cabinets in New York and Chicago. It was the embryonic field of comic books that came to the rescue of their comic strip.

In fall 1937, Detective Comics, Inc., was looking to launch another of the genre books to complement their newly acquired detective anthology. The pressure from Donenfeld and Liebowitz to get an action-oriented book on the stands was so intense that the managing editor, Vin Sullivan, had to pull from a backlog of rejected and second-rate submissions. There were the reliable, if uninspired, soldiers of fortune, five-star reporters, and modern-day buccaneers. The closest thing to an exciting hero was Zatara, Master Magician—a Mandrake rip-off who wasn't fooling anyone.

SUPERMAN

"HE'S GRAND! HE'S GLORIOUS! HE'S TERRIFIC! HE'S EVERYTHING YOU'RE NOT! BRAVE, BOLD, HANDSOME, SUPERB!"

OPPOSITE: Two milestone issues: *Action Comics* hits #50 (1942) and the premiere of *Superman*—the first time a superhero achieved his own title.

Even though he didn't really fly for his first four years in print, Superman took off like no other character in popular culture.

In his debut story in *Action Comics* #1, readers are given all they need to know about Superman's background in a cobbled one-page origin story: Superman was an "infant son" launched to earth by his scientist father from a distant planet destroyed by "old age." When he reached maturity, he discovered he had titanic strength that he could channel to benefit mankind, and became "SUPERMAN!"—champion of the oppressed, devoted to helping those in need. The first panel of his exploits has him literally jumping into the fray—the result, perhaps, of the quick cut-and-paste job performed in Cleveland in order to make a deadline. Then, in the course of the next twelve pages, Superman saves an innocent woman from getting fried in the electric chair, implicates the true murderess, serves a wife-beater his just desserts, rescues Lois Lane from the amorous clutches of a mobster, breaks up the mobster's gang, and coerces a confession out of a crooked lobbyist. As Clark Kent, he also manages to put in a day at the office and set up a disastrous date with Lois Lane in the evening. It was, as historian Bradford Wright put it, "a very busy first day on the superhero job."

Superman was the first among not-quite-equals. The Shadow fought crooks who sought to undermine society, but not in broad daylight and not so colorfully. Flash Gordon had a strong jawline and colorful get-ups, but he performed his derring-do far away on another planet. Popeye was impossibly strong, but no one other than Olive Oyl would have fallen for him. Doc Savage held up an impressive ethical value system for righting wrongs, but if he ever cracked a good joke, it went unrecorded. "People were waiting for this character to come along," said artist Jim Steranko. "He was a very appealing individual. He could essentially fly. Bullets would bounce off his chest. He could bend automobile bumpers into pretzels without even being winded. And he had this beautiful basic colored outfit: red, yellow, blue."

Yet, for all of his appeal, it was a while before Superman's publishers harnessed his considerable strength. He was, essentially, the lead feature (thirteen pages per issue) in *Action Comics*, sharing the sixty-four pages with far duller action-oriented characters. For nearly twenty issues, he alternated cover space with car crashes, boat crashes, even French Foreign Legionnaires. As more and more children demanded Superman on the front cover, *Detective Comics* gradually obliged; legends persist that publisher Donenfeld was embarrassed by the costumed character, but the truth is that, in the days before immediate sales reports, it took the publisher months to gin up the Superman engines. Still, only a year after his debut, Superman was given his own book, which devoted all sixty-four pages to the exclusive exploits of the "Man of Tomorrow," as he was dubbed by his publisher; another first for a comic book hero.

Superman's initial exploits indeed centered around being a friend of the helpless and oppressed. He went after racketeers, corrupt munitions dealers, unscrupulous mine owners, and

Superman—By Jerry Siegel and Joe Shuster   *The Superman Is Born*   (Copyright, 1939.)

hoodlums muscling in on circuses; in one story, he even extorts various criminals in order to raise two million dollars to save an orphanage. His frequent retort to malefactors was, "We'll see about that!" Superman didn't solve mysteries or go out on nocturnal patrols: He Saved Things. And in so doing, he found a receptive audience. Jules Feiffer puts it into context:

> Superman came at a time when, as many people saw it, particularly Jews, a super-hero in a wheelchair had entered the White House—and that was [Franklin Delano Roosevelt]. The notion that you could have a superhero who was going to stand up for you, who would be your advocate, was connected to the hope brought on by this larger-than-life figure in the White House. Crippled though he was, F.D.R. had this secret identity, taking off into outer space and solving problems with the New Deal and creating a whole new feeling with the New Deal. Superman was an underground New Dealer.

Superman's powers increased incrementally, as did the dramatic power of his existence. He could hurdle over twenty-story buildings, lift tremendous weights, was impervious to bullets, had astonishing hearing and eyesight. Although he could jump and leap like a grasshopper on steroids (and often appeared swooping down on things), Superman was not given the full power of flight in the comic book continuity until October 1943 (his radio program, out of necessity, conveyed that gift as early as 1940). Gradually, he gained his X-ray vision and adversaries worthy of his overpowering might. The first of the latter was the Ultra-Humanite, a bald, wheelchair-bound mad scientist who appeared hygienically challenged; his vocation as Superman's arch-enemy was ceded to the ingenious, nefarious (and eventually bald as well) Lex Luthor by 1941. Superman's early stories didn't even exploit the drama of his transformation into Superman—he is often shown in a modestly decorated apartment, putting his feet up on the bed while changing into his costume; he could well be going out for a jog. Even his "S" insignia took a while to develop dimension and plasticity—its early manifestations looked like a poor man's Kiwanis Club badge, and sometimes it appears on the back of his cape, sometimes not.

Part of Superman's appeal was his good looks.
As writer Denny O'Neil phrased it: "It was kind of comforting when people realized that although he was a very nearly omnipotent creature, he is straight from the Chamber of Commerce, or the land in which Norman Rockwell paintings exist." And yet, Superman wasn't from the Midwest, at least not initially—he was from

TOP LEFT AND RIGHT: Superman's origin gets expanded for the daily strip, appearing in January 1939. MIDDLE LEFT AND RIGHT: Flying, jumping, or zooming—Superman's power

another planet. This was one of Jerry Siegel's many twists on science fiction tropes and, in a seminal way, perhaps his most effective. Previous heroic characters, such as Flash Gordon, were all-Americans who were spirited away to other planets to fight alien races; Superman was himself of an alien race whose destiny was to be with us. Author Michael Chabon delves into the mythic and cultural ramifications of this journey:

> Superman is an alien. He comes from Krypton. He emigrated to Earth, he left everything behind. That world is gone. He comes here, he changes his name to something that sounds really Gentile, Clark Kent. It's an unintentional metaphor for the American immigrant experience; just leaving all of that behind, coming to America. He transforms himself into the ultimate symbol of the American way of life, like truth, justice, and the American way of life with the flag behind him and his red and blue and gold colors. That was a powerful expression of both a wish that immigrants felt and also that this is the way that you went about doing it and making good in this country.

Superman's Kryptonian origins also took a while to manifest themselves in the comic books. Although the newspaper strip renditions of his adventures (also written by Siegel) laid out the chronicles of his doomed home planet in detail early on—including the names and identities of parents, eventually burnished into Jor-El and Lara—the traumatic events of Superman's arrival on this planet were not embellished until 1948. And it wasn't until a year later that Superman himself learned of his cosmic origins, by flying back in time to trace down fragments of an errant meteor. Of course the fragments would become known as Kryptonite, but not before Superman—in phantom form—shadows his own father and learns the truth of his own beginnings. How could he have known his own story otherwise? Sympathetically, the splash pages of both Krypton stories have Superman holding his head in his hands, bereft on discovering himself the last remnant of an entire culture—survivor guilt in comic book form. (Interestingly, both stories were written not by Siegel, who was booted off the Superman firm by then, but by Bill Finger, Batman's co-creator.) Still, the Krypton stories opened an important door into Superman's psyche; by going back into the Man of Tomorrow's past, scriptwriters found tremendously fertile scenarios in his future for the next seven decades.

In 1938, however, Superman was having a complicated enough time juggling his day job as Clark Kent with his mission of fighting evil as Superman. In popular culture of the 1930s,

of flight grows incrementally as the 1940s begin. **BOTTOM LEFT AND RIGHT:** Clark Kent's powers of transformation were originally much less glamorous (*Action Comics* #47).

newspaper reporters were often portrayed as enterprising crusaders—there were numerous radio shows, movies, and plays devoted to their exploits—and besides, having Clark Kent work for a "great metropolitan newspaper" was convenient for initiating plot lines. Originally, he worked for the *Daily Star* (although nostalgia or sloppiness put him on the *Cleveland Evening News* in *Action Comics* #2). By 1940, Kent was hanging up his shingle at the *Daily Planet*, working for editor Perry White. His real complication lay with the brunette at the desk across the newsroom: reporter and, as Siegel called her, "sob sister" Lois Lane.

The triangle of Clark Kent, Lois Lane, and Superman has become one of the most intriguing and dramatically fertile dysfunctional relationships in pop culture. The bespectacled Clark Kent chases after Lois Lane, who is only put off by the awkwardness of his ardor. In the meantime, Lois pines after Superman, who is equally put off by the excesses of her devotion to him. And therein lies the irony: because Clark Kent and Superman are the same person, the situation becomes a ménage à trois that actually only involves two people. Superman constantly allows himself to be rejected in the form of a false identity he alone has chosen to affect.

Whatever level of masochism that Superman submitted to in this arrangement, at least he seemed to be in on the joke by *Action Comics* #9. As Clark Kent, he tentatively asks Lois out on a date, to which she responds: "Clark Kent—I DESPISE YOU!" When he summons up the courage to ask if there's anyone else in her life, Lois retorts: "He's grand! He's glorious! He's terrific! He's everything you're not! Brave, bold, handsome, superb!" And, of course, he's Superman. Kent walks dejectedly to his office, only to close the door and laugh himself silly at the irony. The very irony of that triangle is the wellspring that has fed thousands of narrative tributaries over the decades. It took nearly ten years before Lois even suspected that Clark himself might be Superman—a suspicion that sparked another wealth of stories.

In the first decade or so of his existence, Superman lived a uniquely peripatetic existence in modern media. Neither Popeye nor the Shadow nor Mickey Mouse had so many venues to promote their escapades—Superman appeared in comic books, comic strips, radio, even cartoon shorts by 1941. In the devil-may-care days of his early existence, there were often maddening zigzags in continuity, for those who cared about such things. Kryptonite makes an embryonic appearance on radio in 1943, then waits until 1949 to reveal itself as a major plot factor in the comic books. That same year, Superman's editors gave him a "Superroom" of his own: a Fortress of Solitude in the arctic north, for contemplation and reflection, which only he could access by virtue of his superhuman strength. (This complete lift from Doc Savage's mythos is made slightly less egregious by the fact that pulp stories had pretty much ground to a halt by 1949.)

But, for all the eventual complications rolled up into his mythology, Superman's initial appearance was as simple and as bold as a thunderbolt. As artist Jim Steranko says, "The only mystery is, what the hell took you so long to get here?"

PAYMENTS TO ARTISTS

NAME *Siegel & Shuster*

DATE SUBMITTED 3/.4/40
DATE PAID
CHECK NO. 3458

FEATURE	PAGES	PRICE	MONTH	REMARKS
1	Superman	13	×60.	#3	
2	Superman - cover		15 -	#5	
3	"Action" Comics cover		15	July -	
4					
5					
6					
7					
8					
9					

TOTAL ×90 -   SIGNED BY

OPPOSITE, FROM TOP: Superman battles his first real supervillain, the Ultra-Humanite (*Action Comics* #14, 1939); Lois Lane's first (but not last) rejection of Clark Kent; Superman experiences his family destiny for the first time (*Superman* #61, 1949). RIGHT: A work-for-hire pay card from 1940. BELOW: Superman was up, up, in the air by 1940.

Sullivan reportedly asked an associate editor and aspiring cartoonist named Sheldon Mayer if there was anything else in the files that might work. Mayer remembered the Superman strip sent to Gaines. Mayer was barely out of his teens himself, and the gee-whiz excitement of the Siegel and Shuster strip appealed to him.

The strip appealed to Sullivan as well; it was just what the pop-culture doctor ordered. Siegel and Shuster had already worked for Detective Comics at this point (they placed a bumptious soldier of fortune named Slam Bradley in the first issue of *Detective Comics*); the letter Sullivan sent to Cleveland was both pressing and professional: "I have on hand now several features that you sent to Mr. Liebowitz. The one feature I liked best, and the one that seems to fit into the proposed schedule, is that, Superman."

Sullivan sent back the strips to Siegel and Shuster, giving them three weeks to reorganize the strips into thirteen pages of comic book story as the lead feature in *Action Comics* #1. Siegel and Shuster were not about to stand on ceremony; if this was not quite the daily newspaper splash they had intended for the super-creation, it would do. They hastily repurposed the submitted strips; cutting panels, elongating others, writing and drawing new transitions, even extending a brief origin and designing a unique logo. At the end of three weeks, Siegel mailed their retrofitted brainchild back to New York; in return, they were given their usual page rate of $10, a total of $130. They also had to sign a release that gave Detective Comics, Inc., the rights to Superman. The boys demurred, but Jack Liebowitz had no desire to enter into legal wrangling: take it or leave it.

The deal that Siegel and Shuster accepted in order to get Superman into print has evolved into one of the more infamous arrangements in American commerce. Some commentators have called it the greatest rip-off since Peter Stuyvesant convinced the Indians to sell Manhattan Island for twenty-four dollars. Others, usually more seasoned veterans, shrug and say, "That's the way it was—once they bought it, they owned it." The truth is somewhere in between. Indeed, with most of popular culture in the 1930s, the producers owned the product, and anything submitted and paid for was a work-for-hire. In Hollywood, other than the studios, no entity got a piece of anything; not directors, not actors, especially not scriptwriters. At exactly the same time that Siegel and Shuster were being offered the chance to have Superman published, Bette Davis was suing Warner Bros. to get out of her studio contract, which declared that she had to act in whatever roles the studio chose for her. She balked, took the Warners to court, lost, and was forced to return to the backlot for them just to make a living, having been wiped out from legal fees.

But the long trail of tears and disappointments suborned by Siegel and Shuster seemed very far in the horizon. Like some Depression-era Hollywood fantasy, their dream was going to become a reality. Cartoonist Jules Feiffer captures the feeling of the time:

> The American story is that we always believe, we always dream. Someday will come around the corner. Something might work out. There was a spirit as a kid living in the 1930s, there was a spirit of optimism; we may be losers, we may be in bad shape, but we are going to end up victorious. I knew for certain that I would end up being a famous cartoonist, by golly—I was going to get what I wanted. And other kids felt they were going to get what they wanted.

In spring 1938, after struggling with their dream for half a decade, it seemed as if two kids from Cleveland were going to get what they wanted, too.

THE MAN OF STEEL ZOOMS UP OVER THE GREAT CITY!

--UP.. --UP!..

CHAPTER TWO

64 PAGES OF THRILL-PACKED ACTION!
EXPLOSION
OF
AN INDUSTRY!

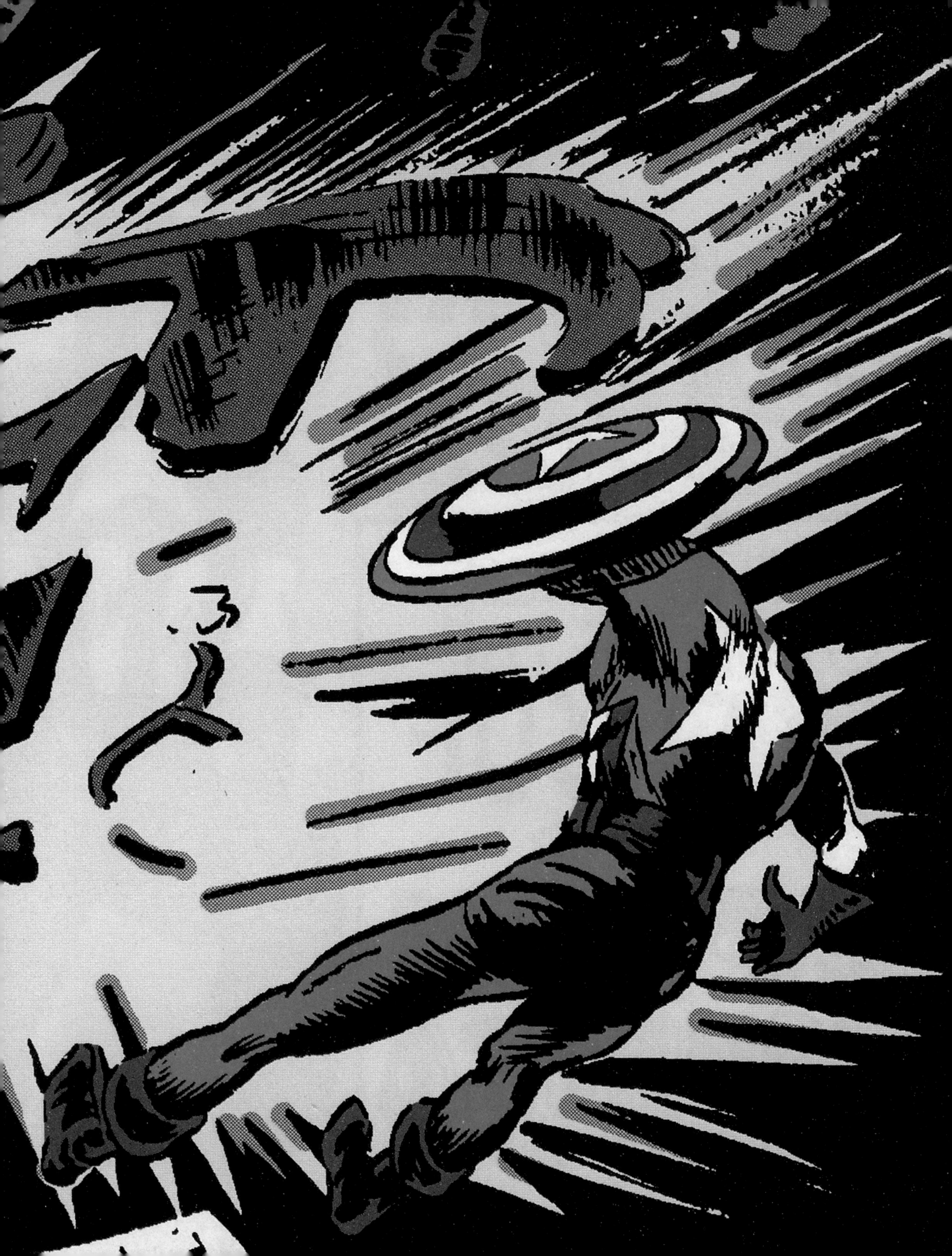

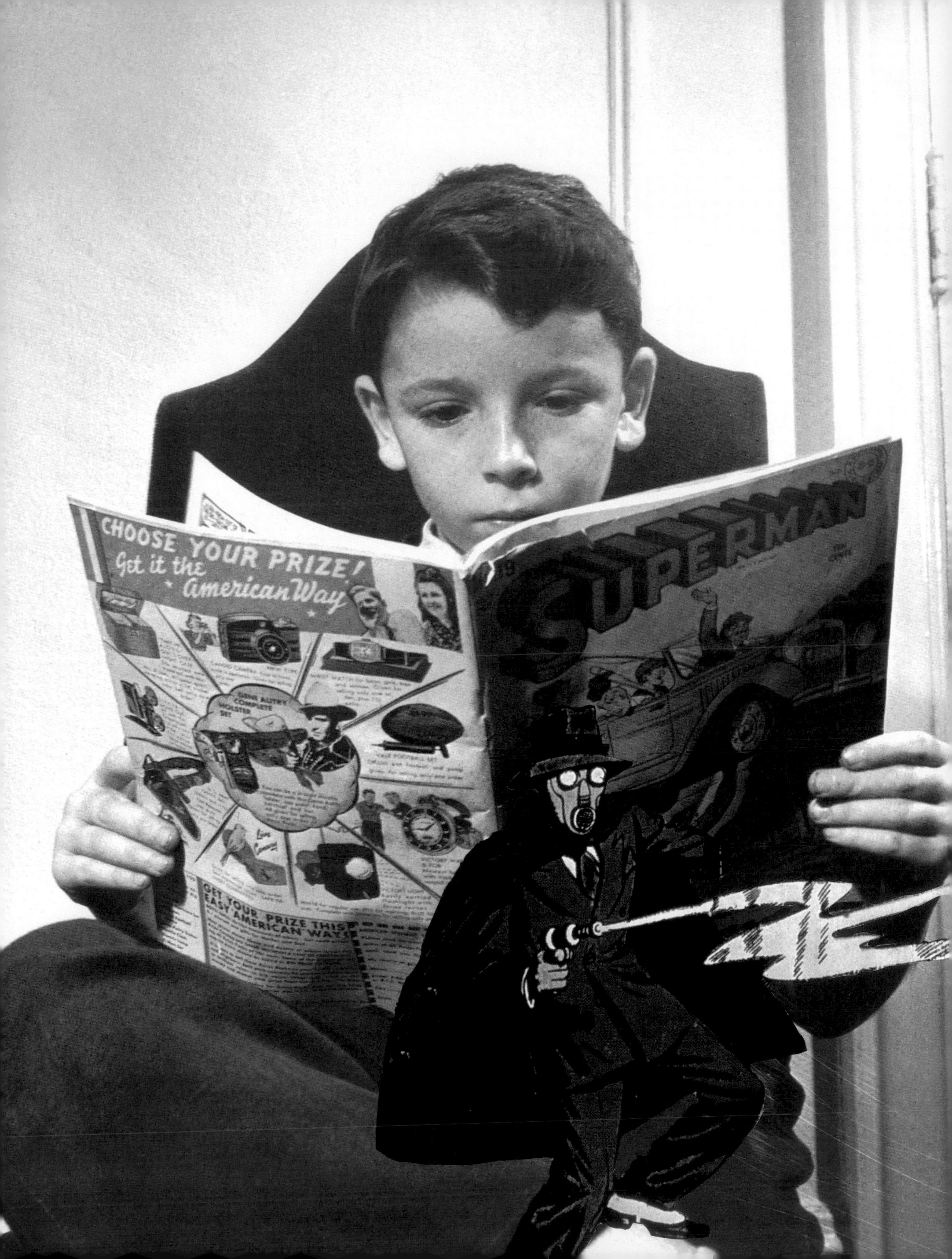
CHOOSE YOUR PRIZE!
Get it the American Way
SUPERMAN
GENE AUTRY COMPLETE HOLSTER SET
GET YOUR PRIZE THIS EASY AMERICAN WAY!

A PIECE OF THE ACTION
The Publishing Phenomenon

lthough the debut of Superman was a bombshell to every eleven-year-old who bought *Action Comics* #1, it took a while for the full implications of a superhero to hit the nascent comic book industry; when they did, they would be an unprecedented event in the history of publishing.

Comic books, in general, were entering the marketplace—newsstands and candy stores—with greater success. Several publishing houses, mostly in New York City, many barely scraping by, were transitioning from pulp novels into comics—diversifying their portfolios, as it were. There were even a few work-for-hire cartoon studios popping up; never mind trying to create an entire pantheon of heroes, costumed or otherwise, from scratch—a publisher could simply order up some characters and pages from a studio. One of the first, and most seminal, was the Eisner & Iger Studio. In 1939, twenty-one-year-old artist and writer Will Eisner was just out of De Witt Clinton High School in the Bronx and schlepping his portfolio around town. Realizing that publishers were going to need more and more original material, he precociously made a deal with Sam "Jerry" Iger, an editor nearly twice his age, to set up a studio and gradually create a bullpen of artists and writers, just in case someone should knock on the door someday.

At the same time, a new wave of action characters who had originated on the radio was becoming popular; they included the Lone Ranger and the Green Hornet. The Green Hornet was another wealthy, young man-about-town who fought crime when the sun went down, this time with a mask, a gas gun, and an Asian sidekick who conveniently happened to be his chauffeur. Two early comic book heroes borrowed heavily from the Hornet— the Crimson Avenger (and his assistant Wang), who debuted in *Detective Comics* #20, four months after Superman, and the uninspired Sandman, who also had a gas gun to go with his baggy green suit and clashing purple cape; he started putting criminals (and some readers) to sleep in the summer of 1939.

When it came to rip-offs, however, nothing beat the day toward the end of 1938 when there was, in fact, an urgent knock at the

OVERLEAF: An explosive panel by Jack Kirby and Joe Simon for *Captain America*. OPPOSITE: One of millions of young Americans entranced by comic book superheroes. TOP: Wonder Man's brief moment in the sun. BOTTOM: Artist/writer Will Eisner at his drawing board.

door of the Eisner & Iger Studio. In walked Victor Fox. Fox had his own publishing house, in the same building as Detective Comics, and was ostensibly privy to the sales figures on Superman. Fox reportedly ordered up a superhero as close to Superman as possible, and in the early spring of 1939 the "daring, superhuman exploits of the Wonder Man" were touted on the cover of *Wonder Comics*. If there were ever a one-hit wonder, it was Wonder Man. Before a second issue could be completed, Fox was hit by an injunction from Detective Comics and the character was never heard from again; a slight shame, if only because Eisner's work on the book was more fluid and more dramatic than Shuster's work for the competition. More important, however, was the implication that superheroes were big business—and Detective Comics meant business, too: it was the first, but by no means the last, litigation to protect the valuable interests of a successful costumed superhero.

Within the course of eighteen months—from the middle of 1938 to the end of 1940—two dozen publishing houses entered the comic book market, putting out a combined 150 different monthly titles. Here are some of the major players:

Centaur Comics, featuring minor entities such as the Arrow and Fantom of the Fair, who protected the World's Fair (and morphed into Fantoman), had begun as early as 1938, but would be out of business four years later.

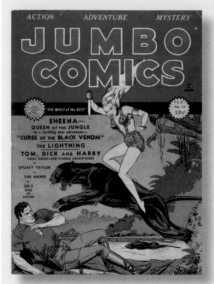

The Fiction House imprint would transition from pulp publishing to comic books in 1938 as well, and subcontracted the Eisner & Iger studio to create characters such as Sheena, Queen of the Jungle.

After the failure with Wonder Man, Victor Fox remained undaunted, solidifying his own Fox Features firm by unleashing a variety of slightly cheesy new super characters by the end of 1939, including the Flame and the Blue Beetle. Artist and comic book historian Jim Steranko defines the Fox style:

> Fox Publications was the poverty row of comic books and their superheroes were completely derivative. Their most important hero was the Blue Beetle. I remember one day I talked to Charlie Nicholas, the creator of the Blue Beetle, and I asked him what was it that inspired him to create this rather unusual character named after a *bug*. And he explained everything about the Fox mentality to me in two words: *Green Hornet*.

The year 1939 would bring other new important companies on line. The two most influential were Marvel Comics and Quality Comics, whose chief, Everett "Busy" Arnold, brought in Will Eisner to create popular characters such as Doll Man, Plastic Man, and the Blackhawks.

The firm variously known as Marvel Comics and Timely Comics was founded by Martin Goodman, another former pulp publisher, although with slightly darker tastes. Marvel/Timely blurred the line between pulps and comics with characters such as the Human Torch and the Sub-Mariner, who often slugged their way through their books without much concern for ethics or clean living.

MLJ Comics, founded by former magazine publishers Morris Coyne, Louis Silberkleit, and John Goldwater, appeared just as the 1930s ended. MLJ trotted out some good titles featuring the Shield and the Black Hood, before ultimately giving their line over to Archie Andrews, the eternal post-pubescent hero of his eponymous comics, in 1947.

Prize Publications featured well-drawn character such as the Black Owl and the Green Lama, who began in the pulps, and who was the first of many superheroes mentored in some obscure Asian monastery.

Hillman, which built its firm in the magazine business, cornered the market on flying aces, a successful staple of the pulp era, only now with superhero costumes. Heroes included Airboy, Skywolf, and the monstrous Heap.

Lev Gleason Publications (also 1939) brought in imaginative artists to create shriekingly dramatic comic characters such as Silver Streak, Daredevil (not the 1960s version), and the first supervillain, the Claw.

Street and Smith transformed their pulp heroes into full-color illustrations with somewhat uninspired renderings of the Shadow and Doc Savage, who was given a ridiculous superhero costume with a magic hood.

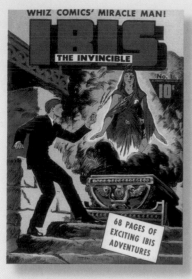

Most important, a firm called Fawcett Publications transitioned from magazines and books for kids into full-fledged comics with the introduction of *Whiz Comics*, the venue for Captain Marvel. Originally based in Minnesota, Fawcett was unique for having a non-Manhattan base and a distribution network centered in the Midwest; they produced comic books that, according to author Gerard Jones, even a Lutheran could love.

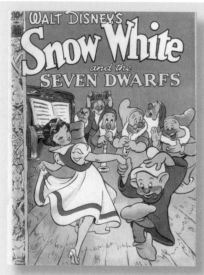

Dell Publications deserves a special cartoon medal of honor; they cornered the market on funny animal comics by sewing up licensing from Walt Disney, Warner Bros. (Bugs Bunny et al.), and Woody Woodpecker; they were far and away the most successful comic book publishers of the 1940s and 50s.

As most of these sixty-four-page monthly comic books were showcases for a variety of characters, hundreds of spanking new superheroes exploded on the American scene within two and a half years of Superman's debut. (The only comparable explosion in popular culture might be the creation of the American Popular Songbook after World War I—the hundreds of Broadway and Tin Pan Alley tunes which entered our national consciousness and remain lodged there to this day—but that took more than two decades to accomplish.) Of course, this phenomenon wasn't due to Superman alone, but more likely to the one-two punch cooked up over at DC Comics in spring 1939.

DC Comics editor Vin Sullivan, who advocated for the inclusion of the Superman character in *Action Comics* a year earlier, had seen the appeal of costumed superheroes and realized that the publishing company needed to boost its stable beyond the Man of Tomorrow. He tapped Bob Kane, a young cartoonist who had been supplying yet another soldier-of-fortune strip to *Detective Comics*. Kane, whose real name was Kahn, had attended the same Bronx high school as Will Eisner, had been trained in art school, and was trying to make it as a freelancer. He took on the assignment to create a new superhero and brought in a casual friend named Bill Finger for advice. Finger, two years older, had also gone to DeWitt Clinton High School, and was an avid pulp fiction reader. Kane was inspired by various flying characters in the comics— birds and bats—and Finger helped him refine the idea into a nocturnal emissary against crime with the terrifying affect of a bat. The character was, in fact, a Bat-Man. "Bob Kane created him with the only kind of innocence you can have as a teenage boy," said artist Neal Adams, "to create something that seems different and borrow it from everything that you can borrow it from."

Sullivan showcased the Bat-Man as the cover character and lead feature in *Detective Comics #27* (May 1939) and sales took off. Within a year, the Batman would gain his own book devoted solely to his adventures (but lose the distracting hyphen in his name), while continuing as the lead feature in *Detective Comics,* as well as another featured strip in the *World's Finest* anthology. Bob Kane quickly took his place among seminal comic book creators, branding each new adventure with his idiosyncratic signature. The reality was more complex. Kane was possessed of an important superpower: *chutzpah.* He had an intrinsic dislike for sharing the stage, while his collaborator, Bill Finger, was introspective and self-effacing; Finger seemingly didn't mind that his younger partner took credit for the plots and mythology that he himself added to the Batman. Kane also managed to outdo even Siegel and Shuster in one critical respect: his father worked for the New York *Daily News* and had an insider's knowledge of the legal ramifications of creating characters for a powerful syndicate. Armed with a lawyer's advice, Kane apparently negotiated a contract with *Detective Comics* that kept him deeply entwined in the creative and financial enterprise of Batman for the next four decades.

In the meantime, on his own merits and seemingly without legal advice, Batman emerged as the other pillar of the DC Comics community; his self-developed skill set and crepuscular persona were the perfect complement to Superman's impervious confidence and

An early Da Vinci-influenced Kane sketch of Batman—how early is a subject of debate: the 1934 date on the sketch is probably fudged. INSET: World's finest detective: The Batman's first appearance.

brightly colored optimism. They represented the same worlds that the Shadow and Doc Savage had respectively in the pulps: darkness and light, mystery and action. As Neal Adams put it, "Within a year, you had Superman, who was so powerful that he could move planets, and then you had Batman who had no powers at all; he was the opposite. All the other superheroes would fit in between these two characters." Superman and Batman were tag-team gods, perched at the very top of the comic book Olympus—between them, they inspired hundreds of characters, characters who would, in turn, inspire the imaginations of millions of Americans, young and old.

In a universe of spectacularly and powerfully endowed superbeings, Batman's most endearing trait was—and is—his vulnerability.

As one of the Caped Crusader's greatest interpreters in the 1970s, artist Neal Adams, puts it:

> The Batman is Sherlock Holmes and one of the greatest athletes on earth all jammed together into one person, isn't he? He had no super powers. He could do nothing. Nothing. Still probably the greatest fictional super hero that has existed on earth since mankind has been doing literature.

When Batman made his debut in a six-page story called "The Case of the Chemical Syndicate" in spring 1939, what you saw with Batman was what you got. His essential external elements were in that first story: "Young socialite" Bruce Wayne shares a jaw with his pal, Police Commissioner Gordon, who invites Wayne to a crime scene. Two pages later, the Bat-Man appears to track down the criminals and solve the crime. In the final two panels, a door to Wayne's study opens, revealing the mysterious identity of the Bat-Man. While Superman bounced around the East Coast in his debut, pulling off a half-dozen feats in thirteen pages, Batman solved one murder mystery, escaped the killer's death trap, and sent him to his doom in six pages. Superman had exploits; Batman had adventures.

Over the next six months in *Detective Comics*, he gradually added to his bat-arsenal of bat-paraphernalia—a utility belt (lifted from Doc Savage), a batarang, a Bat-Gyro (lifted from the Shadow)—and he carried a gun and knew how to use it. His adventures sent him to a mythical country where he rescued the damsel-in-distress by shooting werewolves with silver bullets.

TOP: A rare instance of Batman wielding a gun—he was more potent after he refused to take a life in his battle against crime. RIGHT: Young Bruce Wayne vows his revenge in *Detective Comics* #33 (1939); that vow would drive Batman for the next eight decades.

All of which was compelling to his young readership. All he was missing was his *raison d'être*—an origin story. The editors insisted on one, and Bill Finger delivered for *Detective Comics* #33. The resonance of Superman's roots was about external factors—where he came from, what he could do—but Finger exploited Batman's internal resonance. In a two-pager called "The Batman—Who He Is and How He Came to Be!," we see young Bruce Wayne witness the death of his parents during a botched stick-up and vow to use his inheritance to fight crime. (The source of his father's wealth would evolve over the years.)

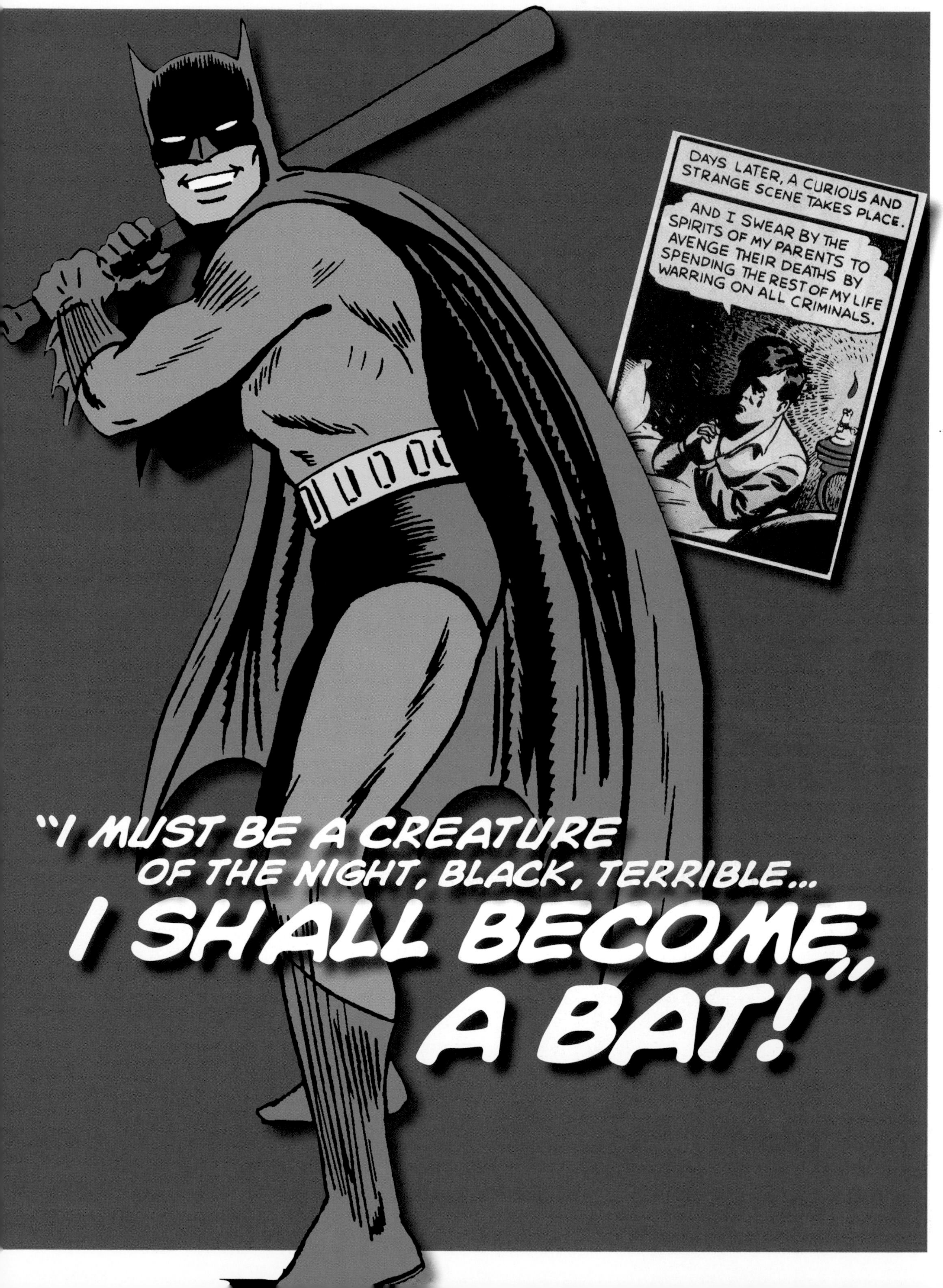
DAYS LATER, A CURIOUS AND STRANGE SCENE TAKES PLACE.
AND I SWEAR BY THE SPIRITS OF MY PARENTS TO AVENGE THEIR DEATHS BY SPENDING THE REST OF MY LIFE WARRING ON ALL CRIMINALS.
"I MUST BE A CREATURE OF THE NIGHT, BLACK, TERRIBLE... I SHALL BECOME A BAT!"

"To avenge their deaths by spending the rest of my life warring on all criminals. Criminals are a superstitious, cowardly lot, so my disguise must be able to strike terror into their hearts. I must be a creature of the night, black, terrible . . . I shall become a BAT!"

It would become one of the simplest and most fertile origin stories in pop culture.

Stan Lee, the cornerstone of the Marvel Comics Universe of the 1960s and beyond, and who knows as much about creating heroic fiction as anyone since Homer, put it this way: "You try to make an origin as dramatic as possible. Now, death has to do with vengeance— Batman's parents were killed, and he wanted to avenge their death. If somebody is killed, and you feel that should not have happened, that was a terrible thing and I'm gonna see that justice is done and make the killer pay, that's a great motivation for a hero." "What more do you need to know—he saw his parents killed," said Denny O'Neil, Batman's most effective scribe in the 1970s. "It was a choice he made, he realizes that he has chosen to do this because it helps deal with the trauma of his parents, but also because it's worth doing, because it's damned interesting. On some level, he enjoys doing it."

Certainly, Bill Finger enjoyed creating Batman's detective challenges. "Everything he did was based on athletics, on using his astute wits and acute observation," Finger said in a 1970s interview. "I didn't want Batman to be a superman; I wanted Batman to be hurt." Batman was given a puzzle to solve or a death trap to escape in every story, and readers got the feeling that "warring on all criminals" wasn't necessarily the easiest job in the world. "With Superman we won; with Batman we held our own," wrote Jules Feiffer in 1965's *The Great Comic Book Heroes*. "Individual preferences were based on the ambitions and arrogance of one's fantasies. I suspect the Batman school of having healthier egos." The Caped Crusader's job was made somewhat harder in 1940 when, according to Finger, DC Comics editor Whitney Ellsworth called him on the carpet for having Batman shoot down a giant monster with a machine gun. Batman would never deploy a lethal weapon again; and if his vow against killing made the vengeance game more difficult, it only affirmed his nobility by rejecting the methods that made him Batman in the first place.

Batman's driven nature was submerged after the appearance of his brightly colored chum, Robin the Boy Wonder, in *Detective Comics* #38, but it reared its cowled head again in an astonishing story from 1948 (written by Finger): in the course of solving a smuggling ring, Batman recognizes the mastermind as the man who killed his parents. "This is one job I'm doing alone. I don't have to explain—you can understand why," he tells Robin. Calling on the killer, Joe Chill, in an abandoned warehouse, Batman reveals his own identity to Chill in order to prove he knows his foul deed and threatens to hound him until he confesses. In a neat ironic note, Chill seeks help from his fellow criminals by admitting he killed Batman's father—but before he can reveal Batman's identity, he is gunned down by his confederates, who blame Chill as "responsible for creating their dread nemesis!"

By adding a kid sidekick almost a year after Batman's initial appearance, the creative team managed to turn the character in a different, nearly perpendicular, direction. A few months into Batman's run, Bob Kane and Bill Finger were joined by Jerry Robinson, a young artist who would wind up contributing pencils, inks, backgrounds, plots, and characters to the Batman storylines. Robinson was on the ground floor in bringing the Boy Wonder into the books: "Robin expanded the story potential— Batman would save Robin, Robin would save Batman. The younger readers could relate to Robin, and the older readers with Batman. There was a lot of interplay between Batman and Robin, with puns and whatnot. It did change the nature of the strip—it became a little lighter." An understatement, to say the least. The Boy Wonder, with his primary colors and relentlessly optimistic nature, took Batman out of the shadows, literally and figuratively.

FROM TOP: Batman in his most Gothic moment; the first appearances of the "baterang" and the "batgyro" (all from *Detective Comics* #31, 1939). OPPOSITE: Three of Batman's most insidious enemies: The Joker, Two-Face, and Catwoman.

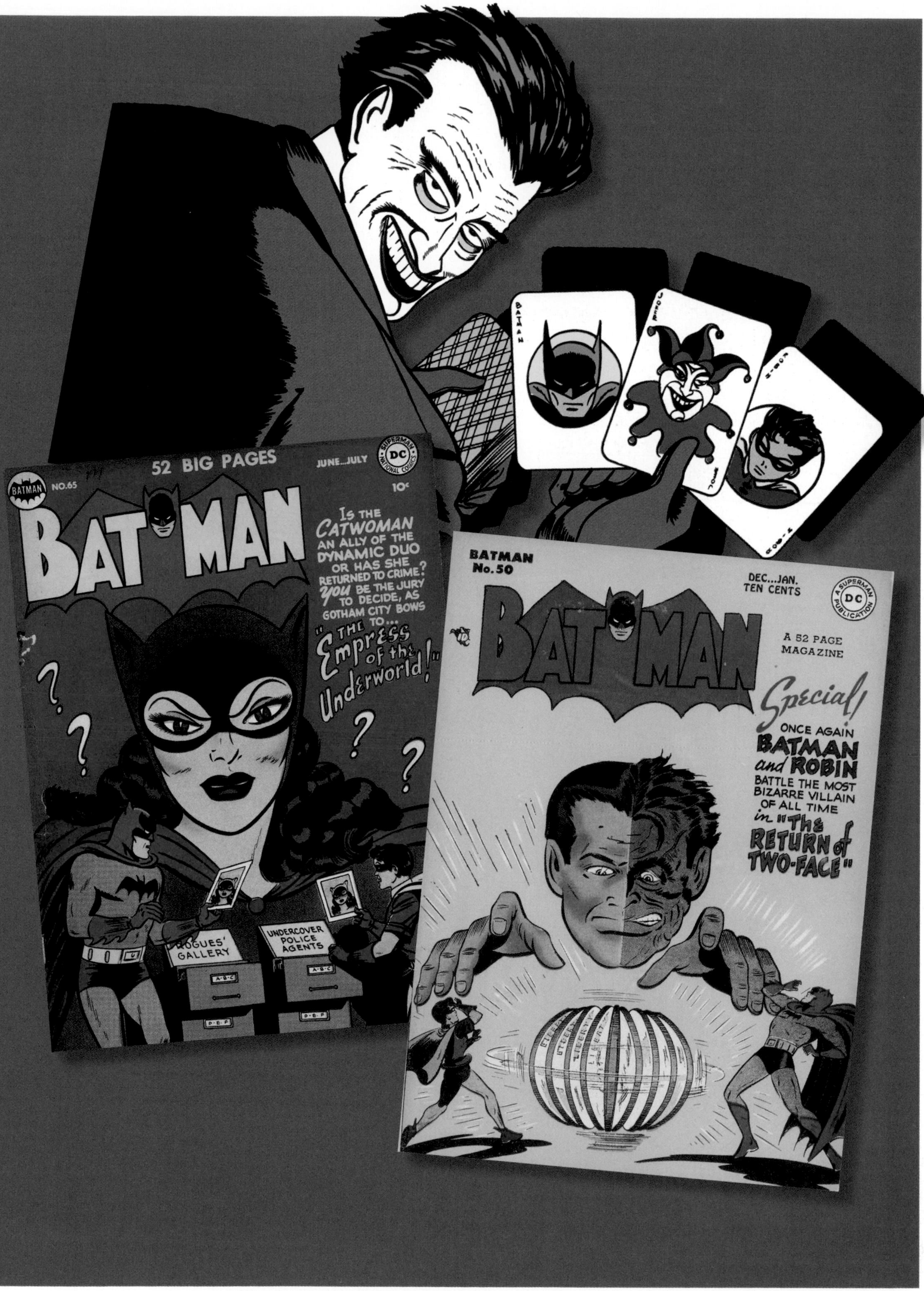
52 BIG PAGES
JUNE...JULY
NO.65
BATMAN
10¢
SUPERMAN DC NATIONAL COMICS
BATMAN
IS THE CATWOMAN AN ALLY OF THE DYNAMIC DUO OR HAS SHE RETURNED TO CRIME? YOU BE THE JURY TO DECIDE, AS GOTHAM CITY BOWS TO...
"THE Empress of the Underworld!"
ROGUES' GALLERY
UNDERCOVER POLICE AGENTS
A-B-C
D-E-F
BATMAN No.50
DEC...JAN. TEN CENTS
A SUPERMAN DC PUBLICATION
BATMAN
A 52 PAGE MAGAZINE
Special!
ONCE AGAIN BATMAN and ROBIN BATTLE THE MOST BIZARRE VILLAIN OF ALL TIME in "The RETURN of TWO-FACE"
LIBERTY

Another crucial contribution by Robinson—arguably more important than the introduction of Robin to the series—counterbalanced the upbeat sensibility of the kid sidekick and reclaimed Batman's stature as a creature of the night (or at least kept one of his Bat-boots in that territory). By early spring 1940, Batman was popular enough to become the second DC Comics hero to earn his own book. *Batman* #1 was a quarterly book, to be filled with sixty-four pages of his adventures and new antagonists. Robinson reached to the top shelf of his imagination:

> I wanted to create a villain that was worthy of Batman; Sherlock Holmes had Profes-
> sor Moriarty, for instance. And I knew that good characters had some contradiction in
> terms, so a villain with a sense of humor would be quite different and once I thought of
> a villain with a sense of humor, I thought of the Joker. In my family, one of my brothers
> was a champion bridge player, so there was always a deck of cards around the house,
> so it was quite natural that I immediately thought of the "Joker" playing card. Just by
> luck, that image—a clown, a jester—had a certain edginess to it that most people don't
> recognize. For example, clowns can be feared by children—and by many adults, too.

Bill Finger drafted the first Joker story and in that initial appearance, the Joker was a serial killer. Although Finger foolishly tried to bump him off after his second appearance, the Clown Prince of Crime quickly became Batman's primary nemesis. His crimes would veer from psychotic to goofy and swing firmly back to psychotic over the years, but his appeal never diminished. Denny O'Neil summed up the attraction of the Joker: "The Joker is one of the most interesting characters in all of pop culture—a serial killer who's a clown. Any pulp writer can go with that, we can work with that. He comes into your room and he may kill you, horribly, or he may give you a new car. And you don't know ahead of time because you can't figure out what's going on in his mind. And maybe he can't figure it out, either."

While the Joker may have been the first among deranged equals, Batman's famous Rogue's Gallery was the most colorful, inventive, and bizarre that any hero faced during the Golden Age. In that same *Batman* #1, the Caped Crusader crossed paths with the Cat, an early version of the Catwoman, a femme fatale who would continue to bewitch, bother, and bewilder Batman for decades. Bob Kane created the bifurcated menace of Two-Face; there were also the lighter provocations of the Penguin and a fairly harmless pair called Tweedledum and Tweedledee. Batman also kept up his membership in the noir club by duking it out with the fearful Scarecrow and the maniacal Clayface, a horror film actor who sought revenge—clearly after watching *The Phantom of the Opera* several times too many.

Batman never really had the time for the soap opera romance indulged in by Clark Kent and Lois Lane. In the late 1940s, a Lois Lane clone named Vicki Vale was desultorily tossed his way (she was a news photographer instead of a news reporter), but she didn't have, as it were, legs. Batman's real passion was for chasing down grotesque malefactors and tossing them into the clink; or, put more simply, he was driven by revenge. No other character in all of comic book history could match Batman's passion for justice. Neal Adams has the last word:

> He was just a guy who was in revenge mode and because he thought he could
> frighten criminals, he wore a bat costume. He can see it in their eyes that they're
> afraid. And he can use that and stop them. And guess what—he actually can do
> it. You know what would happen if you did it or I did it? Bang! One bullet, we'd be
> gone. But Batman makes it through. And in the end he is the guy that we want to be.
> The point is that everybody's Batman. It's stupid to want to be Superman—everybody
> can't be super. But Batman? It's possible.

"THANKS, OLD CHUM!"
Kid Sidekicks

hen Batman shared his secret identity with the young, orphaned Dick Grayson in *Detective Comics* #38 —"moved deeply" by his plight— he probably thought he was doing the right thing. Still, the Caped Crusader has a lot to answer for.

Dick Grayson grew up in the circus, part of a trapeze act with his parents, the Flying Graysons. A mobster named Boss Zucco was shaking down the circus and arranged for an "accident" one night—and young Dick's parents were murdered. The Batman took him under his—there's no other word for it—wing: "I guess you and I were both victims of a similar trouble, all right. I'll make you my aid [sic]. But I warn you, I lead a perilous life!" "I'm not afraid," responds Dick—and for decades to come, he never would be.

After Bill Finger and Bob Kane decided to add a kid sidekick to the Batman serials, they kicked around a lot of names with their associate Jerry Robinson: Mercury, Wildcat, Pepper, Davy (as in "Davy Crockett"), and Socko. Robinson recalls, "I thought of Batman's new partner as a sort of young Robin Hood, and suggested the name Robin. I had been inspired by N.C. Wyeth's beautiful illustrations for the classic edition of *The Adventures of Robin Hood.* Once we agreed upon the name, I suggested adapting Robin Hood's costume for the new character. I recall adding the final touch to Bob's sketch of Robin, the small "R" monogram on his vest." According to artist Jim Steranko, "When comic book creators were interested in promoting younger audiences and unifying their audience with the material, they thought it would be a good idea to use younger characters in the strips." So, young Dick Grayson became Robin, the Boy Wonder, "The Sensational Character Find of 1940," teaming up with the World's Greatest Detective. It didn't take a detective for the comic book publishers to realize who was subsidizing their new fortunes: kids.

By the early 1940s, statistics revealed that more than 90 percent of American boys from seven to seventeen and nearly 90 percent of American girls read some kind of comic book. "You

OPPOSITE, FROM TOP: Batman's tragic origin made him unique among superheroes—a 1948 story dealt with its implications; most of Batman's 1940s adventures were of the goofier variety. ABOVE: Batman introduces his new chum in *Detective Comics* #38 (April 1940).

also have to understand that when you bought a comic book, you were actually buying ten comic books or more," said artist Joe Kubert, "because each one of your friends bought one comic and we'd trade them off so that if you had ten buddies, you had access to at least ten different comic books." It was an industry built on sticky dimes and lunch money.

Cultural historian Bradford Wright suggests that "Comic book publishers bypassed parents and aimed their products directly at the tastes of children and adolescents. This trend was probably furthered by parental guilt over deprived Depression-era childhoods, that young people deserved greater latitude to pursue their own happiness." Gerard Jones adds, "Previously there had been kids' books and there had been pulp magazines [marketed toward adults], but not until comics was there anything marketed, 'Hey, kids!' and yet containing the kind of violence and passion and seediness that they love."

Whether the addition of a kid sidekick to a grown-up super-

hero's adventures actually increased sales of a given title is impossible to know, but once Batman made Robin his "old chum" in crime-fighting, the flood gates were open. Captain America had his comrade in arms, Bucky; the Human Torch encouraged Toro to flame alongside him; the Green Arrow mentored young Speedy; the Shield had Dusty to ride shotgun; the Sandman was given the inevitably named Sandy; Mr. Scarlet gained the less intensely colored comrade, Pinky. Sometimes, the sidekick added an exciting *nom de guerre* to the superhero firm—witness TNT and Dan, the Dyna-Mite. However, the writers clearly ran out of inspiration when they assigned the Black Terror a sidekick named Tim. Jerry Siegel actually created one of the better sidekick variations in 1941: in this case, the teenaged Star-Spangled Kid was the hero and his sidekick was a rather dim-witted adult named Stripesy.

The introduction of the kid sidekick revealed a kind of disconnect between the adult creators of the comics and their adolescent audience. As Jim Steranko puts it, "The sidekick was important

In the 1940s, sidekicks were all the rage. FROM LEFT: TNT and Dan the Dyna-mite; the Black Terror and Tim; Sandman and Sandy (courtesy of Simon and Kirby); the Human Torch and Toro; the Star-Spangled Kid and Stripesy.

because it gave characters somebody to talk to, to relate to, otherwise they'd be walking down the street talking to themselves, which is not a good sign in the superhero world." But, as Stan Lee, who strenuously avoided co-opting sidekicks in his work if he could help it, explained, "I always felt if I were a superhero, the last thing in the world I would want to do is pal around with some teenaged kid! I mean, at the very least, people would talk!"

Cartoonist Jules Feiffer, who was roughly the same age as Robin when he debuted, sums up every twelve-year-old's real reaction to the kid sidekick:

> Robin was just along to attract a young audience. Which seemed dumb because the young audience really wanted to be Batman; they didn't want to grow up to be Robin. I thought, keep the kids out of the comic books—I didn't need a boy superhero who was going to make me look bad.

Captain Marvel also knew how to toss a car; his first appearance in *Whiz Comics* (February 1940).
OPPOSITE: Film actor Fred MacMurray, the model for Captain Marvel.

"WITH ONE MIGHTY WORD"
Fawcett Comics and Their Happy Warrior

There was one kid in comics, however, who posed no threat to any youngster's sense of security, and millions of readers adored him. He was an orphaned newsboy named Billy Batson, who was only one word away from becoming the World's Mightiest Mortal.

In the second issue of *Whiz Comics*, dated February 1940, Billy hawks his newspapers on an abandoned street. A shadowy figure (who actually looks a lot like the Shadow) beckons, then disappears into a subway entrance. Billy follows him, only to find himself alone in an abandoned tunnel. Seated on a throne in front of him is a wizened, bearded man in a simple, floor-length robe; he looks like every Jewish kid's vision of Yahweh.

> SHAZAM: Billy Batson! I have fought injustice and cruelty all my life, but I am old now—my time is almost up. You shall be my successor simply by speaking my name, you can become the strongest and mightiest man in the world—CAPTAIN MARVEL! Speak my name!
> BILLY: SHAZAM!

"As Billy speaks the word, he becomes Captain Marvel!" In Billy's place stood the mighty hero, a character whose similarities to Superman would prove to be his biggest challenge.

Fawcett Publications began in 1919 by publishing *Captain Billy's Whiz Bang*, a joke book (the one excoriated by Professor Harold Hill in the musical *The Music Man*) before moving into magazines such as *True Confessions* and *Mechanix Illustrated*. When they entered the comic books business, they did so as a lucrative firm. As the 1930s ended, they moved their base of operations from Minnesota to tony Greenwich, Connecticut. The story goes that, one day, their circulation director barged into an editorial meeting and ordered up a new superhero for their nascent comic book line. He had to be like Superman, but he had to have the secret identity of an eleven- or twelve-year-old boy. It was a simple formula and it worked like magic.

Fawcett staff writer Bill Parker developed the idea by proposing a team of seven immortal superheroes—**S**olomon, **H**ercules,

Atlas, **Z**eus, **A**chilles, and **M**ercury. When that proved too unwieldly, he gave their cumulative powers to young Billy Batson in the form of Captain Marvel. The fact that this anagram of mythical gods and heroes is rather a mash-up didn't seem to bother anyone; Solomon, of distinctly Hebraic ancestry, apparently can gain membership in a restricted Greek club—and Mercury was, in fact, the Roman god of speed. The Greek god of speed is Hermes, but "SHAZAH!" admittedly doesn't have the same ring to it.

Artist C. C. Beck mitigated Captain Marvel's ancient lineage with a more contemporary costume; Beck admitted that the red-and-gold uniform was based on a combination of a drum major, a chorus boy from a road company operetta, and the outfit of an usher at the Roxy Music Hall. Back in the pulp days, Doc Savage's visage was consciously modeled on Clark Gable's. With Captain Marvel, however, his creators looked to Fred MacMurray, a genial leading man and lighthearted contract player for Paramount Pictures. If anything gave away the demographic aspirations of Fawcett in creating Captain Marvel, that was it.

Otto Binder, who wrote nearly one thousand Captain Marvel stories, summed up his approach to the character: "The Big Red Cheese was a sort of

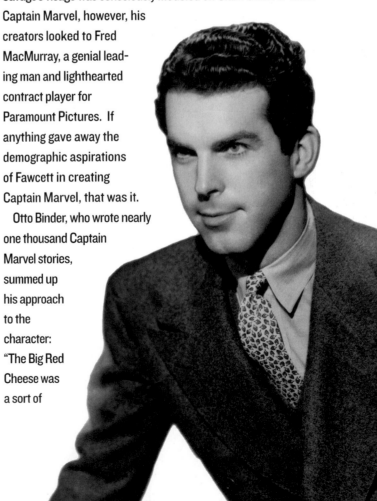

kind, bumbling, hulking crusader without armor, using his super-powers sparingly and subject to the whims and dreams and human fallacies which are all a part of us." Captain Marvel took off immediately, and within a short time, he was starring in three magazines. The first issue of *Captain Marvel Adventures* featured a series of tales hastily written and drawn by Jack Kirby and Joe Simon, who admitted that this particular Captain was not their style: "Charming is the word for *Captain Marvel*. It was enchanting, like a children's story."

Indeed, while Captain Marvel's rivals, Superman and Batman, evolved in the 1940s with origin stories and mythologies that deepened and enlarged their characters, Captain Marvel preferred to explode in place. The artwork was genial, the stories were easy to follow and whimsically unaggressive. Even his arch-nemesis, another balding scientific genius megalomaniac who went by the name of Dr. Sivana, seemed incapable of screwing in a new light bulb without blowing out the fuse box. Jim Steranko contrasts Captain Marvel with Superman: "Superman was very serious about what he did. His job was to kick

the ass of any criminal that happened to come within the city limits of Metropolis. There weren't a lot of laughs in the Superman comics. But with Captain Marvel it was all laughs. And an entire segment of the comic reading public preferred that."

And a vast segment it was. By the early 1940s, Captain Marvel monthly sales were surpassing those of *Superman* and Fawcett was providing real competition with *Detective Comics*, adding other successful characters such as Spy Smasher and Captain Midnight. Still, Captain Marvel won the gold watch around the Fawcett offices every time, selling more than a million comics a month. In 1944, appearing in a variety of magazines, some of which were bi-monthly, Captain Marvel sold 14 million comic books. It's worth remembering that the most popular comics of the 1940s were "funny animal" books; here, too, Captain Marvel hedged his magical bets. During the same month as the attack on Pearl Harbor, Fawcett provided young audiences with an even more sympathetic character than orphaned Billy Batson: a newsboy named Freddy Freeman, who, when injured by the despicable Captain Nazi, is taken by Billy for an audience with the great wizard Shazam. Shazam

OPPOSITE, CLOCKWISE FROM LEFT: Uncle Dudley Marvel; a rare Jack Kirby take on Captain Marvel; a humorous segment, drawn by C. C. Beck (*Whiz Comics* #5, 1940). RIGHT: The immortals who made up "SHAZAM" and Captain Marvel Jr.—the first addition to the fertile Marvel family (art by Mac Raboy).

anoints Freddy with the power of transformation into a mighty young man—all he has to do is speak the name, "Captain Marvel!," and he becomes Captain Marvel Jr., a cadet-sized (and more dramatically drawn) version of our hero. Soon there was Billy's twin sister, removed from the same orphanage at a young age, who emerged to take on similarly magical powers as Mary Marvel; a thoroughly unnecessary Uncle Dudley Marvel; and Hoppy, the Marvel Bunny, who erased any boundaries—if any really remained—between the Fawcett superhero books and their successful funny animal books.

The Marvel Family, as they were known, was the first real superhero franchise and, far from cannibalizing sales from each other, the characters fed the enthusiasm of loyal readers as they fought together in innumerable escapades (even Dr. Sivana got his family into the act to fight them, though with predictably ineffectual conclusions). Captain Marvel even pioneered the idea of product identification. When he offered kids the chance to join the Captain Marvel Club, the promotional device proved so popular that Fawcett had to open a new office just to handle the correspondence. At its height (buoyed by the Captain's eventual appeal to patriotism during World War II), the Captain Marvel Club embraced 400,000 members.

Of course, membership in the Captain Marvel zeitgeist required even less than a dime: it only required that magic word—"Shazam!" Magic words, alas, don't have much purchase in a court of law; it was the harsh reality of copyright and commerce that undermined the fantasy world of Captain Marvel. Eighteen months after Detective Comics vanquished Wonder Man in the courts, their lawyers took on Fawcett, initiating first a cease-and-desist order, then a lawsuit in 1941, claiming that Captain Marvel had infringed on Superman's copy-

right. The legal wranglings between Detective Comics (by then, known as National Periodicals) and Fawcett went on for seven years before the case went to court. According to Joe Simon, National's publisher, Harry Donenfeld, was driven to distraction by Fawcett's superior sales and their comfortable headquarters in leafy Connecticut. Both parties ordered up scrapbooks that culled and pasted both Superman's and Captain Marvel's escapades side by side for point of comparison. The case bounced from court to appeals to court again for years, but in 1951, Judge August Hand ruled in favor of National. Both sides agreed to settle out of court: Captain Marvel suspended publication and Fawcett forked over $400,000 in damages. Apparently, as magic words go, "Shazam!" is trumped only by "So ordered."

It's difficult to cast one's mind back over the decades and imagine that Superman really had a rival who outdid him to such an extent that legal action was needed. It's even harder to imagine when one reads the Captain Marvel adventures—they are so benign, optimistic, and trustworthy. Perhaps Captain Marvel didn't pay enough attention to the second "A" in his name: where Achilles' vulnerability lay in his heel, Captain Marvel's lay in his heart. He was simply too uncomplicated, and the modern age has displayed little sympathy for a heart so pure.

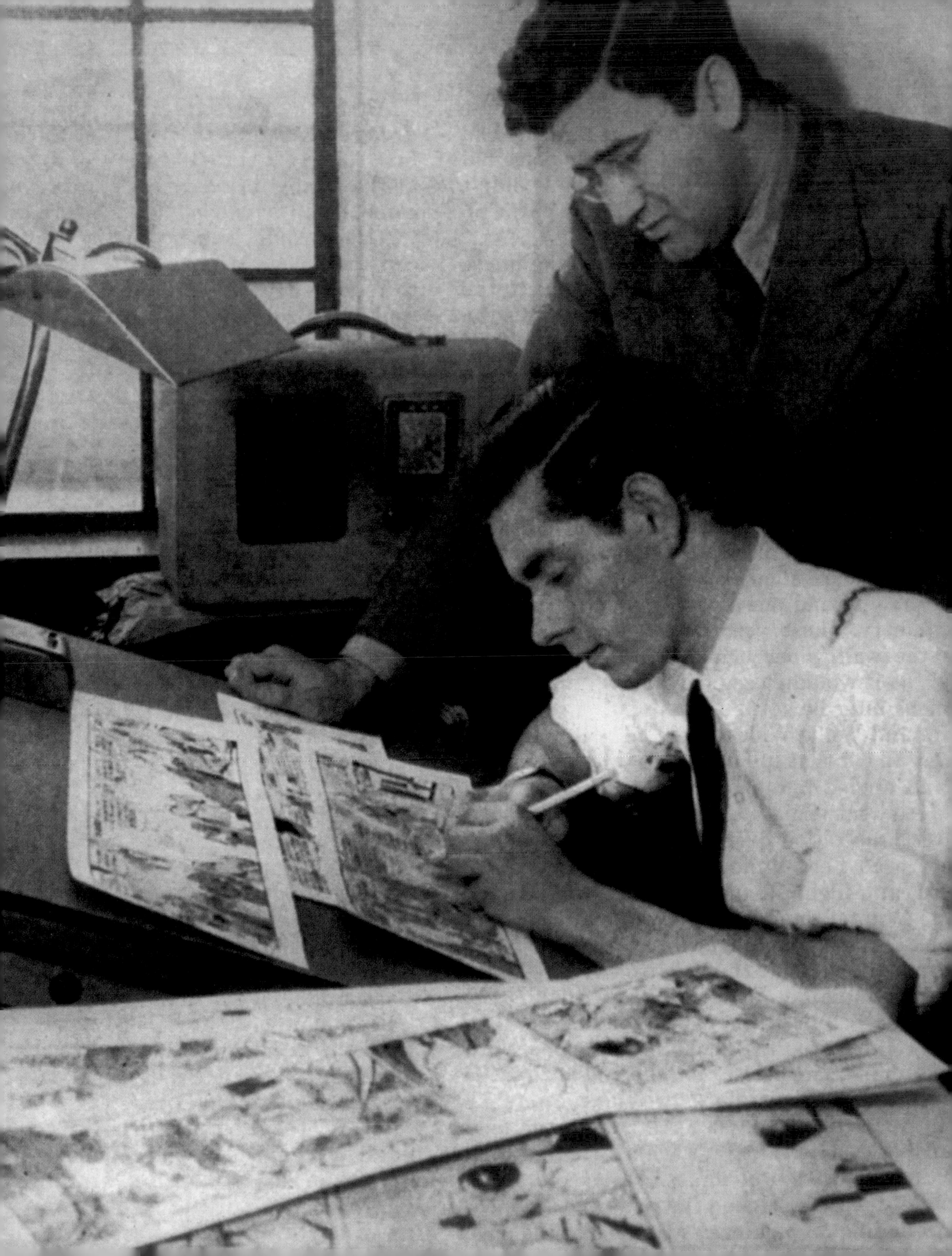

"LOOK UP IN THE SKY!"
And in the Movie Theaters. And on the Radio.

 n the popularity contest between Superman and Captain Marvel the stakes were high, but as the 1940s progressed, the categories in competition expanded faster than a speeding bullet. Superman had an in-house advantage. His publisher, Detective Comics, was clever enough to create a subsidiary division in 1940 under the Superman, Inc. shingle, which was devoted to promoting the Superman brand in various media. It might be argued that the nationwide hunger for all things Superman outpaced even the voracious imagination of the very company created to exploit him; nevertheless, the speed and depth of the media penetration of Superman was unprecedented by popular culture standards.

Characters such as Mickey Mouse, Popeye, and Flash Gordon had been able to infiltrate kids' consciousnesses—and their parents' pocketbooks—in a variety of different products: toys, games, promotions. Superman's march to consumer saturation began in January 1939. Siegel and Shuster's initial dream of a Superman daily strip was realized when the McClure Syndicate, which had turned down their spectacular idea a few years earlier, bought the syndication rights to Superman from Detective Comics and asked Siegel and Shuster to produce the strip out of their Cleveland studio. This made Superman the first comic book character to be licensed as a comic strip. It became a phenomenally successful strip, printed in more than 300 daily papers and read by millions—many of whom were adults who had never read a comic book. In fact, for decades, adult commentators would refer to Superman as a "comic strip" character.

In April 1939, the New York World's Fair opened, celebrating "the world of tomorrow." It was only natural that the Man of Tomorrow would make an appearance, and so he did, impersonated by an unbilled actor named Ray Middleton, on Superman Day, appropriately marked on July 4, 1940. (There is some dispute as to whether Middleton—who would have been the

OPPOSITE: Jerry Siegel and Joe Shuster prepare the Superman daily strip; TOP: Actor Ray Middleton on Superman Day at the World's Fair (1940). BOTTOM: Superman at the Macy's Thanksgiving Day Parade (1940).

RIGHT: Superman was a radio phenomenon, both over the airwaves and in his comic books. OPPOSITE: The animated adventures of Superman (above) took off from the Max Fleischer Studios. Fleischer is at center, below.

first actor to impersonate Superman—was in fact the avatar in question; but by 1946, he was facing off with Ethel Merman eight times a week in *Annie Get Your Gun*, so Middleton must have had some qualities of invulnerability.) November of that same year brought a somewhat bloated, but giant-sized Superman balloon to the Macy's Thanksgiving Day Parade.

The major event of 1940, as regards Superman's expansive empire, was the introduction of a radio show. Radio was, of course, the primary non-printed medium for action and adventure heroes in the 1930s and 40s—the Shadow, the Green Hornet, Little Orphan Annie, the Lone Ranger, and Flash Gordon had all streaked across the airwaves to great success. DC hired a public relations man and a producer named Robert Maxwell to create a Superman pilot and to bring it to the radio; and on February 12, *The Adventures of Superman* debuted as a fifteen-minute serial on WOR in New York. It was quickly picked up and usually broadcast several times a week in the late afternoon— just after kids got home from school and right before dinner. Although the idea of a full-color comic book hero without any visuals would seem counterintuitive, the radio program was a huge success, lasting into the 1950s.

The already fertile imaginations of kids were inflamed by the hard-working sound artists, who reportedly created Superman's flying effect by combining a recording of an artillery shell streaking through the air with a separate recording of a wind tunnel played backward. The effect zoomed over one of the most famous openings in radio history:

"Faster than an airplane, more powerful than a locomotive, impervious to bullets!"
"Up in the sky — look!"
"It's a giant bird!"
"It's a plane!"
"It's SUPERMAN!"
"And now, Superman . . . a strange visitor from a distant planet: champion of the oppressed, physical marvel extraordinary who has sworn to devote his existence on Earth to helping those in need!"

Forced by the conventions of radio to adapt Superman's adventures in an aural medium, the program introduced some innovations: Superman was given a teenaged comrade, a copy boy named Jimmy Olsen—because on radio he *really* needed someone to talk to, and to keep the suspense of the serials going; Clark Kent's paper was now the *Daily Planet*, run by a hard-boiled editor name Perry White; and a radioactive substance from his home planet, Kryptonite, pierced Superman's invulnerable carapace. Even Batman made a guest appearance on the radio show in 1945—the first time these two titans of industry ever met in any medium. As radio historian Jim Harmon put it, "The crossovers where Superman met Batman on the air were equally rare for fictional characters on the radio, where almost nobody but comedians and singers ever visited each other's shows." (The stardust didn't rub off on the Dynamic Duo—Batman and Robin never got their own spin-off.) The real heavy lifting was done by radio actor Bud Collyer who voiced both Superman and Clark Kent for more than 2,000 episodes (and initially did so anonymously in order to keep up the mystery of Superman's existence). He was famous for dropping an octave while ostensibly undoing his tie: "This is a job for—*Superman!*"

If the radio show contributed essential elements to the Superman mythology, his next triumph in the media sweepstakes would allow him to zoom across the silver screen in full color. Paramount Pictures obtained the license to bring Superman to the movies and turned to the renowned animators, Max and Dave Fleischer, who had rendered *Popeye* so entertainingly to the cartoon medium (a particular favorite of Joe Shuster's). The Fleischers were reportedly dubious about the practicalities and made Paramount an exorbitant counteroffer; the studio did not refuse and okayed $50,000 for the first ten-minute Superman cartoon, an incomprehensible amount for the time.

The Fleischers spared no effort and committed to the assiduous job of putting the Man of Steel and his pals through seventeen animated adventures throughout 1943. The installments appeared on movie screens across the nation, whipping up fans, old and new, into a frenzy, while adding new elements to the Supersaga, including non-stop flying and the new introductory phrase (soon to be appropriated by the radio show): "Superman fights a never-ending battle for truth and justice." Perhaps the Fleischers' greatest achievement, ironically, was to make this primary-colored fantasy figure believable: human characters rarely appeared in animated cartoons at the time—let alone as the full cast of characters—and the Fleischer Superman cartoons set a very high standard for elegant, graceful, thrilling cartoon animation.

The Holy Grail was a full-fledged Hollywood film featuring a superhero, but in the era of prestige studios—Metro-Goldwyn-Mayer, Paramount, Warner Bros., and so on—it was a practical and commercial impossibility. Hollywood was decades away from throwing its weight behind a fantasy blockbuster—as far

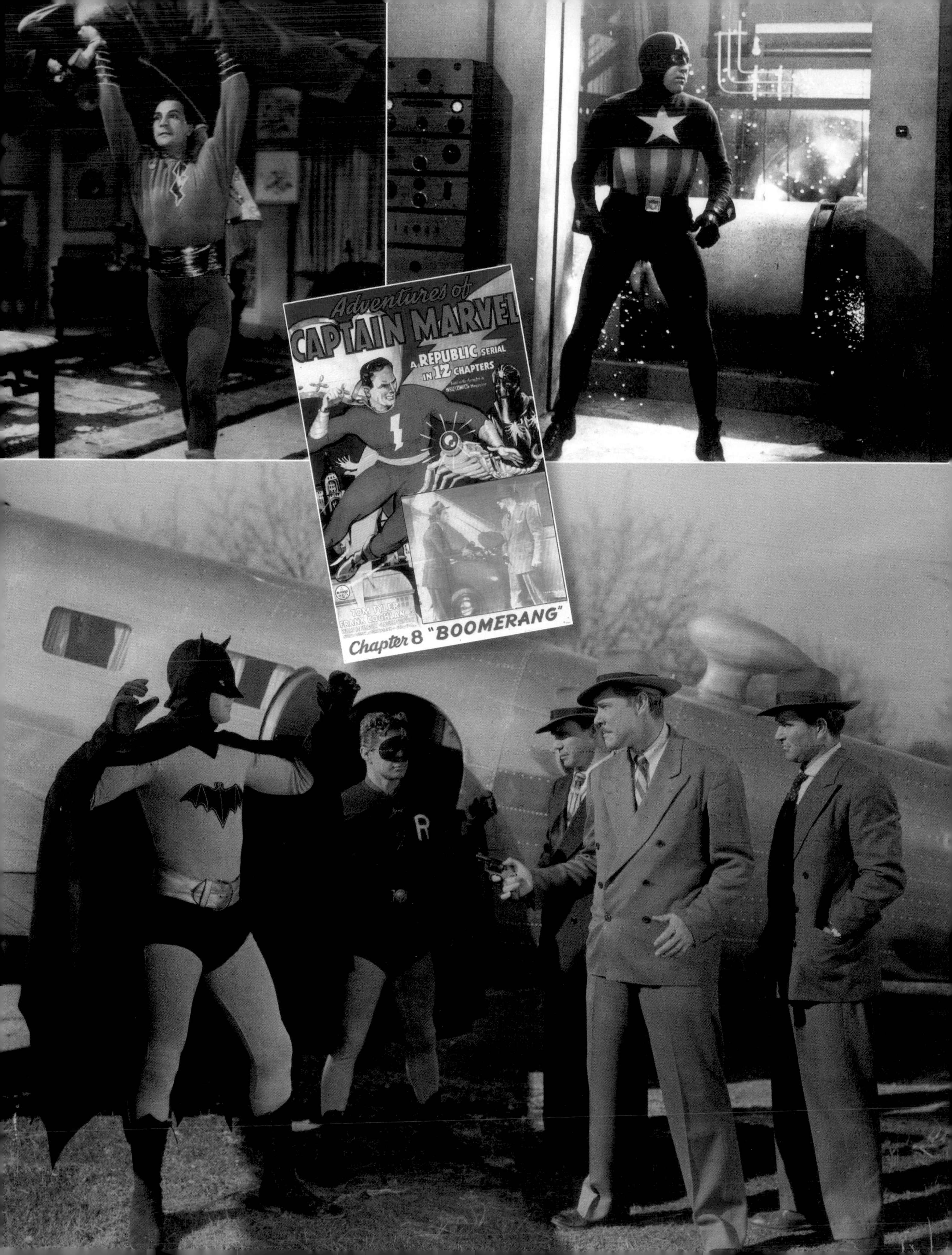
Adventures of
CAPTAIN MARVEL
A REPUBLIC SERIAL
IN 12 CHAPTERS
TOM TYLER
FRANK COGHLAN
Chapter 8 "BOOMERANG"

as MGM's accountants were concerned, the labor-intensive *The Wizard of Oz* in 1939 was barely worth the effort—and certainly these new-fangled comic book heroes were not high-class items. Luckily, there was another way: the Saturday afternoon serials. Serials were two-reel adventures shown in weekly installments; the average serial adventure was twelve episodes long, running a total of about four hours. Typically, the serials were based on Western or detective stories, although Universal had a huge success with its Flash Gordon serials in the late 1930s.

Republic Pictures was the most reliable serial machine in the early 1940s and they set about acquiring the rights to Superman. Either Detective Comics asked for too much editorial control or Paramount had already sewn up the screen rights for the cartoons—no one is sure—but plans fell apart. Republic Pictures turned to the next best thing, superhero-speaking: Captain Marvel. They plunged into production on *Adventures of Captain Marvel* right before Christmas 1940; the final product, all 216 minutes of it, cost $143,000 and was released the following March. The odds would seem to be against it—*Adventures* was the first live-action superhero film, after all—but it was an exciting serial and many aficionados consider it to be the best of its kind. *Captain Marvel* replaced the comic book's lightheartedness with real drama and cliffhanger exploits; it was also well-cast, and—perhaps most admirably—it all seems relatively credible.

Captain Marvel edged out

Superman on the movie front by a long lead: the Man of Steel wouldn't appear on screen in a live-action serial until 1948, when the serial phenomenon was past its prime (Kirk Alyn played him in the fifteen-chapter *Superman*). In the meanwhile, millions of adolescents were roused by the serial adventures of Batman, the Phantom, and Captain America (the only media appearance of a Marvel/

Timely character until the 1960s), thrillingly inserted in-between the Looney Tunes cartoons and the wartime newsreels.

This cinematic setback didn't seem to crimp Superman's style. His likeness was licensed for innumerable puzzles, paint sets, paper dolls, real dolls, games, greeting cards, coloring books, candy, racing cars, tin ray guns, playsuits, socks, shirts, and underwear. You could even have your Superman cake and eat it, too, as it were—there was Superman bread and, according to media executive Ed Catto, there was "Superman milk from the Hourigan Dairy Farm in Syracuse, New York, which seems a little misleading because you're not going to get super powers from drinking that milk." Captain Marvel had his own merchandising engine as well but, impressive though it was, it didn't catch up to Superman's. Other comic strip characters—Popeye, Flash Gordon, Little Orphan Annie—were successfully marketed as licensed products, but few superheroes other than Superman and Captain Marvel were; surprisingly, Batman's commercial potential was almost completely underexploited.

"Underexploited," however, is not a term that could be accurately applied to Superman's creators. In the view of Michael Chabon:

> Piles of money, blizzards of money were going to Harry Donenfeld and to DC Comics, but Jerry Siegel and Joe Shuster had to wait a long time before either of them began to see anything resembling even a fraction of the kind of money that had been made off Superman over the years. The incredible gap between the imaginative leap that those guys had taken and the pennies that they were making off of it. . . . Whether it's good or bad is not really a question for me—there's just something moving and sad about it.

THE FIRST GENERATION:

When the comic book industry exploded at the beginning of 1939, it faced its own labor force dilemma: there were far more opportunities to pencil, ink, or write comic books than there were first-class artists to do the work. Accomplished illustrators from the comic strip or magazine world were unlikely to accept the low pay and rigorous hours of churning out comic book superheroes. A new generation stepped into the breach—young, inexperienced, eager, and usually from a first-generation New York background. They would become their own honor roll of champions. Here are their stories, in their own words:

JERRY ROBINSON: A lot of publishers were Jewish; they were already in publishing, and they had brought their skills from Europe when they escaped the tyrannies in Europe. So they brought their professions with them. They were receptive to this new genre of comic books, which apparently kids loved and bought. And they had to keep the presses going.

CARMINE INFANTINO: You couldn't be a fine artist. You couldn't go to school for that or get the education for that. And we came from the tenements, so you had to find a way to make a living. The comic books were the only way for us.

IRWIN HASEN: When people were rich, we were rich—car, chauffeur. And we lost everything. The Depression, for people who had it and lost it, was terrible. And so I lived through that with my parents in their apartment. We lived together, five of us. How I survived with the charming sense of humor that I have, I don't know. I could have been a drunk and I could have been a dope fiend, the way I lived with my family. So I had to get out of it. And I got out of it by being a cartoonist.

CARMINE INFANTINO: Wherever you went there was a bunch of people sitting, waiting to be interviewed. We were all hungry to be cartoonists. And it was a thriving business in those days, very thriving. So you'd meet people there and the editors would come out and look at your work—and walk away. You'd never hear from them again. But eventually you hooked up with somebody. I went to Quality Comics and I erased pages for a living the whole summer. Then I went to Fiction House and did backgrounds. Everything to move forward. Then I worked for Charlie Biro over at Boy Comics. Again, backgrounds. And then they eventually put me on the main features. I did westerns there.

JULES FEIFFER: One summer, I was hired by one of the sleazier publishers to be his assistant. And it turned out my job was not to pay any of the

JERRY ROBINSON, Artist Entered the business: 1939
Characters include: Batman, Robin, the Joker, London

CARMINE INFANTINO, Artist Entered the business: 1942
Characters include: Jack Frost, Airboy, Black Canary, the Flash

THE PIONEERS

WONDER WOMAN

GREEN LANTERN

1940 - 1952

WILDCAT

guys working on the strips. When I found out they weren't getting their checks, I warned them all. I said, "Don't tell the boss I told you, but you're not going to get paid." Somehow, I lost that job.

CARMINE INFANTINO: After enough under my belt, I brought my portfolio to DC and there was a guy named Eddie Eisenberg come out. He says, we can't use you here, cause they put out *Superman* and *Batman*. He said, but go down the hall and ask for Shelly Mayer, maybe he might be able to use you. He was on All-American Comics. I went down there and the girl said, come on in. I went in. Now, his office was half paneling and half glass. And you sit there, you see the artists working at their desks. And Shelly's sitting there, he's looking at my work. He was about twenty-six years old at that point. All of a sudden, I hear the door open behind me and somebody says, "*En garde!*" And Irwin Hasen is there, with a T-square. And Shelly drops my pages, picks up his T-square and they start dueling all over the room, over the desk, back, forth. I don't want no part of this. Shelly stabs Irwin. Irwin kisses him and he leaves and that was the end of it. And Shelly goes back, picks up the pages and is back at it again, like nothing happened. I thought, I gotta get out of here, this is nuts.

RAMONA FRADON: I would come into the office there at about three o'clock, and this bullpen happened to be right in the center of this building. There were no windows. It was pitch black except for all those lights where the artists were hunched over the tables. And around three o'clock they'd all begin to sort of stir and wake up and then the ethnic slurs would start going back

and forth. And the erasers would be flying. And I would slink into the back and put the drawing board up as high as I could to draw so nobody would see me, because I figured they'd start teasing me.

JULES FEIFFER: When I reached age sixteen and a half, to get a summer job, I looked Will Eisner up in the phone book. He had an office down on Wall Street of all places. I went down there and expected there to be a receptionist, but where the receptionist usually sat there was Eisner at a desk in a dark room drawing the Spirit. Instead of brushing me off, he welcomed me and he sat me down and he looked through my samples and he told me how awful they were and he was absolutely right. Since I was getting nowhere in talking about my work, I began to talk about his work and he found that I knew everything there was to know about him, going back years to his earliest features. Here he had this sixteen-year-old kid who had a dossier on him and just went back to *Hawks of the Seas* and espionage with *Black Ace* and all of the things he had done earlier, so essentially he had no choice but to hire me as a groupie. He needed some support system in his own office.

JULES FEIFFER, Artist Entered the business: 1945
Characters include: the Spirit

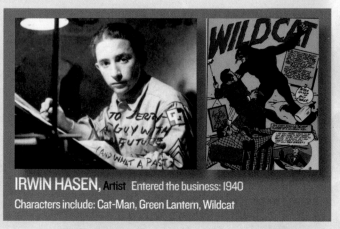

IRWIN HASEN, Artist Entered the business: 1940
Characters include: Cat-Man, Green Lantern, Wildcat

CARMINE INFANTINO:

I got a call from Shelly Mayer about four months later, come on in, we want to see you. I was lucky, the good part for us was there were back features you could begin on, six pages, twelve pages, but never the lead feature. And that's what I did. I went on a thing called *Johnny Thunder,* I think. And then there was the *Black Canary* and other characters—the *Ghost Patrol,* whatever the hell it was. And eventually I moved on to the old *Flash.*

JOE SIMON: As the business developed, it seems that the writers were mostly Jewish, and the artists were mostly Italian. Most of these people that were doing the artwork were sons of immigrants, and almost everybody I knew, including Jerry Siegel and Joe Shuster, their parents were tailors. "Schneiders," we used to call them, "sons of Schneiders." We had a guy named Whit Ellsworth. He was the editor at DC Comics. And he was known as the "company goy." That means "untribely" people. They had to have a front who was not Jewish.

IRWIN HASEN: In a company corporation you need a diversion. Don't let them look at the Jews, let them look at Whitney Ellsworth.

JERRY ROBINSON: At that time, Jews were for the most part barred from colleges, there was a quota system. A lot of the professions were closed to them. Here's one profession that depended on talent. They didn't care who you were, or where you came from, or what your name was.

STAN LEE: Comic books were not respected in those days. People felt they were either read by young children or adults who were semi-literate. And a lot of parents would even say to their children, "I don't want you reading those comic books." I thought someday I would be a writer and I would write books, the Great American Novel, like everybody wanted to write at some time or other. And I didn't want to use my name on these comics, this name that would one day appear on the Great American Novel. So I just shortened my name, which had been Stanley Martin Lieber, a normal name—I shortened the first name Stanley to "Stan Lee," so that I could save my name for these great things I would later write.

JOE SIMON: When I started, I was getting a total of something like five dollars a page. For that you had to write the story, and come up with the idea, got to come up with the character, furnish the characters, do the scripts, get the ideas, draw it—the whole thing! One of our little class jokes in order to make a quick buck, we'd have a big explosion on one page taking up several panels. So, we were kind of getting even with "The Man." [Laughs] Maybe we cheated them out of two dollars!

RAMONA FRADON, Artist Entered the business: 1950
Characters include: the Shining Knight, Aquaman, Aqualad

JOE SIMON, Artist/Writer Entered the business: 1940
Characters include: the Fiery Mask, Blue Bolt, Captain America

IRWIN HASEN: My page rate at that time was the incredible amount of eight dollars a page and we worked our asses off, pardon the expression. Day and night and alone in a room. And these young guys, myself included, sat, got our assignment from the office. Going to the editor, sitting down with the editor. Him telling you what he wants. Him telling you, can you suggest a costume? And that's how it was done. It was like in a shirt factory, piecemeal. Instead of a needle, instead of thread, pen and ink, pen and ink, pen and ink. That's how we lived.

STAN LEE: Well, in the beginning, everything was a little bit frantic, 'cause we were always working—in fact, all the time, we were working against deadlines. You had to have the book finished in time for the printer, because the publisher had arranged with the printer that the presses would be ready for the book at a certain time. If the book didn't arrive to be printed at that time, the publisher still had to pay for the time. So it was like life or death, that book mustn't be late. Things were frantic in the office, usually. The editor, or the publisher, or whoever was in charge was always making sure everything was on time. That was almost more important than the quality of the work, in those days.

JERRY ROBINSON: Basically, we were kids ourselves, so we were writing what excited us, which our audience then related to. We were making up the language as we went along. Every time we created something new, it was exciting.

JULES FEIFFER: At the time I don't think anybody ever intended to stay in comic books. Comic books were a way station toward the world of magazine illustration, which was a big deal in the *Saturday Evening Post* and *Collier's* and some of the other magazines where it was still going on.

JOE KUBERT: Most of us did work on a freelance basis; we either worked by ourselves at home, or in a studio, if you felt you couldn't work at home. There were shops, we called them shops at the time. The first place I came up to, MLJ on Canal Street, had about a half dozen artists working up there. Lined up on the window overlooking Canal Street. There'd be a lineup of artists and letterers and colorists working all at the same time. I've heard them described as sweatshops. Nothing like it. Nothing like it at all. Nobody chained you to a table, nobody, nobody beat you with a whip and ordered you to do the work. It was fun. These people were happy to be able to do this kind of work and get money for it at the same time. For me especially—I was just a kid and I was kind of separated from the other adults because of the age difference. I loved being in the business. I loved every, every minute of it.

STAN LEE, Editor/Writer Entered the business: 1939
Characters include: Jack Frost, Father Time, the Destroyer

JOE KUBERT, Artist Entered the business: 1941 or 1942
Characters include: Hawkman, the Blue Beetle, the Seven Soldiers of Victory

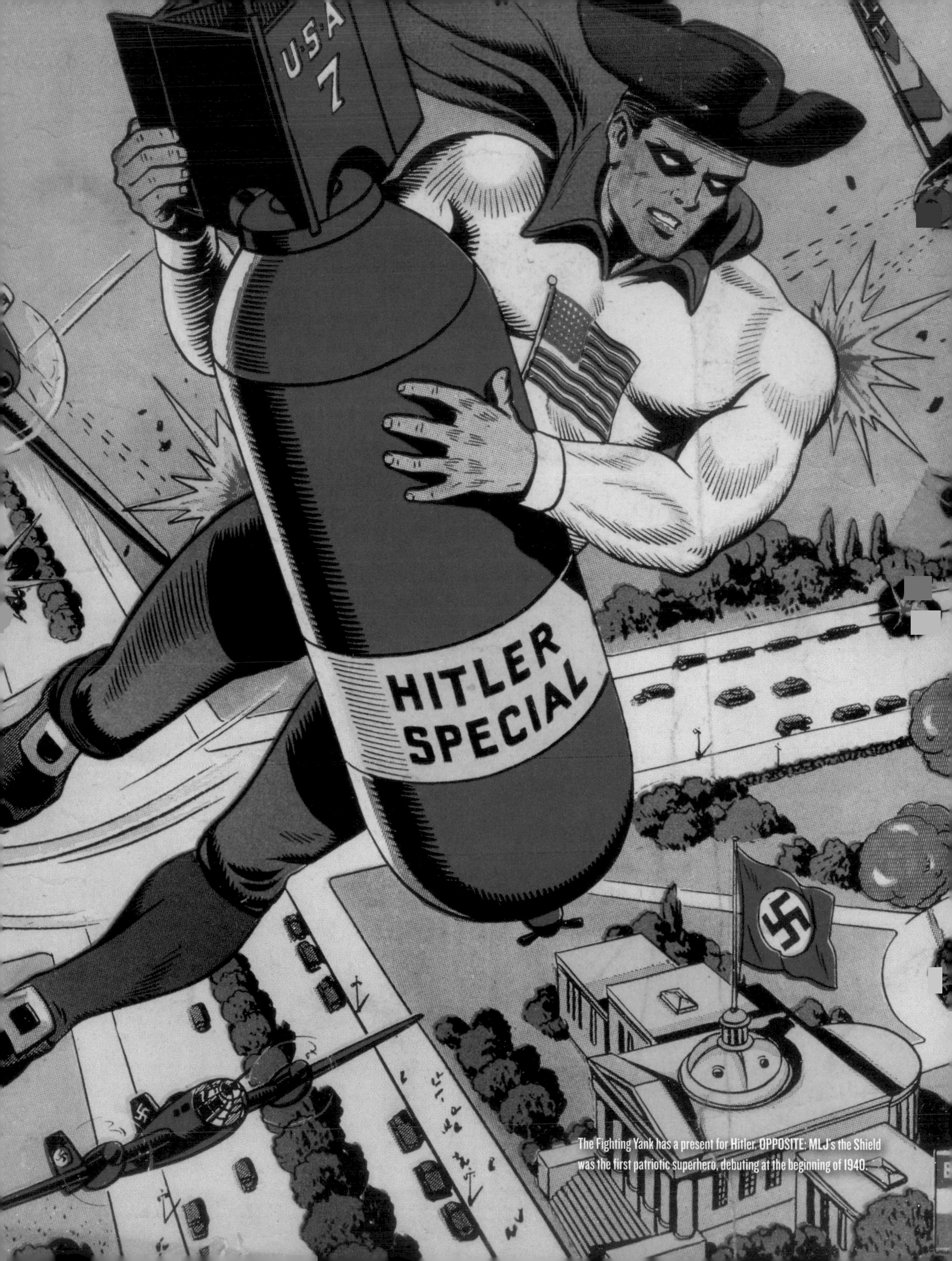
U·S·A
7
HITLER
SPECIAL

The Fighting Yank has a present for Hitler. OPPOSITE: MLJ's the Shield was the first patriotic superhero, debuting at the beginning of 1940.

"EVERY AMERICAN BOY'S MY NEPHEW!"
The March to War

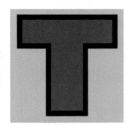he rise of the comic book super-hero occurred in close synchronicity to America's march to war—or, more accurately, the delicate dance of diplomacy required by the Roosevelt Administration.

When the character of Superman first hit the newsstands in spring 1938, Hitler's forces had just pushed into Austria and swallowed up its native government. When Batman first appeared in 1939, Germany and Italy had just announced their Pact of Steel—the beginning of the Axis powers. When Captain Marvel shazammed into view as 1940 began, World War II was already three months old and Germany had just unveiled its plans to conquer Scandinavia. But, if our heroes were physically ready to stand up against the threat from the Third Reich, they were constrained by the impulses of the American people, who were officially neutral and, by appearances in polls and opinion papers in early 1940, intended to remain so.

In Hollywood, the challenge of presenting opposition to Hitler and the Nazis by use of a popular art form presented a real dilemma. Almost all of the studio chiefs were Jewish and would have had little sympathy for isolationism, but they were also affected by economics. Initially concerned about foreign box office—in the late 1930s, nearly 40 percent of their income came from overseas—studio chiefs were cautious about insulting the governments of any country that had the power to restrict their product. But, as the 1940s began, and Hitler marched into various European countries, and as Italy and Japan formed the Axis powers, more and more doors were being closed to Hollywood product anyway. England was practically the only European market left. Despite the official stance of neutrality, Hollywood began to offer more products to American audiences that dealt with the widening European conflict. Newsreels were obviously incredibly popular in the early 1940s, as audiences avidly devoured any news from the continent. As Hollywood geared itself up to support America and American values, it cautiously toed an increasingly shifting line. The scourge of Nazism appeared in narratives that buried the political implications under genre categories such as the espio-

nage picture *Confessions of a Nazi Spy* (1939), and *The Mortal Storm* (1940), which was pitched as a family drama.

The comic book industry, churning out its own voluminous product on the East Coast, was a much more renegade business. Publishers had very little collaboration or cooperation amongst each other, let alone any kind of self-imposed regulation. The pace of producing comic books was such that anything was likely to get into print, whether or not it tipped the industry's hand about the war in Europe. In January 1940, MLJ's *Pep Comics* featured a brand-new superhero: the Shield, a "symbol of Americanism and all America stands for—truth, justice, patriotism, courage." The Shield was Joel Higgins, a young man whose scientist father was developing a secret serum to help the US government; when his father was murdered by Nazis, Joel avenged him by using the serum himself to transform into the strength-enhanced Shield. The Shield, conspicuous in his stars-and-stripes crime-fighting garb, worked for the FBI as his day job, where his identity was known only to J. Edgar Hoover.

A month after the Shield's debut appearance, Superman was drawn incidentally into the European conflict. *Look* magazine commissioned a two-page spread from Siegel and Shuster for its February 1940 issue, asking them to imagine how Superman would handle Hitler and Stalin. In a vignette inspired by the second Superman story in 1938, where two enemy generals are forced by Superman to duke it out, the Man of Steel pummels a Nazi bomb squadron, grabs Hitler by the collar ("I'd like to land a strictly non-Aryan sock on your jaw!," he proclaims, providing ammunition to the Superman-is-really-Jewish lobby), and

LEFT: A *Look* magazine take on tensions in Europe, courtesy of Siegel and Shuster. RIGHT: Minute-Man fought the good fight for Fawcett Comics. OPPOSITE: The superhero version of Uncle Sam was a Will Eisner creation for Quality Comics.

tosses the Führer and Stalin before the judgment of the World Court. (Since Siegel and Shuster were working on the Superman comic strip out of their Cleveland shop, they ostensibly created this piece outside of DC Comics' jurisdiction.)

Although Superman nominally worked for Uncle Sam (or at least with his tacit approval), that great superpatriot made his own bold appearance in the comic book pages, created by Will Eisner for Quality's *National Comics* in July 1940, just as the Battle of Britain was going through its worst days: "The forces of greed, evil, intolerance, and crime threaten the very existence out of which America's greatest character is born! Uncle Sam!" "Whose Uncle are you?" asks an orphaned boy, to which Uncle Sam, rendered as a steroidal version of James Montgomery Flagg's 1917 icon, responds, "Everyone's Uncle—every American boy is my nephew!"

By fall 1940, the real Uncle Sam—or, that is to say, his representative in the form of President Roosevelt—was still unwilling to show his hand. As the President told the *Herald-Tribune* in October, "The fact . . . is that the United States of America, as I have said before, is neutral and does not intend to get involved in war. That we can be neutral in thought as well as in act is impossible of fulfillment because again, the people of this country, thinking things through calmly and without prejudice, have been and are making up their minds about the relative merits of current events on other continents."

The quest for a supremely patriotic character, untrammeled by diplomatic considerations, began at the McGraw-Hill Building on West 42nd Street in New York City. There, publisher Martin Goodman was creating a hothouse for compelling new heroes. Goodman was famous for shifting around the actual titles of his publishing companies as a kind of financial Three-card Monte, but *Marvel Comics #1* in 1939 had been the launching pad for two seminal comic book characters: the Human Torch and Prince Namor, the Sub-Mariner. Both had become popular within a year after their debuts, but it was the Torch who first caught fire, as it were, and was given his own comic book in October 1940. They were idiosyncratic characters, inextricably wrapped up in each other's mythology and adventures. The Torch, created by Carl Burgos, was an android—an artificial being—who could burst into flame (although he had a thoroughly unnecessary day job as Jim Hammond, a New York City cop), and if he was rendered somewhat indistinctly as a sputtering red blob, it didn't singe his popularity.

Prince Namor, on the other hand, had no end of compelling facial expressions. Drawn with whiplash eyebrows and pointy ears by his creator, Bill Everett, the Sub-Mariner could usually be found sneering at surface dwellers or superciliously condemning them to their doom. The child of a human father and a princess of an underwater kingdom (eventually revealed as Atlantis), the Sub-Mariner sought revenge against the human community for wrongs done to his aquatic brethren. Acknowledged to be comic book's first anti-hero (as well as its first flying character, due to a pair of wings, Mercury-like, on each ankle), Namor could also be rather a bore, ginning up his ancient grudge in comic book after comic book. Finally someone on Goodman's staff realized that the Human Torch and the Sub-Mariner would get along like—well, you know—and soon had them squaring off against each other in two consecutive episodes in the pages of *Marvel Mystery Comics* in summer 1940; it would become famous as the first crossover storyline in comic book history. These match-ups (or smack-downs) became increasingly popular, culminating in one apocalyptic storyline at the end of 1940, in which Namor threatened to deluge the island of Manhattan with one enormous, lethal tidal wave. Whether young readers saw this as a metaphor for an imperious

madman who wished to destroy the foundations of democracy is open to conjecture.

By spring 1941, Goodman had hired a comparatively old hand in the business, the twenty-six-year-old Joe Simon, to be his editor.

SALLY O'NEIL

CLOCKWISE FROM TOP LEFT: Joe Simon (left) and Jack Kirby (right) at their studio; the Sub-Mariner didn't wait for a declaration of war to attack the Nazis (spring 1941); By 1941, the Torch and the Sub-Mariner were fighting Nazis side by side. Blue Bolt was a seminal Simon/Kirby creation (1940). OPPOSITE: Star-spangled powerhouses: the first issue of *Captain America* (March 1941) and Standard Comics' American Eagle, who also debuted before the war.

Although there were other costumed crime-fighters at Marvel/Timely (including a mystical creature called the Vision), they were nothing to write home about. Perhaps Goodman and Simon realized that, even though the Torch and the Sub-Mariner were the leading players in their studio, combined they were only one-quarter human. Perhaps it was time for a more relatable hero—a regular guy who could openly stand up for America. The time was certainly right: Roosevelt had just won his unprecedented 1940 campaign handily. He was also forcibly moving the country into supporting its one free ally left standing—the British government—by drafting the Lend-Lease Act, which allowed the English forces to supply themselves with American armaments. Perhaps it was the realization that America had just lost one of its previously unassailable heroes: Charles Lindbergh had just testified before Congress and recommended that the United States should come to an agreement with Hitler.

Artist Jack Kirby was born Jacob Kurtzberg on Suffolk Street in New York's Lower East Side; he attended the school of hard knocks, often reading adventure novels under the dark of the stairs because, in his neighborhood, kids who read books for fun got beaten up. Eventually leaving high school before graduation to become an artist, Kirby worked on various comic books, strips, and animation shorts. When he brought his portfolio to Joe Simon, then at Fox Comics, the older editor was impressed by the work and brought Kirby along to work on *Blue Bolt*, a Flash Gordonesque superhero; the fact that both men had fathers in the pants business provided a sentimental bond that went a long way toward making some of their early projects bearable.

For Simon, Kirby was the natural collaborator for a new super-patriotic character, so he brought Kirby over to Marvel to create Captain America with him. When they brought the character to Goodman, he supposedly loved it, but his only concern was that Hitler might be killed before the first issue hit the stands. With the debut of *Captain America* #1 (where Captain America's punch to Hitler's jaw might have indeed killed him), there was no question about American commitment to defending Europe

against the Nazis, at least in the comic book world. The timing was perfect for a character to stand up to the Third Reich. Jews in Germany had been relieved of their economic and civil rights since November 1938; no matter how secret Hitler's subsequent plans were, American Jews, many of whom still had families in Europe, still knew his tyranny had to be opposed. As Michael Chabon puts it: "A lot of those people in the comic book industry are Jews, American Jews, who are a little more clued in about what's happening over there, and a little more worried about it. They have a greater sense of urgency maybe than the country at large."

Although the majority of the American populace was still against military intervention in Europe as late as November 1941, Captain America opened the floodgates for patriotic characters. Soon, he had to face a different kind of competition—from his own side. Friendly fire in the comic book world came from a battalion of characters: Minute Man, U.S.A., the Patriot, the American Eagle, Fighting Yank, Yankee Doodle Jones, Spirit of '76, the Unknown Soldier, Major Liberty, Liberty Belle, and Miss America. Goodman was forced to put the following squib at the back of the *Captain America* comics:

IMITATORS BEWARE! Now that Captain America has attained such a vast following, many comic books are attempting to copy his costume and his deeds. The publishers of Captain America hereby serve notice that they will prosecute to the full extent of the law any and all acts of infringement. THERE IS ONLY ONE CAPTAIN AMERICA!

Such legal action never came to pass; it was the comic book equivalent of saber-rattling. It would have been, well, un-American in any case. When Japan attacked American naval forces at Pearl Harbor on December 7, 1941, the red, yellow, blue, and green gloves finally came off; with America officially at war, all of the superheroes waded into the front-lines. "OK, Axis, here we come!," was the war cry among the superheroes; cooperation was the order of the day.

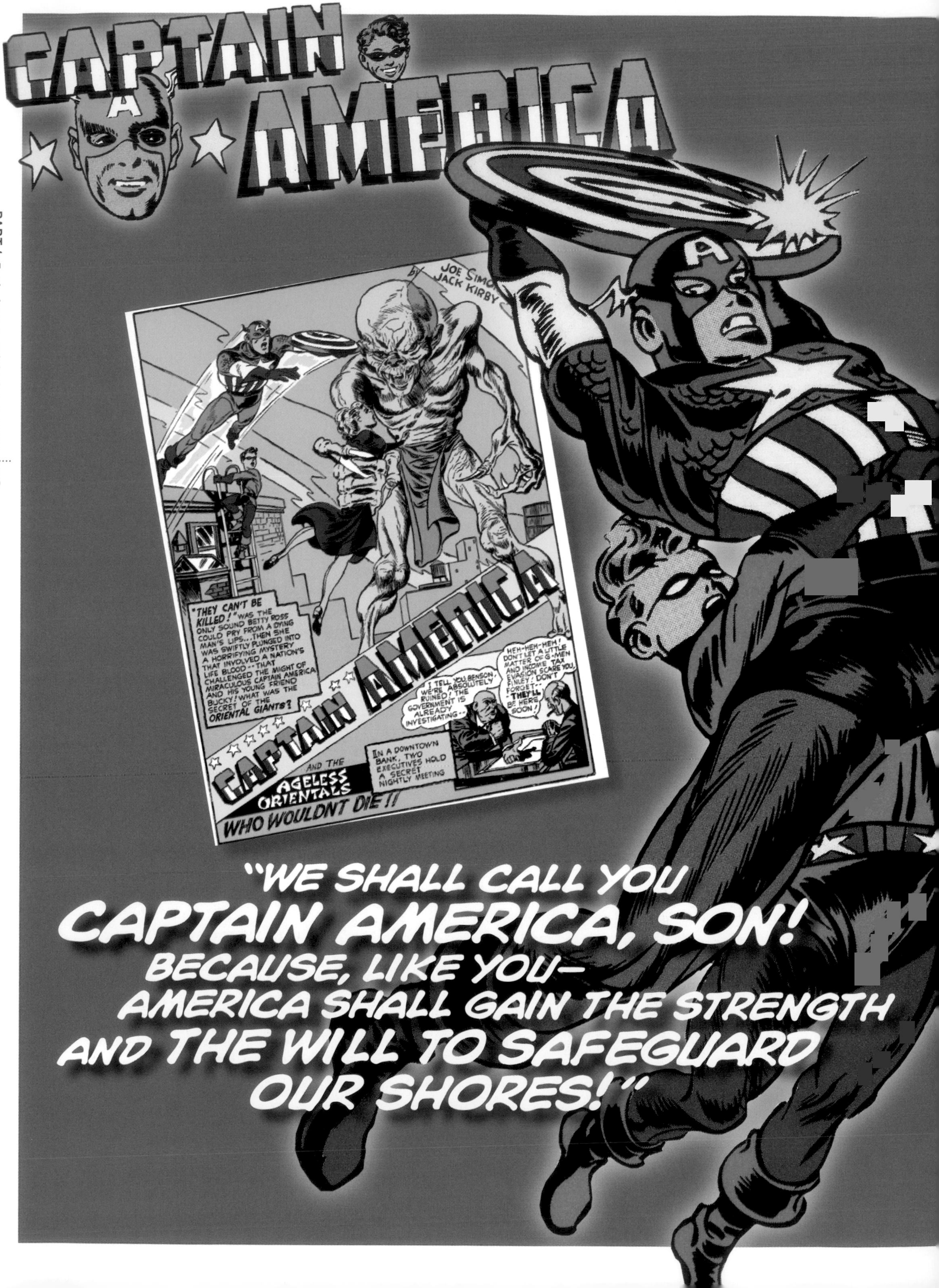
CAPTAIN AMERICA
by JOE SIMO
JACK KIRBY
"THEY CAN'T BE KILLED!" WAS THE ONLY SOUND BETTY ROSS COULD PRY FROM A DYING MAN'S LIPS...THEN SHE WAS SWIFTLY PLUNGED INTO A HORRIFYING MYSTERY THAT INVOLVED A NATION'S LIFE BLOOD--THAT CHALLENGED THE MIGHT OF MIRACULOUS CAPTAIN AMERICA AND HIS YOUNG FRIEND BUCKY! WHAT WAS THE SECRET OF THE ORIENTAL GIANTS?
CAPTAIN AMERICA
AND THE AGELESS ORIENTALS WHO WOULDNT DIE!!
IN A DOWNTOWN BANK, TWO EXECUTIVES HOLD A SECRET NIGHTLY MEETING
I TELL YOU, BENSON, WE'RE ABSOLUTELY RUINED! THE GOVERNMENT IS ALREADY INVESTIGATING--
HEH-HEH-HEH! DON'T LET A LITTLE MATTER OF G-MEN AND INCOME TAX EVASION SCARE YOU, FINLEY! DON'T FORGET--THEY'LL BE HERE SOON!
"WE SHALL CALL YOU CAPTAIN AMERICA, SON! BECAUSE, LIKE YOU—AMERICA SHALL GAIN THE STRENGTH AND THE WILL TO SAFEGUARD OUR SHORES!"

Captain America pulled no punches; certainly not on the cover of his eponymous first issue, where he lands a stunning haymaker smack on the jaw of Adolf Hitler. It was an iconic image: the punch that launched a thousand storylines.

In March 1941, President Franklin D. Roosevelt presented a real-life dilemma to the American people via one of his famous fireside chats on the radio:

> My Fellow Americans in all of the Americas: The pressing problems that confront us are military and naval problems. What we face is cold, hard fact. The first and fundamental fact is that what started as a European war has developed, as the Nazis always intended it should develop, into a world war for world domination.

That same month, in the comic book fantasy of America, President Roosevelt was presented with a pressing problem:

Actually, it *was* a comic book character who came to the rescue. More specifically, it was a scrawny recruit named Steve Rogers. Part of a government experiment overseen (presumably) by the FBI, Rogers is injected with a secret serum, wielded by a scientist with a more-than-passing resemblance to Albert Einstein. "It is working!," crows the scientist. "There's power surging through these growing muscles! Millions of cells forming at incredible speed!" This gimmick actually had been lifted from a *Blue Bolt* comic that co-creators Joe Simon and Jack Kirby had done for Fox the year before. Remembers Simon: "You know, if it's a good idea, and if it's funny or thrilling, it's okay to do it at least eight times."

The government experiment goes awry when a concealed Nazi agent assassinates the scientist—but within moments, the muscle-bound powerhouse that used to be Steve Rogers leaps to action and exacts revenge: "We shall call you Captain America, son! Because like you—America shall gain the strength and will to safeguard our shores!" Soon, "Cap"—as legions of fans

LEFT: Cap and Bucky face a typical Timely fiend in *Captain America* #2.
RIGHT: President Franklin D. Roosevelt appears (discreetly) in *Captain America* #1.

would refer to him—is placed among the trainees at the fictitious Camp Lehigh as a private. There, the goldbricking Rogers leads a miserable, Clark Kent-like existence. His secret identity is immediately stumbled upon by the camp's teenage mascot, young Bucky Barnes, who, in short order, dons a domino mask and becomes Cap's teenaged sidekick. (When pitching the character to publisher Martin Goodman, Simon wrote, "I think he should have a kid buddy or he'll be talking to himself all the time.")

Captain America's appeal was immediate. According to Simon, his debut issue sold at an unheard-of 95 percent rate, and subsequent issues were soon selling one million copies per month. Part of the appeal was his costume, an elegant redistribution of the American flag, with a chain-mail torso. He had buccaneer boots and gloves, which gave him a jaunty look, and a proud "A" on his forehead. (Much later, in a 21st-century adventure, an alien mocks Captain America's courage, to which he retorts, sneeringly, "What do you think this 'A' stands for—France?") Originally, he was given a shield that looked like something out of a Prince Valiant comic, but when the publishers of the Shield objected, flexing their litigious muscles, Simon and Kirby were forced to make a switch. They gave Cap a circular shield, a bull's eye that made him a moving target. It proved to be a felicitous move, as it made Cap more fluid (although he wouldn't toss his shield like a discus for many, many issues).

If ever a comic book character were created out of the zeitgeist, it was Captain America. In a 1988 interview, Jack Kirby said, "There wasn't a day passed by when in the newspaper the war in Europe wasn't mentioned, Hitler wasn't mentioned, liberty wasn't mentioned. And America wasn't mentioned. Everyone was patriotic. It was ridiculous *not* to do Captain America. Because there was an idea that would be bought by everybody." Joe Simon remembered, "People used to wonder what we were thinking—did our Jewish ethnicity have anything to do with it? You know, attacking Adolf Hitler and the German military? We never even thought of it. We were just trying to sell comic books. Hitler was the live villain of the time and Captain America was simply a foil for the comic Hitler. Oh, but it turned out the other way around!"

The adventures of Captain America and Bucky were repetitively bizarre and bizarrely repetitive. Somehow, Cap and Bucky would leap over a fence at Camp Lehigh and emerge hundreds of miles elsewhere to fight a barrage of drooling, slobbering fiends: werewolves, zombies, deranged hunchbacks, mummies, and other grotesque malefactors (usually some sort of saboteur in disguise). Whoever ran the fangs concession over at Marvel/Timely Comics made out like a bandit. In the second issue of *Captain America*, Cap and Bucky get into drag, with Cap as a grandma and Bucky as her "Fauntleroy" grandson, and fly to Germany, where they give Hitler and the German High Command a thorough kick in the pants. Inevitably, they would make it back to Camp Lehigh just in time for roll call, where the sergeant at arms would bawl them out, as if they had escaped, not from Hitler's clutches, but the latest Abbott and Costello *Buck Privates* flick.

What made these escapades unique, however, was the contribution of Simon and Kirby—particularly Kirby—for the first year or so of Cap's existence. As Jules Feiffer observed, "What Simon and Kirby did in *Captain America* was blow up the page. They were the first guys to use steroidal muscled characters before they had steroids, bursting with muscles but also bursting with action, jumping out of the panel, leaping, falling, flying figures here and flying figures there, and if you liked action—and most kids do—that was something that you paid attention to." For Kirby, it was pure common sense, a way to exploit the possibilities of the comic book page:

No other strips really moved. I created the follow-up action, which none of the strips had. In another strip, there would be one action in one panel and an unrelated action in another panel, whereas I would have a continuous slug fight. If a guy parried, he would follow up with a thrust . . . so it gave the strip a little motion. My instincts told me that a figure had to be extreme to have power.

Simon had nothing but praise for his colleague: "I think that Kirby was quite outstanding. He had a style that really changed the whole industry. Kirby had what we call a 'heavy brush.' That means he had a lot of ink on it."

From the start, Simon and Kirby sought to make a direct connection with their younger readers, initiating the Sentinels of Liberty club: ten cents would buy you a tin badge and a membership. Cap and Bucky encouraged youngsters to be part of the larger national struggle and, when the war came along, the Sentinels of Liberty were more explicitly asked, "If you see anything suspicious, even in your own family, report it to the FBI or to the cop on the corner." It was an early example of the "If You See Something, Say Something" public awareness campaign and it made the Sentinels the most popular superhero/kids affiliation after the Captain Marvel Club.

Simon and Kirby were none too popular with grass-roots isolationist organizations such as the America First Party and the German American Bund. Angered by Timely's hero taking such obvious sides against the Nazis, they tried to use their bullying tactics on Captain America's creators by harassing them outside the Timely headquarters in the McGraw-Hill Building. Mayor La Guardia offered police support, but Simon demurred: "We didn't think that we were insulting anybody, but, if we did, so much the better." By the time Captain America's April 1942 issue came out, it didn't matter very much. America was officially at war and Cap proved it by smashing Japan military commander Tojo in the jaw much as he had Hitler a year earlier. "You started it—now, we'll finish it!," he exclaimed on the cover.

The war kept Captain America's adventures in an ever more predictable bubble. He never really evolved, and readers never learned more about Steve Rogers or Cap's beliefs and fears. After the war, Bucky was briefly substituted with a sidekick named Golden Girl. By 1949, Cap's *raison d'être* was so diminished that he was folded into a horror comic before disappearing completely. He would have a brief revival for a few issues in 1955, fighting Communist spies instead of Nazi saboteurs, but the magic was gone; his glory days were during the home-front fervor of the early 1940s. However hackneyed his comic book adventures were, he bestrode them like a patriotic Colossus. To many young Americans, who had a brother or an uncle or even a father fighting on the front in Europe or in the South Pacific, Captain America was a connection to that conflict, a way of filtering grown-up warfare through the simplicity of a child's eyes. It was a great gift to the home front; Superman may have been a metaphor for America, but Cap simply *was* America.

"I always saw him as a modern-day Uncle Sam," remembers Joe Simon. "That's the only way I can describe him. The real Captain America, during my whole lifetime, my whole experience with him, was the kind of a guy, the kind of American that should be your friend, or your son or your father—more of a symbol than anything else. "

CLOCKWISE FROM TOP: An action-packed Kirby panel; an early Simon sketch of Captain America, with note to publisher Martin Goodman; scenes from *Captain America* #1.

CHAPTER THREE

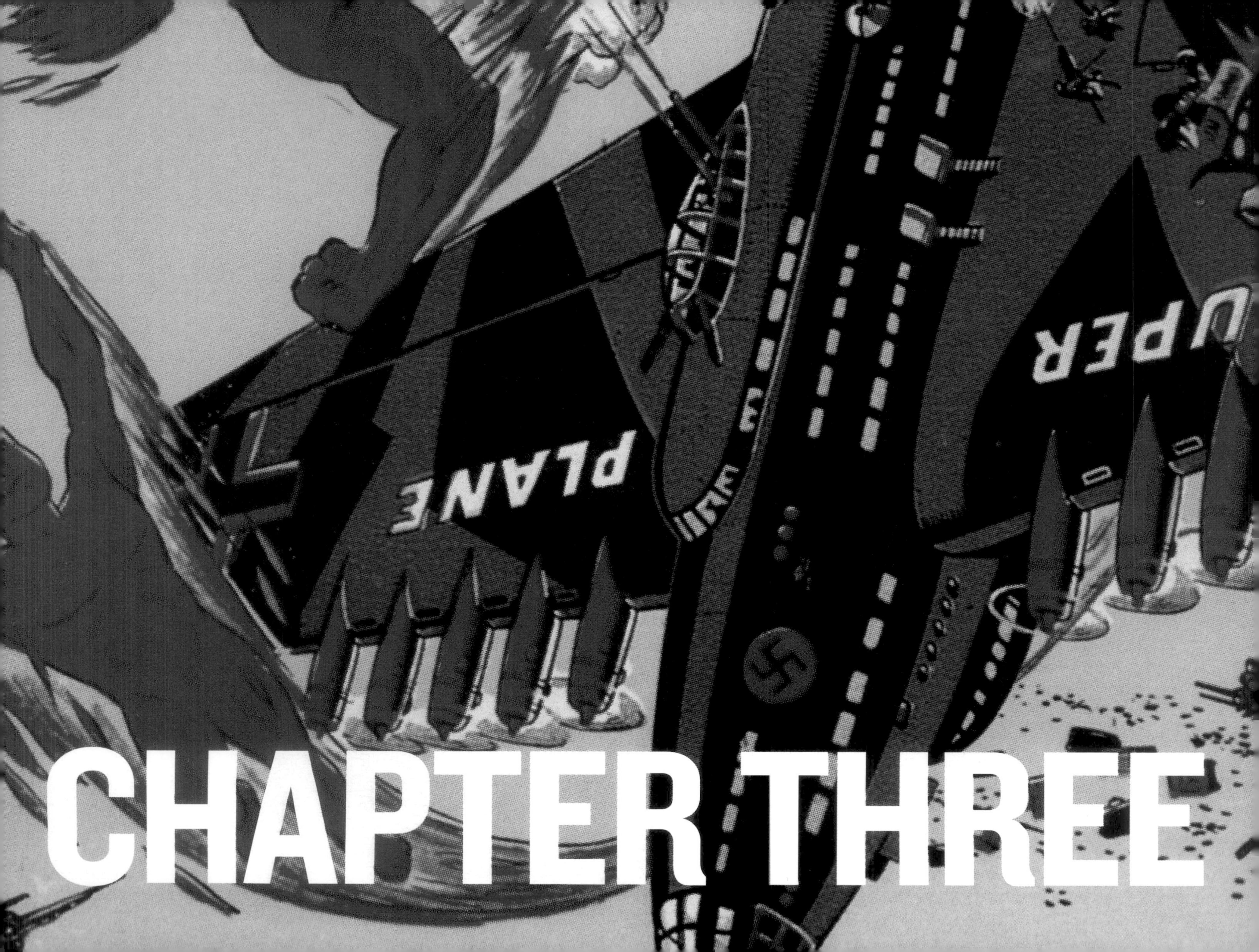
PLANE
UPER

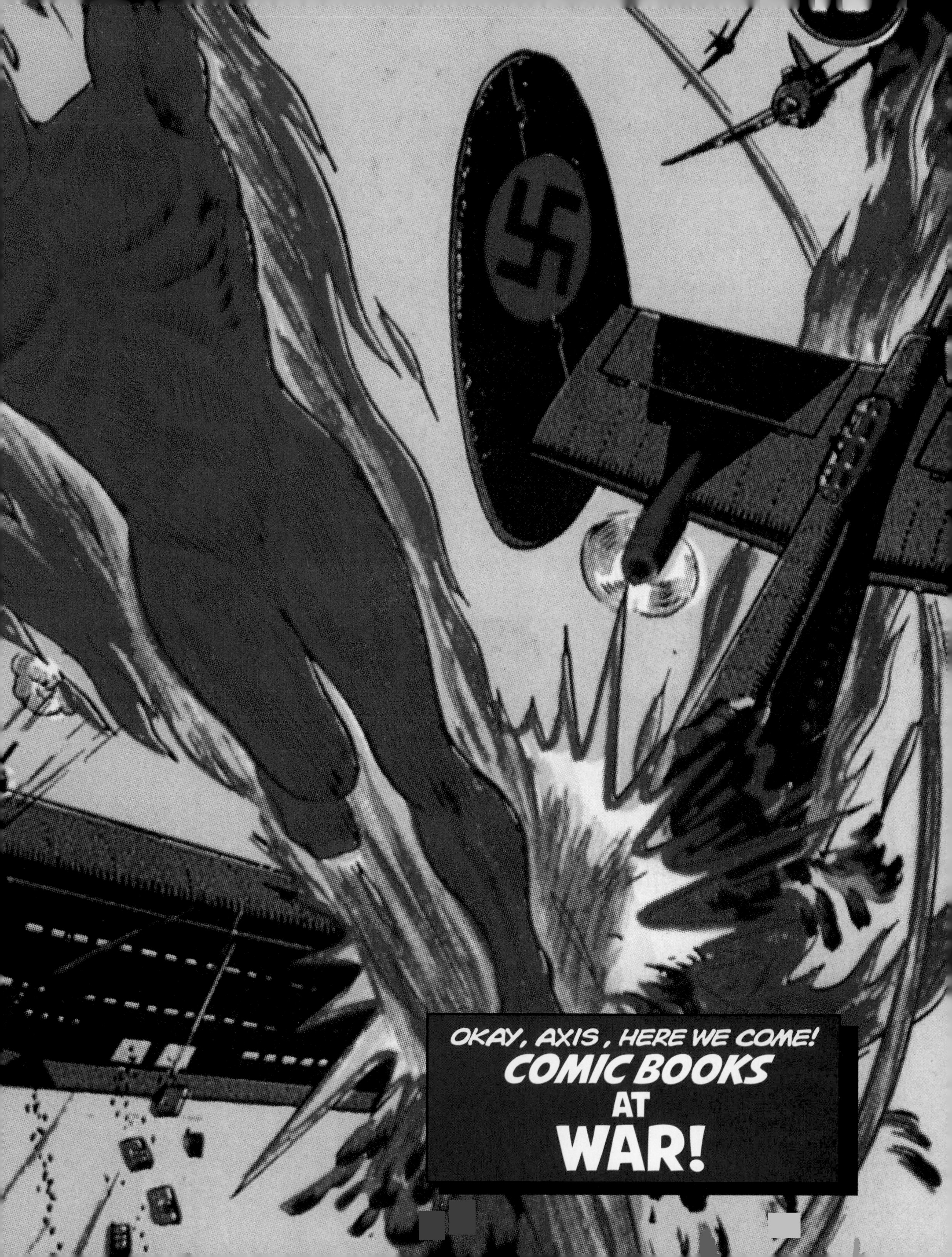
OKAY, AXIS, HERE WE COME!
COMIC BOOKS
AT
WAR!

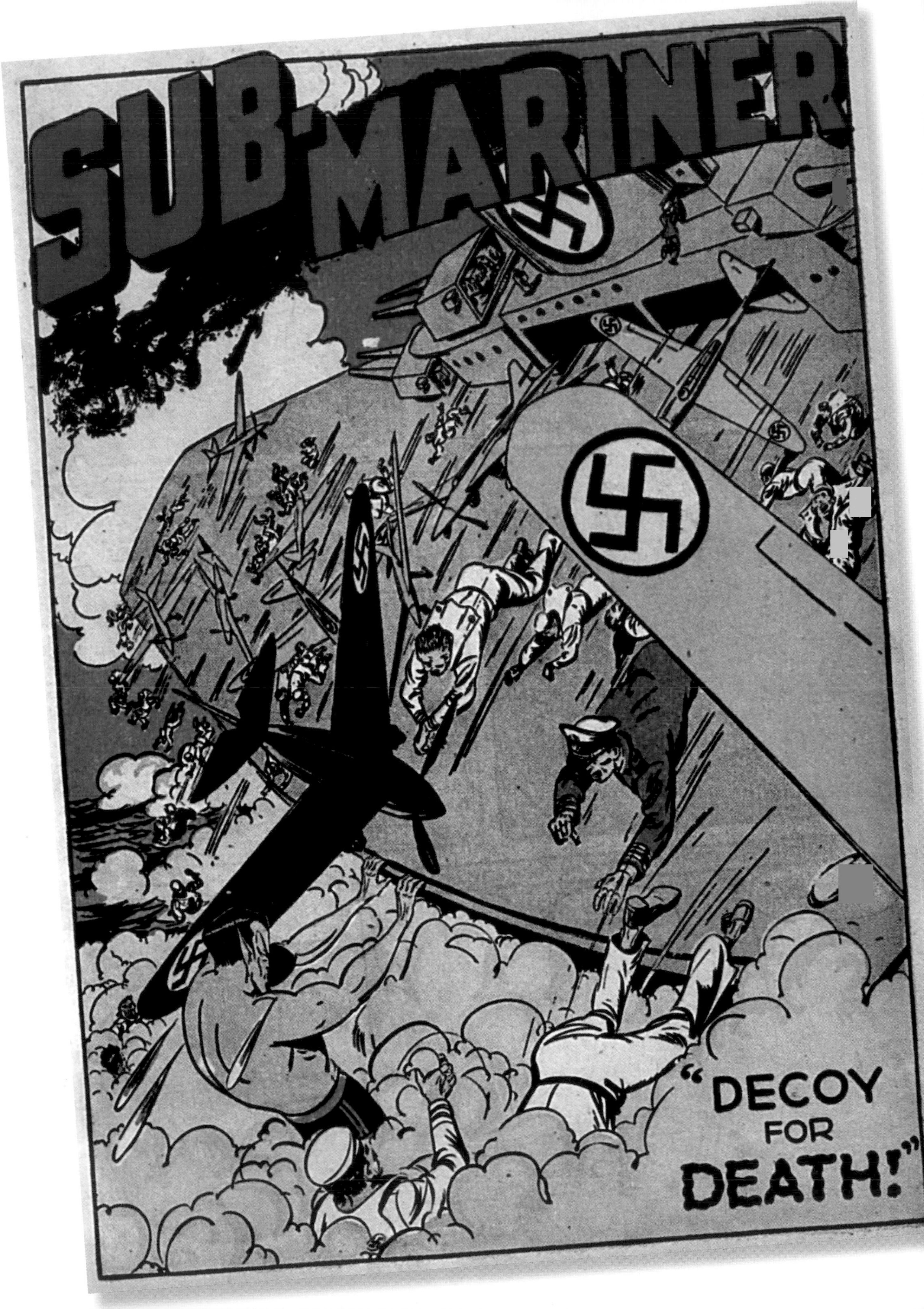
SUB-MARINER
"DECOY FOR DEATH!"

"OKAY, AXIS, HERE WE COME!"
Comic Books at War

**W**ith America's declaration of war against Japan on December 8, 1941, nearly all of the superheroes waded into the front lines. In the atmosphere of home-front morale, they could now throw themselves at Japanese; it was a comic book war on two fronts.

> Right at the moment when they most needed it, comic book superheroes were provided with the ultimate super villain, someone who is much more worthy of their powers than some guy who's trying to rob a bank. World War II cemented and solidified the idea of the comic book superhero.
>
> —Michael Chabon

The scale of the battles fought in comic books was near-apocalyptic. Tights-clad adventurers could single-handedly defeat an entire Panzer division; Prince Namor was easily convinced to rain terror and vengeance on Nazis and the Japanese troops rather than just humanity at large; the Human Torch could be found burning off the arm of an errant German madman who had his hand on some doomsday switch. With their fair-minded ethics untrammeled, the superheroes burst forth with the full extent of their powers—and if it looked like fun, well, that was okay, too.

The only superhero who seemed less than enthusiastic about his wartime opportunities was Superman. Given his invulnerable confidence, Superman had always been a difficult character to put credibly in harm's way, and America's plunge into international conflict complicated matters. He could have easily ended the war in one day if he wanted to, but that would have been hard to explain to the millions of kids who would have had to confront the next day's headlines. The solution to Superman's predicament actually appeared in the daily newspaper strip version in 1942. Clark Kent shows up at an army recruiting center, assuming he'll breeze through the physical exam. Alas, in his preoccupied state to enter the war, Kent/Superman's X-ray vision inadvertently kicks in as he attempts to read the eye chart on the wall, and, by accident, he

OVERLEAF: Timely cover artist Alex Schomburg lovingly displays the Human Torch's capacity for destruction in *Marvel Mystery Comics* #44. OPPOSITE: Sub-Mariner creator Bill Everett's elegant splash page from *Marvel Mystery Comics* #48. TOP: The first *Captain America* cover after Pearl Harbor. BOTTOM: Clark Kent flunks his exam, from the newspaper strip, 1942.

reads the chart in the adjoining room instead. Rejected as 4-F, he muses, "Can you beat it? Here—I've got the most powerful body the world has ever known—and thru a sad trick of fate, the army turns me down as hopeless."

In his comic books, Superman resolved to serve the American war effort by policing America's home front, declaring, "The

several "dumbed down" issues of *Superman*, with simpler vocabulary, available at induction centers.) At PXs in Europe and the South Pacific, comic books were outselling publications such as *Readers Digest* and *Saturday Evening Post* by ten to one. Despite wartime restrictions on paper, by December 1943, monthly comic book sales had climbed to 25 million copies, with retail sales of nearly $30 million. During World War II, market research showed that 70 million Americans—about half the total population—were reading comic books.

While the Marvel/Timely characters bravely stormed Hitler's fortress of evil, some of their creators did as well—at the very least, they were either drafted or enlisted. Joe Simon served for the Coast Guard and Jack Kirby fought on the European front. "Jack went into the war already a very compassionate man, with a lot of violent thoughts in the appropriate places. But when he came out, those thoughts were much more intense and he knew how to use them in his work," said Mark Evanier, Kirby's biographer. The overworked Captain Marvel writer Otto Binder said, "I think I'll be glad when I'm drafted and can get a rest." Sometimes, the comic book creators' skills gave them an entrée into special government work: Jerry Siegel worked on various service publications stateside, while Will Eisner created magazines, service manuals, and posters as a Chief Warrant Officer in Washington from 1942 to 1945. Stan Lee, who got his start at Marvel/Timely while still the teenaged cousin-in-law of Martin Goodman, found himself being trained to cut down enemy transmission wires on the front lines. When his superiors discovered that the twenty-year-old Stan Lee had a gift for writing, he was assigned to pen scripts for training films instead of shipping out with the infantry. He even managed some freelance work from his barracks: "Timely would occasionally send me a request: 'Can you do a ten-page story of this character or that? And let us have it by Tuesday.' So at night, when everybody was sleeping, I'd bang out a story and I'd sent it back to them."

Cooperation and team spirit were preached on the home front, as millions of Americans put aside their petty differences and marched together, shoulder to shoulder, ready to make sacrifices for the greater good. The stage was set for such comradeship in winter 1940, when the Justice Society of America convened for the first time in the pages of *All Star Comics* #3. The origins of the

United States Army, Navy, and Marines are capable of smashing their foes without the aid of a Superman." Batman also took a back seat in his Batmobile to the war in Europe, holding down the fort in Gotham City instead. No matter: Superman, Batman, and Robin were enlisted as buoyant morale boosters, giving over cover space to shill war bonds, stand shoulder-to-shoulder with various members of the armed forces, and promote self-sacrifice at home. One thing the DC Comics torchbearers did not have to sacrifice, however, was the sixty-four-page allotment of their adventures. Although wartime rationing suctioned up 30 percent of the nation's pulp paper supply for the war effort, Harry Donenfeld, using DC's superior sales and contacts, managed to keep churning out comic books when many of his competitors found themselves wanting for the paper on which to print them.

If Superman never made it to the European front, his exploits certainly did. Superhero comic books were now more popular than ever. One out of every four magazines shipped to troops overseas was a comic book; every month 35,000 copies of *Superman* were earmarked for servicemen. (Apparently, there were

OPPOSITE: At DC Comics, the real heroes were the enlisted men (from the anthology, *World's Finest Comics*). CLOCKWISE, FROM LEFT: Superman, Batman, and Robin inspire youngsters to participate in wartime paper drives; from the European front; a paratrooper in training takes a break (1944).

Wonder Woman's rise to prominence in the superhero field in winter 1941 was a precursor to the expanded role of women on the home front. RIGHT: The Flash makes the first plea for comic book unity in the pages of *All Star Comics* #3 (1940).

Membership in the Justice Society of America had a peculiar meta-quality to it. According to the JSA charter, once you got your own comic book with your name in the title, you had to recuse yourself from active membership. This is why Superman and Batman were naught but honorary members and why, in 1941, the Flash and Green Lantern had to streak away to parts unknown, so that they could shoulder comic magazines of their own. If this lent a slight bargain-basement quality to the remaining members, it didn't matter to fans—the idea of a superhero team was irresistible. As writer Jim Harmon put it: "Bound by similar interests and occupations, how could the masked and more-than-human crusaders who eventually became the Justice Society of America not become the closest of compatriots? Their conspiracies, their goals, their passions were all the same, and the same as ours, their admirers."

The Justice Society highlighted the importance of having all hands on deck; on the real-life home front, no one could be left behind—everybody counted. The most pronounced change in American society during the war was the introduction of women to the workforce in massive numbers. The female workforce grew by more than 50 percent, with more than 6 million women taking on new jobs—mostly in the defense industry and in civil service. And if women were taking on traditionally male jobs in real life, why not in comic books, too? A year into the Justice Society's existence, All American Comics introduced the character of Wonder Woman, and she quickly joined their ranks. (She was initially consigned by Hawkman to be "our secretary while we are at war," but that was really because she soon had her own book, too—those superheroes sure knew their JSA charter by heart!)

Justice Society of America lie partly in the spirit of comradeship, partly in the spirit of commerce. In 1938, Detective Comics had essentially given a franchise to M.C. Gaines to develop his own line of comic books under the "All American" banner. The heroes created there, often by Sheldon Moldoff, were admired but not nearly as successful as Superman and Batman, and none of them had his own book. Gaines' suggestion was to join all the second bananas in one bunch, thereby creating the first superhero team.

The Justice Society was composed of the Flash, comics' preeminent super-speedster; Hawkman, a high-flying crusader abetted by an anti-gravity Nth metal; the sorcerer Dr. Fate; the emerald ring-wielding Green Lantern; the chemically enhanced Hourman; the Sandman, he of the somnolent gas gun; the pint-sized Atom; and the Spectre, a sepulchral figure with powers from beyond the grave. In their first call to order, the JSA met to recount their most exciting stories at the behest of Johnny Thunder, a plainclothes youngster with a magic genie, who was probably comics' first official pest. For the next three dozen issues, the JSA would meet in the first few pages, acknowledge some dire threat, and then the members would split off into separate adventures, solve the problem, and return for the conclusion in a metaphorical gloved handshake of congratulations.

Other members eventually came on board to join Wonder Woman—Starman, Dr. Mid-Nite—and after more than three years, All-American took a gamble and created adventures in which the JSA members fought crime together as an actual team. During the war, the JSA displayed international solidarity with stories of shipping food to ravaged European countries and raising money for war orphans.

Gardner Fox, an inventive writer who created the Justice Society's exploits and sustained them for years, summed up the credo that kept such a disparate group of adventurers together:

I believe in the brotherhood of man and peace on earth. If I could do it all with a wave of my hand, I'd stop all this war and this silly nonsense of killing people. So I used the superheroes' powers to accomplish what I couldn't do as a person. The superheroes were my wish fulfillment figures for benefiting the world.

The popularity of the Justice Society superteam was noticed over at Marvel/Timely, which quickly put their heavy hitters—Captain America, the Human Torch, and the Sub-Mariner—together in the pages of *All Winners*, but here, too, their respective adventures were mostly separate. For only two issues, after the war, they were joined by some B-level heroes to become the All-Winners Squad. But, when it came to the issue of the wartime enemy, Gardner Fox's notion of the "brotherhood of man" would have hardly been of inter-

LEFT: The debut appearance of the Justice Society (Winter 1940); the Sandman displays an aptitude for public speaking in *All Star* #16 (April-May 1943). TOP: A self-portrait by Jack Kirby, P.F.C. BOTTOM: *Kid Komics* (Timely) offered a double-dose of racism: Japanese villains and black Americans.

est to the characters in the Marvel/Timely world, or to any of the other anti-Axis publishers, for that matter.

"During the war fever," according to comics historian Gerard Jones, "you have some appallingly racist portrayals of Japanese as animals, as demons. The portrayal of Japanese in war-time comics was more appallingly racist than in any other medium— even in the movies—and that's saying something." Somehow, the notion of a non-Caucasian enemy unleashed unprecedented revenge fantasies from a battery of artists and editors ensconced in studios in Manhattan: "The Japanese in comics all wore glasses and had buck teeth (or, often, fangs) and claw-like fingernails," wrote Don Thompson, in 1970. "Their skins were usually yellow, often greenish yellow. They were the Enemy, so it was all right to derogate them racially." If anyone complained about stereotypical depictions during wartime, those objections went unrecorded. Jules Feiffer remembers:

> That's what it was in those days and I was doing it myself. It's important to say that, with all their good points, one of the negative points about comic books was how racist and stereotyped it was in terms of minorities. Jews drew blacks who were cowards and ran from fights; the Japanese were frothing at the mouth; the Germans were blond hulks who underneath it all were terrible cowards. It was a tradition.

Still, in the heat of a horrendous battle that had young Americans fighting on two fronts across the world from each other, the comic book heroes sustained our fighting men and women, as well as the folks back home who supported them. Stan Lee observes:

> The troops, the soldiers, loved those comic books. Our books very often had Captain America fighting the Nazis, which was great for the troops, 'cause we always won in the comic book stories. It's a shame all wars couldn't be done via comic books. We'd always win and nobody would ever be hurt.

RIGHT, FROM TOP: Bulletgirl was this hero's sidekick; William Moulton Marston deploys one of his polygraph tests; Invisible Scarlet O'Neil was a leading lady in comic strips beginning in 1940.

LIKE THE CRASH OF THUNDER FROM THE SKY COMES THE WONDER WOMAN, TO SAVE THE WORLD FROM THE HATREDS AND WARS OF MEN IN A MAN-MADE WORLD! AND WHAT A WOMAN!

Wonder Woman is one of the most indelible characters of the comic book pantheon; her creator, William Moulton Marston, was one hell of a character, too.

Marston was part self-made promoter, part Harvard-educated psychologist, part mountebank, and an all-American original. Most comic book writers of the Golden Age were either star-struck kids or hacks with few options; Marston actually auditioned for the role at the age of forty-seven. His scientific background consisted of odds and ends; an interest in the relation between blood pressure and conscious duplicity, for example, and a fascination with the erotic implications of domination and submission. Based on the former, he contrived an early version of the polygraph test; based on the latter, he wrote a series of books and articles promoting the notion that if men willingly submitted their authority to women, it would yield both parties great erotic satisfaction and the world would be a better place. Neither of these two concepts proved financially sufficient to raise a family (perhaps because Marston lived in a *ménage à trois* with two women, but that's another story), so Marston supplemented his income by serving as a consultant to various public relations interests in Hollywood.

Casting about for some sort of reputable (and lucrative) forum, Marston famously gave an interview to *Family Circle* magazine in October 1940, where—against the intellectual grain of the day—he praised the imaginative powers of comic books and had some fine words to say on behalf of Superman's publisher. DC Comics (and All American Comics) already retained an advisory board to vet their titles, so it was an easy move for M.C. Gaines to offer Marston a position on the board. It was the spotlight that Marston had been craving for decades. He used the opportunity to put forward a new comic book character who could embody all of his philosophies: "Women's strong qualities have become despised because of their weakness," he wrote to Gaines. "The obvious remedy is to create a feminine character with all the strength of Superman plus all the allure of a good and beautiful woman." In spring 1941, Marston submitted Suprema, the Wonder Woman, and, after changing her name and hiring the artist Marston himself selected, Gaines and editor Sheldon Mayer gave Wonder Woman her debut as a nine-page back feature in *All Star Comics* #8—which means the star-spangled heroine would have hit the stands a few months before Pearl Harbor.

Wonder Woman was not technically the first female superhero, although she was far more colorful than her predecessors. There was Olga Mesmer, the Girl with the X-Ray Eyes, who had appeared in an October 1938 issue of *Spicy Mystery Stories*, and Invisible Scarlet O'Neil, who turned invisible by touching a nerve in her left wrist. And it wasn't as if there were no women characters in comic books. But according to comics historian Trina Robbins, there was a difference: "In the 1940s, in most comics the role of women was to be the girlfriend who was either a pest or was always getting into trouble and had to be rescued, and in that case was still a pest. You had Dollman and Doll*girl*. You had Hawkman and Hawk*girl*. Bulletman—Bullet*girl*. They were the ladies auxiliary in the costume but they were there to be rescued."

Wonder Woman took a back seat to no one. If Captain Marvel's origin was a primer on Greek mythology, Wonder Woman's lineage was a veritable graduate course. She began her existence

as Diana, princess of the Amazons of Paradise Island, an enclave of immortal women who have been living in seclusion on a hidden island for the past 3,000 years. Her mother, Queen Hippolyte, created Diana out of clay (propagation by a male was clearly a non-starter on Paradise Island) and the goddess of love, Aphrodite, breathed her into life. One day, an American pilot, Captain Steve Trevor, is wrecked on Paradise Island and the goddesses Athena and Aphrodite appeal to Queen Hippolyte to send Trevor back to America, "the last citadel of democracy, and of equal rights for women." The queen throws a tournament to designate the worthiest and the most capable Amazon to go forth from their little island; Diana enters in disguise and, to her mother's chagrin, reveals herself to be "the strongest and most agile of all the Amazons." Queen Hippolyte gives her a unique costume—with its eagle-adorned bustier and star-spangled culottes, it's just *made* to be worn in America—and, "like any other girl with new clothes, Diana cannot wait to try them on!" In love with Trevor, Wonder Woman brings him back to America, assumes the bespectacled guise of an army nurse named Diana Prince, and, in the words of artist Phil Jiminez, "begins her mission—to teach men the ideals of peace, equality, and loving submission."

After her brief appearance in *All Star Comics*, Wonder Woman soon became the lead feature in *Sensation Comics* and, as America's involvement in the war began heating up, found herself buoyed to new heights of popularity. There was certainly nothing else like Wonder Woman in comics at the time. Marston himself wrote every story (under the pseudonym Charles Moulton) and ruthlessly policed the editorial direction of the character. The depiction of Wonder Woman was largely delegated to only one artist, Harry G. Peter, a much older drafts-man who, in great contrast to the more fluid artists of the time, drew with an arcane style, a sort of Maxfield Parrish rendered in woodcuts.

And then, there was the paraphernalia. Wonder Woman was given a magic golden lasso that compelled anyone gripped in its noose to obey her and tell the truth. A pair of thick magic bracelets was a gift from Diana's tournament days on Paradise Island; they had the power to deflect bullets, but were often used by Wonder Woman's enemies to confine her in chains. Even the casual reader would have noticed a propensity toward bondage in Wonder Woman's adventures: she would bind malefactors with her golden lasso; they would capture her and bind her in some sort of ropes or chains; there was also the occasional paddling as punishment. The male superheroes of the time were hardly beyond reproach—after all, they wielded shields, batarangs, and ray-guns—but even Wonder Woman's more defensive accessories raised eyebrows. According to comics historian Gerard Jones, "You see a lot of characters in chains and manacled to the wall with leashes and collars. Really a lot—virtually every page. So, it was an interesting comic book. It had a wide readership, some of which I'm sure was little girls who wanted a heroine of their own. But I'm sure some of it was male and it was probably not all kids and teenagers either."

Marston's worldview did not go unnoticed. In 1942, *Wonder Woman* appeared on the list of

books banned by the Catholic church's National Organization for Decent Literature. When another member of the All American advisory board complained to publisher M.C. Gaines about the recurring images of bondage, Marston shot back:

> Since binding and chaining are the one harmless, painless way of subjecting the heroine to menace and making drama of it, I have developed elaborate ways of having Wonder Woman and other characters confined.... This, my dear friend, is the one truly great contribution of my Wonder Woman strip to moral education of the young. The only hope for peace is to teach people who are full of pep and unbound force to enjoy being bound.

While acknowledging Marston's predilections, Trina Robbins points out, "Kids don't see that. What they see is this fabulous strong woman and what they also see is a whole island of strong women—*and no boys allowed.*"

Marston continued Wonder Woman's chronicles nearly until the day he died in 1947. By then, Wonder Woman had joined Superman and Batman as the commercial trinity of DC Comics. In addition to her appearances in *Sensation Comics*, she earned her own title, as well as being featured in two other magazines. Wonder Woman's combined sales in the mid-1940s were judged to be somewhere around 2.5 million copies a month. And yet, her actual adventures lacked the jazzy spontaneity of most other comics from the era. Perhaps it was the result of her unlikely creative team—two middle-aged men with no real experience of comic books, one of whom had a huge psychosexual ax to grind. Her stories often read like the equivalent of "dad dancing." But through it all, the sheer bravura of her character, her noble strength, colorful costume, and unique position shone through, turning her into an American legend. Of all the great superheroes of the 1940s, it might be said of Wonder Woman that her whole transcended the idiosyncratic parts that went into her creation.

Jerry Robinson's Atoman first appeared in the wake of the atom bomb, in 1946. RIGHT: Captain Marvel fights an atomic villain (1947); Superman covers an atomic blast (1946) and gets bombarded with radiation in 1945.

IMAGINARY STORIES
Post-war Superheroes

The popularity of superheroes after World War II may have well ended in a whimper, but it began with a bang. The detonation of two atomic bombs on the Japanese populace in August 1945 unleashed the kind of devastation that was beyond the range of even the most powerful superheroes. In fact, Superman—and his publishers— almost courted disaster in the months leading up to Hiroshima and Nagasaki by flirting with atomic energy. The *Superman* comic book was preparing a story for publication in late 1944 that involved Lex Luthor attacking Superman with an "Atomic Bomb." The publishers at National obviously had no idea that the Department of Defense was preparing its own real-life atomic bomb, so when government officials stepped in and demanded that the story be put on hold indefinitely, the editorial staff was chagrined, to say the least. (How the Department of Defense knew about the storyline is unclear.) The "Battle of the Atoms" issue was eventually published in early 1946. The editors of the Superman comic strip had their own headaches when they published a few dailies in mid-April 1945 about Superman being bombarded by a nuclear cyclotron. The Defense Department once again stepped in and asked for the remaining strips to be pulled, although secret documents unearthed years later revealed that the government thought that if an inconsequential comic strip mentioned centrifuge, it was actually pretty good subterfuge.

The atomic bomb may have also functioned as a subliminal dose of reality. In much the same way that an actual antagonist to America's interest such as Hitler helped to provide an exciting context for comic books, the atom bomb's immense power may have conversely diminished the fictional fantasy of comics. Here was something more powerful than even the most imaginative writer could cook up. The brutality of the war also

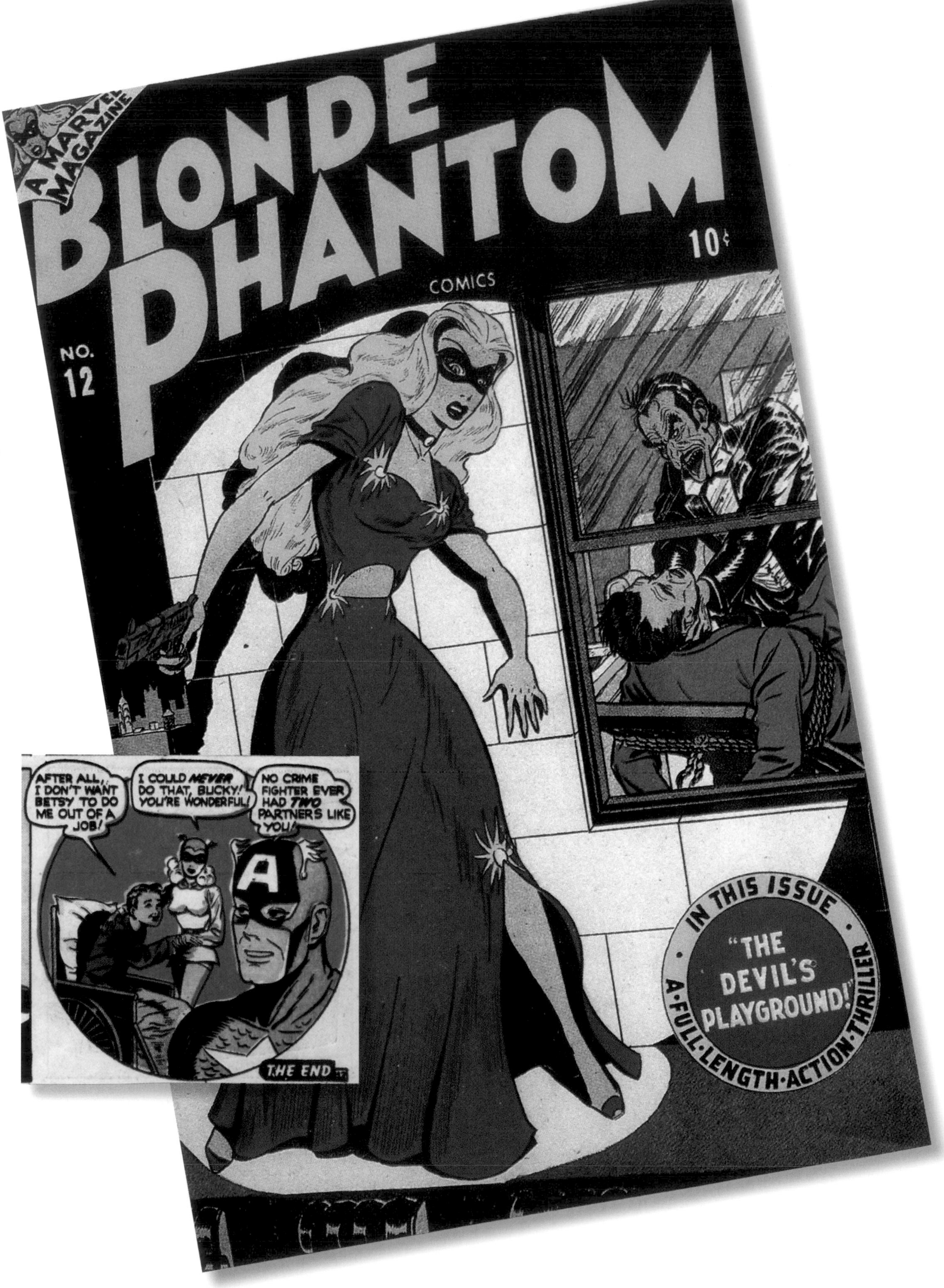
A MARVEL MAGAZINE
BLONDE PHANTOM
10¢
COMICS
NO. 12
IN THIS ISSUE
"THE DEVIL'S PLAYGROUND!"
A·FULL·LENGTH·ACTION·THRILLER
AFTER ALL, I DON'T WANT BETSY TO DO ME OUT OF A JOB!
I COULD NEVER DO THAT, BUCKY! YOU'RE WONDERFUL!
NO CRIME FIGHTER EVER HAD TWO PARTNERS LIKE YOU!
THE END

OPPOSITE: The Blonde Phantom carried the superheroine baton for Timely/Marvel after the war; Bucky is replaced by Golden Girl in *Captain America Comics* #66 (1948).
ABOVE: The Green Arrow (drawn by Jack Kirby) and Aquaman (Ramona Fradon) were respective back-up features in *Adventure Comics.*

contributed to a re-assessment of the superhero. Author Michael Chabon puts it in context:

> A lot of GIs who might not otherwise have read comics came back from the war and were willing to keep reading comics, but weren't so willing to keep reading comic books about guys wearing tights, flying around, wearing masks and driving Batmobiles. For someone who's fought in a war, has known the reality of fighting "evil," it doesn't coincide quite with what's going on in the pages of a Superman comic book where he just flies over to Japan and then slugs Hirohito across the jaw.

Superheroes were no longer box office champs by the time Harry Truman was elected president in 1948. Only one new superhero would appear as a title character immediately after the war: Marvel/Timely's Blonde Phantom, who fought crime elegantly, but inefficiently, with a revolver, in a mask and a red satin evening dress, slit generously up the side. Captain Marvel's sales had

dropped by 50 percent; Marvel/Timely's characters either would be shunted into horror anthologies or phased out entirely by 1949; Plastic Man was the only major Quality character to stretch into the 1950s. DC Comics (now National) had Superman, Batman, and Wonder Woman as anchors with which to weather the storm, but many of the anthology titles—*More Fun, Adventure*—divested themselves of superheroes or consolidated them into other books. Two minor characters from the DC pantheon managed to secure themselves a safe berth in the back pages of more reliable titles: the Green Arrow, a Batman knock-off; and the self-explanatory Aquaman who, according to his premier artist Ramona Fradon, "had the power to communicate with fish. He didn't have any others except punching people once in a while."

The year 1948 signaled a hallmark for Superman —it would be his ten-year anniversary—but for his creators, Jerry Siegel and Joe Shuster, it also meant the end of their initial agreement with DC Comics. Siegel felt increasingly estranged from his creation. During his wartime service, he relinquished his writing chores on both the comic books and the daily strip

Lois Lane got her own title in 1958, highlighting her romantic (mis)adventures with the Man of Steel; likewise, *Sensation Comics* (1950) concentrated on Wonder Woman's love interest, Steve Trevor. OPPOSITE: It's a dog's life: super-pets come to comics. Ace the Bat-Hound first appeared in 1955.

to other writers—"ghosts," they were called—and if the readers noticed, they didn't mind. (Joe Shuster, declared 4-F because of his failing vision, used other artists as well, and there was actually a noticeable improvement in Superman's artwork.) The top brass at National, guided now by editor Mort Weisinger, didn't mind either. Siegel's absence allowed them greater control over the character, who had easily proven to be a top earner in a variety of fields. Siegel ruefully observed the heights to which Superman was climbing and felt the impending termination of the decade-long arrangement required decisive action. He decided, perhaps under less-than-sage advice, to sue National for control of the Superman copyright and for $5 million in damages, which included, he claimed, the fact that he and Shuster should be credited with the propagation of the entire superhero industry.

It was a huge gamble, if a worthy one, but it didn't pay off. National stuck to their rights per the original arrangement and countered that, over the previous decade, Siegel and Shuster had made more than $400,000 in ongoing production fees as writer

and artist—no small sum in the 1940s. On Superman's tenth anniversary, the court decided that the authors "had no property rights in Superman since they had assigned all rights to the publisher." Siegel was awarded the rights to Superboy—a back-feature he had created about the adventures of Superman when he was a boy—but he quickly sold the character to National for less than $100,000 in order to pay for his legal fees. Even their creation's heat-ray vision could not have burned a bridge faster. Siegel and Shuster's lawsuit meant that they were no longer employable at National; worse, they had to endure the indignity of seeing their names as the creators of Superman redacted from the comic book splash pages for more than a quarter of a century. The ongoing phenomenal commercial success of Superman would prompt litigation for decades to come.

At the dawn of the 1950s, however, this provided a huge relief for National Periodicals. The lawsuit provided National with complete Super-vision of their most lucrative asset. The direction of Superman's "career" was now under full editorial control and Weisinger, in collaboration with Whitney Ellsworth and Robert Maxwell, could create a new Superman universe. In this they succeeded, certainly in terms of scale, if not necessarily in quality. The Man of Steel would now stand for the avuncular, reassuring values espoused by the Eisenhower era. This 1950s Superman would have been unrecognizable to his scrappier late-Depression era incarnation. He could now take literal flights of fancy into the past, the future, or into the world of "Imaginary Stories," which allowed him to explore—for one month at a time, at least—the idea of becoming the husband of Lois Lane, say, without damaging the title's ongoing continuity. Superman also gradually developed powers beyond consequence (or common sense), which ran the danger of making him inconsequential.

Taking a cue from the [Captain] Marvel Family, Weisinger famously oversaw not only the development of Superboy into his own "gee-willikers" kind of feature, but the introduction of Krypto, the Superdog; Supergirl, Superman's cousin (who had apparently gotten her own intergalactic exit visa from Krypton before it exploded); the "lost city of Kandor" (a Kryptonian Avalon miniaturized by a new villain, Brainiac, and kept in a very large bottle by a protective Superman); and a number of other super-sized pets and animals. This fantastical franchisement of the Super-brand even insinuated itself into the Batman comics. Batman was given an official police badge, took part in daylight parades, and was saddled with an incredibly unattractively designed Bat-family—Batwoman, Batgirl, even Ace the Bat-Hound— who at least had the discretion to wear a mask, so he wouldn't be embarrassed if spotted by his pals from the dog park. There was not a trace to be found of the late 1930s Batman in this cheery, earnest incarnation of the Caped Crusader—a character as creepy as the original Batman wouldn't have even cut it as a *villain* in the 1950s.

However egregious the changes were to the twin pillars of the superhero community, at least they kept the franchises alive. By 1951, protracted legal wrangling between National and Fawcett

finally killed off the Captain Marvel character. Ironically, it wasn't as if comic books themselves were doing badly after the war; quite the contrary—by the end of 1947, there were nearly 200 hundred titles on the market, which represented a 30 percent increase of the prodigious sales during the war. Studies showed that nine in ten children between the ages of eight and thirteen were reading comics—they just weren't clamoring for superhero comic books anymore. For Stan Lee, the high publication numbers came from a variety of other genres: "There were so many new fields, it might have been the Westerns, it might have been the crimes stories, it might've been the teenage adventures, but there was always something coming along. Whatever the field was would last for a year, year and a half, something like that, and then the new thing would come along." Romance comics had been lucratively pioneered by Simon and Kirby with *Young Romance* in 1947. Television and Saturday morning serials had propelled Western gunslingers into

the stratosphere; by the end of the 1940s, comic book publishers marketed their likenesses and exploits into publications that were selling in the millions. Crime comics had begun during the war, pioneered by Lev Gleason's *Crime Does Not Pay*; by 1946, circulation on that title had quadrupled. Violent crime comics hit a high spike in 1949, when they made up 15 percent of all comics on the market. The next new thing was the horror comic, brought into the market after the war and burnished into a grotesque, gory sheen by E.C. Comics starting in 1950; by 1952, horror comics, published by a variety of smaller, cheaper houses, but still led by E.C., cornered a third of the comic book market.

Taken together, this variegated competition spelled the temporary eclipse of the superhero comic book. Throughout the war years, superheroes of all stars and stripes fought against mad scientists and doctors who were devoted to their complete and utter destruction, and who often brandished a German accent. The comic book versions of these monomaniacs, such as Dr. Sivana in the Captain Marvel comic books, were laughable, one-dimensional, and easily defeated. The real-life scientist who emerged to eradicate the superhero in 1948 would not be so easily vanquished.

Comic books lose their innocence in the 1950s:
ABOVE: Marvel/Timely ventures into ghost stories,
while E.C. Comics, in an infamous Johnny Craig cover,
dives headfirst into horror. OPPOSITE: Lev Gleason's
crime comics were equally disturbing.

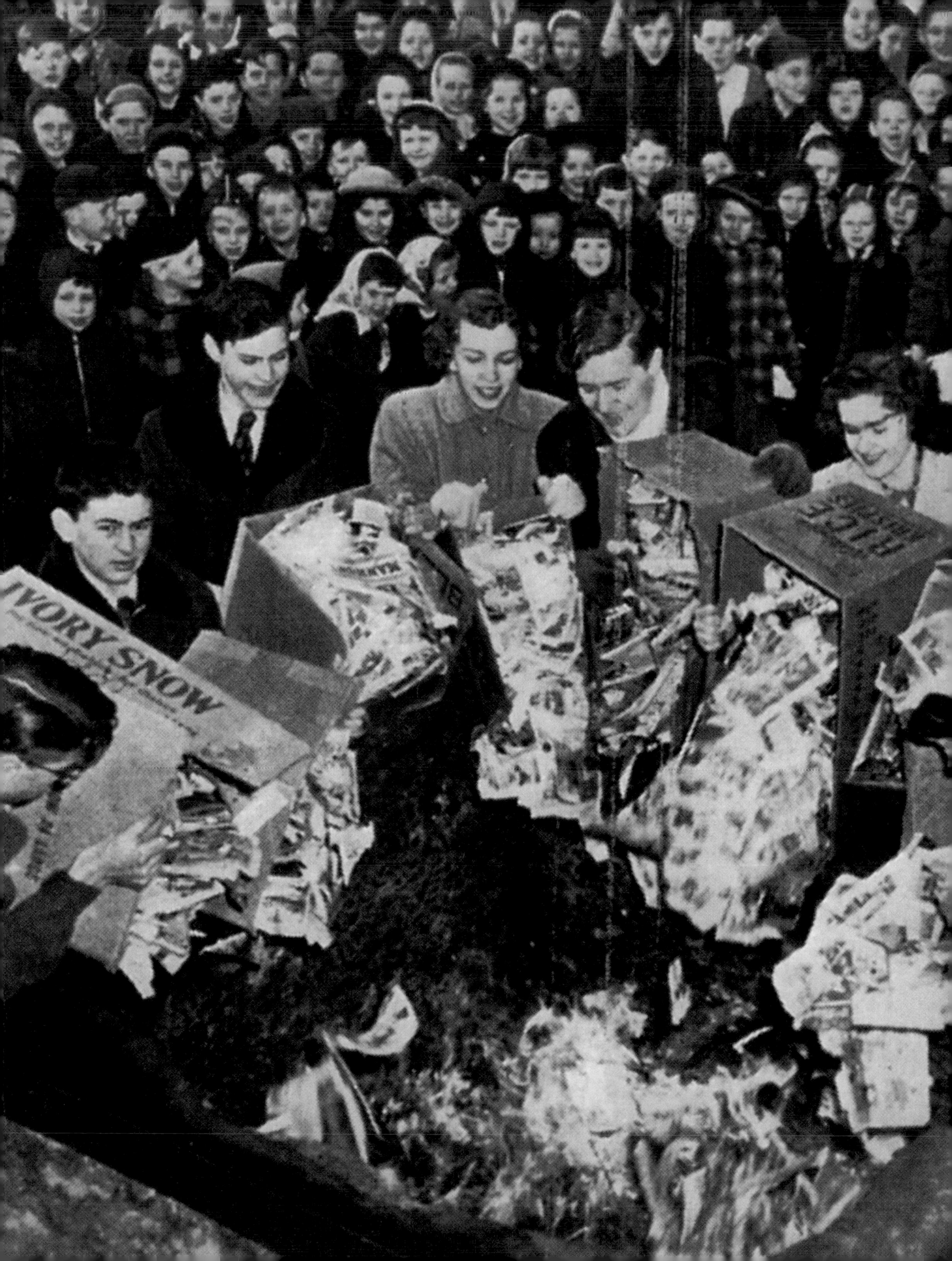
IVORY SNOW

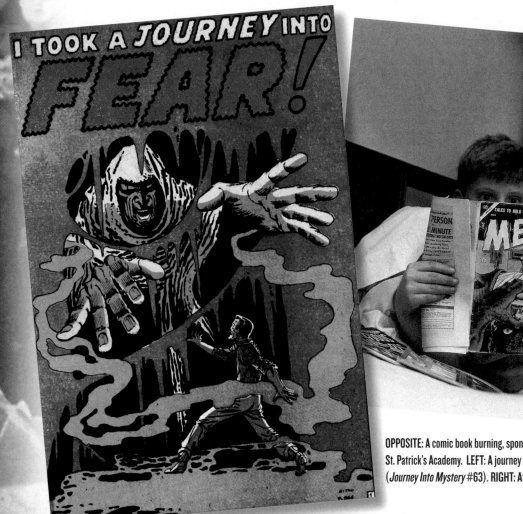

OPPOSITE: A comic book burning, sponsored by St. Patrick's Academy. **LEFT:** A journey into fear, courtesy of Steve Ditko (*Journey Into Mystery* #63). **RIGHT:** At home, darker tastes prevail.

SEDUCTION OF THE INNOCENT
The War Against Comics

Criticism of comic books came hot on the heels of the new medium. The first outright attack on comic books came in May of 1940, when Sterling North, a literary critic at the *Chicago Daily News*, penned a scathing attack entitled "A National Disgrace: And a Challenge to American Parents":

> Badly drawn, badly written and badly printed—a strain on young eyes and young nervous systems— the effects of these pulp-paper nightmares is that of a violent stimulant.

North's screed was so effective that thousands of readers, educators, and clergymen wrote in to get copies of the piece.

In a way, it was understandable; the very uniqueness of comic books was also their source of vulnerability. Comic strips had the tacit approval of whomever brought home the family newspaper, and pulp magazines were rarely bought by those with "young eyes and young nervous systems." Comic books, on the other hand, were both thrilling and accessible to youngsters, and the speed of their absorption into the "bloodstream" of American youth was unprecedented.

Historian Amy Kiste Nyberg notes, "the three groups that criticized comics were teachers and librarians who attacked the lack of literary quality of the material; the church and civic groups who were more concerned about the morality of comics; and, finally, the child study groups and psychiatrists who were concerned with the media effects on children's behavior." Some publishers, such as National and Fawcett, had recruited advisory boards to vet their material early in the 1940s, but the spike in anti-comic book crusades occurred right after the war. For writer Denny O'Neil, "It was a perfect storm of opportunism. A kind of maybe national disillusionment that World War II did not solve the problems and in fact we had juvenile delinquency. They looked for someone to blame and comic books were a very easy target because they weren't organized. They didn't have the means or the knowledge to resist the attacks made on them."

As 1948 wore on, the attacks became more frequent and frequently fierce. Grass-roots organizations and community groups organized public burnings of comic books around the country—despite the obvious association with Nazi Germany—and kids were often wrangled to join the proceedings. O'Neil remembers how one young attendee handled the bonfire:

> One of the towns that decided to burn comic books was Jackson, Missouri. And that was the home of Roy Thomas who eventually became a major writer for comics. You have to love Roy for what he did: He was a big comic book fan, and he and his mother attended that comic book burning and he brought a few comics that he didn't want and threw those on the fire, and then took some comics that he wanted to read and went home with them.

The more organized forces tried to put pressure on their local legislators, seeking some kind of government restriction against the publication of comic books. From 1948 to 1954, nearly a dozen attempts to regulate comic books were introduced in local legislatures from Los Angeles to New York. Despite fervent lobbying, they all failed. The First Amendment maintained a Superman-like imperviousness to these well-meaning assaults, and in many cases, lawmakers couldn't reach a consensus on how to define a comic book properly.

The anti-comic book lobby needed a champion; the one who came along was a most unlikely candidate. Fredric Wertham was a German-born psychiatrist who had emigrated to America in 1922. Ten years later, he opened a clinic in Harlem to provide inexpensive psychiatric treatment to black residents and their children. It was there, at the Lafargue Clinic, that Wertham began to observe children who were what we would now call "at risk"—and he found that most of them read comic books. For Wertham, comic books were the thin end of a thick wedge, a wedge of desensitized violence that allowed children to misapprehend the consequences of what was being presented to them. He saw it as his mission to make sure that every possible lever in the judicial system would be pulled to keep comic books from falling into the hands of impressionable readers.

By 1948, after various lectures and articles, Wertham became the poster boy against the tainted influence of comic books, backing up his assertions with a veritable portfolio of every objectionable panel or story he could find. Viable clinical data was harder to come by. Stan Lee took exception:

> He claimed that comic books were responsible for all the ills that befall mankind, especially amongst kids. He said he had proven that he went to a reform school somewhere, and ninety percent of the boys there read comic books. I used to say, "Well, a *hundred* percent of 'em drank milk!" It's very convincing when you have the name "Doctor" in front of your name and he got a lot of attention.

Wertham did receive a lot of attention—much of which he created for himself. In 1954, he collected several articles and speeches, with accompanying graphics, into a book entitled *Seduction of the Innocent.* Much of the book took on the fairly egregious panels and graphics of various crime and horror magazines, especially those published by E.C. Comics since 1950. Perhaps the worst of a bad lot was an illustration of a woman about to be jabbed in the eye by a hypodermic needle; ironically, it came out of a crime comic drawn by Jack Cole, the same jolly old soul who had drawn the antics of Plastic Man for more than a decade. Superheroes were not outside Wertham's brief, and he made a vehement case for Superman, Batman, and Wonder Woman as exemplars of fascism, homoeroticism, and sadomasochism.

Wertham's observations about Batman were mildly amusing:

> At home they lead an idyllic life. They are Bruce Wayne and "Dick" Grayson. Bruce Wayne is described as a "socialite" and the official relationship is that Dick is Bruce's ward. They live in sumptuous quarters, with beautiful flowers in large vases. . . . Batman is sometimes shown in a dressing gown. . . . It is like a wish dream of two homosexuals living together.

But many readers were bewildered by his attack on Superman:

> Superman (with the big S on his uniform—we should, I suppose be thankful that it is not an "S.S.") needs an endless stream of ever-new sub-men, criminals and "foreign-looking" people not only to justify his existence but even to make it possible. Superman has long been recognized as a symbol of violent race superiority.

Wertham's critique of the comic book industry might have been a provocative sidebar had it not been for a political opportunity seized by a member of Congress. Beginning in the late 1940s, elected officials investigated many of the perceived threats to American society. Senator Joseph McCarthy's investigations were the most infamous, but Senator Estes Kefauver's hearings on organized crime in 1950 were a live television spectacular unparalleled at the time. Kefauver, a Democrat from Tennessee, had been angling for a presidential nomination and was looking for a political football he could put in play to his advantage. In 1954, he joined with Senator Robert C. Hendrickson to convene a Senate subcommittee investigating juvenile delinquency. For two days in April, and one in June, they brought their hearings to New York City, the center of the comic book industry, to see if there was any demonstrable proof of the effect of comics on juvenile delinquency and, if so, what might be done about it.

On the first day of testimony, the subcommittee called on Wertham, who was their star witness. Wertham was treated

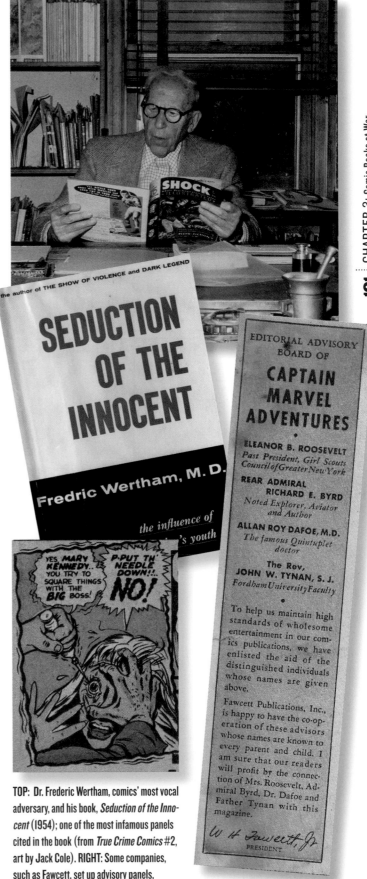

TOP: Dr. Frederic Wertham, comics' most vocal adversary, and his book, *Seduction of the Innocent* (1954); one of the most infamous panels cited in the book (from *True Crime Comics* #2, art by Jack Cole). RIGHT: Some companies, such as Fawcett, set up advisory panels, including this one with Eleanor Roosevelt.

with deference and held forth about the deleterious effects of Superman comics and E.C. Comics, among others. The next person to testify, unfortunately, was William Gaines, the son of M.C. Gaines, and, as the publisher of the execrable E.C. Comics, the most vulnerable of all the chiefs of the comic book industry. Gaines, who never suffered pretentious self-promoters gladly, took it upon himself to be the St. George who would slay the dragon that was singeing his sales. Alas, he was so wound up that he appeared both belligerent and incoherent. To his ever-lasting shame and regret, Gaines' self-serving performance gave the subcommittee all the ammunition it was looking for.

While the hearings made front-page news, they didn't really give Kefauver the gold ticket he was seeking. Again, clinical testimony was inconclusive and the final report issued by the subcommittee could only strongly imprecate the publishers to reform from within. Though the publicity was ruinous to the comic book industry, Wertham was furious about the final report, which he found to be much milder than his own recommendations, which included a prohibition against selling comic books to anyone under sixteen years of age. (In this regard, Wertham was quite prescient; he was arguing for a ratings system—something the movie industry never got around to doing until the early 1970s.)

However collateral the damage done to the comic book industry, it was damage enough. As Joe Simon remembered, "The news dealers were getting quite disturbed and scared—and they had all these mothers' groups that all were organized against comic books." For some artists and writers, the scandal touched them personally as well as professionally. Artist Carmine Infantino recalled, "Kefauver was using us. They went after us pretty hot and heavy, to the point where I changed my name in the books. I wouldn't use my name anymore, because it was like 'comic book' was a dirty word."

Ironically, 1954, the year that produced *Seduction of the Innocent* and the Senate Subcommittee, was the most successful in comic book history: more than 650 titles bringing in roughly $90 million. But by 1955, that number would be

ABOVE: The comradely relationship between Batman and Robin was open to misinterpretation: at play (*World's Finest Comics* #61, 1952) and at home (*Batman* #84, 1954).

Superman's superiority alarmed Wertham (*Superman* #22, 1943).

cut in half. Stan Lee recalled, "A lot of comic book companies either went out of business or had to cut the amount of books they published considerably, and because of that a lot of artists and writers lost their jobs and so forth. So, it was pretty tough."

There was another problem: television. A year after the war ended, there were only six million sets in home across America; by the time that the Kefauver hearings were being broadcast, half the homes in America could have viewed them on their consoles. Television manufacturers were clever at manipulating the new medium's appeal to children—sets were marketed as

a way of bringing families together. The rudimentary airwaves were quickly clogged with cartoons, space rangers, and Western heroes, especially in the afterschool hours—the exact time when a healthy American child might have been spending his time (and his allowance) at the corner candy store, sipping an ice cream soda and leafing through *World's Finest Comics*. The tiny black-and-white video screen had drastically cut into the revenue of both full-color widescreen movies and twelve-cent full-color comic books.

Who was going to come to the rescue of the superhero business now?

HEROES WE HAVE KNOWN

THE SPIRIT

First appearance: June 1940, "The Spirit Section"

Though not a true superhero in the technical sense, the Spirit looms large—as large as the moniker in his signature splash panels—over comic book history. In 1940, writer/artist Will Eisner was given the chance to create his own comic book as a sixteen-page insert for the newspapers owned by the Register & Tribune Syndicate. He jumped at the chance because, in the words of his eventual assistant, Jules Feiffer, "with a newspaper strip audience, he could get away from kids. Eisner thought, 'I'll do it for grown-ups' and he started using

his considerable layout skills and storytelling skills to write stories with satire and commentary, but with plenty of action to mask what he was doing."

The mask itself was essential to the Spirit—Eisner's only concession to superhero tastes—who began life as Denny Colt, a police detective thought to be murdered in the line of work. Using the exaggerations of his demise for crime-fighting purposes, the Spirit sequestered himself in a well-furnished apartment in the "tangled weedy growth" of Wildwood Cemetery. In Eisner's description from a 1948 strip: "Accepted by the police as a friendly 'outlaw' and feared by the underworld, his true identity is still a mystery." Although the Spirit often tangled with a criminal mastermind named the Octopus, he was much more at home tracking down swindlers, spies, and bank robbers on behalf of Police Commissioner Dolan, who conveniently was the father of Denny Colt's girlfriend. Women seemed particularly attracted to the Spirit, who was often willing—usually femme fatales with outrageous names such as Lorelei Rox and Sand Saref, who must have been a favorite among copy editors.

Off the record, Eisner said, "The Spirit, you could say, was a pure existentialist. He was living in and dealing with the world as it was and solving crimes for no apparent reason.... The movies always influenced me; doing the Spirit strip was like making movies. It gave me a chance to be an actor, producer, author, and camera-man all at once." Feiffer concurred, citing the Spirit's seven-or eight-page newspaper adventures as being more complex than the average comic—or movie, for that matter: "Every week, he did the equivalent of a B movie, except his B movie was often consider-ably better written than the ones at the movie theaters."

Indeed, although "The Spirit Section" —the supplemental insert— promoted "ACTION–MYSTERY–ADVENTURE" above the splash page, they were more often than not human interest stories with a nominal crime fighter in the middle of them. The Spirit himself was less of a superhero and more like a quizzical Jimmy Stewart playing the part

AND LOVED

of Philip Marlowe. The stories appeared in twenty major newspapers, from 1940 through 1952—read by almost 5 million people every week—and were eventually reprinted in the pages of Quality Comics. Eisner tapped into the dissonant uncertainty of an America that was trying to redefine its meaning after the war; his crime-fighting avatar fit glove-in-fist with the new, tense, morally ambiguous spirit of *film noir* that was appearing in American cinema.

PLASTIC MAN

First appearance: August 1941, *Police Comics* #1

Eel O'Brien was a petty crook whose cronies left him for dead after a foiled heist in a chemical factory; unbeknownst to them, Eel had absorbed some of the chemicals and woke up to discover he could become completely—and outrageously—pliable.

Cartoonist and creator Jack Cole had an equally pliable imagination and took Plastic Man on one of the wildest rides in comic book history. The character was given his name by Quality Comics' editor, "Busy" Arnold, who suggested that the character might get a, well, bounce, from the new substance being celebrated at the Hall of Industrial Science at the New York World's Fair—plastic. Plastic Man was introduced in *Police Comics*, and the first stretchable hero got his own magazine two years later. Cole soon stretched the boundaries of the comic book form, ingesting comedy, surrealism, and pure adventure. An advertisement kept readers on their toes:

If you should see a man standing on the street and reaching into the top window of a skyscraper, that's not astigmatism—it's Plastic Man! If you happen upon a gent all bent up like a pretzel, don't dunk him—it's Plastic Man! All this and bouncing, too!

Plas, as friends and readers called him, enjoyed an initial run of fifteen years, supplying the long arm of the law with a pretty long arm. Cole's biographer, artist Art Spiegelman, described his charms aptly: "Cole, a fantasist, made the point that in comics, anything one could dream, one could draw."

Quality Comics also gave fans the first "shrinkable hero": **Doll Man**—also created by Eisner—and the **Human Bomb**, yet another unwilling recipient of a "secret formula." This time, the formula turned Roy Lincoln into an explosive personality—literally. When he took off his insulated gloves, anything he touched exploded to smithereens. An impressive talent in the superhero game, it probably didn't do Roy any favors on the cocktail circuit.

MISS FURY

First appearance (in newspapers): April 1941;
(in comics): January 1943, *Miss Fury* #1

Miss Fury was not really a superhero, nor the first female superhero, but she was the first female action character created by a woman. June Tarpe Mills discarded her first name when she introduced and drew Miss Fury for the Bell Syndicate in a daily strip that ran until 1952. Miss Fury was Marla Drake, a bored socialite who put on a skin-tight cat suit on her way to a costume party and discovered it not only worked for fighting crime, but gave her something to do in the evenings. Miss Fury's adventures were collected and reprinted in Marvel Comics during the 1940s.

DR. MID-NITE

First appearance: April 1941, *All-American Comics* #25

Dr. Charles McNider was the victim of a bomb attack intended to keep him off the witness stand. When an owl pulled the bandages off his eyes, he discovered he could see in the dark; the addition of a pair of special goggles allowed the blinded McNider to see in the daylight. The first blind superhero (although it is churlish, but accurate, to point out that he was actually able to see most of the time), Dr. Mid-Nite used "blackout" bombs to disorient criminals in his *All-American* appearances; the resourceful owl became his pet sidekick, Hooty—one of the many redundant pet and goofy sidekicks given to All-American and DC Comics heroes during the war.

THE SPECTRE

First appearance: April 1940, *More Fun Comics* #52

Jerry Siegel gave the world its most important superhero in 1938, but two years later, for *More Fun Comics*, he created (with Bernard Baily) one of its most intriguing. The Spectre was originally a cop named Jim Corrigan who was killed in the line of duty; some generic Heavenly Fathers decided that although his number was up, his duty on earth wasn't. He was reincarnated as the chalk-white Spectre—the "Ghostly Guardian." The Spectre,

who could manipulate metaphysical time and space, proved to be as omnipotent in his own creepy way as Superman was in his—and that also made him a difficult character for whom to create ongoing suspense. Still, no hero who could isolate a criminal's brain in mid-air in order to read his thoughts should be discounted; until he gave up the ghost in 1945, the Spectre made life—and death—pretty interesting over at DC Comics.

THE DESTROYER

First appearance: November 1941, *Mystic Comics* #6

Yet another superhero given his powers by a secret formula, the Destroyer had the advantage of a slightly more interesting background (concocted by the young Stan Lee). Keen Marlowe was an investigative reporter poking into Nazi atrocities; for his curiosity, the Nazis gave him a one-way ticket to a concentration camp. There, he befriended a German (and presumably Jewish) scientist who gave him a power-enhancing serum before he died. Marlowe took the serum, escaped, and became the Destroyer, a powerhouse with a relentless hatred of Nazis. One of the few heroes who fought their battles exclusively on the European front, the Destroyer exhibited a fearful mien that placed him firmly within the Marvel/Timely camp, as did the extremity of his violent rages. His striped tights, however, made him unique outside of a revival of the musical *Kiss Me, Kate*.

AND VILLAINS WE LOVE TO HATE

MR. MIND

First appearance: March 1943,
Captain Marvel Adventures #22

In a story line that lasted nearly two years, Captain Marvel was driven to distraction by a mysterious voice that had organized and unleashed the Monster Society of Evil against him. A few issues later, the criminal mastermind was revealed to be a little green worm from another planet, whose mutations gave him the power of speech (through a tiny radio) and a mental capacity far beyond those of mortal men—or mortal larvae, for that matter. Mr. Mind was the paradigmatic example of the gentle and beloved ludicrousness of the Captain Marvel comic books.

THE RED SKULL

First appearance: March 1941, *Captain America* #1

If the Red Skull had a membership card in the National Socialist Party, he was probably identified as number "2." Hitler's most trusted agent in carrying out atrocities and malefaction on behalf of the Third Reich appeared as one of Captain America's very first villains. The Red Skull was revealed to be an American industrialist with nefarious plans on the home front and died at the end of his debut story. Fans clamored for his return, so Simon and Kirby—who knew a good, lurid, leering villain when they saw one—resurrected him six issues later. This Red Skull was the genuine article, although whether he wore a mask or was some grotesque mutation was left up in the air. As much as Captain America was the symbol of all that was good in the U.S. of A., the Red Skull symbolized everyone's worst fears of the Nazis' intentions. The Red Skull and Captain America squared off against each other throughout the war, all the way to Cap's last appearance of the Golden Age in 1949, where they drag each other into the pits of Hell. When the Red Skull re-appeared in the 1960s, his origin became more complex, but during the war years, the enormity of his evil schemes required no such naturalistic explanations.

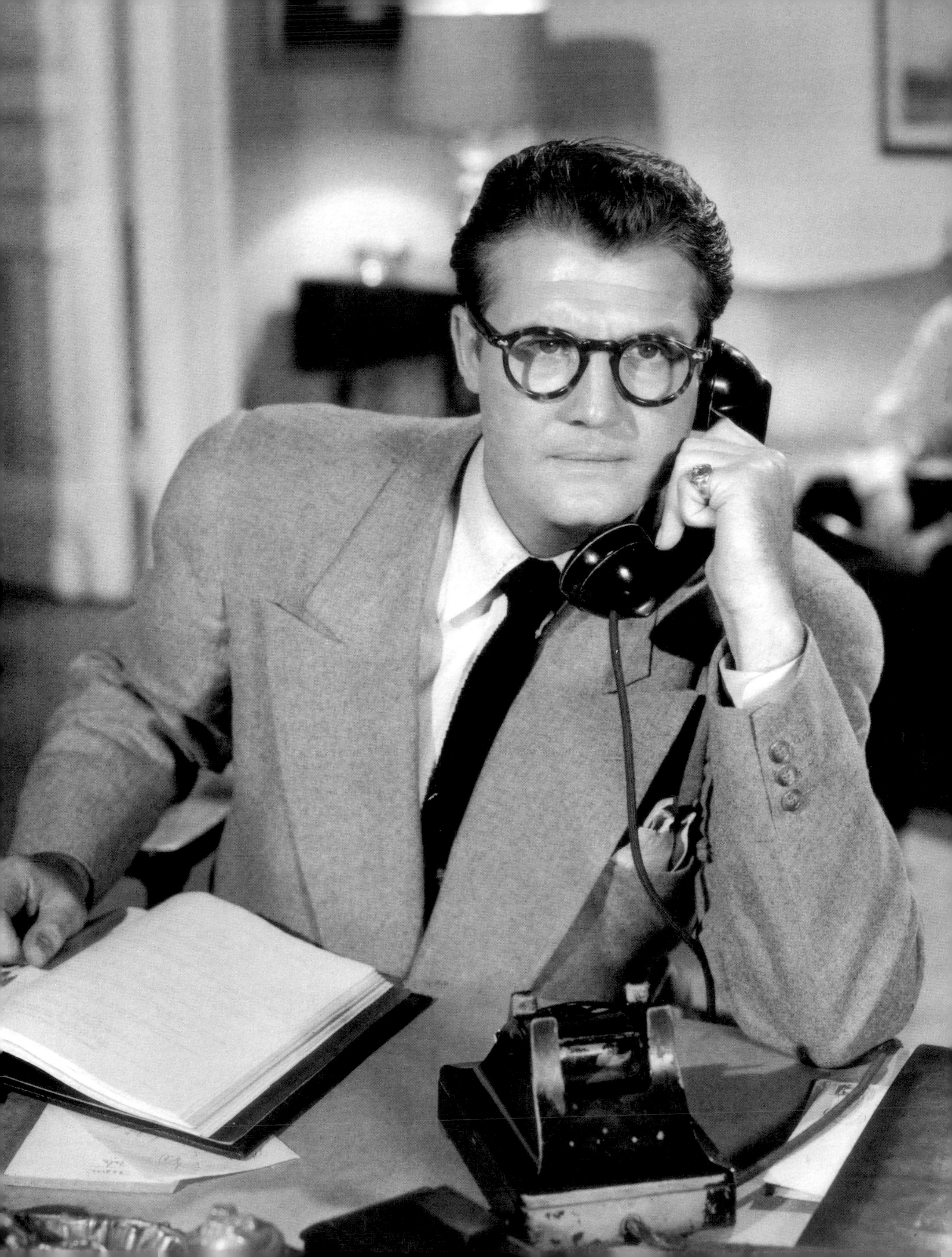

TO BE CONTINUED:
"And They Call *Me* Superman!"

In 1951, the Man of Tomorrow looked into the future and saw a tiny black-and-white screen.

Radio dramas and Saturday afternoon serials were in a death spiral; the radio adventures of Superman had come to their conclusion in 1951, and the final chapter of the Superman movie serials had posted "The End" the year before. Television was the new medium with which to be reckoned. There were already successful Western heroes and space heroes on television—Superman seemed a natural.

National Periodicals dispatched Robert Maxwell, the radio producer who guided Superman to the airwaves, to Los Angeles to see if he could make a deal to put Superman on screen. He decided to make a short film as a pilot, called *Superman vs. the Mole Men;* it involved some underground creatures appearing to terrorize an oil town, only to discover that they are being terrorized themselves by hostile townspeople. Superman intercedes and restores order and decency. The film was released briefly to considerable success among the kiddie matinee audience; almost immediately, the producers of *Adventures of Superman* began grinding out the remaining episodes for the twenty-six-part series on the RKO backlot in Culver City.

The executive producer, National Periodicals—and kids around the country—were blessed with their choice of a Superman. George Reeves, a former boxer, was a trained actor and had been a Hollywood stand-by for two decades (he appeared in *Gone with the Wind* as well as several successful "A" films during the war). He was thirty-seven and experiencing a career downturn when he got offered the job of Superman. He shrugged his soon-to-be-padded shoulders: "Why not?" he purportedly said. "I've played every other type of part you could think of."

It wasn't easy being Superman on television. The budget was tightly corseted—the crew would shoot, say, all the Daily Planet scenes for the entire season in a row—and the special effects were primitive. Still, Reeves brought something special to the Super-party. No actor before him had impersonated a superhero

OPPOSITE: George Reeves brought an engaging humor and sense of purpose into his Clark Kent persona. TOP: DC editor Whitney Ellsworth brings his Super-Vision to the set with Reeves. BOTTOM: The trial balloon for the *Adventures of Superman* was a brief feature in 1951.

so persuasively; many fans would argue that no other actor after him would do as well in such a preposterous assignment. Reeves eschewed any kind of transformative change between Superman and Clark Kent. His Clark Kent, who always wore the same grey doubled-breasted suit and fedora (again, due to budget constraints), was a hard-nosed, crusading reporter with a great deal of tenacity and charm, while his Superman was a hard-nosed, crusading superhero with a great deal of tenacity and charm. Reeves pursued a more contrasting alter ego in real life: off the set, he appreciated the value of a martini or three at quitting time, and his love life involved a long dalliance with the wife of a powerful MGM producer. But he took his public image of Superman seriously, often suiting up for charity appearances (where he endured more than one punch to the stomach from a competitive eleven-year-old) and making sure children knew that only Superman had the power to fly—he pressured National to place prominent warnings to that effect on licensed Halloween costumes.

The first twenty-six episodes of *Adventures of Superman* were picked up for national broadcast in 1953. They were compelling pot-boilers which owed more to film noir than to the fantastical Superman in the comic books; in one episode, Superman grimly stranded three malefactors on a snowy mountaintop. Still, the series caught on quickly, but National was distressed by the tone of the show, which was skewed toward adults who liked crime stories. Whitney Ellsworth, a DC Comics editor since 1940—he was known as the "company goy"—was dispatched to Hollywood to take over from Maxwell and reformat the series for kids and for a new sponsor, Kellogg's cereal. Years before the word "synergy" was invented, it fell to Ellsworth (who would eventually co-write a dozen of the show's 104 episodes) to make sure the published Superman and the video Superman stood for the same values. Occasionally, a television script would become a comic book story, or vice versa, but the main thing was that, within the confines of the production budget, Superman and his chums would now deal less with vicious gangsters and more with befuddled professors, incompetent smugglers, gullible crooks, and adoring children. During the

1954 season, while the Senate hearings about juvenile delinquents were being televised in the afternoon, Superman was the unblemished idol of millions of children on television before they went to bed.

In fact, at the same time that the Kefauver hearings were gearing up, the US Treasury Department worked with Ellsworth to create a special short subject, after the regular season's filming for *Adventures of Superman* had come to a close, that made the Man of Steel their official spokesperson for National Stamp Day.

> SUPERMAN: Hiya, boys and gals. There can only be one Superman, of course, but do you ever think about some of the super things you yourself can do? You can put some of your allowance into United States Savings Stamps at school. So, boys and girls, be super citizens—and have a super future— by saving regularly with United States Savings Stamps at school! Keep making me and everyone as proud of you as we are today!

For the federal government to request the imprimatur of a superhero during the overheated days of the Seduction of the Innocent hysteria was like a gift from another galaxy, and the Superman television show seized on the opportunity. The complete video vindication of Superman as a role model for Americans—large and small, super and ordinary—could be found at the beginning of each episode. The times demanded nothing less. The television series copied the introduction to the 1940s cartoon series—but added one searing concluding phrase that brought the Superman myth into compelling, irresistible focus:

> Superman—who can bend steel with his bare hands and change the course of mighty rivers. And who, disguised as mild-mannered reporter Clark Kent, fights a never-ending battle for truth, justice—*and the American way!*

Reeves guest-starred on a famous *I Love Lucy* episode in 1957; alas, his name was never used in the credits; when *Adventures of Superman* went to color in 1954, it gained a new legion of young followers.

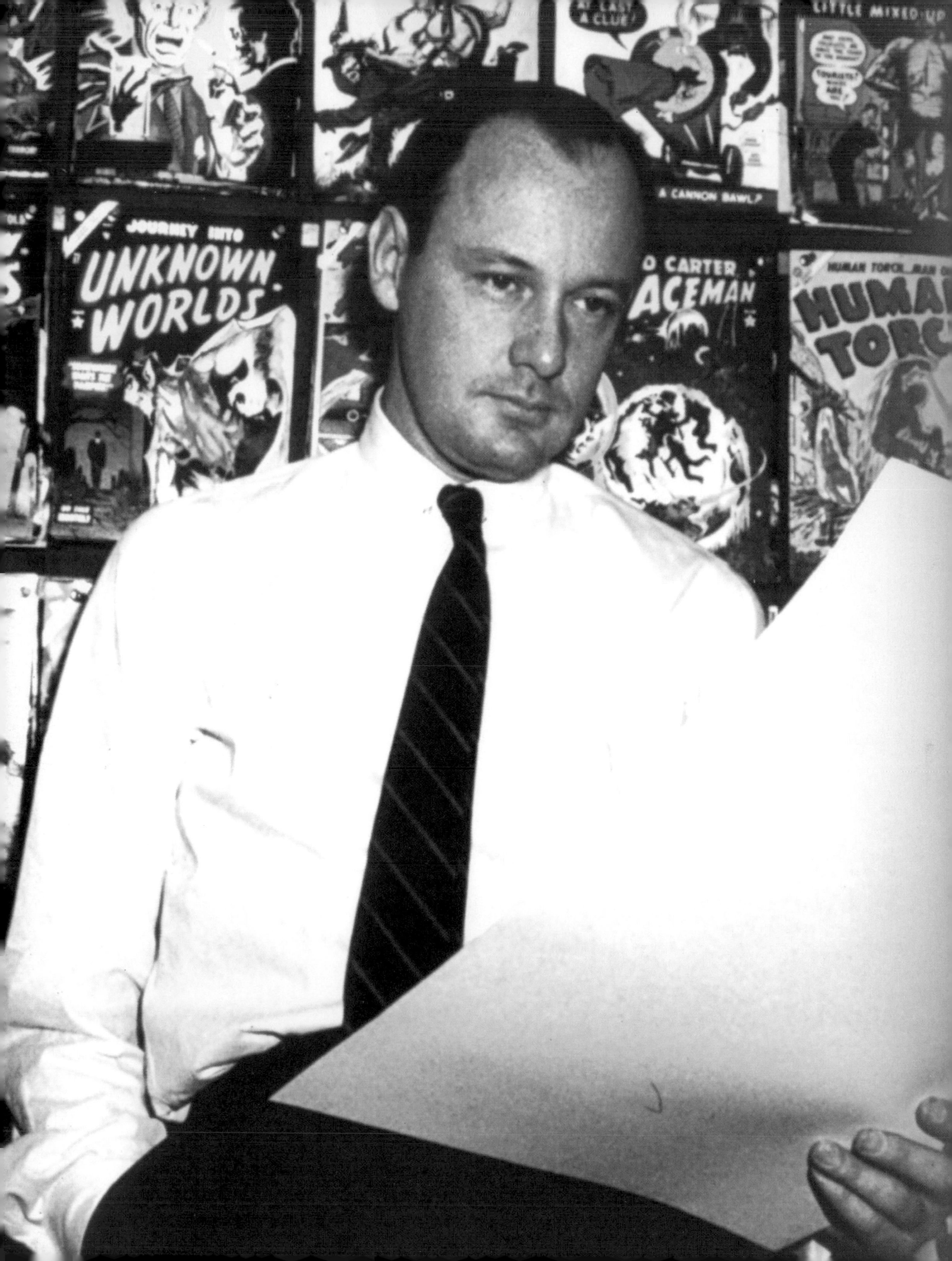
JOURNEY INTO
UNKNOWN WORLDS
A CANNON BAWL?
LITTLE MIXED-UP

Part Two

GREAT ★ POWER
GREAT RESPONSIBILITY

After two decades spent writing hundreds of comic books, Stan Lee was fed up. The postwar years had been difficult times at the publishing company owned by his boss, Martin Goodman. The ground had shifted so often that even the company had shifted names three times: Timely to Atlas to Marvel, the latter so unceremoniously that, by 1960, their covers only bore a tiny "MC" indicia.

Still, Timely/Atlas/Marvel was a survivor, more than could be said about a dozen other firms that weren't able to crawl out of the 1950s. One might charitably say that publisher Goodman threw whatever he could at the wall to see what would stick; unfortunately the kinds of derivative titles he threw had already stuck to his competitors' walls.

Goodman put Stan Lee into the driver's seat of whatever used vehicle he was pushing that month; Lee had to grind out several stories every week to keep up with the schedule. He was a self-admitted "hack," convincing himself he could get interested in the romantic trials of *Linda Carter, Student Nurse* or the gunslinging exploits of *Kid Colt, Outlaw,* or the less-than-astonishing threats from Titano, the Monster That Time Forgot in *Tales to Astonish.* Lee contented himself by presuming that some of the firm's dwindling readership might be interested, too—besides, banging out the outrageous monster stories was occasionally fun. Stan's job as editor was decidedly less fun. Goodman frequently switched distributors, which played havoc with the lineup, and twice since 1948, Stan had to call the freelance artists he worked with to tell them either that the company was only going to use back inventory they had already paid for, or, worse, that there wouldn't be any work for them at all. That was the part Stan hated the most.

OVERLEAF: Stan Lee in the Marvel Comics office, circa 1954; hopefully he's perusing some submitted artwork, not the business ledger. BELOW: Marvel Comics' stable of staples in the early 1960s: romance, westerns, and monster books.

I really had had it up to here. I wanted to quit and try something else. I wanted to try to write something for people, hopefully, with a higher IQ. So I told my wife, "I'm gonna quit." So she said, "You know, Stan, before you quit, why don't you do one book the way you'd like to do it. The worst that can happen is Goodman'll fire you, and so what? You want to quit anyway."

By then, it was literally the dawn of the 1960s. One day, Goodman walked into the office and mentioned to Stan that their distinguished competition—National, which was cleaning their clocks, saleswise—had a book with a bunch of superheroes. "How about you coming up with a bunch of superheroes in one story?" he asked Stan. Lee had cut his teeth on superhero comics in the early 1940s and had periodically nudged Goodman into releasing a title or two, but those attempts were met with bitter ends. Having nothing to lose, Stan figured, "Okay, I'm gonna try it, but I would do it my way."

Lee's "way" would require the best artist in the business. Jack Kirby had weathered the vagaries of the comic book industry, partly because of his successful partnership with Joe Simon and partly out of his own unique, spectacular talent. But, by the end of the 1950s, he and Simon had gone their separate ways, and although Kirby had created some pseudo-superheroes at National—including Challengers of the Unknown, a complementary quartet of daredevil adventurers—since 1959, he had been hanging his shingle, more often than not, over at Marvel. Lee and Kirby had been working cheek by jowl (Lee's cheeky sense of humor, Kirby's jowly gruffness) on various permutations of the same monster-from-another-world formula. Kirby was five years older than Lee and had known him back in the day at Timely when Kirby was illustrating million-selling issues of *Captain America* and Lee was the office boy.

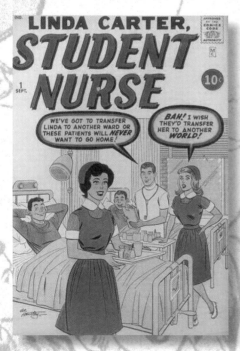
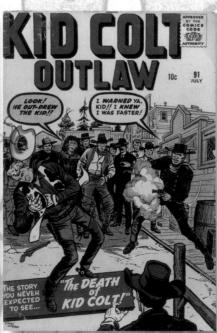

But now Lee was in charge and he yoked Kirby to his new superhero project. He typed out a two-page précis for the superhero group: The Fantastic Four. The Fantastic Four were something old (the Human Torch, now a human teenager), something new (their personalities); something borrowed (Reed Richards, Mr. Fantastic, was stretchable, like Plastic Man; Susan Storm, the Invisible Girl, could disappear from view, like Invisible Scarlet O'Neil; and poor Ben Grimm transformed into the Thing, a carbuncled behemoth not unlike the Lee-Kirby monsters), and something blue (their uniforms, although they would fight evil in their street clothes for the first two issues).

Lee conceived the team as accidental heroes: egghead scientist Reed Richards convinces his girlfriend, her brother, and his friend—a "surly" test pilot—to join him on an expedition to Mars (although in a neat bit of Cold War humor, Lee writes to Kirby: "At the rate the Communists are progressing in space, maybe we better make this a flight to the STARS, instead of just to Mars, because by the time this mag goes on sale, the Russians may have already MADE a flight to Mars!"). The quartet is besieged by cosmic rays (in the atomic age, radiation replaced secret formulas) and crash-land on earth, only to discover their bodies—and their lives—have been unalterably changed. But, famously, the Fantastic Four would never be "one for all, and all for one"—again. As Lee wrote, "To keep it all from getting too goody-goody, there is always friction between Mr. Fantastic and the Thing, with Human Torch siding with Mr. F."

Kirby went to town on Lee's synopsis, creating an introductory sequence of the new team, attempting to lead "normal" lives in midtown Manhattan, and providing the twenty-three-page story with his inimitable action sequences, dramatic tableaux, and ornery monsters. In September 1961, only weeks after Gherman Titov, a Soviet cosmonaut, paced the space race by orbiting the earth seventeen times, *The Fantastic Four* hit the newsstands.

The Fantastic Four #1: a plainclothes superteam, courtesy of Kirby. BELOW: The last panel from that issue.

The team would revolutionize comic books. The leader was a loquacious big shot, whose authority was consistently undermined by a cigar-chomping, Lower East Side-born curmudgeon. Still, they managed to overcome their differences for the common good and worked as uneasy comrades on dozens and dozens of far-flung amazing adventures.

The Fantastic Four—the other team—didn't do so badly either.

Stan Lee's initial frustration at the limited imagination of his publishing company would be the cosmic ray that transformed puny Marvel Comics into the reigning powerhouse of the industry. As Lee and Kirby put it at the end of the Fantastic Four's origin story: AND THE WORLD WOULD NEVER AGAIN BE THE SAME.

CHAPTER FOUR

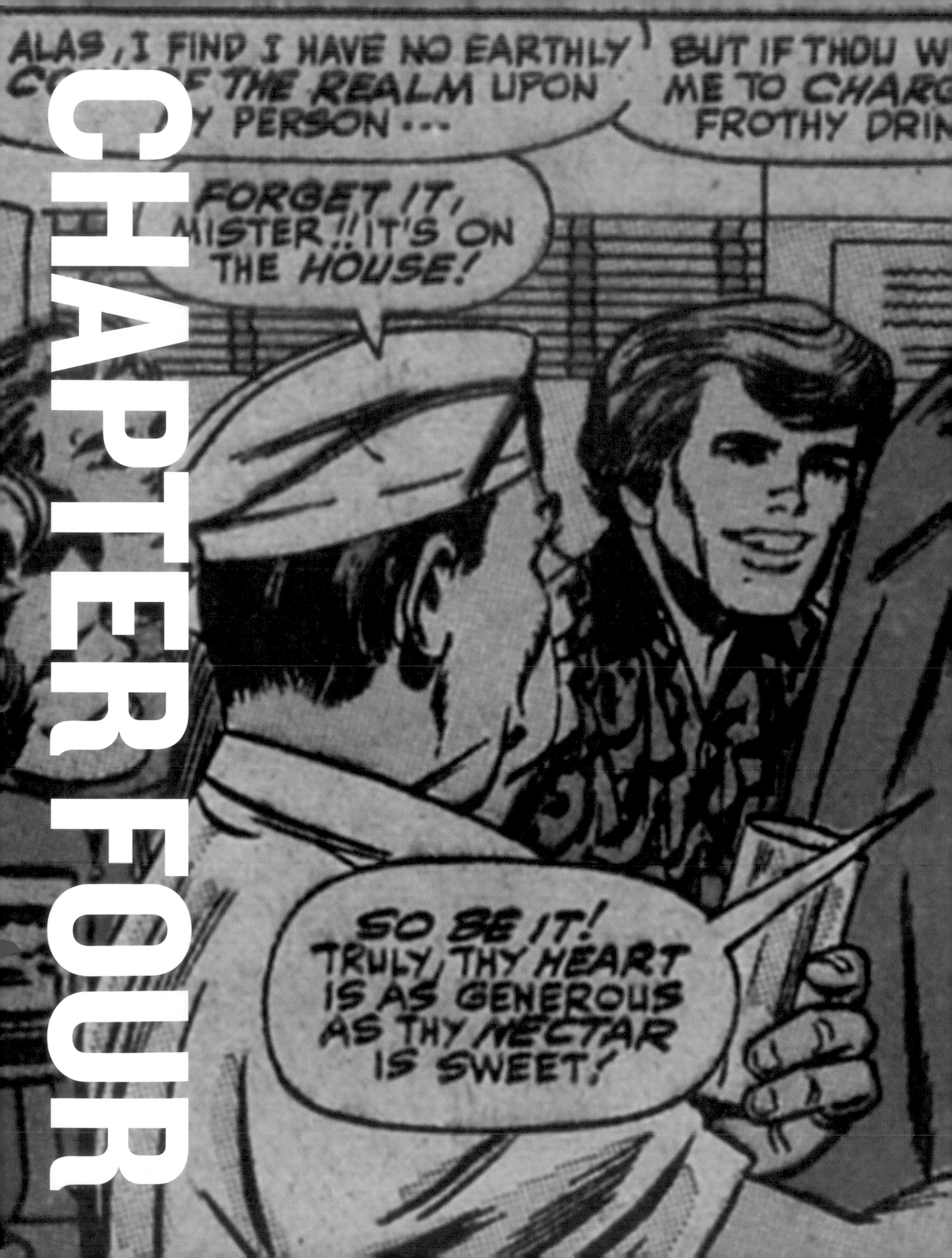
ALAS, I FIND I HAVE NO EARTHLY
THE REALM UPON
PERSON ...
BUT IF THOU
ME TO
FROTHY
FORGET IT, MISTER!! IT'S ON THE HOUSE!
SO BE IT! TRULY, THY HEART IS AS GENEROUS AS THY NECTAR IS SWEET!

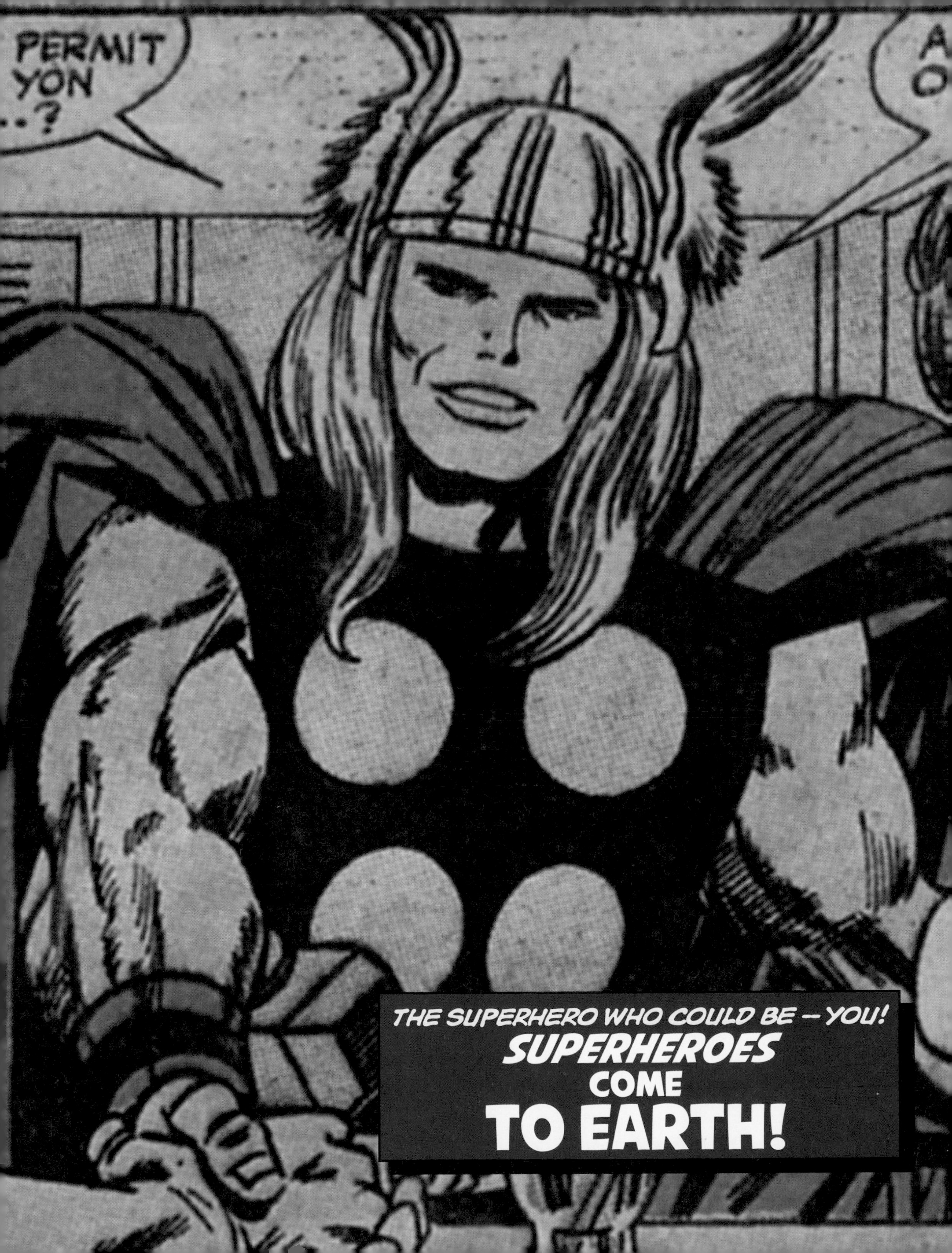
PERMIT YON ..?

THE SUPERHERO WHO COULD BE -- YOU!

SUPERHEROES COME TO EARTH!

CODE-APPROVED COMIC MAGAZINES are WHOLESOME ENTERTAINING EDUCATIONAL

APPROVED BY THE COMICS CODE (A) AUTHORITY

Look for this seal on the cover!

CODE OF THE COMICS MAGAZINE ASSOCIATION OF AMERICA, INC.

Adopted on October 26, 1954, the enforcement of this Code is the basis for the comic magazine industry's program of self-regulation.

CODE FOR EDITORIAL MATTER

General Standards   Part A

1) Crimes shall never be presented in such a way as to create sympathy for the criminal, to promote distrust of the forces of law and justice, or to inspire others with a desire to imitate criminals.
2) No comics shall explicitly present the unique details and methods of a crime.
3) Policemen, judges, government officials and respected institutions shall never be presented in such a way as to create disrespect for established authority.
4) If crime is depicted it shall be as a sordid and unpleasant activity.
5) Criminals shall not be presented so as to be rendered glamorous or to occupy a position which creates a desire for emulation.
6) In every instance good shall triumph over evil and the criminal punished for his misdeeds.
7) Scenes of excessive violence shall be prohibited. Scenes of brutal torture, excessive and unnecessary knife and gun play, physical agony, gory and gruesome crime shall be eliminated.
8) No unique or unusual methods of concealing weapons shall be shown.
9) Instances of law enforcement officers dying as a result of a criminal's activities should be discouraged.
10) The crime of kidnapping shall never be portrayed in any detail, nor shall any profit accrue to the abductor or kidnapper. The criminal or the kidnapper must be punished in every case.
11) The letters of the word "crime" on a comics magazine cover shall never be appreciably greater in dimension than the other words contained in the title. The word "crime" shall never appear alone on a cover.
12) Restraint in the use of the word "crime" in titles or sub-titles shall be exercised.

General Standards   Part B

1) No comic magazine shall use the word horror or terror in its title.
2) All scenes of horror, excessive bloodshed, gory or gruesome crimes, depravity, lust, sadism, masochism shall not be permitted.
3) All lurid, unsavory, gruesome illustrations shall be eliminated.
4) Inclusion of stories dealing with evil shall be used or shall be published only where the intent is to illustrate a moral issue and in no case shall evil be presented alluringly nor so as to injure the sensibilities of the reader.
5) Scenes dealing with, or instruments associated with walking dead, torture, vampires and vampirism, ghouls, cannibalism and werewolfism are prohibited.

General Standards   Part C

All elements or techniques not specifically mentioned herein, but which are contrary to the spirit and intent of the Code, and are considered violations of good taste or decency, shall be prohibited.

Dialogue

1) Profanity, obscenity, smut, vulgarity, or words or symbols which have acquired undesirable meanings are forbidden.
2) Special precautions to avoid references to physical afflictions or deformities shall be taken.
3) Although slang and colloquialisms are acceptable, excessive use should be discouraged and wherever possible good grammar shall be employed.

Religion

1) Ridicule or attack on any religious or racial group is never permissible.

Costume

1) Nudity in any form is prohibited, as is indecent or undue exposure.
2) Suggestive and salacious illustration or suggestive posture is unacceptable.
3) All characters shall be depicted in dress reasonably acceptable to society.
4) Females shall be drawn realistically without exaggeration of any physical qualities.

NOTE: It should be recognized that all prohibitions dealing with costume, dialogue or artwork applies as specifically to the cover of a comic magazine as they do to the contents.

Marriage and Sex

1) Divorce shall not be treated humorously nor represented as desirable.
2) Illicit sex relations are neither to be hinted at or portrayed. Violent love scenes as well as sexual abnormalities are unacceptable.
3) Respect for parents, the moral code, and for honorable behavior shall be fostered. A sympathetic understanding of the problems of love is not a license for morbid distortion.
4) The treatment of love-romance stories shall emphasize the value of the home and the sanctity of marriage.
5) Passion or romantic interest shall never be treated in such a way as to stimulate the lower and baser emotions.
6) Seduction and rape shall never be shown or suggested.
7) Sex perversion or any inference to same is strictly forbidden.

CODE FOR ADVERTISING MATTER

These regulations are applicable to all magazines published by members of the Comics Magazine Association of America, Inc. Good taste shall be the guiding principle in the acceptance of advertising.
1) Liquor and tobacco advertising is not acceptable.
2) Advertisement of sex or sex instruction books are unacceptable.
3) The sale of picture postcards, "pin-ups," "art studies," or any other reproduction of nude or semi-nude figures is prohibited.
4) Advertising for the sale of knives, concealable weapons, or realistic gun facsimiles is prohibited.
5) Advertising for the sale of fireworks is prohibited.
6) Advertising dealing with the sale of gambling equipment or printed matter dealing with gambling shall not be accepted.
7) Nudity with meretricious purpose and salacious postures shall not be permitted in the advertising of any product; clothed figures shall never be presented in such a way as to be offensive or contrary to good taste or morals.
8) To the best of his ability, each publisher shall ascertain that all statements made in advertisements conform to fact and avoid misrepresentation.
9) Advertisement of medical, health, or toiletry products of questionable nature are to be rejected. Advertisements for medical, health or toiletry products endorsed by the American Medical Association, or the American Dental Association, shall be deemed acceptable if they conform with all other conditions of the Advertising Code.

COMICS MAGAZINE ASSOCIATION OF AMERICA, INC.

300 PARK AVENUE SOUTH   NEW YORK, N. Y. 10010

OVERLEAF: The God of Thunder entertains questions from teenagers in the local malt shop (Lee/Kirby: *The Mighty Thor* #143, 1967). ABOVE: An educational pamphlet from the Comics Code Authority, 1954. OPPOSITE: Code president Charles Murphy promotes acceptable emendations, 1954.

"GOOD SHALL TRIUMPH OVER EVIL"
The Comics Code Authority

t was the postage stamp that stopped an industry in its tracks.

In spring 1954, when the Senate Subcommittee on Juvenile Delinquency attempted to move to a speedy conclusion to its deliberations, it found itself blocked from enacting any legal restrictions that would regulate the comic book industry. Despite the outcries of various parents, church groups, and one psychiatrist in particular, the free market would be allowed to work its magic. However, the conclusion was clear: the comic book industry had to reform from within. Kefauver's attitude toward the industry was the same as a mother asking her eleven-year-old son to clean up his room: do it, or else. Besides, it would be good for you.

The comic book publishers, never a group that had worked concertedly in their own mutual interests, realized that last point was inarguable: from a public relations standpoint—which really means a business standpoint—the industry had to clean up its act. It had tried once before, in 1948, when a subset of publishers came together as the Association of Comic Magazine Publishers and drafted a general six-item resolution, but the group soon fell apart. National and Fawcett already had in-house restrictions in place since the early 1940s which worked out very well for them. But there needed to be something formal, something that everyone could endorse.

In summer 1954, thirty-eight members of the comic book industry—publishers, printers, engravers—met in New York to form the Comics Magazine Association of America. They would hire an independent "czar" to oversee the final publications, a former judge named Charles Murphy; they would give him a budget to hire a staff; and they would draft a code of standards. Every important publisher signed on, except for William Gaines, who took his E.C. Comics football and went home, and, surprisingly, Dell Comics, whose wholesome "funny animals" line was actually the industry's indisputable giant. Dell, who felt they did a perfectly fine job of policing Woody Woodpecker on their own, thank you very much, apparently didn't want to belong to any club that would accept the other members as a member.

Five days before Halloween 1954, the CMAA published its code. In tone and breadth, it took its inspiration from the Motion Picture Production Code, which had been in place since 1930, but not seriously enforced until 1934. There was an initial section that encompassed what the movies' Code referred to as "compensating moral values": i.e., criminal or antisocial behavior would be punished and the social fabric (usually authoritarian) would be upheld. Specific to comic books, the CMAA forbade the use of "Crime," "Horror," or "Terror" in a magazine title, and presented restrictions against gruesome depredations, slang and obscenity, and sexual deviancy, while upholding respect for religion, racial groups, and the sanctity of marriage. It also required advertising in the comic books to be in "good taste."

Judge Murphy's policy was for all the publishers to submit their initial artwork—"boards," as the roughly 2' x 3' white cardboard

pieces were called—for review. Changes and alterations would be requested by the authority, if necessary, and despite the dilatory and frustrating nature of the request, publishers were forced to comply. Once the correction was made, the comic book cover would bear a stamp affixed to its upper right-hand corner: "Approved by the COMICS CODE AUTHORITY." No business-minded publisher would dream of sending his product out on the stands without the stamp of approval, so a good deal of silliness and busy-work was endured. Stan Lee was submitting a host of science-fiction comics, romance books, and Western titles on behalf of Atlas Comics:

We got one page back in a Western book that showed a close-up of a hand shooting a gun, the cowboy was shooting a gun, and there was a puff of smoke coming out of the barrel of the gun, and a straight line indicating the trajectory of the bullet. That's it: the gun, the puff of smoke, the straight line. And that panel was rejected. I had to phone the Code office, and I said, "What's wrong with that panel?" And I will never to my dying day forget the answer. "The puff of smoke was too big, that made it violent." So we redrew it. I mean, it just shows how ridiculous this whole thing could be.

Writer Denny O'Neil dealt with the absurdities of the Code into the early 1970s. He was particularly baffled by the way the CMAA split hairs in the realm of the supernatural; writers couldn't use the word "zombie," but they could use the word "ghoul." In other words, O'Neil speculated, you couldn't have the walking dead eating people's brains, but once they sat down, it was okay.

The Comics Code was, to say the least, an imperfect document—largely because it was a reactive document, not an organic way of creating an ameliorating standard. In fact, if the given task were simply to draft legislation that would put E.C.'s horror line out of business, it succeeded admirably. (Gaines eventually threw in the towel, put all his chips on a little satirical

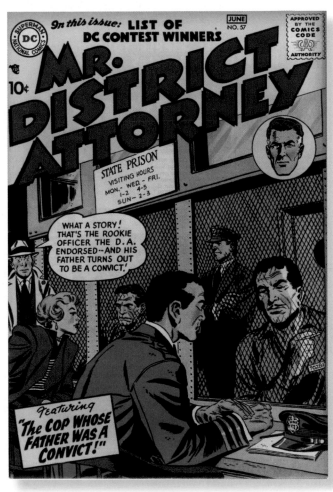

OPPOSITE: *MAD* #1, 1952: the only E.C. comic book to survive the Code—by ignoring it. ABOVE: Comedian Jackie Gleason and the stalwart radio show star Mr. District Attorney kept DC (National) going in the late 1950s.

rag called *MAD* magazine, influenced generations of anarchic souls, and became a millionaire in the process.) It also was pretty late in the game for any media industry to begin policing its standards, as times were changing quickly. Within a decade of the Comics Code's inception, the Motion Picture Production Code would start to unravel, besieged by an inexorable wave of shifting social forces. The Comics Code seemed to be the last remnant of the McCarthy era, and it did more to slow down the production process, and to encumber business sales and the creative imagination, than it did to uplift and inspire an industry.

It was a tough time to be weathering the comic book market in any event. In 1955, a federal anti-trust suit demolished American News Company, the distributor that serviced 50 percent of the industry, which left publishers scrambling to find anything that would attract new readers. The previously successful crime and horror comics were no longer an option, so publishers, according to Carmine Infantino, "started putting out adventure comics, westerns, romance, science fiction and whatever they could try. And everything was flopping, one thing after another." National Periodicals started adding titles devoted to comedians and television stars, such as Jerry Lewis and Jackie Gleason. Their most daring adventurer was called Mr. District Attorney. Artist Neal Adams recalled going to their offices as a young artist right out of high school to show off his portfolio:

A nice older guy came out to the lobby and he briefly flipped through it. And he said, "Look, kid, I can't take you in there. Confidentially, in a year or two there's not going to be comics. We're phasing them out." This—at DC Comics.

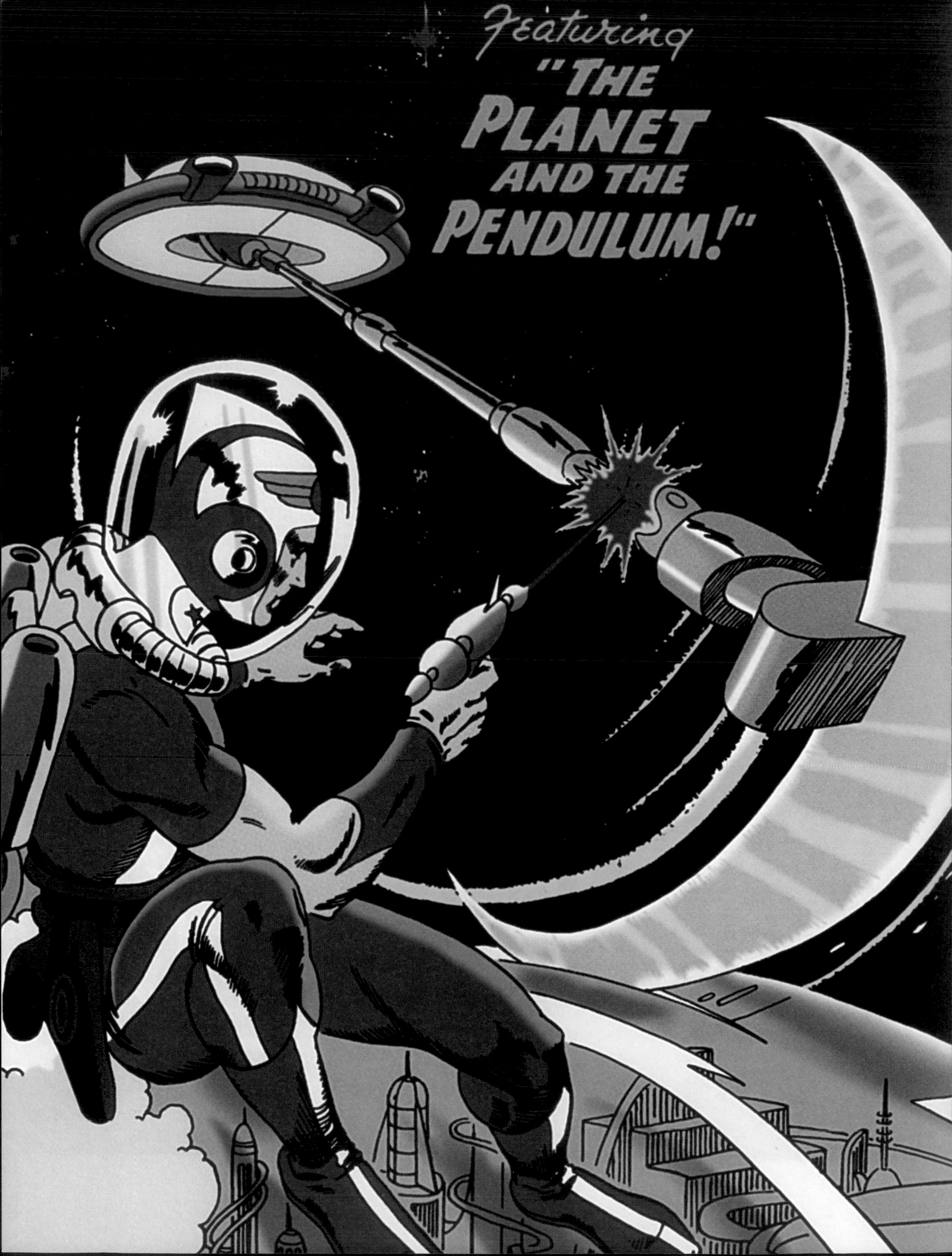
Featuring
"THE PLANET AND THE PENDULUM!"

WHIRLWIND ADVENTURES
The Silver Age of DC Comics

OPPOSITE: *Showcase* #17 gave spaceman Adam Strange his debut (1958), courtesy of artist Gil Kane. TOP LEFT: Artist Carmine Infantino (left) and editor Jules Schwartz (right) led the DC (National) team of retrofitted superheroes. BOTTOM LEFT, AND RIGHT: Almost superheroes: the debuts of the Manhunter from Mars (*Detective Comics* #225, 1955) and the Phantom Stranger (1952).

Beyond their trinity of heavy-hitters—Superman, Batman, and Wonder Woman —one might say that National Periodicals' attitude toward superheroes in the mid 1950s was akin to the attitude that business executives have when they murmur "Let's have lunch" to each other: I'll call you if I need you.

There had been a few half-hearted heroes under the "DC" logo, but they were hybrids with other genres: mystery (The Phantom Stranger), space rangers (Captain Comet, Adam Strange), even a man from Mars, who suited up in a blue cape and matching underwear for some terrestrial detective work (J'onn J'onzz, Manhunter from Mars). National staff artist Carmine Infantino had been a company regular since the mid 1940s; he had long given up his original assignments such as the first incarnation of the Flash in the 1940s—"a guy with a tin hat, running like

crazy," in his words—and was contenting himself with executing National's stable of space rangers. Infantino was as surprised as anyone when he received a call from editor Julie Schwartz in spring 1956.

> He says, "Come in, I want to talk to you." I said, "Fine." He says, "We're going to do superheroes again." I said, "That's nice, good for you." He says, "We want to do the Flash." I said, "That's nice," again. He says, "You're doing it. Go get us a character, draw a character for us."

Working with writer Robert Kanigher, Infantino reconceived the Flash for the mid 1950s, effectively "re-booting" a character for the first time in comics. Gone was the tin hat, replaced with a zippy red suit emblazoned with yellow lightning bolts that emerged improbably from the hero's signet ring. The revised

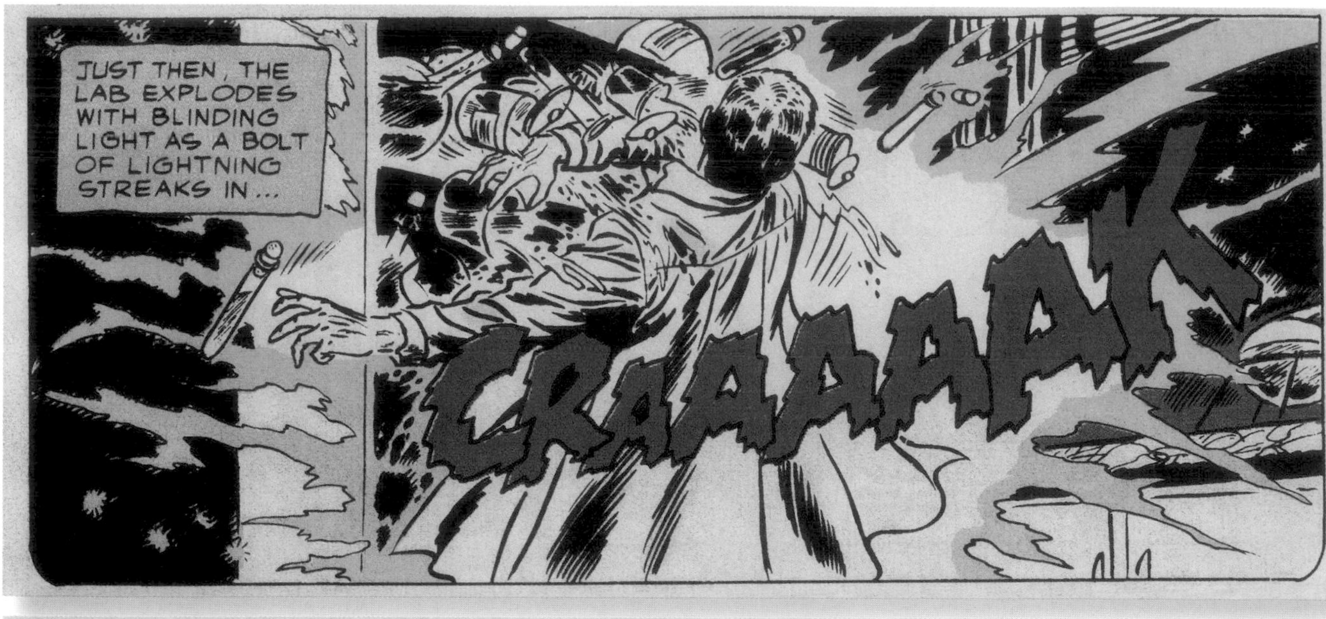
JUST THEN, THE LAB EXPLODES WITH BLINDING LIGHT AS A BOLT OF LIGHTNING STREAKS IN...
CRAAAAAK

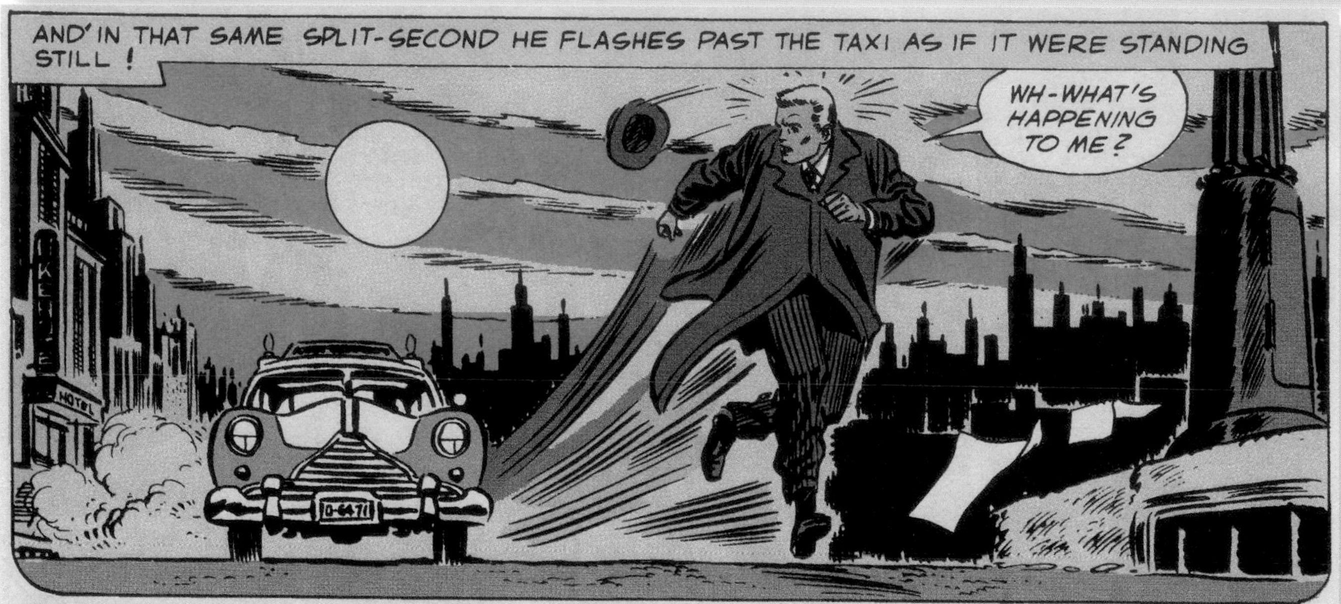
AND IN THAT SAME SPLIT-SECOND HE FLASHES PAST THE TAXI AS IF IT WERE STANDING STILL!
WH-WHAT'S HAPPENING TO ME?

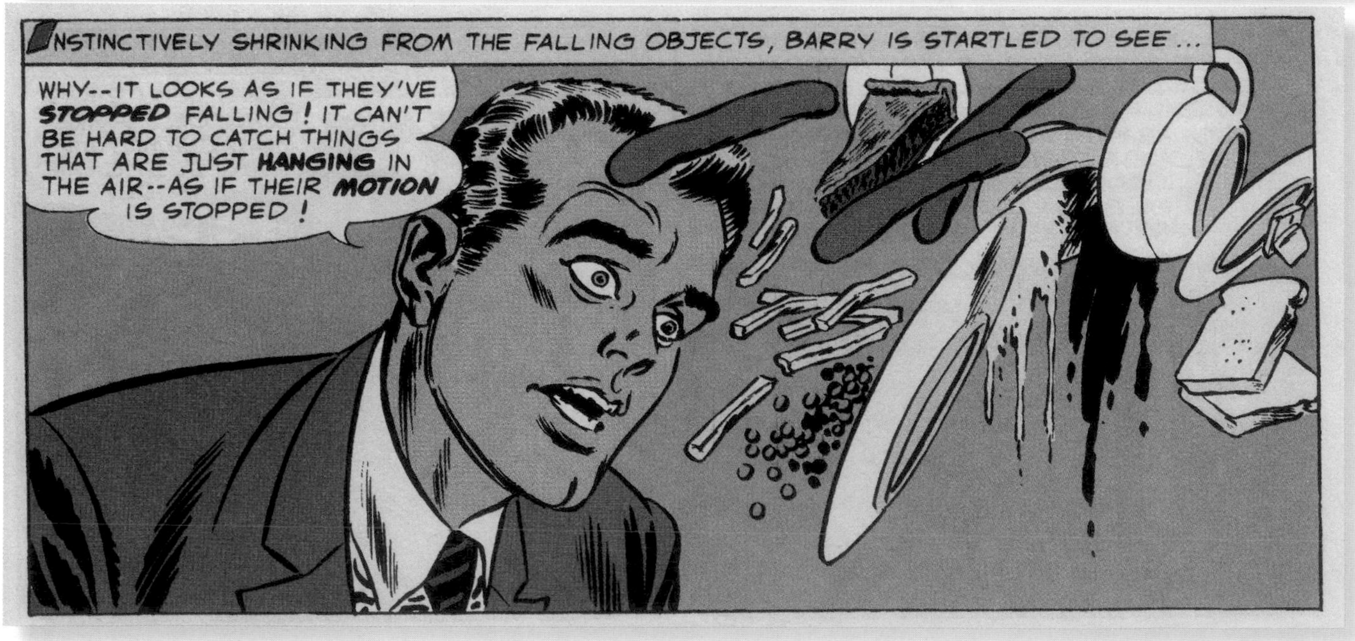
INSTINCTIVELY SHRINKING FROM THE FALLING OBJECTS, BARRY IS STARTLED TO SEE...
WHY--IT LOOKS AS IF THEY'VE STOPPED FALLING! IT CAN'T BE HARD TO CATCH THINGS THAT ARE JUST HANGING IN THE AIR--AS IF THEIR MOTION IS STOPPED!

WHIRLWIND
ADVENTURES OF THE
FASTEST MAN ALIVE!

OPPOSITE: Barry Allen gets the shock of his life (Infantino panels from the origin story). LEFT: A cinematic debut for the fastest man alive: *Showcase* #4 (1956).

National released the Flash tepidly, as the October 1956 cover feature of their magazine that showcased new strips called, appropriately, *Showcase.* "The Fastest Man Alive" would appear there three more times over the next two and a half years before he got his own title magazine in 1959 (National executives apparently weren't as swift as their hero). But, as Julie Schwartz intuited, the time was right again for superheroes, and the Flash led the pack by several lengths. He was the perfect character for his times. His adventures had a rare puckish sense of humor; he had the niftiest "Rogues Gallery" since Batman in the early 1940s; and he mirrored the speed-freak mentality of the late 1950s. American car companies were retooling European sports cars for mass commercial production—Chevrolet brought out the Corvette in 1954 and Ford would compete with the Thunderbird in 1955. If land speed records weren't tantalizing enough, the space race had begun the year before the Flash's debut, when both the United States and the Soviet Union announced their intentions to put an unmanned satellite in orbit. It was a good time to be a superhero who mirrored every kid's gym-class fantasy.

The success of the Flash among young readers encouraged National to launch another crew of superheroes into orbit as well. Green Lantern, one of the previous Flash's wartime comrades, was reconceived with space-aged flair, thanks to the acrobatic elegance of artist Gil Kane, in the October 1959 issue of *Showcase.* The Lantern was now part of a vast, universe-wide police force, overseen by a bunch of interstellar (and

concept brought out the best in Infantino's work: the whole get-up was designed for maximum aerodynamics; the new Flash (a police scientist named Barry Allen who is caught in an accident between a lightning bolt and some unknown chemicals) was lithe, like a track star, and Infantino often drew him banking to one side, the better to gain momentum. The Flash was bristling with animation; even the panel arrangements on the page were built for speed. Flash's Central City was all sleek, modernist architecture; everything was streamlined for fast, modernist adventure. If Frank Lloyd Wright had ever designed a comic book, it would look like Infantino's *Flash* series.

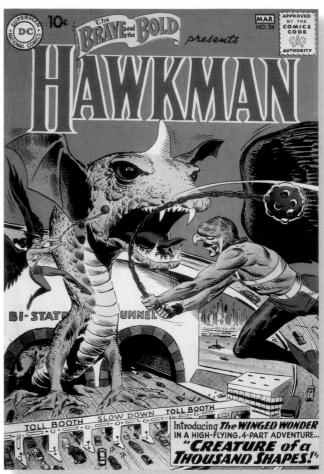

cranky) blue-skinned guardians. As the 1960s began, editor Julie Schwartz put all of his extant A-listers, new and old, into a reconstitution of the Justice Society of America, now called the Justice League of America, as "league" had a preferable intramural resonance for Schwartz. Hawkman was taken out of mothballs for the March 1961 anthology *The Brave and the Bold* and, in October of that year, the Atom—who in the 1940s was simply a pee-wee-sized athlete—reemerged as a microscopic crime fighter. A Plastic Man knock-off named the Elongated Man bounced back and forth in various titles.

Eventually, as National's new stable of champions was amassing an invigorated fan base, some readers wondered what happened to their favorite heroes from the 1940s. Schwartz obliged their curiosity in *Flash* #123 (in fall 1961), when he commissioned writer Gardner Fox to team the new Flash together with the old Flash who was, apparently, still fighting crime on Earth-Two (although, technically, as he was the antecedent, the older Flash should be fighting crime on Earth-One—but no one had quite pondered the consequences of his reappearance). The crossover classic—"The Flash of Two Worlds"—threw open the

barnyard door for a multitude of "alternative universe" adventures, the magnitude of which would be felt for years to come.

National deserves a good deal of credit for taking some undervalued assets and dusting them off in an imaginative way. Almost all of the revived heroes benefitted from the space age and from changing times. Green Lantern's adventures had a yearning, visionary, science-fiction element to them; Hawkman (along with his high-flying wife, Hawkgirl) was now a policeman from a faraway planet; the Atom derived his new molecular metabolism via a thorough study of astrophysics. They all brought their new technologies as a symbol of heroic enlightenment to the readers of DC Comics; for these new heroes, scientific breakthroughs ennobled mankind to save itself and move forward (indeed, in the Atom's origin story, he contrives a way to shrink down in order to save a bunch of kids lost on a camping trip in an underground cavern).

Fans and comic book historians would consecrate this era as the dawn of the "Silver Age of Comics." Looking back on this visionary time, which coincided almost identically with the nomination, election, and inauguration of John F. Kennedy, it seemed more like the New Frontier.

OPPOSITE: Green Lantern got his own comic quickly (*Green Lantern* #4, 1961), art by Gil Kane. Hawkman, lovingly rendered by Joe Kubert, had to wing it in the pages of *The Brave and the Bold* (1961).
TOP: The first crossover in the comic book universe: "The Flash of Two Worlds" (*The Flash* #123, 1961).
BOTTOM: John F. Kennedy places the space program at the forefront of the New Frontier (1961).

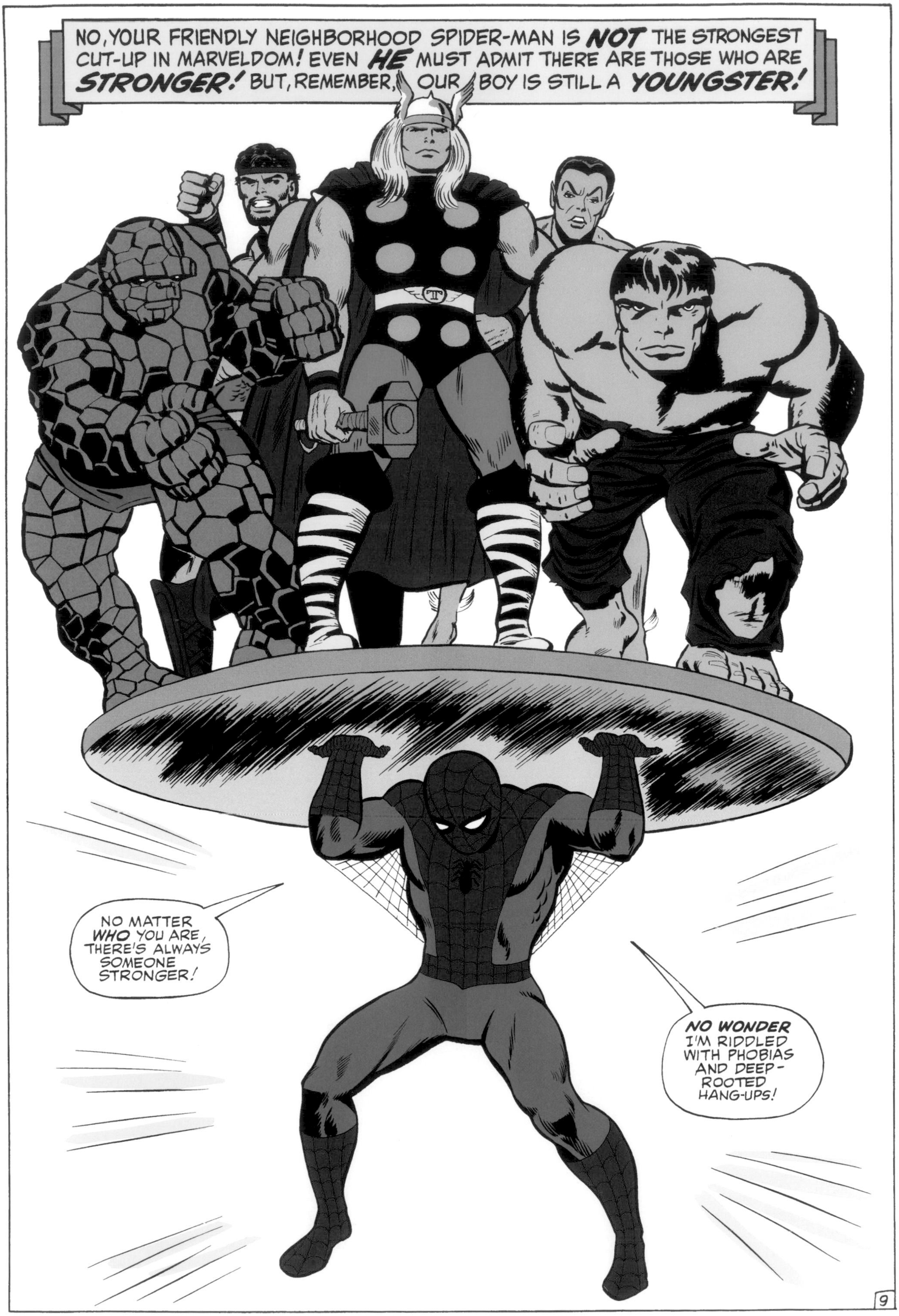
NO, YOUR FRIENDLY NEIGHBORHOOD SPIDER-MAN IS NOT THE STRONGEST CUT-UP IN MARVELDOM! EVEN HE MUST ADMIT THERE ARE THOSE WHO ARE STRONGER! BUT, REMEMBER, OUR BOY IS STILL A YOUNGSTER!
NO MATTER WHO YOU ARE, THERE'S ALWAYS SOMEONE STRONGER!
NO WONDER I'M RIDDLED WITH PHOBIAS AND DEEP-ROOTED HANG-UPS!
9

"MAKE MINE MARVEL!"
The Marvel Age of Comics

f science and technology provided the visionary goalposts for the superheroes at National Periodicals, over at what would be called the Marvel Universe, science was the metaphor for the anxiety of the age, providing only transformation, terror, ambivalence, guilt, and, ultimately, responsibility.

Marvel's editor and chief scribe, Stan Lee, would be loath to consider himself the progenitor of a worldview, but, when one co-creates a dozen new characters and titles within thirty months, there are—much like developing a gamma radiation bomb—a certain amount of unintended consequences. Toward the end of 1961, once it appeared that the Lee-Kirby title *The Fantastic Four* was going to be a hit, Lee would turn to his publisher Martin Goodman time after time, asking him to allow yet another superhero title onto Marvel's corseted repertory of titles. Adding a new character or title meant cancelling another—it was like a game of musical chairs—and it taxed Lee's creative imagination as editor; he often would sneak superhero characters into mystery or science fiction titles to see if, like the Human Torch, they would catch fire. At the same time, Lee was editing and/or writing the entire Marvel lineup, which continued to include Westerns, teen humor books, romance titles, and the occasional monster anthology.

Perhaps this was why, as some commentators have pointed out, Lee seemed to hedge his bets by adding characters that were more grotesque than exemplary. "Stan's attitude," according to comic book writer Len Wein, " was just in case readers don't like the superhero, look, here's a monster in this book, they might want to buy it for that. Let's try it, what the heck's going to happen? Worse of it is, we'll be doing Westerns again next week." That made the next Lee-Kirby creation a logical extension of the monster books: the Incredible Hulk. Debuting in his own title at the beginning of 1962, the Hulk emerged out of perhaps the most potent and resonant stew of ideas in the

Marvel canon. Nuclear physicist Bruce Banner is employed by the government to develop a "gamma bomb"—another collage of military ambitions, experimentation, and radiation. Lee tapped into the contemporary anxiety over nuclear destruction: "I am the least scientific person you'll ever know," he admitted. "I wouldn't know a gamma ray if I saw it, but if it sounds good, I'll use it." And use it he did: when Banner saves a teenager who strays onto the gamma-bomb testing field, he absorbs the gamma rays' unknown poisonous potential himself. When the sun sets, Banner transforms into a glowering, brutish monster with the strength of a score of ordinary humans. "Human? Why should I want to be human?" this hulking brute questions a fleeing soldier, not unreasonably.

The Hulk was admittedly a mixture of the Dr. Jekyll and Mr. Hyde dialectic, along with a heavy dose of misunderstood monstrosity care of the Frankenstein creature. (For a while, there was a little of the Wolf Man mixed in as well, as Dr. Banner only transformed into the Hulk when the sun went down.) Jack Kirby's yeoman's service drawing Marvel's various monster books over the previous few years came in good stead. His Hulk had the Frankenstein monster's beetle-brow, but was far more expressive—there was something even balletic in the way the Hulk wielded his densely packed muscles, leaping over several counties in a single bound.

OPPOSITE: Spider-Man carries the burden of a new generation of comic book superstars.
ABOVE: Stan Lee banged out the outlines, vivified by Jack Kirby. A Kirby rendering of a fantastical team-up with him and Stan (*What If?*, 1978).

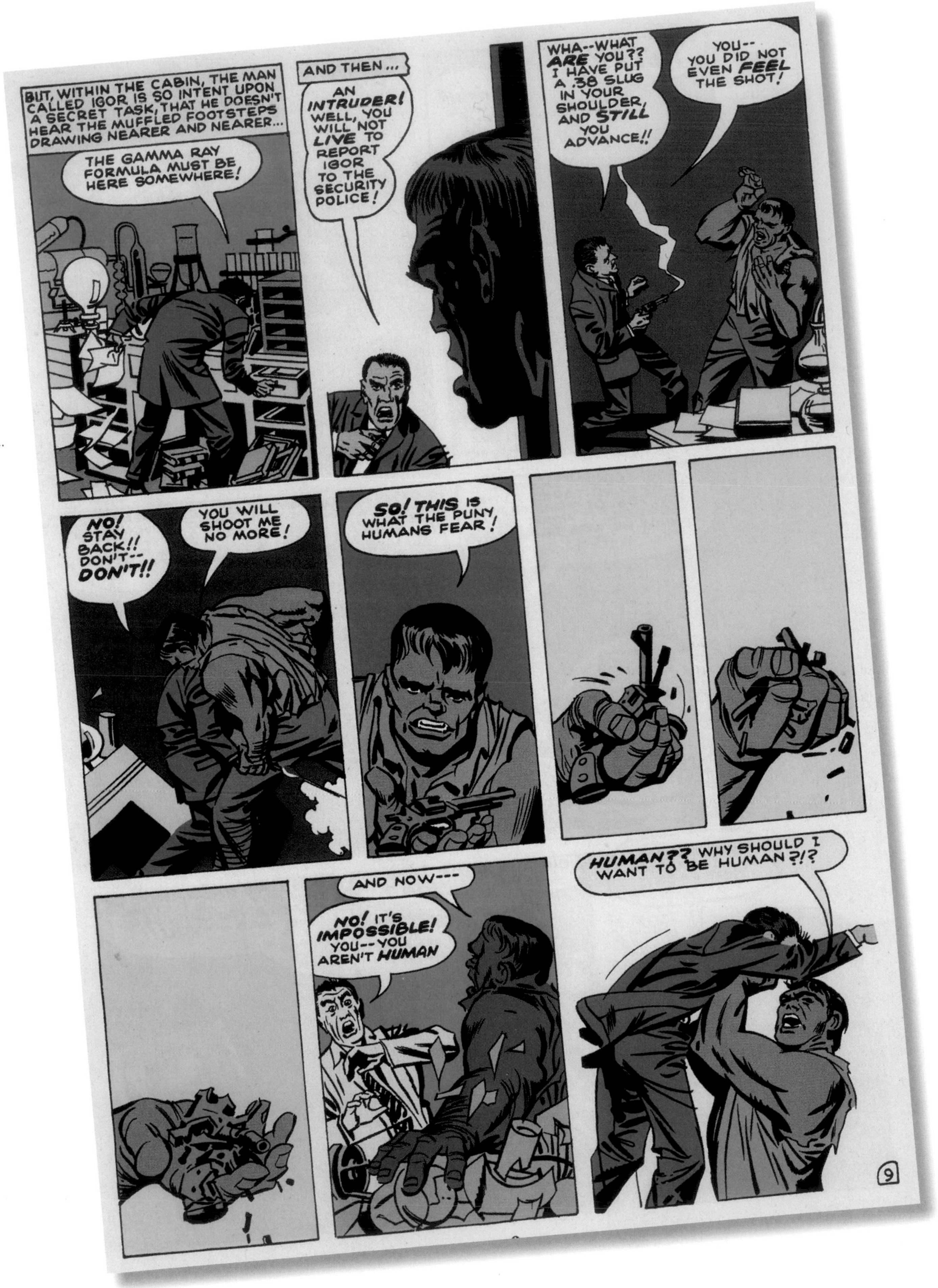
BUT, WITHIN THE CABIN, THE MAN CALLED IGOR IS SO INTENT UPON A SECRET TASK, THAT HE DOESN'T HEAR THE MUFFLED FOOTSTEPS DRAWING NEARER AND NEARER...
THE GAMMA RAY FORMULA MUST BE HERE SOMEWHERE!
AND THEN...
AN INTRUDER! WELL, YOU WILL NOT LIVE TO REPORT IGOR TO THE SECURITY POLICE!
WHA--WHAT ARE YOU?? I HAVE PUT A .38 SLUG IN YOUR SHOULDER, AND STILL YOU ADVANCE!!
YOU-- YOU DID NOT EVEN FEEL THE SHOT!
NO! STAY BACK!! DON'T-- DON'T!!
YOU WILL SHOOT ME NO MORE!
SO! THIS IS WHAT THE PUNY HUMANS FEAR!
AND NOW---
NO! IT'S IMPOSSIBLE! YOU-- YOU AREN'T HUMAN
HUMAN?? WHY SHOULD I WANT TO BE HUMAN?!?
9

(Apparently Kirby and Lee wanted the Hulk's skin rendered as a dull grey flesh, but—felicitously—the printer couldn't accomplish that with any consistency, so he was soon rendered in an appropriately alienating chartreuse.)

In his initial appearance, the Hulk is captured by a deformed Soviet agent named the Gargoyle and transported to a lab in Moscow for observation (portraits of a lugubrious Khrushchev loomed over the corridors). Eventually, Banner helps the Gargoyle regain a vestige of humanity, but no such luck for the scientist himself, who is sent back to the United States via a remote-controlled jet plane, only to be persecuted as the Hulk for another half century. And "perhaps the beginning of the end of Red tyranny, too!" suggests the last caption, dogmatically, if hopefully.

The Hulk is the official outlier in the Marvel Universe. Indeed, he was even the first real failure of the new cadre of superheroes, as his own magazine was cancelled after a half-dozen issues. He was destined to bound across different titles (the Hulk bounded like no one else in comics), fight every other hero in the lineup, and then bound away, misapprehended and shunned—the most powerful being in the world, yet incapable of making the simplest human connection. As the Hulk himself grew increasingly inarticulate and incapable of parsing a simple sentence ("Hulk smash!"), the dilemma of his alter ego, Bruce Banner, grew more existential; one of humanity's most useful scientists, Banner was now an exile and a pariah, unable to manage the raging beast inside him.

The next hero to emerge from the fecund factory at Marvel was a pariah to begin with. Lee conferred unsought heroism onto a character not unlike many of his readers: a bespectacled teenager who was shunned by the popular kids in high school. "I really hate teenage sidekicks," claimed Lee, "but I thought it would be fun to get a character who's a teenager who isn't a sidekick, but a real hero himself. That would be a first!" The actual origins of Spider-Man are shrouded in a web of conflicting stories. Apparently, Joe Simon had developed a spider-themed character with Jack Kirby in the 1950s, but it came to nothing. When Stan Lee was looking for new characters to add to the Marvel roster, he either shopped ideas back

and forth with Kirby and this one emerged, or he came up with an arachnid-oriented hero on his own. At any rate, Lee brought a much more unique version of the spider character to his publisher, Martin Goodman, and, according to Lee, "He said to me, 'That's the worst idea I ever heard. Stan, first of all, people hate spiders. You can't call a book *Spider-Man*. Nobody'll buy it.'"

Lee had developed his first two characters in close collaboration with Kirby, but there was something about Kirby's steroidal powerhouse creations that seemed ill-suited to the Spider-Man alter-ego, a nerdy high-schooler from Forest Hills, Queens. Instead, Lee turned to another artist in the overworked Marvel bullpen, Steve Ditko. Ditko had been working as a cartoonist since the early 1950s, apprenticing first with Jerry Robinson, then Simon and Kirby. He had done some horror comics for Charlton Comics, an economy-minded firm based in Connecticut, and developed a few superheroes for them. Marvel (then Atlas) beckoned to Ditko in the late 1950s and he created some very effectively paranoiac suspense tales with Stan Lee for various anthologies.

Lee pitched the Spider-Man idea to Ditko and the artist created the costume and the various gizmos used by Peter Parker—the teenager who would become, in yet another freak accident of nuclear science, endowed with "the proportionate strength of a radioactive spider." Ditko proved to be the right man for the job, making Spider-Man appear both creepy and appealing, dully realistic and amazingly fantastical. Kirby's fantasy world was visionary and futuristic—his scientific gizmos looked as if they wouldn't be invented for decades—but Ditko toiled in a crepuscular, almost grimy world of late-Depression-era melancholy. His scientific gizmos, for example, looked like vacuum cleaners from the 1940s and most of his characters—heroes or villains—had the rumpled affect of an unmade bed. Still, Lee opted for a Kirby-rendered cover when Spider-Man made his debut in *Amazing Fantasy* #15 in June 1962, a sort of end-run around Goodman, as the title was about to be cancelled.

While Lee and Ditko were awaiting readers' reactions to Spider-Man's eleven-page origin story, which was tucked among other science fiction stories in the anthology, two more superheroes debuted under Lee's aegis that same month: the Mighty Thor (or "Thor, the Mighty," depending on which panel you were reading) debuted in *Journey into Mystery* #83 and the lead character in a previous horror tale was repurposed as Marvel's first microscopic hero—the Astonishing Ant-Man, who defeated villains aided by a battery of ants under his radio control, in *Tales to Astonish*. While helping to create the characters and plot their initial adventures, Lee jobbed out scripting chores for both characters to his younger brother, Larry Lieber. The next month, the teenaged Human Torch would break out from his home franchise, *The Fantastic Four*, and get his own solo showcase in *Strange Tales* #101.

At the conclusion of the insanely productive year of 1962, Lee introduced yet another character in initial collaboration with Kirby, Iron Man, appearing in the anthology *Tales of Suspense* #39. Although there had been mechanically oriented superheroes in the 1940s, Iron Man represented a particularly original approach. Not only was his automated armor equipped with modern transistors, his alter ego and origin were very much part of an early 1960s ethos. Iron Man was, in reality, Tony Stark, a self-made billionaire and technological genius. He was the logical extension of the "wealthy young men about town" who had inhabited popular fiction for decades, but Lee had based Stark on the more solipsistic Howard Hughes, even giving him a moustache—always suspect in the superhero universe.

But Stark was also under a government contract to "solve [your] problems in Vietnam," as he explained to some military brass. While developing a weapon that would wipe out the "red guerrillas" in jungles of Southeast Asia, Stark was captured by a Vietcong leader and forced to create a weapon for his troops; instead, he secretly developed his mechanized armor, foiled their plans, and returned to the States to run his multibillion-dollar empire. (This origin story has close parallels to Lee's 1940s hero, the Destroyer, who began life as an experiment in a concentration camp.) Appearing only months after the American government committed to aid South Vietnamese forces by conducting combat raids, Iron Man's origin played on the resonance with contemporary headlines that had eluded superhero comics since the end of

OPPOSITE, TOP: A rare photo of artist Steve Ditko, circa 1959. BOTTOM: Ah, to be a fly on the wall! From *Amazing Spider-Man Annual* #1 (1964). ABOVE: The one-shot appearance that spun a new industry: *Amazing Fantasy* #1 (1962).

World War II. Tony Stark's conflicted relationship with his own industrialist enterprises would also make Iron Man one of the few truly ambiguously heroic characters of the time.

Stan Lee kept moving forward in 1963, scripting the hallucinatory peregrinations of Steve Ditko's shadowy magus Dr. Strange in *Strange Tales* in April and, three months later, putting Thor, Iron Man, the Hulk, and Ant Man and his paramour, the Wasp, into an uncomfortably comprised team called the Avengers. Unlike the Justice League of America, who always seemed impeccably civil, the *Avengers* fought over their own membership, their own mission—even over Robert's Rules of Order—during their meetings. The Avengers would go on to become one of Marvel's most elastic and surprising titles. Also in July, Kirby and Lee collaborated on a team of young superheroes, each mutated at birth in a different way to manifest an extraordinary superpower. They were originally to be called the Mutants, but, ostensibly, publisher Goodman got squeamish about the name and so Lee redubbed them the X-Men. Thus, from their very beginning, there was something suspect and off-putting about the group; one felt sympathy for their leader, a middle-aged mentor named Professor Xavier, who knew intuitively how different—and vulnerable—his charges would be. According to Lee, "he was afraid that people would fear the X-Men if they knew about their power. So he kept them hidden in what seemed to be a school for gifted youngsters, but nobody knew how gifted they were."

In February 1964, Lee released his final major new superhero, an acrobatic crimefighter named Daredevil, the "Man Without Fear." Blinded by an errant canister of radioactive material (even on the streets of Manhattan, the Marvel characters weren't safe from nuclear anxiety), the young Matt Murdock developed a compensating acuteness among his other senses, including his own personal radar. Initially illustrated by Bill Everett, who created the Sub-Mariner in 1939, Daredevil took a

TOP: *Tales of Suspense* #39 featured the metal-morphosis of Iron Man (1962, art by Don Heck). BOTTOM: Howard Hughes was the conscious role model for billionaire Tony Stark.

LEFT: *Journey into Mystery* gave the Asgardian god, Thor, an earthly home (1962). RIGHT: Ant Man's costumed debut in the *Tales to Astonish* anthology (1962).

while to find his own style and his own audience. Still, he held up the rear as the tenth signature superhero title created at Marvel Comics in less than three years—an even more amazing feat when one considers that Lee and Goodman were still juggling Western gunslingers, fashion models, and howling army commandos at the same time.

Creating characters is one kind of skill, but creating a mythos is another ball game entirely. By accident, design, or both, Lee created a personality and style for Marvel Comics that was larger than the whole of its disparate, dysfunctional, dynamically powered parts. The first was what came to be called the "Marvel Method." Partly because he was overextended with sixteen separate storylines, partly because he trusted his artists, Lee typically didn't type up an entire script, with panel-by-panel descriptions (the way it was usually done), but would present a premise or outline to his artist—Kirby, Ditko, Don Heck, Wally Wood, etc.—and then tighten up the story and render dialogue when the artist returned the penciled layouts. He described his m.o. with Jack Kirby:

> See, in the beginning, I would just give Jack the plot, but I didn't tell him how to draw. Jack would take an idea and . . . he would often add many thoughts and ideas and concepts that hadn't even occurred to me. . . . We were such a good team because we fed off each other. I gave him ideas, he gave me ideas— I was able to run as far as the dialogue and captions were concerned with the ideas he gave me.

Kirby, in particular, enticed readers to dive headfirst into the Marvel Universe. In addition to creating the look for most of the line's superheroes and villains, he could also be called upon

issue, it was Lee's dialogue and characterization that sealed the deal and instilled brand loyalty. First, he simply looked at comic book characters differently:

> When I was young, my favorite superhero was Sherlock Holmes. Sherlock Holmes was just a superior human being. So, to me, he was as super as any superhero. We tried to make our characters realistic at Marvel, even though they had super-powers. Now we're talking about fantasy stories, but I tried to say, "If such characters existed, how would they act in the real world," and that's where we tried to inject a little bit of reality. . . . I had always felt that if I had a superpower (which is not to say that I don't), I wouldn't immediately put on a mask and a costume. . . . And, also, I wouldn't go around looking for bad guys to fight: I'd be thinking, "How can I make some money on this? Maybe I can get a guest shot on Jay Leno's show? I wonder what they'd pay me?"

In other hands, such sentiments might make a superhero a figure of derision or mockery, but Lee gave his heroes a kind of mortal dignity. Whether they still lived at home with their aunts (or even their ants); or bickered with each other; or couldn't pay the rent; or even questioned their very avocation as superheroes, the Marvel characters had the courage of their restrictions. DC Comics artist Ramona Fradon summed up the difference between Marvel and what Lee called the "Distinguished Competition":

> You would never think of having Superman be neurotic or have doubts or anything like that. That was true of all the DC characters. [To me,] it was like Greek drama: there was Aeschylus, where the

to render an eye-catching cover, especially for an all-important debut issue. Already the most explosive—and prolific—artist in comics, the "Marvel Method" freed up Kirby to take even larger creative chances. Artist Neal Adams describes Kirby's evolution at Marvel: "I don't even know how to describe it except to say that he was fearless. You could say, 'Draw a universe' and he would." Writer Len Wein concurred, "Jack was a machine who had infinite capacity to create ideas, one after the other, in any genre you ever wanted them. There was no genre where he wasn't capable of coming up with something that topped everybody else in the room."

But if Kirby's action-packed frescoes and Steve Ditko's detailed narratives got readers to part with their twelve cents per gods were in their heavens, unquestioned, and then Euripides came along and decided to analyze them and bring them down to a human level. Maybe it was time—you can't have those characters running around forever without beginning to wonder what they did in their off-hours.

Lee demystified his characters' environment as well; rather than creating fictitious towns to live in—Metropolis or Gotham City— all the Marvel characters lived in New York City. This made it easier for crossover adventures, which certainly couldn't have hurt sales, but it also gave the Marvel Universe literal common ground with its characters, its creators, and its audience. It also, not coincidentally, made continuity easier.

It also didn't hurt that Lee reached to a higher shelf when writing dialogue or constructing characters: "Well, I would like to think that we wrote our stories as if the readers were a little older and a maybe little smarter than our competition." One Daredevil villain would be called Mr. Hyde; another, the Jester, had formerly been an actor famous as Cyrano de Bergerac; most of Thor's Asgardian colleagues were borrowed either from Alexandre Dumas or William Shakespeare, who, for better or worse, had always inspired Lee to create farragoes of bombasti- cally elevated dialogue. And, intentionally or not, the Marvel Universe contained a hierarchy of paternal, avuncular, or pedagogical authority figures. Some were inspirational, such as the benevolent Ancient One, who mentored Dr. Strange in the mystic arts, or Professor Xavier; some were nefarious, such as General "Thunderbolt" Ross, who was always using his military command to flatten the Hulk into a big green pancake, or Magneto, who was constantly trying to enroll errant mutants into his Evil Brotherhood. Young readers, who had to contend with such authority figures in their real lives, were drawn into the character-building exercise of choosing right from wrong.

Still, the Marvel Universe was hardly a series of pompous *bildungsromans*: Lee's dialogue bristled with a sense of humor, often taking the piss out of the very idea of comic book super-

OPPOSITE: Eternity showing his powers to Dr. Strange (*Strange Tales* #138, art by Steve Ditko). TOP: Bill Everett was the first artist to render the Man Without Fear (*Daredevil* #1, 1964); Everett departed the feature five issues later—the yellow costume quickly followed suit. BOTTOM: The Hulk never played well with others: from *Avengers* #2 (1963).

ABOVE: Kirby's universe unleashed on Manhattan (*Fantastic Four* #50, 1966).
BELOW: The X-Men's high-flying Angel (1965).

The Ultimate Marvel Superhero interior monologue: Peter Parker comtemplates his existential destiny in *The Amazing Spider-Man* #50, art by John Romita.

hcrocs. For example, when the helmet-clad Magneto marches onto an army base in *X-Men* #l, fully intent on eradicating it to smithereens, the sentry guard shouts at him, "Hold it, mac! If you're looking for a masquerade party, you've come to the wrong place! Beat it!" Meaningful interior monologue was a rarity in comic books, but Lee upped the ante there, too. "I used thought balloons heavily, because a thought balloon could show the reader what the character was thinking of as well as what the character was saying, and you get to know the character better that way." Lee even extended his approach to readers as an editor, speaking to them from his "soapbox" as if the company and the consumer belonged to the same club—and after a while, they did.

> I could come up with slogans, like "Make Mine Marvel," "Marvel Marches On" and a membership club, "The Merry Marvel Marching Society," things like that. You could give a mood and a feeling to the company. I really tried to treat everything like a big ad campaign. I wanted the readers to feel they're part of this exciting little world that we have.

Carmine Infantino, eventually Lee's opposite number at National, gave him credit for redirecting the dynamic: "Stan made it very personal. He was marvelous at that. He was buddy-buddy and we were not that way. At DC, we were: 'We talk, you listen.' That was the difference."

The difference between DC and Marvel was also one of professional priorities. DC had maintained an unbroken corporate structure since the l930s, with all the privilege and decorum that conveys; Marvel was a renegade company, which had almost disappeared down the sinkhole a few years earlier. DC's workforce numbered in the dozens: artists, writers, editors, and administrative assistants who were expected to show up for work in suits and skinny black ties. By contrast, the entire Marvel staff could have fit into an elevator with room to spare. According to comic book writer and historian Mark Waid, "because Marvel didn't have to answer to corporate shareholders, the buck stopped at Stan. It's whatever he wanted to do that day, that's what got published." In contemporary parlance, it was the *Mad Men* culture vs. the beatnik culture. "Whenever Stan was writing, he would always have Peter Parker call coffee 'java,'" recounted artist/writer Walt Simonson. "I think 'java' was out of date forty years earlier, but it sounded like something college kids drank."

Indeed, Marvel's first line of attack was the college campus. Not only was there the occasional Spider-Man story about campus unrest (in between sips of java), but baby-boomer college students were embracing the fractured, flawed superheroes of the Marvel Universe as comrades of their own. In September 1966, *Esquire* magazine published an unprecedented story about Marvel Comics, tellingly, in its "Back to College" issue. Jack Kirby created an original full-color illustration of ten of Marvel's major superheroes, and various college students spoke of their allegiance to the company and its characters. One Southern Illinois University student was quoted: "My favorite is the Hulk. I identify with him. He is the outcast against the Institution." Stan Lee himself brought his outcasts into the Institution, delivering lectures for college campus organizations across the country, including at Princeton's tony Debating Society.

As the sixties moved forward, Marvel Comics provided DC Comics the first real competition that they'd had since the days, ironically, of Captain Marvel. Artist Jim Steranko suggested that the success of Marvel came about because, "Stan, of course, is a consummate pro and he surrounded himself with other veteran artists who really couldn't draw a bad panel if they wanted to." But perhaps the most revolutionary concept initiated by Stan Lee and Co. could be contained in a small all-caps squib at the bottom of various splash pages and advertisements: "FROM THE MARVEL HOUSE OF IDEAS!"

Ideas? In a comic book? As Ben Grimm, the transformed Thing, used to say, "Who'da thunk it?"

FROM TOP: Two authority figures: one enraged (General "Thunderbolt" Ross, *The Incredible Hulk* #1) and one enlightened (the Ancient One, *Strange Tales* #115); the Merry Marvel Marching Society reached out to fans (and their parents' pocketbooks)—theme song included.

LEFT: The blockbuster John Romita cover showed college-age readers which hero swung to their side (1969). RIGHT: A house ad for Marvel from *Fantastic Four* #14 (1965).

Like costumed heroes? Confidentially, we in the comic mag business refer to them as "long underwear characters"! And, as you know, they're a dime a dozen. But we think you may find our Spider-Man just a bit . . . different.

Normally, a blurb like that, which appeared at the top of the first Spider-Man story in *Amazing Fantasy* #15, would be dismissed as typical Stan Lee hyperbole. But, if anything, Lee uncharacteristically undersold his product: Spider-Man was more than a bit different. And that difference would go a long way toward creating the most popular comic book superhero of the second part of the 20th century.

First, Lee took the teenaged sidekick and turned him, appropriately for a spider, upside down. Batman's Robin had been cavorting about as a jocular teenager for two decades, but his highly contrived circumstances had always annoyed Lee. "Real teenagers have problems," he said. "In those days especially, it was hell being a teenager. [This teenager] never had enough money, he wasn't the most popular kid in school, he didn't always do well with girls. . . . I wanted Peter Parker—Spider-Man—to have a lot of problems. His life isn't that easy."

The bespectacled bookworm, Parker resembled, for all the world, a junior varsity version of the hapless Clark Kent, but with one major difference: "Clark Kent was a disguise," writer Len Wein puts it concisely, "Peter Parker was a fact." Teenaged Parker wasn't entirely a hopeless loser—he had a proficiency for science, which would come in very handy. "Transported to another world—the fascinating world of atomic science!," Parker attends a science exhibit on "radio-activity," where he is accidentally bitten by an atomically enhanced spider. Soon, he discovers he has the ability to scale buildings, balance on a thread, contort himself gymnastically through the air, and exercise "the proportionate strength of a spider"—one of Lee's pet, and admittedly inane, phrases.

But, true to the new Marvel ethos, Parker initially decides not to right wrongs, but to pocket some much-needed cash. Apparently orphaned (a complicated situation resolved decades later), Parker lives with his Uncle Ben and Aunt May in a "neat frame two-story house." Their strapped financial situation is spotlighted when Uncle Ben scrapes his pennies together to buy Peter a new microscope. Parker uses his scientific talent to fashion a pair of web-shooters that dispense a miraculous web-like substance; then, he dons a red-and-blue spider-emblazoned costume, and he's off to the races.

Lee even has his lead character become a sensation on the actual *Ed Sullivan Show*, where the newly minted Spiderman (he would lose and gain his hyphen several times over his initial appearances) racks up not only a fistful of dollars, but an uncharacteristic sense of arrogance. Refusing to help the police apprehend a passing thief, he blithely lets the criminal slip by. Days

LEFT: A Ditko spectacular (*The Amazing Spider-Man* #8). ABOVE: Seminal moments from *Amazing Fantasy* #15.

later, as Peter Parker, he discovers that his beloved Uncle Ben has been shot dead by a burglar. Swinging into action as Spider-Man, he tracks down the burglar—only to discover that the burglar was the same thief that he brushed off earlier. Young Parker's sense of guilt is overwhelming, but he transmutes it into something more virtuous and more useful: responsibility. In one of the most memorable phrases in comic book history, the story concludes, "A lean, silent figure slowly fades in to the gathering darkness, aware at last, that in this world, with great power, there must also come great responsibility."

Peter Parker's personal loss was the most resonant since Bruce Wayne's; Stan Lee had effectively combined Batman's tragic history with Robin's youth and Superman's alter ego.

Intended as a one-off, Spider-Man enflamed young readers' enthusiasms almost immediately. By the beginning of 1963, he was given his own bi-monthly book, *The Amazing Spider-Man*; by the summer, it went monthly. Spider-Man appealed on a variety of levels. Steve Ditko had given the character a variety of cool gizmos, including web-shooters and a spider-beam (eventually discarded), but beyond the tried-and-true appeal of a red-and-blue suit was the mask that covered Parker's entire face. While this may have limited Spider-Man's expressivity, it allowed generations of kids of all types and races to project themselves inside his suit, which no doubt extended his popularity. Besides, the acrobatic gyrations that Ditko conceived for Spider-Man were far more expressive than the faces rendered by most artists.

Peter Parker's personality was unique in comic books at the time; an inveterate wise-cracker, he frequently compared his ghoulish adversaries invidiously to movie characters, rock 'n' roll stars, or contemporary politicians. Tweaking various civics lessons, he often referred to himself as "your friendly neighborhood Spider-Man" and Lee frequently called him "Spidey" ("I could never imagine calling Superman 'Supesy,'" Lee once said). Along with the Thing from the Fantastic Four, Spider-Man was the first meta-superhero, aware of the basic absurdity of his situation. When Dr. Octopus threatened to "end [Spider-Man's] career for good," our hero responded, "Yeah, some career! No vacations, no pension plan! Not even a salary! Go ahead and end it . . . who cares!!?" Parker was even denied the basic fantasy outlet of every other teenaged kid: "Boy! When I used to read comic mag adventures of super heroes, I always dreamed about how GREAT it would be if I could become one! It's great, alright—for everyone except Spider-Man! Aw, NUTS!"

Spider-Man's villains were a colorful lot, gnomish and cranky, frequently deformed (a veteran scientist who lost his right arm in World War II tries to grow it back and instead is transformed into the gnarly Lizard) and often intricately woven into his personal life. For example, the Green Goblin, who was slow to emerge as his arch-nemesis, would be revealed as the father

OPPOSITE, FROM TOP: Peter Parker's alter ego always stood between him and happiness (*The Amazing Spider-Man* #30, art by Ditko); Spider-Man confronts his uncle's killer: a shock so severe, it produces a rare shot of pupils in our hero's eyes; the first Marvel hero to break out of an anthology and achieve his own magazine (1963). TOP: Spider-Man becomes a celebrity, even without a hypen (*Amazing Fantasy* #15).

of Peter Parker's best friend and would ultimately deal the web-slinger his most painful emotional blow. In another storyline, the eight-limbed "Doc Ock" almost married Parker's widowed Aunt May.

Yet, although Ditko rendered Spider-Man's encounters with his adversaries in epic proportions, sometimes it seemed as if the colorful villains were the least of his problems—and therein lay a great deal of the series' charm. Parker was always being bullied at school by the arrogant jock Flash Thompson—the irony being that Flash Thompson was Spider-Man's most fervent enthusiast. The irony extended into Parker's workplace; using his unique access to Spider-Man to take brilliant snapshots of his escapades, Parker sold his photos to the *Daily Bugle*. (Imagine if Clark Kent and Peter Parker had been assigned to work the same story!) The publisher and editor of the tabloid newspaper was a xenophobic blowhard named J. Jonah Jameson who, for complicated reasons (jealousy, family tragedy, dyspepsia, you name it), took on Spider-Man as his life-long animus. Jameson was dedicated to smearing Spider-Man at every turn, in every headline and editorial; his megalomaniacal rants began to resemble Donald Trump's incoherent screeds. It didn't matter: the more "J.J.J." turned up the heat, the more readers loved it; the fact that Peter Parker was financially dependent on his publisher's tightfisted payroll made the irony all the more delicious.

If that didn't make Parker's life complicated enough, there were the girls. Initially spurned by the "chicks" at Midtown High, Peter Parker eventually became an assured ladies' man (his alternate career must have boosted his confidence). He dated his school's most comely blonde, his boss's secretary, his aunt's best friend's niece—almost always screwing up his love life because some deadly adversary had clambered into town and required his attention instead. Clark Kent and Lois Lane were, for decades, trapped in the same immovable triangle, but Peter Parker's romantic peregrinations were sometimes more involving than his knock-down, drag-out fights. It's worth remembering that while Stan Lee was writing *The Amazing Spider-Man* (which he did for nearly 100 issues), he was still writing teen comics and romance comics (*Millie the Model*, et al.) for the Marvel line; his skill at creating soap opera for those titles came in handy. Author Michael Chabon sees Peter Parker's emotional life as the essential truth of the character:

> He's a boy. He's a real teenager. He's self-doubting. And there's a poignancy in that idea that you could have all these powers, these great powers, but you know what doesn't come with great power? A love life. You're still a hopeless case; even if you have the ability to swing from skyscrapers over the streets of New York, it's not going to help you get a date on Friday night.

Even with these problems—because of these problems—Spider-Man was the most evolving character of his time. He was in a constant state of flux; he was, as it were, always spinning. He was unable to get his checks cashed, because he didn't have any I.D. beyond his costume; he would come down with the flu and get his clock cleaned by Doc Ock; he would suspect that he was schizophrenic and attempt to see a psychiatrist—only to realize he would be putting his secret identity at risk. As the years went on, Peter Parker would grow up, attend college, date more interesting women (sometimes simultaneously), lose one of them tragically, settle down with another, and move toward maturity, even stability, to varying degrees of success.

But, more than anything, Spider-Man had a painful duality to his very existence, an ambivalence that resonated mightily in a decade that challenged the very assumptions of heroic authority:

> I can never forget that I'M partially to blame for Uncle Ben's death! And the fact that I'm the only one who knows it doesn't make it any easier to live with! And now, no matter what I do … no matter how great my spider powers are, I can never undo that tragic mistake! I can never completely forgive myself! Sometimes, I hate my Spider-Man powers! Sometimes I wish I were just like any normal teen-ager!

The ultimate genius of Spider-Man was that there were millions of so-called "normal teen-agers" who saw in the web-slinger an avatar of their own problems and conflicts—and they loved him as much for his screw-ups as Peter Parker as for his triumphs as their friendly neighborhood Spider-Man.

FROM TOP: Publisher J. Jonah Jameson was, in many ways, Spider-Man's ultimate foe; his attacks on the webslinger even complicated Spidey's love life (with Betty Brant). Another classic Romita cover—the ultimate identity crisis (*The Amazing Spider-Man* #50).

TOP: Roy Lichtenstein's *Whaam!* (1963). BOTTOM: The Bonwit Teller window display that made Andy Warhol's career, thanks in no small part to Superman (1961).

"WHAAM!"
Pop Art

One wouldn't necessarily expect the vanguard of the avant-garde to announce its presence in the store windows of a high-toned women's clothing store on Fifth Avenue, but in spring 1961, there it was.

Andy Warhol had moved to New York City in 1949 to pursue a career in graphic design, while spending his free time developing his own projects, most often using the silk-screen reproduction process. By 1960, he was pursuing studio art full-time. His first public commission came from Bonwit Teller, a prestigious New York women's department store. He was asked to "do" their windows; for the up-and-coming Warhol, this was a huge break.

He exhibited five silk-screened canvases: three were based on comic strip characters: the Little King, Popeye, and Superman (taken from an actual 1959 *Superman* comic panel by Kurt Schaffenberger). There was nothing particularly pointed about Warhol's choice of comic strip characters—growing up as a sickly child in Pittsburgh, his mother frequently read to him from comics of Popeye, Dick Tracy, and Superman. In fact, much of his work from 1960 to 1961 revolved around a number of comics characters: there were several Dick Tracy canvases and another that replicated the Batman logo of the 1940s. "We all read a bunch of comic books, and it just happened to come out then [in the early 1960s]," he said in an interview. "Because comic books make things appear the way they are really today. I mean, you pick up a newspaper and it's just like a comic book of eight years ago. There's so much action." By literally blowing up the images of his childhood heroes, Warhol was blowing up the New York art world while transforming into the High Priest of an international style known as Pop art.

As a movement, Pop art had its roots in Great Britain during the 1950s. After years of deprivation following World War II, a group of artists embraced art that was mass-produced, ephemeral, available to all, and eye-catching: popular, or even imagery that "popped." As the 1960s began, a similar movement was coalescing in New York. Warhol's genius was to memorialize those commercialized

TOP: *Batman* silkscreen by Warhol, using the character's 1950s logo (1960). BOTTOM: Justice League of America nemesis Dr. Light (art by Mike Sekowsky, 1962) gets his moment in the spotlight, via Lichtenstein's *Mad Scientist* (1962). OPPOSITE: Andy Warhol and sidekick Nico pose as Batman and Robin.

images by freezing them in time and expanding them vastly beyond their original use.

While Warhol was installing his canvases at Bonwit Teller, another artist was memorializing the popular image along a parallel track. Roy Lichtenstein, a World War II vet, also turned to images from the past; in his case, Mickey Mouse and Donald Duck. *Look Mickey* (1961) was his breakout canvas, and although Lichtenstein was originally stymied that Warhol had beaten him to the punch, as it were, with a Popeye canvas, Lichtenstein's own version of Popeye socking it to Bluto enhanced his reputation as the other great apostle of Pop art.

Warhol would quickly move on to reproducing consumer goods such as Campbell's soup cans and Brillo pads, but Lichtenstein delved further and further into the world of comic strips and comic books. In the first half of the 1960s, he repurposed more than 100 comic book panels into enormous canvases, usually sketching the panel by hand, projecting it onto a canvas, and then altering it by hand, repainting it in bold outlines and primary colors (often rendering the unique Ben Day dots used by printers). Critics have pointed out the irony of Lichtenstein taking a mechanically produced comic book, re-drawing it by hand, projecting it mechanically, then painting the final image.

Lichtenstein availed himself of the genres of comic books popular in the early 1960s, most famously romance comics and war comics. He used superhero comics panels most specifically twice; the first, *Image Duplicator* (1963), was based on a Jack Kirby illustration of Magneto from *X-Men* #1; the second, *Mad Scientist* (1963), used a panel from a Justice League of America comic. One should also contend with *Whaam!* (1963), which was taken from a war comic, but did more to memorialize a comic book sound effect than anything before it.

Lichtenstein was promiscuous in his use of previously published comic books—rather than craft an original panel, he borrowed

images from artists as prestigious as Kirby, Joe Kubert, Russ Heath, John Romita, and Mike Sekowsky. The fact that Lichtenstein would take a comics panel for which an artist was paid a fraction of, say, $15 a page, repurpose and recomposite it, then sell it for hundreds of thousands of dollars a canvas, was an inequity that did not go unnoticed. It didn't help Lichtenstein's reputation among comic book artists and fans that he was quoted as saying, "The comics really haven't anything I would call art connected with it. They are really using a craft ability almost entirely and artistic sense only slightly. There's composition connected with comic strips, but in a very superficial way."

For the Pop artists of the 1960s, the comic book conformed immediately to their purposes: they were mass-produced, they were resonant with nostalgia, they were already graphically appealing, they were pleasurable and popular. Pop art may have obliterated the narrative form of comic books by reproducing only one panel at a time, but it elevated the vocabulary of comic book art into fine art, or, at very least a vibrant discussion about what constituted high art and low art.

For the comic books themselves (if not for the repurposed artists), the emergence of Pop art was a cultural windfall. Less than a decade after the Senate Subcommittee debacle, comic book art was being talked (and argued) about in the most erudite art journals and newspaper columns. It would have been foolish for comic books not to ride the crest of this public relations bonanza. For a while, Marvel Comics even rebranded their comics as "POP ART PRODUCTIONS"—whatever that meant—on their covers.

Inevitably, Pop art would be appropriated by the very genre it borrowed from initially. It would take a few visionary artists—Neal Adams, Jim Steranko, to name two—to reverse the polarity of Pop art's electricity. They didn't create million-dollar canvases, but no comic book fan worth his or her salt would ever dream of parting with their works of art—even at twelve cents a pop.

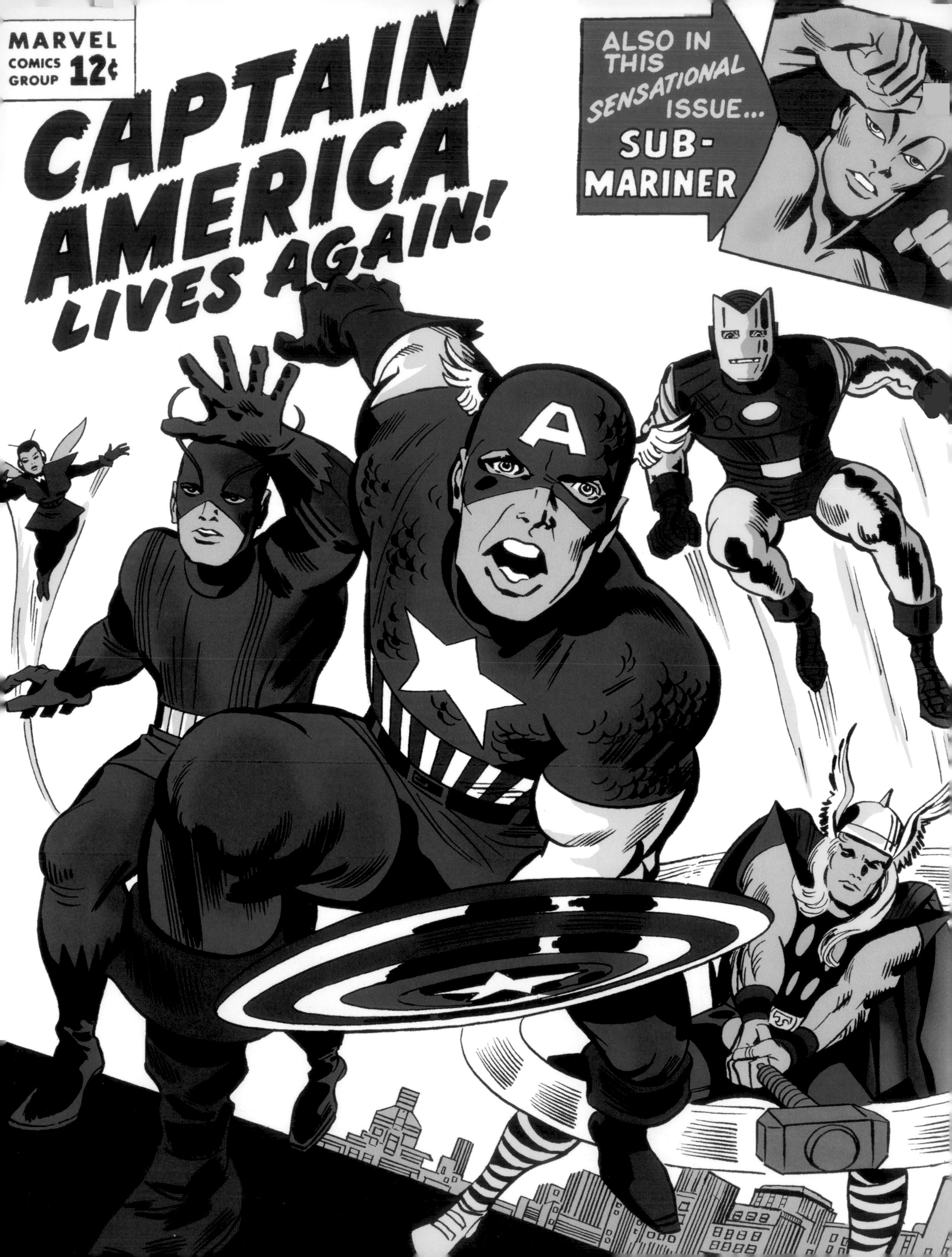
MARVEL COMICS GROUP 12¢
CAPTAIN AMERICA LIVES AGAIN!
ALSO IN THIS SENSATIONAL ISSUE... SUB-MARINER

REPORTING FOR DUTY
"Captain America Lives Again!"

OPPOSITE: Comic books' favorite patriot rallies the country once again in the pages of *The Avengers* #4 (1964). ABOVE: Out-of-town tryout: Lee and Kirby float a revival of Captain America in the pages of the Human Torch omnibus *Strange Tales* #114 (1963).

he term "retcon" has a military feel to it—like something Captain America might have done in some adventure: "Cap and Bucky retconned the impenetrable fortress of the fiendish Red Skull!" "Retcon" actually refers to "retroactive continuity"—a term that bubbled up at a comic book convention in the early 1980s, referring to the need to go back into the past to alter a narrative for the present. It's only fitting that Captain America was the first retconned character of the 1960s.

Among his buddies from the Timely days of the 1940s, Cap's erstwhile partners the Human Torch and the Sub-Mariner had already appeared on the new Marvel scene, but the Torch was a completely reinvented character, reconstituted as teenager Johnny Storm. The Sub-Mariner, for his part, hadn't really changed at all, swimming along in his usual antisocial manner. Captain America was the only major character left unexamined as the fateful fall of 1963 beckoned.

On August 28, 1963, as Martin Luther King, Jr., addressed the throngs gathered at the Mall in Washington DC, and by extension John F. Kennedy, who was listening at the White House, *Strange Tales* #114 hit the streets, with a cover story of young Johnny Storm fighting—"out of the Golden Age of Comics!"—Captain America. It was the first time that Jack Kirby had drawn his star-spangled creation in almost two decades. By the time the tale had concluded, readers were disappointed to learn that it wasn't Cap at all, but an impostor villain called the Acrobat. Still, Stan Lee, who had initiated and written the story, had used the Acrobat as a stalking horse—would readers be interested in seeing the real Cap back in print? The answer was a resounding "yes."

But before Captain America could be launched in a new form, the vibrant young president who had become the new icon of America was assassinated in Dallas that November. At the Marvel Comics offices on Madison Avenue, all work stopped as the staff listened to the sad news on the radio. Within weeks,

Stan Lee would begin to re-create Captain America for a nation in mourning, a nation that had lost a symbol of aspiration and youth, devoid of cynicism. If there were any doubts about the power of resurrection, they were dispelled in early 1964 on the cover of *Avengers* #4, which proudly displayed: "Captain America Lives Again!" And there, rocketing toward the reader, was Captain America as only Jack Kirby could render him, a powerhouse of patriotic passion.

> The mighty Marvel Comics Group is proud to announce that Jack Kirby drew the original Captain America during the Golden Age of Comics . . . and now he draws it again! Also, Stan Lee's first script during those fabled days was Captain America—and now he authors it again! Thus, the chronicle of comicdom turns full circle, reaching a new pinnacle of greatness!

After that ennobling epigraph, the story spun into action: the Avengers, hot in pursuit of the Sub-Mariner up near the Arctic Circle, discover the submerged figure of a man, floating in the sea, encrusted in ice. When Giant-Man pulls the man inside their ship, they notice that his shield and mask could only belong to one person: Captain America. When he awakes, Cap thinks the Avengers are Nazi agents, but is eventually subdued and recounts his story: the last thing he remembers is fighting in World War II, side-by-side with his comrade, Bucky. Against Cap's wishes, Bucky decides to defuse a bomber as a last-ditch effort and is, effectively, blown to smithereens. Captain America falls into the sea, where he drifts to the Arctic, and is frozen in a state of suspended animation. Completely disoriented after his retrieval by the Avengers, he lashes out at them, but by the issue's conclusion, he accepts them as worthy comrades and joins the team, eventually becoming their leader, off-and-on, for the next five decades. The new narrative allowed Lee to redact the awkward Captain America adventures from the mid-1950s, when he'd grappled unconvincingly with Communists.

For Lee and Kirby, Cap's resurrection was fraught with both possibilities and obstacles. Kirby would, indeed, get the chance to tackle his creation again, this time with the formidable storytelling skills he had refined over two decades; imagine Michelangelo, who sculpted his *David* while still in his twenties, getting the chance to return to the same subject after having completed the Sistine Chapel—a wiser, sadder man. Lee—who conveniently airbrushed Joe Simon out of the narrative—would also be returning to a character whom he could now imbue with irony and tragic dimension. The post-1964 appearances of Captain America, in both *The Avengers* and his own exploits published simultaneously in *Tales of Suspense*, focused on spectacular adventure, to be sure, but usually had some scene where an older cop, moved by the sight of his child-hood hero, brushes away a tear, or where some World War II army vet—now in his forties—trades combat stories with the seemingly immortal Captain America. For two World War II army veterans—recall that Kirby and Lee had to go into suspended animation from working on Captain America in the mid-1940s so they could fight

Captain America had fans—both in the comic books and in real life—that stretched across several generations (*Tales of Suspense* #79, 1966). OPPOSITE: As the 1970s dawned, and the Viet Nam War raged a world away, Captain America suffered an existential crisis. Story by Stan Lee, art by Gene Colan (*Captain America* #122, 1970).

the war—it must have been a gratifying way of recounting old war stories; Kirby, in particular, had some combat exploits he must have been eager to exorcise.

Cap himself was not so lucky. Tortured by the guilt of letting Bucky die in his stead, he moaned over his partner's demise to a point that was almost unseemly; he was sometimes in danger of becoming more like Dickens's Miss Havisham than a fearless champion of democracy. He took on another partner, a teenager named Rick Jones, who was usually pestering the Hulk instead, and groomed him to replace Bucky. Occasionally, Lee and Kirby took a break from the modern-day hand-wringing and returned to some actual Captain America and Bucky tales from 1940, rewriting and redrawing them with greatly improved graphics and dimension; they seemed to revel in a return to the less politically ambiguous days of the battle against Hitler.

But the revived Captain America's narrative potency came from his contemporary adventures. As comics historian Danny Fingeroth puts it, "Everybody else that Steve Rogers had known and loved is either dead or a quarter-century older. He survived an era and survived a war where his peers didn't. There's some traumatized thing that I think *Captain America* hooked into and Lee and Kirby were astute enough to understand that and really let it play out." Steve Rogers was, like his namesake Buck Rogers many decades before, a man literally out of his own time—always good for a compelling tale—but he was also the symbol of America, so what did *that* mean?

Just as the country would attempt to regain its footing after Kennedy's death, so, too, did Captain America try to regain his footing after his own rebirth. Within the next decade, he would confront his own obsolescence and his country's at the same time. In one of Stan Lee's favorite lines, he had Marvel's greatest iconic character ponder his situation in a 1970 comic: "I've spent a lifetime defending the flag—and the law! Perhaps I should have battled less—and questioned more!"

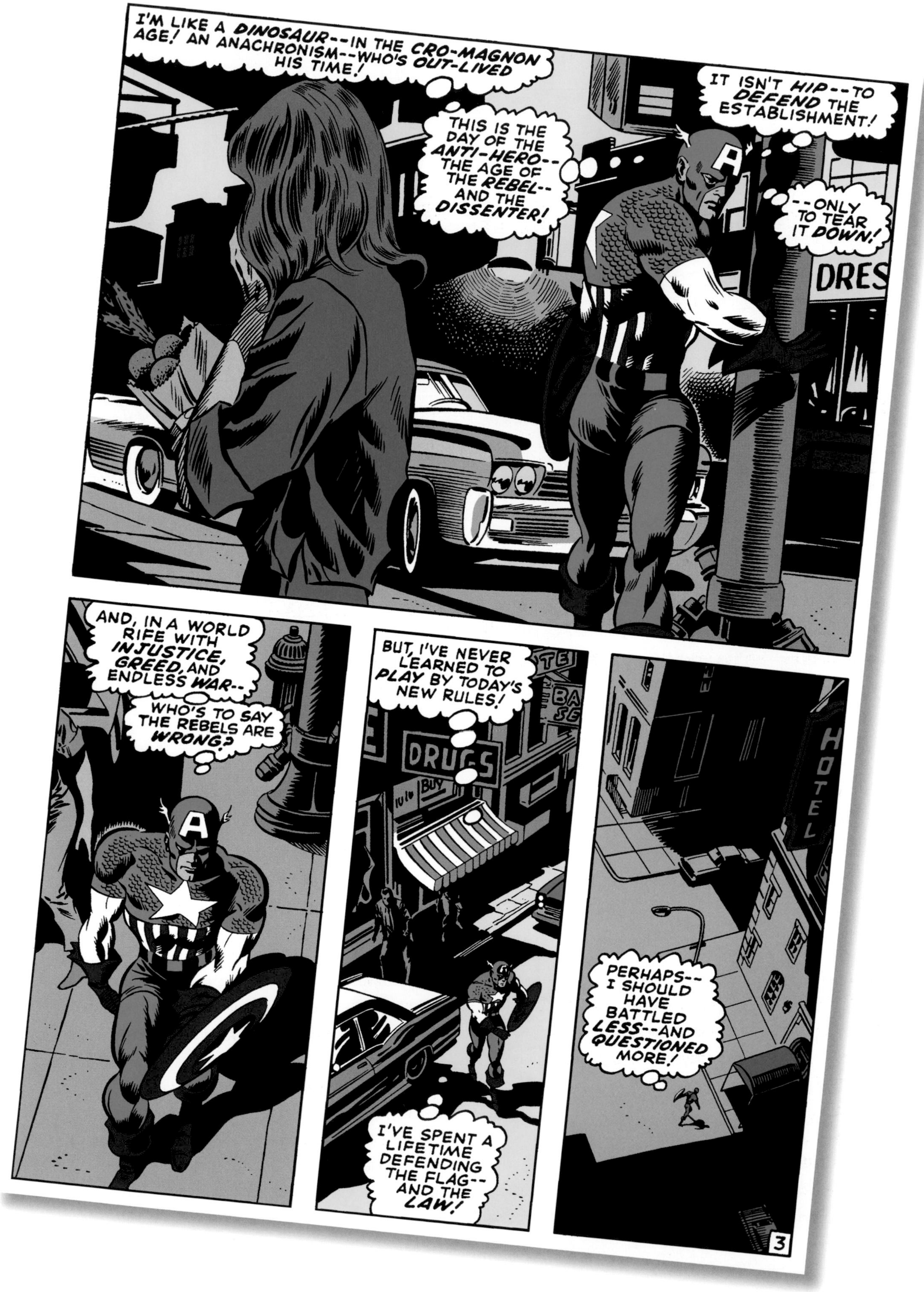
I'M LIKE A DINOSAUR--IN THE CRO-MAGNON AGE! AN ANACHRONISM--WHO'S OUT-LIVED HIS TIME!
THIS IS THE DAY OF THE ANTI-HERO--THE AGE OF THE REBEL--AND THE DISSENTER!
IT ISN'T HIP--TO DEFEND THE ESTABLISHMENT!
--ONLY TO TEAR IT DOWN!
DRES
AND, IN A WORLD RIFE WITH INJUSTICE, GREED, AND ENDLESS WAR--
WHO'S TO SAY THE REBELS ARE WRONG?
BUT, I'VE NEVER LEARNED TO PLAY BY TODAY'S NEW RULES!
DRUGS
I'VE SPENT A LIFETIME DEFENDING THE FLAG--AND THE LAW!
HOTEL
PERHAPS--I SHOULD HAVE BATTLED LESS--AND QUESTIONED MORE!
3

THE SECOND GENERATION:

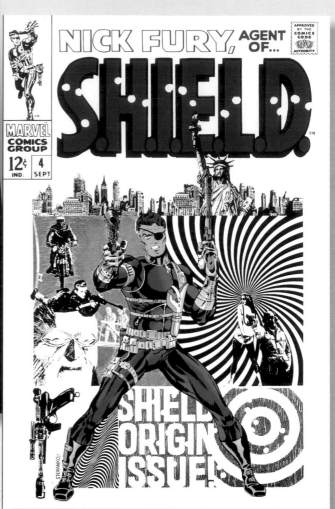

FROM LEFT: Writer/artist Jim Steranko at a 1971 comic book convention; Steranko availed himself of advertising art techniques circa 1968 with *Nick Fury, Agent of S.H.I.E.L.D.* #4; the page and four panels from the opening silent sequence of *Nick Fury, Agent of S.H.I.E.L.D.* #1 (1968).

Jim Steranko burst on the scene in the mid 1960s.
After a few false starts at other companies, he came to Marvel in 1966, where he was put on one of their worst-selling books, *Nick Fury, Agent of S.H.I.E.L.D.* Because there was little to lose, Steranko threw himself at the James Bond knock-off with, well, unshielded fury, bringing dozens of new innovations to the comic book page. His career at Marvel was brief—only three years—but unforgettable. Graphics historian Arlen Schumer puts it this way:

Many people consider Jim Steranko the Jimi Hendrix of comic book art in the late 1960s, because just like Hendrix he came on like a comet, an overnight sensation. And just like Hendrix left in 1970,

Steranko pretty much leaves comics for good in 1970, but creates a body of work that its influence and impact is in inverse proportion to the actual quantity of comics he turned out.

Steranko himself: "Our competition was superheroes who could fly, who could knock down walls, who had colorful costumes, really great. Here's a guy, Nick Fury, all he had was a cigar butt and an eye-patch, for god's sake. How do you compete? Well, I used all of these things. I used modern music. I used modern design. I used psychedelic art. I brought surrealism into the mix. I brought expressionism. I brought Pop art, Optical art. I used everything I could to update comics and bring them into today. *S.H.I.E.L.D.* was very forgiving and it allowed me to do that very easily.

"I did this three-page silent sequence. And it began with Nick

JIM STERANKO

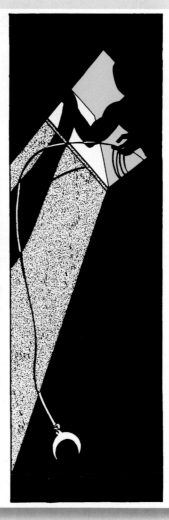

Fury penetrating an enemy fortress. It's a monolithic structure of stone. And he was climbing up, climbing up, using some special tools, broke into the fortress, got down and then the next two pages played out in a little scene where he gets killed at the end. But it was all done silently. And when I say silently, I mean there wasn't even a thought balloon. There wasn't even a caption. There were no words anywhere. Three pages of silence for the first time in comics. I took it in and showed it to Stan and he went, 'Oh my god.' I said, 'What's the matter?' He said, 'Don't you know what you did here?' I said, 'Why don't you tell me?' He said, 'Distributors and bookstores are going to think that this is misprinted, that we forgot the balloons and the captions.' I thought, 'Oh, come off it.' He was probably right about that in a certain way.

"I thought I was bringing a new concept, something really different to the House of Ideas, but I was getting rejected at the same time. So I took the pages in to production where Sol Brodsky held court. And Sol looked over the story, which I think was a twenty-pager. And he said, 'I can't pay you for writing these first three pages, there's nothing here, so I can only pay you for seventeen.' Now look, the pages were written—it's all done visually. The writing is there. But when he said he couldn't pay me for it, I hit the roof. We were on the eighth floor, I grabbed this guy by his shirt and I said, 'I'm going to throw you out this window if you don't pay me for those three pages. I swear to God you're going to be out on Madison Avenue in a moment.'

"Well, in his infinite wisdom he decided to pay me for the three pages and we were cool about it. And those three pages, by the way, were imitated subsequently over and over again in the history of comics. So I kind of felt justified in creating that sequence."

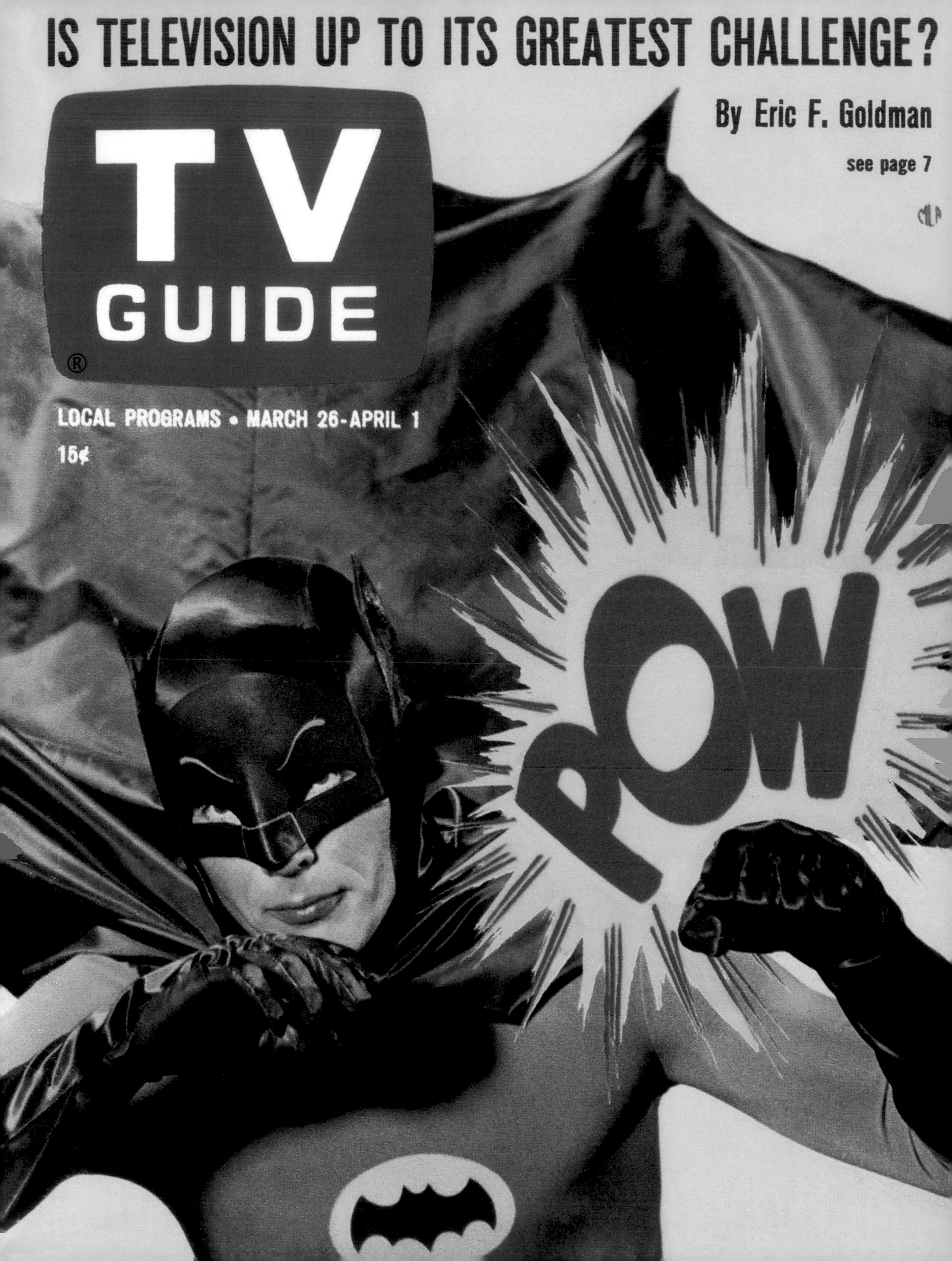
IS TELEVISION UP TO ITS GREATEST CHALLENGE?
By Eric F. Goldman
see page 7
TV GUIDE
LOCAL PROGRAMS • MARCH 26-APRIL 1
15¢
POW

HOLY ZEITGEIST, BATMAN!
The Dynamic Duo on TV

I n his nine-decade history, Batman could always be relied upon to use his bat-ingenuity to get himself out of an infinite number of death traps; his most remarkable escape gimmick would turn out to be a twelve-inch color TV screen.

Although Marvel Comics was publishing exciting exhumations of 1940s characters in the early 1960s, the Distinguished Competition was having a tough time keeping the second of their two major characters commercially viable; according to DC artist Carmine Infantino, Batman's titles were selling about 20 percent each month. The Caped Crusader had lost his way, completely unmoored from his original intention. Batman and Robin—that most unique of comic book duos—had become generic super-heroes, plopped down in any situation: science fiction, monster movies, comedy. The only mystery left in Batman was why National even bothered to keep him in print.

Infantino recounts that he and writer John Broome were called into editor Julie Schwartz's office in 1963, as Schwartz bran-dished a couple of poorly selling *Batman* issues at him: "You two have six months to bring him back or he's dead, finished." Schwartz suggested that the team bring Batman back to his detective roots, jazz up the covers, maybe even jazz up Batman. Infantino was the right man on the National staff for the job, add-ing a yellow bull's-eye around Batman's forlorn bat-insignia and creating covers that intrigued and tantalized readers, beginning

OPPOSITE: Roy Lichtenstein was brought in by the editors of *TV Guide* to memorialize the Batman phenomenon for the 3/26/1966 cover. LEFT: Kids across America found Utility Belts and other Bat-paraphernalia under the Christmas tree, starting in 1967. RIGHT: Another death trap for Batman: the cover of *Detective Comics* #329 celebrates his "new look."

with *Detective Comics* #327 in May 1964. Sales picked up, but whether or not these cosmetic changes (called the "New Look") alone would have restored Batman to his anointed spot on the comic-book Olympus is a question rendered moot by a series of decisions made a continent away in Hollywood.

Television demographics were shifting in the mid-1960s; more families had color television sets and executives were looking for programs that might bridge the divide between kiddie shows and grown-up shows, moving toward what would eventually be called "family shows." Programs with bizarre and fantastical characters began to litter the primetime broadcast landscape— *My Favorite Martian, The Addams Family, The Munsters* were all appealing to youngsters—but there hadn't been a comic book hero on the air since *Adventures of Superman* called it a day in 1958. (Two years later, George Reeves was infamously found shot in his bedroom under still-mysterious circumstances; perhaps his tragic end cast a long shadow over enthusiasm to revive a superhero for television.)

ABC executives thought that comic strip crime-buster Dick Tracy might make a suitable addition to the primetime line-up, but, outbid in a preemptive strike by NBC, they reached a bit further down into the pile and came up with Batman. There's a bit of murkiness about how the idea of the Batman character came to the attention of the programming directors at ABC—rumor had it that Hugh Hefner had been running the old 1940s Batman serials for laughs over at the Playboy Mansion—but nonetheless, by early 1965, ABC had jobbed out the series to 20th Century Fox to produce a pilot. Veteran producer William Dozier was tasked with developing the character for television and flew to New York to meet with the ABC top brass. Dozier apparently took the meeting on faith, knowing nothing about Batman or comic books; he grabbed a handful of Batman comics to read on the transcontinental flight, burying the covers deep in his attaché case, so as not to be mocked by his fellow first-class passengers.

Dozier thought he was in over his head, until it occurred to him that "the idea was to overdo it. If you overdid it, I thought it would be funny to adults and yet it would be stimulating to kids. But you had to appeal on both levels, or you didn't have a chance." Dozier hired Lorenzo Semple, Jr., to draft the pilot episode; Semple delivered, with a story highlighting a minor comic-book adversary called the Riddler. The story equally balanced comedy and adventure, making Batman into an incontrovertibly stolid pillar of civic virtue (i.e., a "square") devoted to maintaining law and order in the vaguely unhinged, swinging '60s. Dozier set his staff and crew to re-creating the Batman universe for color television from the ground of the Batcave up; costumes, sets, props, and a working Batmobile would be designed with unprecedented imaginative freedom. Even the music for the show, scored and arranged by Nelson Riddle, Frank Sinatra's favorite arranger, was hip, jazzy, and unexpected.

Finding the face behind the cowl would be a challenge. The television Batman had to be suitably heroic, yet have a comic touch—and much of the time, the actor's face would be obscured by an inflexible, silk-covered mask. Luckily, actor Adam West got the joke right off. A reliable player in various adventure and detective series and films, West was about to leave the country to make a spaghetti Western, when he was called in to read for Dozier. West doubled over with laughter reading Semple's script and, supposedly, that was all the producer needed to know: West was signed to play Bruce Wayne. Youthful ward Dick Grayson proved harder to find, but, at the last minute, an inexperienced actor with some karate training named Burton Gervis walked onto the Fox lot. He fit the bill admirably, and soon Burt Ward, as he would now be known, completed the Dynamic Duo. West reveled in the challenge of creating TV's first superhero of the 1960s: "In the comic books, Batman was lighthearted and he cracked wise from time to time. Now all I had to do was expand on that. But I wanted to let people watching know that anyone pretty much could become Batman, or become someone admirable, by doing good in the world. And that's kind of the way I played it for the kids."

The pilot episode was filmed in October 1965, and spotlighted the impressionist and actor Frank Gorshin in a career-making performance as the Riddler (his contorted paroxysms in the part would earn him an Emmy nomination). ABC executives made the inventive decision to split the hour-long show in two parts every week, providing a cliffhanger for audiences, and began screening the pilot episode to focus groups. Although Batman tested so poorly that the marketing department was convinced that the reaction monitors were broken, ABC and Dozier kept the faith and ordered sixteen weeks of the two-part weekly program for a January 1966 debut, smack in the middle of the traditional television season. Everything on the program—from its eccentric camera angles, to its saturated color palette, to its melodramatic voiceovers, to the Pop-art title cards that punctuated each knock-down-drag-out fight with "POW!" and "ZONK!," to the ranks of under-employed character actors from the 1940s and 1950s who were knocking over themselves to show up on the program costumed as freakish supervillains—everything had been conceived with originality and underwritten with a generous budget to create a vibrant video equivalent of a comic book. Besides, as the "third network," usually consigned to the ratings basement, ABC had nothing to lose but its conventionality.

CLOCKWISE, FROM RIGHT: Adam West and Burt Ward became national heroes as the Dynamic Duo, twice a week on prime time. The Batman phenomenon overtakes the comics themselves: a Pirandellian cover from *Batman* #183 (January 1967), and a promotional ad.

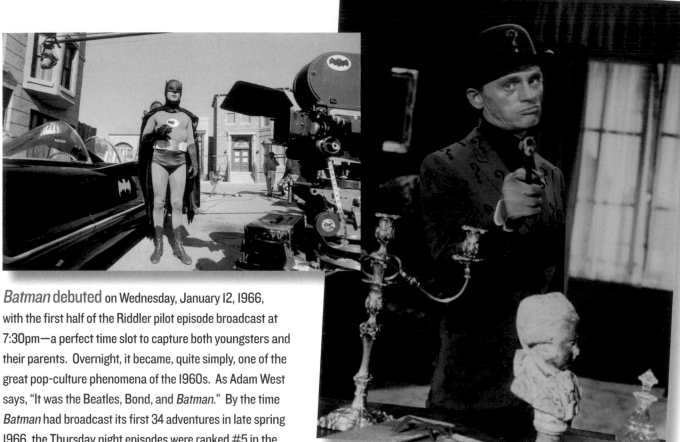

Batman **debuted** on Wednesday, January 12, 1966, with the first half of the Riddler pilot episode broadcast at 7:30pm—a perfect time slot to capture both youngsters and their parents. Overnight, it became, quite simply, one of the great pop-culture phenomena of the 1960s. As Adam West says, "It was the Beatles, Bond, and *Batman*." By the time *Batman* had broadcast its first 34 adventures in late spring 1966, the Thursday night episodes were ranked #5 in the Nielsen ratings and the Wednesday night episodes were #10; no show had ever had two weekly episodes in the Top Ten. "Bat-mania" gripped the nation and, in March 1966, Batman (in the guise of Adam West) became the first superhero to grace the cover of *Life* magazine. Even the Batman comic books, perilously close to extinction only two years earlier, were now selling in the millions.

Batman also hit the marketplace in a manner that far outpaced even Superman at his height: it was an unprecedented Bat-bazaar. Part of this was the nature of the show itself. "We were everywhere and on twice a week in color," says West. "It was different. Anywhere you looked on the set, there was a bat-prop that I could use or a set dressing or something. We had props up the wazoo. So immediately, the merchandizing departments got into the act." Marketing expert Ed Catto reflects that the show was "a game-changer that brainwashed an entire generation of kids, myself included. It had this crazy vibe that no one had seen before. Batman has so many tools and toys and gadgets and friends and villains—and all those things are just ripe for licensing. So, by Christmas of 1967, all these little boys got Batmobiles under the Christmas tree and Batman figures and Bat capes and Batarangs."

The television series succeeded beyond ABC's wildest dreams of unifying a children's audience and an adult audience: it was the first time in media history that all generations could sit around the living room and enjoy a superhero saga. For kids, the derring-do appeal was obvious; for adults, *Batman* offered a window into some of the more complicated cultural conflicts of the 1960s. Pop art made several appearances, including one where the Clock King (a criminal actually borrowed from a Green Arrow comic) masquerades as Progress Pigment—"the true apostle of Pop art!"—in an episode written by none other than Bill Finger, Batman's co-creator. Batman's comic book origins were confined to one throwaway line in the first episode, where Bruce Wayne refers to the "dastardly criminals who murdered my parents," but the character became an effective spokesman for civic virtues and Victorian respectability in an anxious time. Batman championed the use of safety belts, studying your homework, a refreshing glass of milk, and following the straight and narrow. The *Batman* series could pivot on a dime into satirical commentary. In one episode, the nefarious Penguin decides to run for mayor, so that he can pilfer the Gotham City Treasury. When the Caped Crusader tosses his cowl into the ring against the Penguin, he decides to run "a nice, clean campaign, without vaudeville tricks—after all, Robin, the public is interested

OPPOSITE: Adam West on a recycled Gotham City on the backlot of Desilu Studios, 1966; Frank Gorshin's archvillain, the Riddler, was consciously modeled on screen heavy Richard Widmark. ABOVE: *Life* magazine devoted unprecedented attention to a superhero, March 1966.

in the issues." Of course, it turns out to be the dullest political campaign in Gotham City history.

Not everyone was thrilled with Batman's transition into a stuffy, caped prism of contemporary sensibilities. Denny O'Neil, who would go on to create groundbreaking comic book scenarios for Batman in the 1970s said:

> The *Batman* TV show was pretty much a one-line joke: "I loved this stuff when I was six years old and now—that I am twenty-seven, and I have a closet full of Nehru jackets, and a twice-weekly appointment with a therapist and a little tiny drug habit—look how silly it is." In New York, you would go to the most literary bar in the city, the White Horse Inn, on one of the two days that they had the *Batman* shows on, and the cream of Village intelligentsia—at least the ones who liked to go to bars—were looking at that show behind the bar.

However, as the villain Bookworm might have quoted Shakespeare, "So do quick bright things come to confusion." The highly anticipated second season of *Batman* debuted in fall 1966 with even more overacted and underbaked villains, poorer scripts, and strained sensibilities; none of its episodes landed in the Top Twenty. For the third season, the budgets were slashed and the episodes scaled back to once a week; but even the addition of the sassy Batgirl failed to provide enough engines to power or turbines to speed. One-hundred-and-twenty episodes later, Bat-Time had officially come to an end.

West, who has reveled in his iconic presence for six decades now, is philosophical: "I think of our Batman as 'The Bright Knight.' The kids loved it and we were funny for the adults. And that was our intention. If you play it that way, the show stays fresh and always kind of spinning around out there in its own little world, and people get into it once they get past three or four years of age." Or, as Commissioner Gordon put it, five minutes into the first *Batman* episode, speaking for television executives, comic book executives, and eleven-year-old boys alike: "I don't know who he is behind that mask of his, but we need him—and we need him *now*."

PARODY AND SATIRE

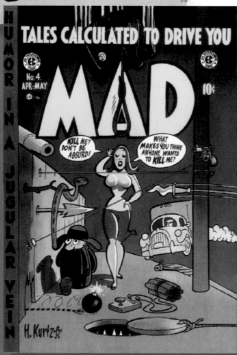

CLOCKWISE, FROM TOP LEFT: Mighty Mouse was the first animated spoof of the super-hero game (1945). *MAD* magazine had been spoofing Batman since 1953, both the comic book (below) and the TV show (1966—although they got Robin's underwear wrong), as well as the Shadow (*MAD* #4).

When William Gaines stomped away from the proceedings of the Comics Code Authority in 1954, turning his back on the successful publishers of superhero comic books, he was no doubt plotting his revenge. The revered saying, "living well is the best revenge," might have been revised by Gaines as, "laughing well is the best revenge."

The one successful comic book that Gaines had left in his portfolio was an anarchic four-color parody magazine called *MAD*. *MAD* would eventually gain a storied reputation for satirizing just about every aspect of American culture worth mocking (which is to say, most of American culture) as a black-and-white magazine beyond the reach of the Code in 1955. But the early, crazy issues of the *MAD* comic book displayed a particular animus toward its colleagues in the funny pages and comic books.

Superheroes had been rather gently but rarely satirized since they arrived on the scene; there might be some jokes at, say, Superman's expense on the Fred Allen radio show. Actual parody came in 1942 with the cartoon shorts featuring Mighty Mouse, who originally began as Super Mouse (even before that, the Terrytoons studio thought of creating a super-powered housefly called—wait for it—Super Fly), but it might be fair to say that, in the 1940s and 1950s, superheroes weren't taken seriously enough to satirize.

The "usual gang of idiots" at *MAD* changed all that. In the fourth issue (1953), MAD took on both the Shadow and Superman, who was exquisitely rethought as "Superduperman!." Harvey Kurtzman, who wrote the spoof, and Wally Wood (a tremendous artist who would render beautiful work on "serious" superhero comics in the 1960s) tapped right into the essential improbabilities of the hero, from Lois Lane derogating Clark Kent as a "creep" to Superduperman's fight to the finish with "Captain Marbles," a rival superhero with a dollar sign on his chest and possessed of a magic word—"Shazoom"—in which the "M" stood for "Money." Four issues later, the same team tackled the Caped Crusaders as a pint-sized "Bat Boy" and his gangly sidekick, "Rubin," chasing down a suspected vampire criminal. The final panel revealed that

it was Bat Boy all along who possessed the real fangs—and knew how to use them. "Woman, Wonder!" (in *MAD* #10) undermined the basic premise of Wonder Woman—her boyfriend, Steve Trevor, had no intention of her being more powerful than he (and he was particularly pleased to catch a glimpse of Woman Wonder changing into her costume inside her invisible plane). The *MAD* parodies were not only clever, they were perceptive—they knew how to get inside the characters' basic absurdities in order to turn them inside-out.

When *Batman* debuted on national television in 1966, *MAD* weighed in almost immediately with "Bats-Man," in which "Sparrow, the Boy Wonderful" disguises himself as a villain in order to knock off Bats-Man, so he can finally hang up his cape and date girls and sniff airplane glue like all the other teenagers in Gotham City. That issue (#183) was billed as the "Special Summer 'Camp' Issue," referring to a cultural phenomenon that had excited literary circles two years before the television show premiered.

Susan Sontag had published her influential essay "Notes on 'Camp' " in the *Partisan Review* in 1964, attempting to give coherence to a disparate set of aesthetic sensibilities that she identified in fifty-eight separate markers. Although Sontag only mentioned comic books once, in a passing note about "old Flash Gordon comics," her comments about science fiction films could be equally well applied to superheroes:

> The reason . . . books like *Winesburg, Ohio* and *For Whom the Bell Tolls* are bad to the point of being laughable, but not bad to the point of being enjoyable, is that they are too dogged and pretentious. They lack fantasy. There is Camp in . . . numerous Japanese science fiction films (*Rodan, The Mysterians, The H-Man*) because, in their relative unpretentiousness and vulgarity, they are more extreme and irresponsible in their fantasy—and therefore touching and quite enjoyable.

Although it was hard to know when the term was being applied accurately or not, "camp" became a convenient label among critics, and the television version of *Batman* appeared to be a poster

CLOCKWISE, FROM TOP LEFT: Broadway actor William Daniels turned goofy in primetime in *Captain Nice* (1967). *MAD* artist Don Martin came up with the amiable adventures of Captain Klutz. *Not Brand Echh* was Marvel's parody omnibus; in issue #2 (1967), it provided fans with an early, if irreverent, crossover. OPPOSITE, TOP: The Johnson Administration provided suitable mockery at the height of the superhero satire movement: a one-shot from 1966. BOTTOM: *SpongeBob Comics Freestyle Funnies* (2012) matched artist Ramona Fradon, who defined Aquaman for DC in the 1950s, with Mermaid Man, his komedy kounterpart.

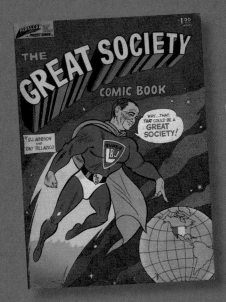

child for a sensibility that, in Sontag's definition, "incarnates a victory of style over content, aesthetics over morality, of irony over tragedy." Apparently, there was no sillier occupation than being a superhero; but since superheroes took it all so seriously, the whole enterprise couldn't possibly be serious—it must be silly. Defining something as "camp" was also a way for folks with heightened sensibilities to enjoy superheroes or comic books without having to admit they actually enjoyed them.

Whether they were technically camp or simply exhaustingly derivative, there was a wave of satirical superheroes after *Batman* appeared. Exactly a year after *Batman*'s debut, network television immediately came up with two witless parodies, *Captain Nice* (NBC) and *Mr. Terrific* (CBS), which premiered on the same night—and were also cancelled on the same night, five months later. (ABC decided to play it straight by hiring William Dozier to produce *The Green Hornet*; it, too, was a flop but it was effective crime drama.) *Underdog* and *Atom Ant* had preceded *Batman* on Saturday morning television, but soon other animated spoofs— *Batfink, Frankenstein Jr. and the Impossibles, Super Chicken*— joined the kiddie line-up. Comic book publishers—no fools, they—saw the commercial possibilities in biting the fans that fed them. Marvel put out a parody anthology devoted to superheroes called *Not Brand Echh* (referring to DC), with their own mascot, Forbush-Man; DC countered with *The Inferior Five*, a hapless quartet who were the grown-up children of parody versions of the DC pantheon. There were also dozens of funny superhero comics from lesser publishers.

The inimitable *MAD* magazine artist Don Martin turned in an amusing paperback book character called Captain Klutz, whose unforgettable alias was Ringo Fonebone. Perhaps the oddest of this odd-lot was

The Great Society Comic Book, a 1967 one-off parody, published by an independent company, that recast the Johnson Administration as superheroes. The president himself was Super LBJ and his nemeses were not supervillains, but the fraternal-hero team Bobman and Teddy—the Kennedy brothers, recast as pretenders to LBJ's seat in the White House.

As long as superheroes run around at night in their underwear and tights, they'll always be targets for parody. Most of the sideswipes are obvious, but a few are so perceptive that they stand a good chance of living on as long as their inspirations. *Saturday Night Live*'s animated parody of Batman and Robin—"The Ambiguously Gay Duo"—is like a Frederic Wertham nightmare come true, and the geriatric pair of aquatic heroes on *SpongeBob SquarePants*, Mermaid Man and Barnacle Boy, not only head-dunk every cliché about undersea heroes, their comic book adventures are drawn by none other than Ramona Fradon—the glorious artist of Aquaman's Golden (and Silver) Age of comics. Imitation is clearly the sincerest form of parody.

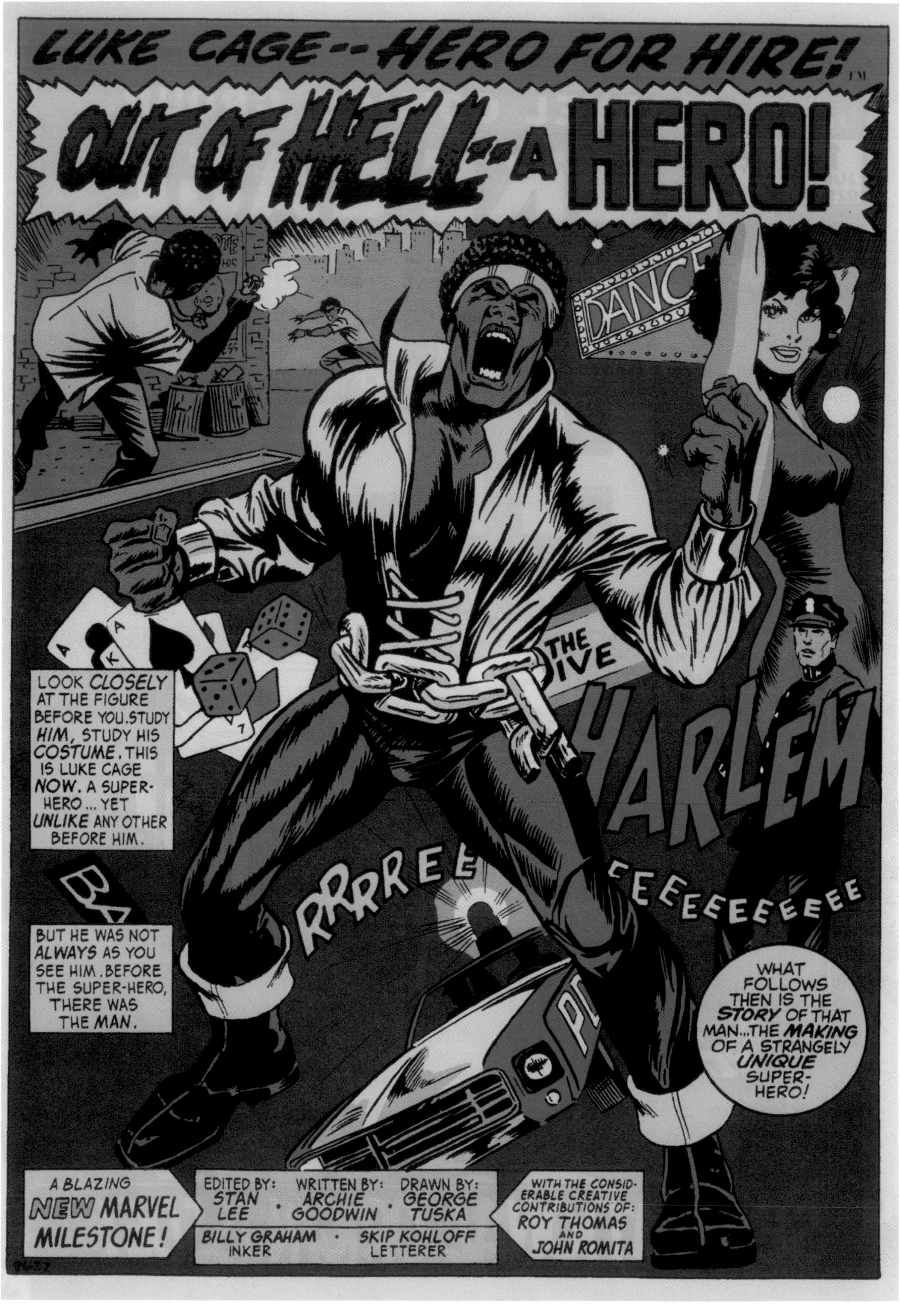
LUKE CAGE--HERO FOR HIRE! TM
OUT OF HELL--A HERO!
DANCE
THE JIVE
HARLEM
LOOK CLOSELY AT THE FIGURE BEFORE YOU. STUDY HIM, STUDY HIS COSTUME. THIS IS LUKE CAGE NOW. A SUPER-HERO ... YET UNLIKE ANY OTHER BEFORE HIM.
RRRREEEEEEEEEEEEEEE
BUT HE WAS NOT ALWAYS AS YOU SEE HIM. BEFORE THE SUPER-HERO, THERE WAS THE MAN.
WHAT FOLLOWS THEN IS THE STORY OF THAT MAN...THE MAKING OF A STRANGELY UNIQUE SUPER-HERO!
A BLAZING NEW MARVEL MILESTONE!
EDITED BY: STAN LEE · WRITTEN BY: ARCHIE GOODWIN · DRAWN BY: GEORGE TUSKA
BILLY GRAHAM INKER · SKIP KOHLOFF LETTERER
WITH THE CONSIDERABLE CREATIVE CONTRIBUTIONS OF: ROY THOMAS AND JOHN ROMITA

"SWEET CHRISTMAS!"
Black Powerhouses

OPPOSITE: Splash page from Luke Cage's debut in *Hero for Hire* #1 (1972): "Sweet Christmas!" was Cage's anodyne epithet (art by George Tuska). LEFT: The Black Panther Party made its political positions known to the world a few months after the comic book character debuted (from 1966). RIGHT: "Robbie" Robertson was the *Daily Bugle*'s editorial voice of reason (*The Amazing Spider-Man* #52, December, 1967).

hen the Marvel Universe coalesced around Manhattan, it was inevitable that, one day, they would wake up to recognize that New York City contained the largest black population in the United States.

With the exception of the music world, African Americans had traditionally been underrepresented in popular culture, but the world of comic books was perhaps the slowest genre to recognize blacks in any meaningful form. By the early 1940s, there were black stars on Broadway, black musicians on the song charts, even an African American winner of an Academy Award. But, as stereotypical as Hollywood portrayals of black characters could be, they seemed practically enlightened by comic book standards. When comic books deigned to portray black characters at all, they were usually gullible, inarticulate sidekicks, caricatured physically as well as culturally, with names like Whitewash Jones or Ebony White, the Spirit's cab-driving sidekick. According to comics historian Gerard Jones, "Some beautiful stories by Will Eisner about the Spirit are to some extent forever marred by his caricatured black sidekick."

As Marvel Comics moved into the 1960s, the hermetically sealed comic book world would slowly open up. Jack Kirby, who was drawing most of Marvel's cityscapes, occasionally inserted a black spectator pointing up at the Fantastic Four's Baxter Building, for example. A World War II comic, created by Kirby and Stan Lee, *Sgt. Fury and His Howling Commandos*, which debuted in 1963, featured a black commando named Gabriel Jones (although the printing plant was so surprised to see a black character that they accidentally colored him white in the first issue). A 1964 Captain America adventure has Cap venturing behind enemy lines into North Vietnam to rescue a downed black pilot; over at the *Spider-Man* book, artist John Romita gave J. Jonah Jameson an African American editor at the *Daily Bugle* named Joseph "Robbie" Robertson in 1967. "There was a time when I realized, we don't really have any black characters," said Stan Lee. "I felt we should be representative of the whole world—every type of person should be represented in these stories."

The first major black superhero appeared in the pages of *Fantastic Four* #52, which would have hit the stands in late spring 1966, nine months after the passage of the Voting Rights Act and the horrendous devastation of the Watts riots. The hero was the completely masked Black Panther, a lithe, mysterious figure who summoned the Fantastic Four to a jungle kingdom in Africa called Wakanda. After outwitting the team, the Panther pulls back his mask to reveal that he is the African chief T'Challa, whose kingdom owns a mine of Vibranium, a rare metal that is the source of their great wealth and astonishing technical expertise.

TOP: The identity of the Black Panther was an easy guess—but in 1966, comic book readers were shocked when he was revealed to be a black superhero. LEFT: Two real Black Panthers: Bobby Seale and Huey Newton at an Oakland rally. RIGHT: A Kirby splash page for a groundbreaking character (*The Fantastic Four* #52, 1966). OPPOSITE: Artist Gene Colan let the Falcon fly for the first time in the pages of *Captain America* #117 (September 1969).

Unfortunately, the vibranium renders Wakanda vulnerable to looters and poachers (one of whom murdered T'Challa's father, the previous Black Panther). The Panther was created by Stan Lee and Jack Kirby, who had conceived an earlier black character, the Coal Tiger, that never made it to the starting gate. Introducing a black superhero busted down enough doors to begin with, but the subtle twist in the two Black Panther issues was the depiction of Wakanda as the most enlightened and tech-savvy country in the world; even the cynical Thing, who yawns that he has "seen [the jungle action] in the movies before," is suitably impressed with the tiny African nation before he returns back home.

Intentionally or not, the character was packed with several conflicting themes from African American culture, dating all the way back to the early 20th century, when activists such as W. E. B. DuBois were trying to define the role of blacks within a larger social structure. Writer Gary Phillips frames the issue:

> There's always that tension, particularly in pop culture, in terms of uplifting the race, of showing the best, one true example of the race. In a lot of ways, the Panther exemplifies that. On one hand, he is the noble savage, but on the other hand, he's this king of this hidden, scientifically advanced kingdom that has purposely hidden itself from the world so as to avoid a lot of conflicts of racism that have taken place on the African continent and, by extension, in America.

The Panther would bestride both continents as a fixture in the Marvel Universe from 1966 on, earning several different versions of his own title, and becoming a loyal member of the Avengers for decades. He ran into some public relations problems when the Black Power group devoted to social revolution called the Black Panther Party emerged out of Oakland a few months after the character's comic book debut (the two occurrences were completely unrelated). At one point, the character changed his name to the Black Leopard but, realizing he wasn't fooling anyone, changed it back: "I did not want my personal goals and tribal

heritage confused with political plans made by others. . . . I am not a stereotype. I am myself. And I am—the Black Panther!" Ironically, the character far outlasted the political party, which was dissolved by 1982.

African American comic book fans were still waiting for a hero of their very own. Marvel artist Gene Colan nudged Stan Lee into creating a rival character for Captain America called the Falcon. A social worker in Harlem with a gift for remarkable telepathy with a falcon named Redwing, Sam Wilson donned his own pin-feathered costume and became the Falcon in 1969. By 1971 the Falcon was Cap's full-time partner; and, thanks to some Wakandan technology, he eventually gained the power to fly on his own steam. Alas, there wasn't enough technology to make him a particularly interesting character; luckily, in spring 1972, the Blaxploitation movement in films and music had opened another opportunistic door in the Marvel Universe.

In the early 1970s, when Marvel was undergoing a feverish expansion, new characters usually appeared first in "showcase" comics, but Luke Cage, Hero for Hire, was given his own eponymous magazine right off the bat. The time was right for a streetwise, gritty black hero. With Roberta Flack, Al Green, and the O'Jays topping the charts, and the black detective film *Shaft* earning back seven times its original investment (and with *Super Fly* about to open), even mainstream white teenaged readers were ready to embrace Luke Cage. In homage to Captain America, a stubborn black prisoner named Carl Lucas, stuck in an impenetrable penitentiary where he is constantly victimized by white guards, agrees to participate in a strength-enhancement experiment in exchange for parole. When the experiment goes horribly awry, he is transformed into a being of incredible power and invulnerability. Lucas escapes prison, returns to Harlem, and re-invents himself as Luke Cage, Hero for Hire—a super-powered mercenary, complete with business cards and a costume with a huge chain for a belt, just in case anyone might miss the symbolism. "Yeah! Outfit's kinda hokey," Cage admits, "but so what? All part of the super-hero scene."

"Reading those early Luke Cage comic books you can almost hear the soundtrack of Isaac Hayes or Curtis Mayfield playing in the background," writes comics historian Bradford Wright. Cage would be part of the superhero scene for the next five decades, undergoing various transformations (he was Power Man for a while), but still an essential lodestar for different groups and titles, including the Avengers. Actor Nicolas Cage has said that he changed his last name from "Coppola" in honor of the character, but the character's greatest contribution was representing a real African American superhero that spoke to all audiences, even though it was a risky choice to render him as an unapologetic troubleshooter who charged for his services. Gary Phillips recalls that the Panther was "all regal wisdom and graceful power, the Sidney Poitier of the Marvel Universe; Luke Cage was street-savvy, stubborn, and built for hellacious mayhem—Jim Brown without the referees."

DC Comics was much slower to enfranchise black heroes and characters.

According to comics historian William Foster, "Marvel was the young maverick, so they could make changes, they could move quickly. They were like a speedboat, unlike DC Comics, which was more like an aircraft carrier. They couldn't maneuver as easily with the changing times." In 1968, up-and-coming writer Marv Wolfman attempted to add a black superhero named Joshua

to the *Teen Titans* comic book, but for reasons never completely confirmed, the character didn't make it out of the starting gate.

DC tried with some one-off stories, the most remarkable of which was the episode in the November 1970 of *Superman's Girl Friend, Lois Lane*, #106: "I Am Curious (Black)." Written by DC veteran scribe Robert Kanigher, the issue borrows heavily from the 1961 nonfiction book *Black Like Me*, where a white writer tints his face so that he can "pass" as a black man in the America South. In the comic book, our intrepid lady reporter is moved to better understand the tensions in "Little Africa" (Metropolis's answer to Harlem). Lois seeks Superman's help, who obliges her with an effective, but presumably little-used, device from his home planet Krypton that can turn white-skinned people black for twenty-four hours. During her one-day adventure, the dark-hued Lois Lane does in fact do her bit for racial equality and brotherhood, but in the end she is a little more concerned whether Superman would still love her if she were black. DC's more effective commitments to African American characters included John Stewart, a black architect who was selected by the Guardians to become Green Lantern's "understudy" in 1972, as well as characters such as Black Lightning and Cyborg.

In the early 1980s, comic book writer and editor Roy Thomas lamented, "You could get blacks to buy comics about whites, but it was hard to get whites to buy comics in which the main character was black." But even with a slow start, the comic book industry has eventually embraced the possibilities inherent in multi-racial characters. The results are imperfect; Hollywood movies and, to a lesser degree, television programs also still wrestle with how to place African American characters, along with other races and ethnicities, at the center of their mainstream narratives. But, there is no denying that in the late 1960s and early '70s, it was the Black Panther and Luke Cage who kicked the door down. Writer Gary Phillips recalled:

> When I was a kid growing up in South Central back then, you were kind of considered a chump and a sissy if you were reading DC Comics. Marvel was where it was at—not only because you had the Hulk and Spider-Man, with their angst and their worries and what have you, but the fact that that's where you had some black superheroes showing up.

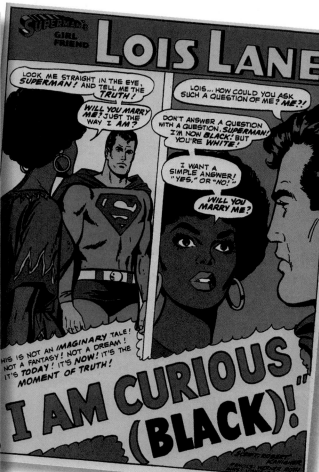

CLOCKWISE, FROM TOP LEFT: Black Lightning debuted in the April 1977 edition of his own DC comic, but never really sparked with readers; Lois Lane undergoes an incredible transformation in "I Am Curious (Black)" in the pages of *Superman's Girl Friend, Lois Lane* #106 (1970); Luke Cage fearlessly travels deep into the enemy territory of Latveria to reclaim the 200 bucks owed to him by the world's most despotic villain, Dr. Doom (*Luke Cage* # 9).

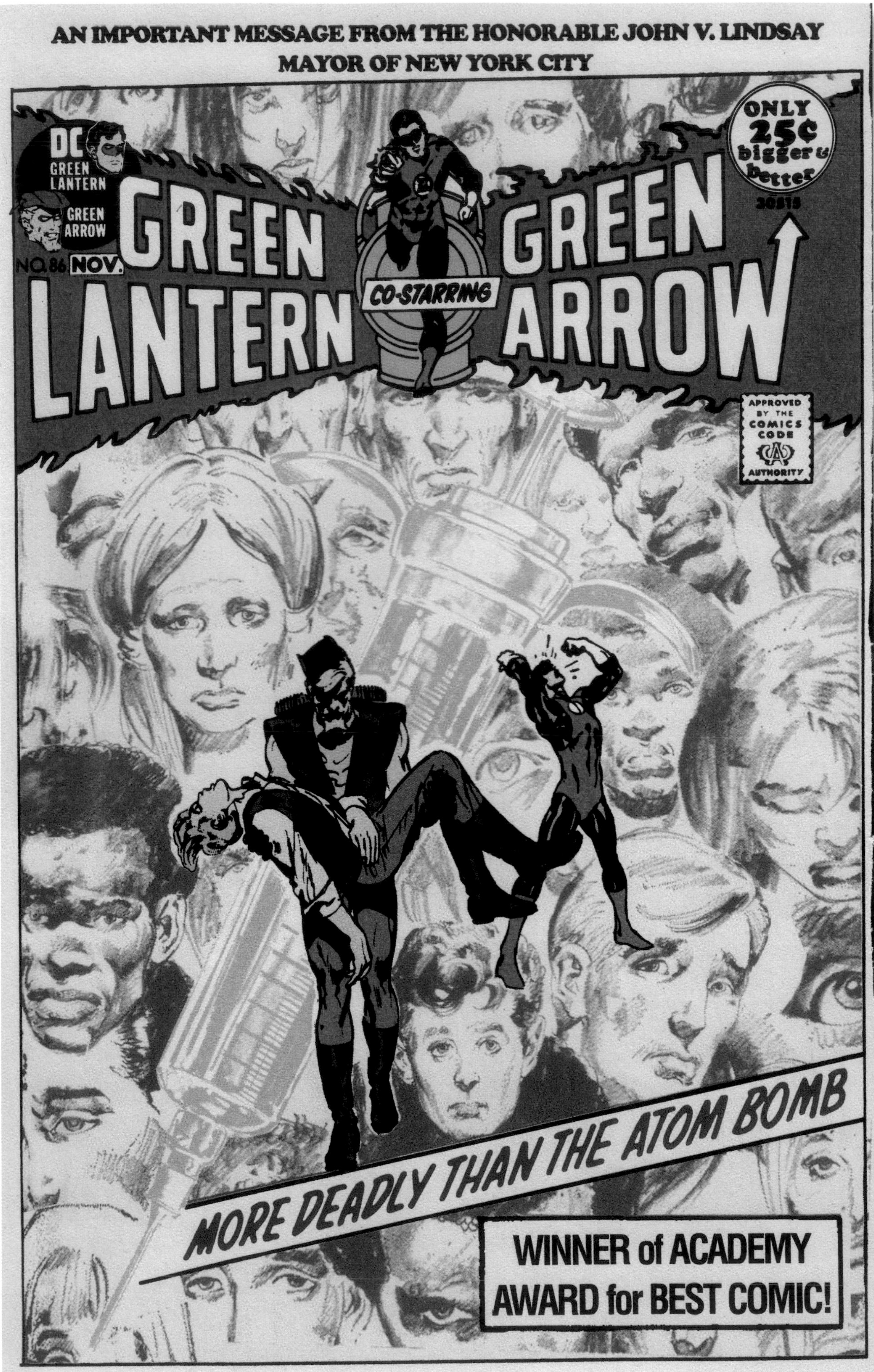
AN IMPORTANT MESSAGE FROM THE HONORABLE JOHN V. LINDSAY
MAYOR OF NEW YORK CITY
DC
GREEN LANTERN
GREEN ARROW
NO. 86 NOV.
GREEN LANTERN
CO-STARRING
GREEN ARROW
ONLY 25¢ bigger & better
30815
APPROVED BY THE COMICS CODE AUTHORITY
MORE DEADLY THAN THE ATOM BOMB
WINNER of ACADEMY AWARD for BEST COMIC!

"ALL-NEW! ALL-NOW!"
The Adventures of Captain Relevant

s the 1960s turned into the 1970s, there were a variety of problems facing the American people —the war in Viet Nam, urban poverty, street riots, assassinations, a devolution of law and order—but, perhaps only one directly confronted a comic book-reading teenager at the time: drugs.

The counterculture of the 1960s had embraced marijuana and hallucinogens as part of their creed, but more powerful narcotics were entering the illegal marketplace, especially heroin. A senate committee revealed that 10 to 15 percent of American combat troops were addicted to heroin; the government had just backed the Comprehensive Drug Abuse Prevention and Control Act of 1970, which tightened the medical supply lines; and President Nixon had declared the illegal drugs were "Public Enemy Number One." Hadn't comic book superheroes been created to fight public enemies?

The Department of Health, Education, and Welfare evidently thought so. Early in 1970, Stan Lee received a letter from a representative in the government agency: "It was something like: 'Recognizing the influence that your character, Spider-Man, has on young people, we think it would be very beneficial if you would do an anti-drug story in *Spider-Man*.' Well, no kid wants to be lectured to, so I wasn't about to do a story that said, 'Don't take drugs!'" The story that Lee did come up with, illustrated by Gil Kane, was a three-part series that began in *The Amazing Spider-Man* #96 and focused mainly on his arch-enemy, the Green Goblin. While Spidey is swinging across the city, he saves a young black man, perched precariously on a rooftop, obviously strung out on drugs. ("I had never taken drugs so I know nothing about them," admitted Lee. "I just wrote that he overdosed on something.")

The story arc was smart enough to leave that issue alone for awhile, as Spider-Man pursued the Green Goblin, only to discover his roommate, Harry Osborn (who is actually also the son of the Green Goblin's alter ego), is also "pill-popping" a combination

OPPOSITE: The shocking cover by Neal Adams (inked by Dick Giordano) to *Green Lantern/Green Arrow* #86 (November 1971)—ripped from the day's headlines. ABOVE: Three panels from *The Amazing Spider-Man* #96 and 97 display the perils of drug abuse: art by Gil Kane.

of uppers and downers. Stuck between helping his friend battle his addiction and battling the Green Goblin himself, Spider-Man resolves the conflict neatly by the third issue in the series. Would that Lee and Marvel Comics could have resolved the conflict with the Comics Code Authority quite so easily.

When Lee and his publisher, Martin Goodman, submitted the three-issue story arc to the Code office for approval in June 1970, it was summarily rejected. Lee's recounting of the discussion:

> They said, "You're not allowed to mention drugs in the comics." I said, "But we're not telling the kids to take drugs, it's an anti-drug message!" "Sorry." I said, "But we were asked to do this by the Office of HEW in Washington." "Sorry."

While the story languished in the limbo of the Code Office, a parallel development was occurring over at DC Comics. It involved two superheroes on the verge of extinction and a pair of young comic book creators who shared a visionary sense of comic books' possibilities. Denny O'Neil was a former journalist from the Midwest and Neal Adams was a former advertising artist; they were both of the first generation that had grown up reading comics to enter the field, and they had secured a berth at DC Comics in the mid 1960s, where they had worked together to get Batman back on his feet after the cancellation of the television show.

In summer 1970, O'Neil was called into the office of editor Julie Schwartz and was told that both Green Lantern and Green Arrow were about to be cancelled and, as a last-ditch effort, he was going to combine them into one title. The only real rationale for combining the swashbuckling Green Arrow and the space-age Green Lantern was that they shared a nominative color. O'Neil thought the only way to make sense of this shotgun marriage was to take it all in a completely new direction:

> What if we plotted the stories from the headlines? What if we did the stuff that as U.S. citizens, and veterans, and fathers, we were really concerned about? So I don't know how detailed a plot I gave Julie for that first one. But we agreed on a direc-

tion and a story and then I went home, writing, and thinking that the usual *Green Lantern* artist would get the art job.

Green Lantern/Green Arrow #76 wasn't much of a story, but it had a hell of a premise. Green Lantern flies through an urban ghetto to stop an apparent beating in progress, only to discover that his old pal, Green Arrow, is on the other side of the angels: the "victim" is an avaricious landlord. Green Arrow lectures Green Lantern that he has spent too much time fighting mad scientists in outer space to see the evil right in front of him in the real world. The point is driven home by a scruffy, aged black man who lives in the landlord's tenement. When O'Neil saw the page proofs, he realized for the first time that the book had been given to Neal Adams to illustrate:

> I looked at the first page and thought, my God, this is great. And got to the end of the first chapter and he did that black guy's face and I thought, this is the tragedy of slavery encapsulated in this one incredible drawing. And we were off and running.

The conclusion of the story literally had Green Lantern and Green Arrow off and running, deciding that true superheroes needed to, in Green Arrow's words, "forget about chasing around the galaxy and remember America." Lantern and Arrow (accompanied by one of Green Lantern's "blue-skinned" alien guardians) decide to go on an extended road trip incognito: "Seeking an identity, an answer—to find America, to learn why this land of the free has become the land of the fearful." It was, in many ways, the comic book equivalent of the 1969 film *Easy Rider*, with the soundtrack to Paul Simon's lyrics from the following year: "And we walked off to look for America."

For the next eight issues, Green Lantern and Green Arrow (eventually joined by the Black Canary, a middle-rank heroine from the 1940s who served as Green Arrow's paramour) traversed the country, confronting inequity, prejudice, and cruelty among striking workers, oppressed native Americans, polluters, brainwashed schoolchildren, and would-be Messiahs. In essence,

In *Green Lantern/Green Arrow* #76, our two heroes square off; they are left speechless by an unnamed black man, who became one of the most iconic figures in comic books.

they battled the same kind of bullies and miscreants tackled by Superman in Siegel and Shuster's stories from the late 1930s. But O'Neil and Adams crafted their stories at a level never previously seen in comic books. In particular, Adams' photo-realistic art style and innovative composition matched O'Neil's hardcore journalistic style; the work looked as if it were torn from that day's front pages. Of course, there were the obligatory action sequences—also rendered with a heart-racing momentum, courtesy of Adams—but Green Lantern's extraordinary powers were taken down several notches to make the character's *wanderjahr*

reasonably credible. Like the Lantern and the Arrow, O'Neil and Adams were on a mission. Reflected Adams, "I grew up at a time when I was told many times that comic books were analogous to toilet paper. So we made our own little statement in our comic book. It reminded college students and high school students that comic books weren't just crap."

O'Neil and Adams had tackled most of the statements about which they felt passionate, but the issue of drug abuse was still closed off to them by the Comics Code. It was an issue that Adams wanted to explore more deeply, and he had a notion—perverse,

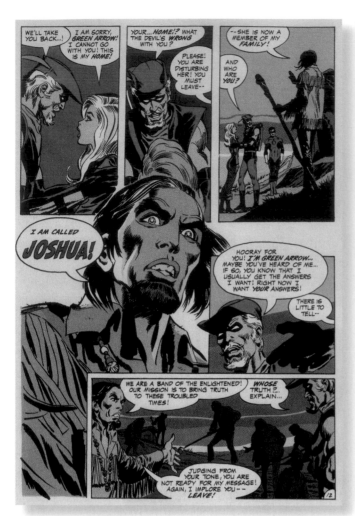

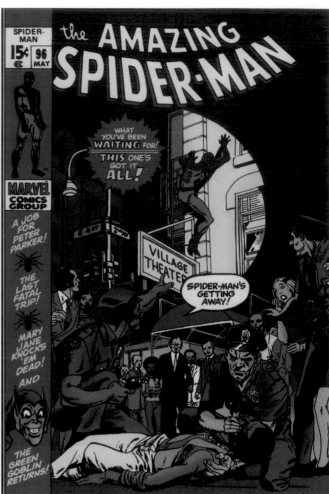

LEFT: The Green Lantern/Green Arrow comics often drafted-in thinly veiled versions of contemporary figures: in *GL/GA* #78 cult leader "Joshua" is a dead ringer for Charles Manson.
RIGHT: The first major title to be released without the seal of approval from the Comics Code Authority: *The Amazing Spider-Man* #96.

perhaps—that Green Arrow's trusty ward from the old days might be a useful character to investigate the problem: his name was Speedy—a resonant name for a potential heroin addict. That idea had too much street potency, so it was tabled by DC's editorial staff. But over at Marvel Comics, Stan Lee was moving forward with his drug-related series in *The Amazing Spider-Man*. He felt so strongly about it that he wanted to publish it without the Code's seal of approval. Publisher Goodman supported him, and *The Amazing Spider-Man* #96 hit the streets in late February 1971; it would be the first mainstream (non–funny animal) comic book to be published without the Code's seal of approval since its inception in 1955, as were the two subsequent issues in the series.

The roof did not cave in. Comic book distributors still put the magazine on their racks and stands (it was one of the most popular titles in the business, after all). "The book sold like it always sold,"

recalled Lee, "but we got more mail from teachers and parents and doctors and everybody all over the country, saying how much they loved that book and how delighted they were! And the folks in Washington liked it. So after that they got a little bit more lenient at the Comic Code office." Indeed, that spring, the Code loosened their restrictions somewhat, especially in the area of narcotics, some sexual situations, and, amusingly, monsters. This allowed O'Neil and Adams officially to tackle the monster of drug addiction.

"The next book that came out was [*Green Lantern/Green Arrow* #85, in summer 1971]," said Adams. "Denny sat down and wrote a two-parter for that [heroin] cover and we put it out. One of the most revolutionary covers there ever was. But it took Stan to get it sold. Incredible." "Snowbirds Don't Fly" was the first of a two-part series where Green Arrow investigates a heroin ring, unaware that his neglected ward, Speedy, is at the center of it. In the next issue, "They Say It Will Kill Me . . . But They Won't Say When!,"

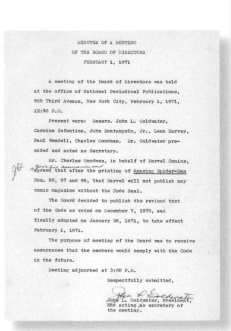

LEFT: Minutes from the Comics Code Authority from February 1, 1971, regarding the groundbreaking (and code-breaking) issues of *The Amazing Spider-Man*. RIGHT: One of the most searingly topical panels in comic book history: Green Arrow lectures the Guardians of Oa in the epilogue from *Green Lantern/Green Arrow* #76 (1970).

Green Arrow discovers Speedy's addiction and uneasily guides him toward withdrawal. Unlike anything before it in comic book history, the narrative of the adventure was woven directly and thrillingly into the tragedy of the times—at one point, the henchman of a drug kingpin injects Green Arrow and Green Lantern with heroin in order to incapacitate them.

This new trend of comics for grown-ups made the front page of the *New York Times Magazine*, the first time comic books had been given that kind of showcase, let alone praise. In "Shazam! Here Comes Captain Relevant" (published on May 2, 1971, after the Spider-Man stories, but before the Speedy storyline), the author wrote, "Today's superhero is about as much like his predecessors as today's child is like his parents." Alas, *Green Lantern/Green Arrow*—the most critically acclaimed and media-celebrated comic book of its day—also suffered from a dichotomy between fans and consumers; three issues after the drug abuse storyline, the title was cancelled, due, ostensibly, to poor sales.

Perhaps its day in the sunlight of topicality had peaked; "[The title] was in danger of becoming 'Cause-of-the-Month' comics," said O'Neil. Many fans, and some insiders, felt uneasy that a superhero title would sell its action-packed birthright for a pot of message. Still, in its time, *Green Lantern/Green Arrow*, a contrived title if ever there was one, attained an exceptionally high standard as a groundbreaking work of art. Far more explosively than Green Lantern's power ring and far more incisively than Green Arrow's weaponry, O'Neil and Adams had used their narrative powers to destroy the wall that arbitrarily separated comic book fantasy from the real world. The shockwaves that reverberated when fantasy combusted with reality would be felt for the next four decades.

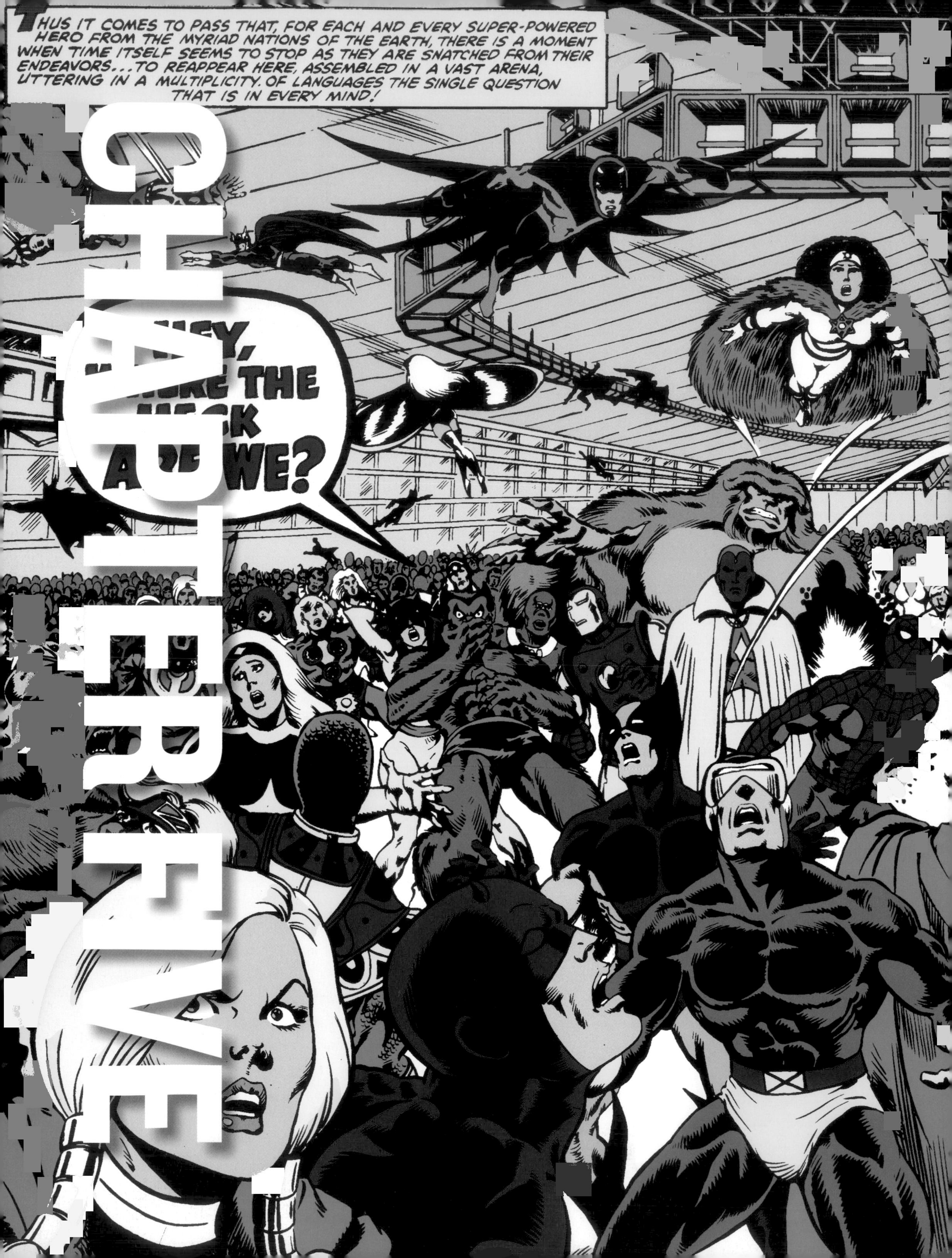
CHAPTER FIVE
THUS IT COMES TO PASS THAT, FOR EACH AND EVERY SUPER-POWERED HERO FROM THE MYRIAD NATIONS OF THE EARTH, THERE IS A MOMENT WHEN TIME ITSELF SEEMS TO STOP AS THEY ARE SNATCHED FROM THEIR ENDEAVORS...TO REAPPEAR HERE, ASSEMBLED IN A VAST ARENA, UTTERING IN A MULTIPLICITY OF LANGUAGES THE SINGLE QUESTION THAT IS IN EVERY MIND!
THE WE?

WORLDS WILL LIVE, WORLDS WILL DIE!
THE EXPANSION OF A UNIVERSE!

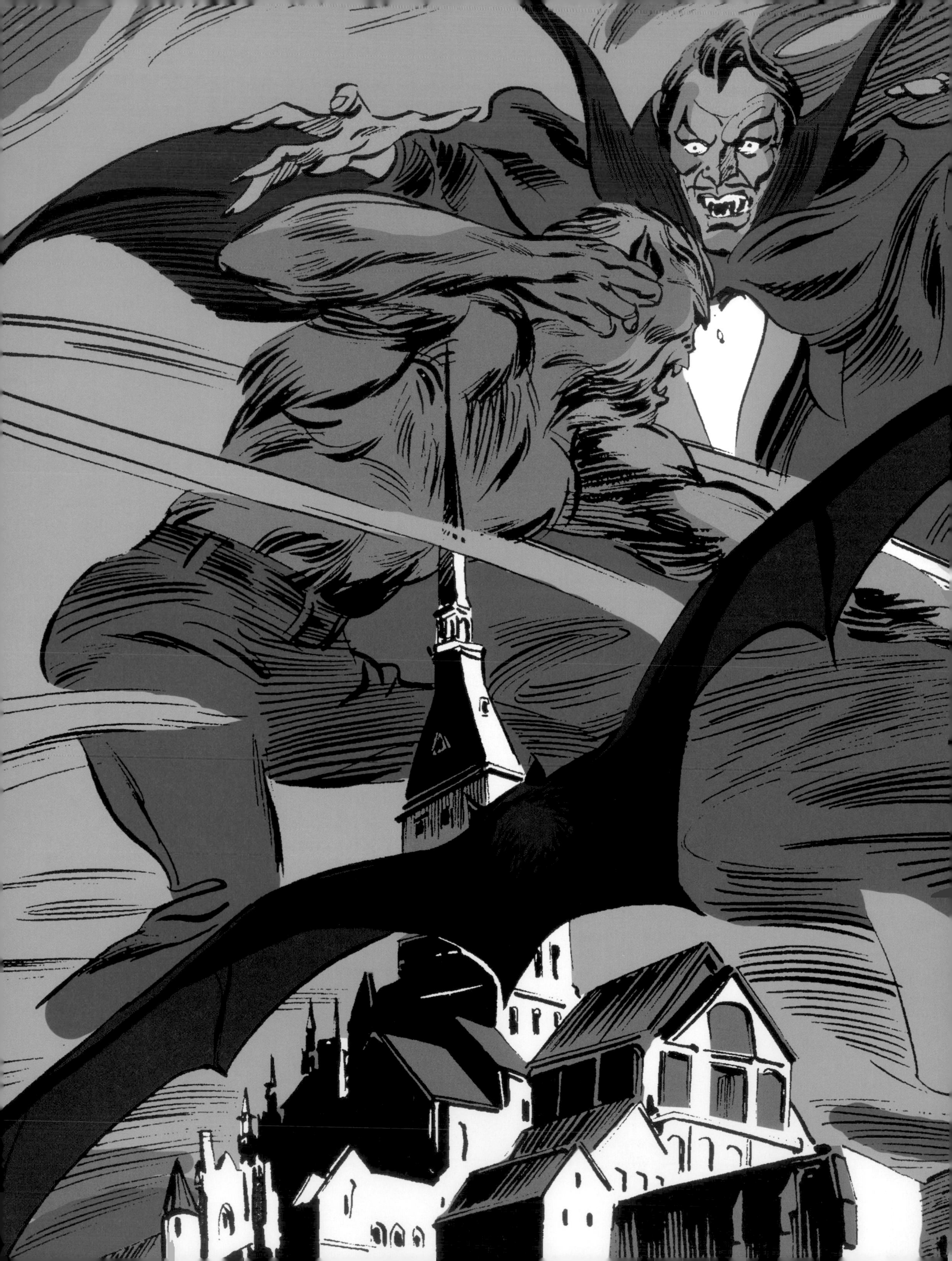

"THE HORROR, THE HORROR!"
Titles from the Crypt

I f your name were Marv Wolfman, imagine how tough things could get during your junior high school recess in Flushing, Queens. But even worse, perhaps, would be having your name restricted by the Comics Code Authority. DC Comics published an on-again, off-again mystery anthology entitled *The House of Secrets*, whose anodyne title was prescribed by the Code. Writer Len Wein, who contributed a variety of scripts to the series, pointed out, "For years, under the Code, you couldn't use the word 'horror,' you couldn't use 'terror.' And so for a while we fudged around the edges. You know there was *House of Mystery*, there was *House of Secrets*, but nothing that was *House of Scary* anything." In 1969, young comics writer Marv Wolfman contributed a story to *House of Secrets*: "It's my real name," he said. "God knows, nobody would choose that." Back then, the writers of the anthology tales were never given a story credit. The title's editor, Gerry Conway, wanted to acknowledge his bullpen in some way, and had the narrator of the comic book refer to a tale told to him by a "wandering wolfman." When that issue of *House of Secrets* was submitted to the Comics Code Authority, they demanded that "wolfman" be removed, citing its restrictions against werewolves and other lycanthropes. "What if it's the guy's actual name?" asked Conway. In that case, the Code Authority gave a practical dispensation; if DC pasted up a blurb to that effect, they would relent. And that's how Marv Wolfman got his first writing credit in a comic book.

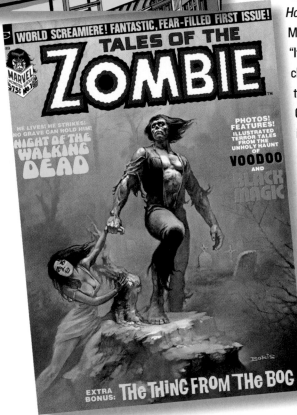

If *The House of Secrets* had been able to keep its powder dry two more years, it wouldn't have mattered. When the Comics Code Authority made its revisions in February 1971, it broadened the possibilities of reintroducing horror (and terror) into the world of comics: "Vampires, ghouls, and werewolves shall be permitted to be used when handled in the classic tradition, such as Frankenstein, Dracula, and other high caliber literary works." The crypt gates were flung wide open and the tomb-raiding began.

OVERLEAF: An explosion of superheroes from *Contest of Champions* #1 (1982, art by John Romita, Jr.). OPPOSITE: Gene Colan brought literature's most famous vampire back from the dead in the pages of *The Tomb of Dracula* (1974). TOP: In the wake of the relaxation of Code restrictions, Marvel Comics opened the crypt doors for every conceivable monster and ghoul in full-color and black-and-white magazines (*Tales of the Zombie* #1, 1975)—sometimes even crossing over to each other's titles: *The Tomb of Dracula* #18 (1974).

Marvel Comics exploited the possibilities with abandon almost as soon as the Code ruling was announced. Under its new editor-in-chief, Roy Thomas, they floated the idea of a scientific vampire supervillain called Morbius in the pages of *The Amazing Spider-Man*. The character was enthusiastically embraced by readers, so Marvel quickly moved ahead with various showcases and titles featuring a shuffling swamp-vegetation humanoid called "The Man-Thing"; a wolfman in *Werewolf by Night*; the godfather of all vampires in *The Tomb of Dracula*; a motorcylist daredevil with a flaming skull for a head in *Ghost Rider*; the eponymous *Monster of Frankenstein*; a mummy character, conceived as a mummified Nubian slave revived in 1972; Brother Voodoo, who fought the undead in Haiti; the self-evident Zombie; several daughters and sons of Satan; even the Golem, that statuesque defender of the Jewish people, was revived to fight the after-effects of the 1973 Yom Kippur War in the Holy Land.

The monster explosion also occurred in a series of parallel publications produced by a new venture of Marvel's publishers: black-and-white magazines, which were larger in size and volume and utterly unrestricted by the Comics Code Authority. As tantaliz-ing and as unfettered as these horror omnibuses were, they didn't last out the 1970s. The monster characters found a more congenial home in the full-color comics, which makes a kind of sense, since the monstrous Hulk and the Thing had already straddled both the superhero and the monster genre; even Batman was at his best as a creature of the night. Speaking of bat-men, the most successful of Marvel's horror ventures was *The Tomb of Dracula*, which con-tinued an epic and convoluted narrative over seven years, guided inestimably—and almost entirely—by the artist Gene Colan (the only comic book artist who could draw fog convincingly) and its scriptwriter, none other than Marv Wolfman. The Ghost Rider spun his wheels into a couple of movies in the 21st century and Blade the Vampire Hunter, who was created for the *Tomb of Dracula* series, also became a Hollywood fixture in three separate films.

DC Comics was clearly outdrawn, as it were, by Marvel's buck-shot approach to monsterdom, but the revised Code also cleared the way for Len Wein and artist Bernie Wrightson to expand on a character they had created in 1971 for *The House of Secrets*: an-

OPPOSITE: Morbius had one fang in the supervillain world, another fang in the monster world (*The Amazing Spider-Man* #101, art by Gil Kane); the swamp monster Man-Thing had a long history at Marvel, beginning in the b&w magazine *Savage Tales* (May 1971). LEFT: Marvel tossed a platoon of new characters at readers in the early 1970s: the Haitian Brother Voodoo (*Strange Tales* #169, art by Gene Colan); the fast-paced Ghost Rider (*Marvel Spotlight* #5, art by Mike Ploog); the Golem (*Strange Tales* #174, art by John Buscema); and the kung fu-inspired adventures of Shang-Chi (art by Paul Gulacy).

other sentient vegetative humanoid called Swamp Thing. Swamp Thing was given his own title in 1972. Along with the Man-Thing at Marvel (in a very different, but equally imaginative series of tales), there was something about sentient vegetative humanoids that leant themselves to wonderfully metaphoric suspense tales: perhaps it was all the concern about the environment and ecology in the mid 1970s. In any event, Ghost Rider, Man-Thing, Swamp Thing, and even Dracula have survived the '70s surge and been successfully assimilated into the universes of their respective publishers.

As much as the younger writers and artists of both companies may have enjoyed tackling the forbidden creatures of yesteryear (the titles were almost uniformly given to up-and-coming creators), the vast expansion of these titles had as much to do

with business practice as it did with the new freedoms of the Comics Code. By 1969, Marvel publisher Martin Goodman had shed his onerous newsstand distribution deal that had corseted the company for years. Space was finally freed up to give almost all the main characters their own books; combined with the new ventures into horror, within three years Marvel had almost quadrupled the number of titles they put out every month. Many were anthologies and reprints of both superhero and monster books from the early 1960s, but just as many were new characters, such as the science fiction-tinged Warlock or the kung fu masters Shang-Chi or Iron Fist. Guided by Roy Thomas, Marvel also dove headfirst into the licensing business, an area previously reigned over by Dell or Gold Key Publishing. The pulp sword-and-sorcery pioneer Conan the Barbarian began his long and violent history

TOP: Pulp characters from the 1930s were licensed by Marvel and DC and briefly joined the superhero stable: Doc Savage meets the Thing, while Batman historically crosses paths with his inspiration, the Shadow. BOTTOM: Artist Wally Wood brought an elegant style to one of the first comic books based on a toy, *Captain Action* #1 (1968). The action figure took on Superman in toy stores, too (original packaging). *OPPOSITE: Star Wars* #1 (art by Howard Chaykin), a collaboration between Marvel and Lucasfilm, began a successful decade-long run in spring 1977.

with Marvel in 1971, and even Doc Savage made a brief, if well-drawn, appearance in 1972. Not to be outdone, DC Comics licensed Tarzan, revived the Captain Marvel character in a series called *Shazam!* (the "M-word" was now off-limits), and reintroduced the Shadow to comic books in some very atmospheric tales. (At the time, Stan Lee joked that if DC licensed the pulp hero the Spider, Marvel would have to license the Black Bat.) But Marvel really hit pay dirt when Thomas had the foresight to license an under-promoted science fiction movie before its 1977 release: *Star Wars.*

Licensing was also extended beyond properties and characters that existed in the print media. In the 1960s, there had been limited spin-offs that provided certain toys with their own comic books. Captain Action, a 12-inch doll who could wear the costumes of other superheroes, was the granddaddy of all action figures (the first in fact to use that term) and had a brief run at DC Comics. But, from the late 1970s on, there were more complicated relationships between toy companies and comic book publishers. A posable robot called Rom the Space Knight was licensed to Marvel to create stories that would provide both a narrative and a buzz for the product (the comic was more successful than the toy); *The Micronauts* comic book was a Marvel initiative, where the comic book piggybacked on a line of miniature toys originally produced by a Japanese company. In the early 1980s, the Hasbro toy manufacturer acquired another line of Japanese toys—little robots which could transform themselves into cars, planes, toaster ovens, you name it—and worked with Marvel and some of its best writers, including Denny O'Neil, to create a mythos and a backstory for the toys: it became *The Transformers*, a dominating titan in the industry. The relationship between toys and comics was no mere child's play: the respective industries would work together into the 21st century, creating complex, multi-platform launches that would encompass endless narratives supporting a battalion of robots, aliens, and action figures who marched down the

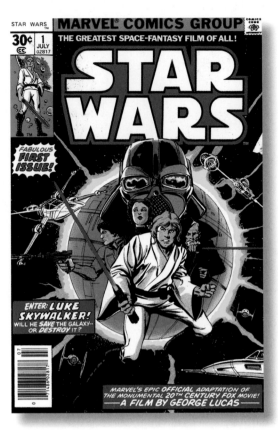

aisles of K-mart and Toys "R" Us for decades.

These expansive relationships with large corporations were manifestations of the fact that both Marvel and DC Comics would become part of corporations themselves and would undergo tremendous structural transitions as a result of corporate buy-outs. Marvel would become a subsidiary of Cadence Industries, a publishing company that had gotten its start in pharmaceuticals, and DC Comics would be taken over by Kinney National Company, a conglomerate built on parking lots and construction, which would soon metamorphose into Warner Communications. The pressure to produce was tremendous; neither of the corporate entities was run by folks who came out of the thirty-odd-year-old comics industry; soon the carefully cherished characters and narratives had to square off against a new adversary: the Bottom Line. As a parting shot to his Distinguished Competition, publisher Goodman raised the price of his comics from fifteen to twenty-five cents and doubled the page count; when DC followed suit, Goodman immediately reversed his policy, cut back the size of the books and charged twenty cents per copy. DC hung in there for a while with the twenty-five-cent price tag, but had been essentially undercut in the marketplace, and was now stuck with overpriced comic books. Kids could buy five Marvel books for a dollar, rather than four with the DC Comics logo. DC never quite recovered.

By the time the Watergate scandal had ousted Richard Nixon from the White House, another authority figure had been routed: DC had ceded their three-decade market share to Marvel Comics. It would require a game-changer to reshuffle the deck. Luckily, DC Comics owned the first, and most super, game-changer of them all.

X-MEN

Giant-Size X-Men #1 (May 1975, art by Dave Cockrum) was the ultimate stealth comic, turning a flop into a titanic hit.

"WILL ANY OF MY NEW X-MEN BE EQUAL TO THE TASK THAT LIES BEFORE YOU? OR WILL YOU CARRY THE WORLD DOWN INTO RUIN?"

THE GRANDEUR AND THE GLORY BEGIN ANEW WITH...

"So the last shall be first, and the first last: for many be called, but few chosen," it says in Matthew 20:16, and that makes a good epigraph for the X-Men, a comic book series that would develop as large a cast of characters and as vast an apocrypha as the New Testament itself.

In many ways, the original X-Men were pretty much "the last" of the Marvel Universe. Invented by Stan Lee and Jack Kirby in 1963, the band of young mutants was abandoned by its creators after about a dozen issues: again, fittingly, because many of the mutant characters in the book had been abandoned by their own families, who were terrified or bewildered by its superpowers. Without a consistent creative team behind them, the *X-Men* seemed doomed to bring up the rear of the Marvel vanguard for the first seven years of their existence, always selling poorly, but not poorly enough to be cancelled.

In retrospect, it's curious as to why the X-Men were so undervalued; they seemed to have an awful lot going for them. They were young, they were different, they were trained at a special school, they bickered with each other and yet clearly admired each other. Their powers were pretty cool, too: Warren Worthington III was the scion of a wealthy family who could fly thanks to a pair of white wings; he became Angel. Hank McCoy had steroidal feet and hands and could bound about like a Beast (originally the boisterous "Thing" of the group, he soon developed a loquacious and literary manner of speaking). Iceman was young Bobby Drake, who could turn himself (and the air's very molecules) into ice, making him pretty popular at cocktail parties. Jean Grey became Marvel Girl, thanks to her powers of telekinesis, allowing her to move objects without lifting a finger; this skill, in addition to her red-haired attractiveness, made her a little standoffish. Scott Summers was the scout leader of the group—a serious fellow, in love with Jean Grey and cursed with the ability to shoot powerful red beams from his eyes. He couldn't turn them off without a special visor and earned the name Cyclops. Putting these teenagers through their paces was Charles Xavier, known as Professor X, as beneficent a mentor as one could find, and also possessed of a mutant attribute that made him the world's most powerful telepath.

TOP: An earlier iteration of the X-Men, courtesy of Jack Kirby. BOTTOM: The persecution of mutants were part of the early X-Men comics of the 1960s; here Cyclops is chased by a mob in *X-Men* #14 (1965).

Professor X trained his students at the Xavier Institute for Higher Learning. As Stan Lee recounted, "He was afraid that people would fear the X-Men if they knew about their power. So he kept them hidden in what seemed to be a school for gifted youngsters, but nobody knew how gifted they were." From the beginning, the X-Men had a compelling duality to them: they were powerful and vulnerable in equal measures. Much of the *X-Men* subtext had to do with the prejudice against them as mutants. In issue #14, they were hunted down by immense robotic Sentinels, who were designed by a mad doctor intent on keeping mutants—*homo superior*, as they were called—from infecting the world of *homo sapiens*. On the other end of the spectrum was the X-Men's grand nemesis, Magneto, who could manipulate any kind of metallic object. Himself persecuted as a mutant (and revealed many years later to have been an inmate at Auschwitz as a child), Magneto vowed to revenge himself on humanity's small-mindedness by destroying them and elevating mutants to become the natural rulers of the planet. In his mad mission, Magneto placed himself in direct opposition to Charles Xavier, and their Manichean struggles for the souls (and talents and membership status) of the Earth's mutants accounted for many, many storylines.

Although some first-rate artists, such as Jim Steranko and Neal Adams, were brought onto the magazine in the late 1960s, there wasn't much hope for the young mutants. In 1970, they were the first to be last—the first superhero title of the early Marvel Age of Comics to be cancelled. Cyclops, the Beast, and Co. puttered around other titles, in various incarnations, until the marketing-minded Roy Thomas thought that the team could be reconstituted along international lines. In other words, as writer Len Wein put it, "Since a lot of the Marvel books were selling very well internationally, if they put together a team of characters who would represent the countries where these books were already selling, they could sell this new book even better in—name the country."

Wein was already working on *The Incredible Hulk*, and created a fierce Canadian upstart called Wolverine, just so Marvel could have a Canadian superhero at their disposal, if the situation ever called for it. Little did Wein know that he would be the writer assigned to reconstitute the X-Men team for *Giant-Size X-Men* #1 in spring 1975. The artist of the new series was Dave Cockrum, whose characters were both action-oriented and affable; he had cut his teeth on the largest superhero group of all time, the Legion of Super-Heroes, at DC Comics. Apparently, no one ever gave Wein and Cockrum that magic list of designated countries, so they assembled a new team out of some old sketches for other projects and their gut instincts.

The new X-Men were vital and diverse, to an almost dizzying degree. The metal-clad Colossus hailed from Soviet Russia (he questioned whether or not his power belonged to the state); the shrieking Banshee was from Ireland; the elemental goddess Storm was the reigning deity in Kenya; the indigo-colored Nightcrawler was a hobgoblin from Germany; and Wolverine dutifully, if grumpily, represented Canada. A Japanese hero named Sunfire bailed after the first issue, and a Native American warrior named Thunderbird went on a suicide mission in the third issue; no one much missed him—he was not a team player. The new group was recruited by Professor X and was unofficially led by Cyclops, the one X-Man who decided to stay on. "We never ever to this day found out what countries we were supposed to have used," said Wein. "I guess maybe I should have had a Spanish guy, I don't know. We just did the group we thought was fun."

Readers thought they were pretty fun, too. Wein almost immediately left the book, to be replaced by Chris Claremont, whose seventeen-year tenure on The X-Men was, and is, unparalleled in the annals of comic books. Claremont had a particular gift for creating sympathetic characters, especially female ones, and he could spin out issue upon issue of epic space operas. He also understood that the X-Men's collective Achilles heel—their ostracization by humanity—was the key to their narrative appeal. "I'm out here, saving the universe, I've done it three times, and I still get a weird look when I walk down the street?," Claremont imagined an X-Man as saying: "Thanks a lot. Well, no good deed goes unpunished."

Claremont and Cockrum had made the X-Men viable again, and the book snowballed in popularity as it moved into the 1980s. A heart-wrenching saga involved Jean Grey morphing into a powerful entity called the Dark Phoenix, with the power to wreak havoc on human- and mutant-kind alike; she committed suicide rather than submit to the dark forces within her.

LEFT, FROM TOP: The New Mutants were the first successful spin-off of the blockbuster new X-Men franchise (1982); Nightcrawler is singled out for some Congressional bigotry (1982); *Uncanny X-Men* #137 features the shocking mercy suicide of Jean Grey, who unleashed the power of the Dark Phoenix (1980). ABOVE: The Angel poses a question in *Giant-Size X-Men* #1: it would be answered by a multitude of comic book readers.

Imaginatively crafted younger mutants arrived to Xavier's school to fill out the ranks; a particularly intriguing young woman named Rogue was incapable of touching another human being without absorbing all of their memories and abilities—and it was her curse. She was, in many ways, the logical extension of the tortured characters created by Stan Lee in the 1960s. "They were underdogs," said Louise Simonson, who edited the series in the 1990s. "Although they were extremely powerful characters, they perceived themselves as the underdogs."

Readers suddenly couldn't get enough of the X-Men—but where were all these fans in 1969? The short answer is that they probably hadn't been born yet. The X-Men and their manifold spin-offs—the New Mutants, X-Factor, Excalibur, X-Force, to name but the first few—touched a particular chord in young people. Christina Strain, a Marvel colorist who was born in South Korea and emigrated to the United States, sees the appeal of the multiracial, multigenetic group:

> They were a band of misfits who came together because they all were different. It's like high school. You get to watch all of these people who don't like each other have to work together as a group, and somebody is betraying somebody else and somebody has got a super secret that they're trying to keep and there's romance within the ranks. And everybody can identify with high school.

Perhaps the X-Men's heroic dilemma was embraced because they were the first truly multicultural superhero team; by the early 1980s, cultural diversity, political correctness, and ethnicity had entered the national discourse. Many of these conflicts of difference and community were played out directly—and painfully—in colleges, workplaces, and neighborhoods around the country. Claremont sees the parallel:

> In the X-Men's case, we have an impossible obstacle, but we have to find a way to win—that's an echo, a parallel for what goes on within the culture of the country itself. Over the last thirty-five years, how many people of extraordinarily varied persuasions have come up and said, "The X-Men speak to me"? I'm gay, I'm black, I'm Asian, I'm an immigrant. Why? Because they're outsiders trying to fit in and getting no credit for all the good that they do but not losing faith in the struggle. Still determined that the goal is worth the effort and the sacrifice. And that has a resonance.

By the end of the 1980s, it seemed as if everyone who had ever considered him or herself an outsider was buying *X-Men* and/or its affiliated titles; it became the most successful comic book conglomerate of all time, spawning hundreds of characters and dozens of storylines. Claremont assessed that, if all the X-Men-oriented comic books were spun off from Marvel Comics, they would constitute one of the largest comic publishers in the country. The last were now officially first.

At the very end of *Giant-Size X-Men* #1, in 1975, the Angel pondered a simple problem: "What are we going to do with thirteen X-Men?" Had he but known that, within four decades, the number of X-Men—and their devoted following—would be legion.

Early publicity shots of *Superman: The Movie* put Christopher Reeve in NYC's Central Park; in the film, he appears as Clark Kent with Margot Kidder as Lois Lane. **OPPOSITE:** The "Verisimilitude" sign in director Richard Donner's office.

BELIEVING A MAN CAN FLY
Superman: The Movie

I n the entire contents of Mario Puzo's submitted 500-page screenplay for the first major motion picture based on Superman, there was not one word as important as the one that director Richard Donner ultimately had emblazoned on his office wall:

the picture, and begin shooting at England's Pinewood Studios in March 1977, there was a parallel phenomena of dumping superheroes onto the primetime television schedule (as well as Saturday morning television cartoons). Spider-Man and Captain America fared poorly, while Wonder Woman (embodied with statuesque pep by Lynda Carter) came off more successfully. (The Incredible Hulk launched a successful television run right before *Superman* debuted in movie theaters.) An ill-conceived Doc Savage motion picture was barely released in 1975. The superhero brand had been relegated to the living room console by this kind of exposure, so the road to Superman's multi-million-dollar motion picture showcase was littered with skeptics.

Jerry Siegel couldn't even have been counted on as a skeptic; Superman's co-creator was an outright antagonist to the project. In 1975, as press releases and promotional gimmicks kept perpetuating the eventual release of a Superman film, Siegel sent a nine-page letter out to the media, detailing his outrage at National Periodicals and the profligate expenditures on the upcoming film: "I, Jerry Siegel, the co-originator of SUPERMAN, put a curse on the SUPERMAN movie! I hope it super-bombs. I hope loyal SUPERMAN fans stay away from it in droves. . . . You hear a great deal about The American Dream. But Superman, who in the comics and films fights for 'truth, justice and the American Way,' has for Joe and me become An American Nightmare." The letter detailed every perceived ignominy suffered by Siegel and Shuster—but the basic thrust was true: since their failed lawsuit in the late 1940s, neither man had an ongoing sustainable career in comics—Shuster, in fact, was almost legally blind and living in near-poverty. And their ongoing credit as Superman's creators hadn't appeared in print for a quarter of a century.

Superman's journey to the multiplex was one of his more arduous adventures. Toward the end of 1973, two foreign film producers, Alexander Salkind and his son Ilya, were contemplating their next project. They had just put together a mammoth international version of Dumas' *The Three Musketeers* (so mammoth, it would eventually be released in two parts, an unprecedented event in itself) and were looking for something equally adventurous and monumental. Although, rumor has it, the elder Salkind had never heard of Superman, he was persuaded by his son that it was just the property they needed, and the Salkinds set about acquiring the rights from Warner Communications.

It may be difficult to imagine a time when there had never been a full-length, big-budget Hollywood film about a superhero, but with the exception of a hastily patched-together 1966 movie with the *Batman* television cast, the Salkinds' project was without precedent. Luckily, the producers had the temerity (if not quite the means) to break the mold in a superlative way. In the four years it took them to negotiate the rights from Warner Bros., commission a screenplay (initially from Mario Puzo, famed for his novel and screenplay for *The Godfather*), acquire a director (several had come and gone before Richard Donner signed), cast

The media was slow to pick up the story, but artist Neal Adams, who had been an outspoken advocate for creators' rights for years, teamed up with Golden Age pioneer Jerry Robinson, who was also head of the National Cartoonists Society, to orchestrate a series of press conferences, media appearances, and general

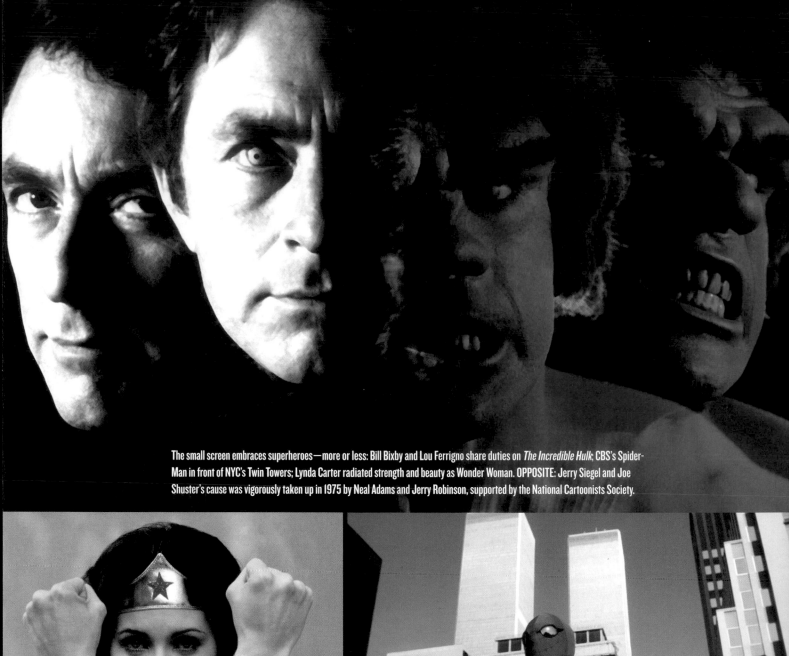

The small screen embraces superheroes—more or less: Bill Bixby and Lou Ferrigno share duties on *The Incredible Hulk*; CBS's Spider-Man in front of NYC's Twin Towers; Lynda Carter radiated strength and beauty as Wonder Woman. OPPOSITE: Jerry Siegel and Joe Shuster's cause was vigorously taken up in 1975 by Neal Adams and Jerry Robinson, supported by the National Cartoonists Society.

drum-beatings that might force Warner Communications' hand. Thanks to Adams and Robinson, it turned out to be a very popular story—the resonant appeal was obviously in the common-man-against-oppression trope that had served Superman so well during the Depression. As 1975 drew to a close, a series of back-and-forth negotiations between Warner and Robinson/Adams (representing Siegel and Shuster) ramped up, all in the shadow of the upcoming film: "That worked in our favor," said Robinson. "That gave us even more leverage. [Warner] didn't want any bad publicity on eve of the movie."

A settlement was reached: Siegel and Shuster were to receive $20,000 each a year, for life; they would get incremental raises; medical coverage; a one-time bonus of $17,500 each; and, most important—an issue haggled over most intensely—their credit as Superman's co-creators would be restored. Warner held out on one point—any credit on toys and action figures was out of its hands—but the important elements were in place. The deal was concluded on the afternoon of December 23, 1975, making it a Christmas present of Dickensian proportions. Siegel and Shuster joined Robinson at his West Side apartment that night, along with other champions of their cause, and watched the *CBS Evening News* together as Walter Cronkite broke the scoop on the deal, which Robinson had personally let him in on. "And finally, truth, justice, and the American Way won out," intoned Cronkite, as everyone lifted their champagne glasses. "I'll tell you," recounted Robinson, "There wasn't a dry eye in the house."

Meanwhile, as they say, production work on the film was taking an unbearably long time. Puzo's immense script draft proved unwieldy, so the Salkinds brought in Robert Benton and David Newman, who had not only written the screenplay for *Bonnie and Clyde*, but the book to a witty if short-lived Broadway musical called *"It's a Bird . . . It's a Plane . . . It's Superman"* in 1966. As the team (along with Newman's wife, Leslie) tried to focus the screenplay and make it compelling to contemporary America, the Salkinds searched in vain for their leading man. It was a near-impossible task, as the role was considered too demanding (so said Robert Redford), too ridiculous (Paul Newman's reason for saying "no"), too square (thereby knocking sexy Burt Reynolds out of competition), too All-American (sorry, Sylvester Stallone—who was dying to play the part), and too unremunerative (James Caan priced himself out). Months dragged on, as Olympic decathlon champ Bruce Jenner, Muhammad Ali, Perry King, and even someone's dentist were all considered and rejected.

Alexander Salkind decided to put his quickly evaporating chips on another part of the table; with a stellar supporting cast, he could raise money and credibility quickly. Marlon Brando accepted $3.7 million to play Superman's father, Jor-El, plus exorbitant percentages of the gross receipts; he would wind up working only twelve and a half days and tweaked the press by claiming he wanted to play the part as a floating green bagel, arguing that Superman's background needn't be humanoid at all (however kooky, Brando made an undeniably sensible point). Gene Hackman was signed to play Superman's arch-foe, the bald-pated Lex Luthor, although to maintain some fleeting sense of dignity (Hackman was embarrassed to be in a comic book movie), he refused to shave his head. The clout of Brando and Hackman allowed Salkind to leverage more money, and to save some overhead, he moved his production to eight sound stages in England's Shepperton Studios, which came with a tax credit. Director Richard Donner was brought on board and he firmly insisted on that "verisimilitude": "It's a word that refers to being real . . . not realistic—yes, there IS a difference—but real," explained Donner. "It was a constant reminder to ourselves that, if we gave into the temptation we knew there would be to parody Superman, we would only be fooling ourselves."

As 1975 stretched into 1976 and into 1977 without a starting date, Donner enlisted screenwriter Tom Mankiewicz, whose witty way with pulp material had enlivened several James Bond movies, to focus the script one more time: it was now being planned by the Salkinds as a two-part movie with a $26.5 million

Two box-office powerhouses lent their clout to the Superman project: Marlon Brando as Jor-El and Gene Hackman as Lex Luthor (from *Superman II*). OPPOSITE, TOP: A high-flying Christopher Reeve in the 1978 film blockbuster; BOTTOM: the opening credit that made comic book fans across America cheer.

budget. Still, the project was lacking a star and a convincing technical method that would get Superman airborne. On a flier, as it were, the producers took one last desperate look at a skinny Juilliard-trained actor from New York, who had some Broadway and soap opera experience. Christopher Reeve nearly didn't make his meeting with Salkind in New York, because, rather likc Hackman, he didn't think the material was serious enough. But his good looks convinced Salkind to arrange a screen test, where, apparently, it was his charming approach to Clark Kent that put him over the top. George Reeves (no relation) barely suggested a difference between Superman and his mortal disguise on the television show, but Reeve was inspired by the bumbling, bespectacled Cary Grant in *Bringing Up Baby.* For Reeve, Clark Kent was "a deliberate put-on by Superman . . . there's some of him in all of us. I have a great deal of affection for him—it's not just that he can't get the girl, he can't get the taxi." Reeve saw himself as "custodian of Superman in the 1970s" and seemed privileged to play the character. When he signed on for a mere $250,000 at the end of February 1977, everyone involved in the project sighed a superbreath of relief.

Filming finally began in March 1977, when the last, essential challenge was solved: how to make it credible that Superman could fly. After testing a variety of different effects to no avail,

the producers were persuaded by an optic effect created for the film called Zoptic, which allowed Reeve to lie ramrod straight on a gurney, while the specially designed zoom lenses did the rest; no pesky wires were required. Filming stretched on into fall 1977, and then into early winter 1978. Donner essentially had to edit two films at once, and was in constant budget battles with his producers; luckily—in the midst of being sued by both Brando and Mario Puzo—the Salkinds managed to offer premium film composer John Williams enough money to score an unforgettably heroic soundtrack.

Donner's completed film took the entire Superman mythos seriously without compromising its giddy charm as an essential myth in American popular culture. *Superman* was stylistically divided into thirds. The first part is icy, deliberate, science fiction on the minimalist, sleek, crystalline planet Krypton, where Jor-El, after sentencing three criminals to the Phantom Zone, vainly attempts to get his elder colleagues to heed his warnings about his planet's imminent destruction. He wearily, but stoically, sends his tiny young son to the planet Earth, via a shimmering, jagged pod.

Once young Kal-El arrives on earth, the second third of the story—his upbringing in Smallville—takes on the yearning frontier spirit of a John Ford movie, as if it were art directed by

sparking banter usually found only in Cary Grant/Katharine Hepburn films.

Proceeded by an ad campaign that riskily taunted audiences that they would "believe a man can fly" and despite its beleaguered history, *Superman* opened across the country on December 15, 1978, to largely enthusiastic reviews— most of them concurring that Reeve had pulled off a titanic task with persuasive flair. By spring 1979, most of the cast and crew returned to begin filming the sequel, much of which was already in the can. Although Donner had had enough dealing with the Salkinds and was replaced by Richard Lester, the sequel further refined the elements that had worked in the first place and in some cases—superior fight scenes with the power-enhanced criminals who escaped from the Phantom Zone, for example; an existential dilemma faced by Superman that stretched all the way back to Greek tragedy—actually improved on the original.

Still, the original *Superman* had a fortress full of happy endings for everyone: for the Salkinds, whose film made nearly $300 million worldwide, providing a profit even after all the settled lawsuits; for Reeve, who went from Hollywood Superman to Hollywood superstar; for audiences, who really did believe a man could fly; for Warner Bros., which mined three sequels out of the project; for fans, who felt that their standard bearer had been rendered in a cinematic version that was worthy of his eminence. But the happiest ending of all happened at the very beginning, some three minutes into the film: two weary comic book creators had the chance to see a boldly animated credit soar across the screen:

Andrew Wyeth. When he turns eighteen, Clark Kent discovers his alien roots via a hologram of his father, who imparts his wisdom in theological tones:

> Live as one of them, Kal-El, to discover where your strength and your power are needed. Always hold in your heart the pride of your special heritage. They can be a great people, Kal-El, they wish to be. They only lack the light to show the way. For this reason above all, their capacity for good, I have sent them you . . . my only son.

Then, the story turns to Metropolis—location filming in New York City proved to be a very persuasive substitute—where Clark's vocation at the *Daily Planet* and his subsequent unrequited affair with Lois Lane was rendered with all the spark and bite of a cynical 1970s urban film, which *Superman* was, after all. In an impressive blend of action, adventure, comedy (nicely rendered largely by Hackman's Luthor who, despite his claims of having "the greatest criminal mind of our time," certainly hires the two most incompetent cohorts in history), and romance, the movie soars to a thrilling conclusion. The romance was charmingly supplied by Reeve and his co-star, Margot Kidder, who brought to the screen the kind of

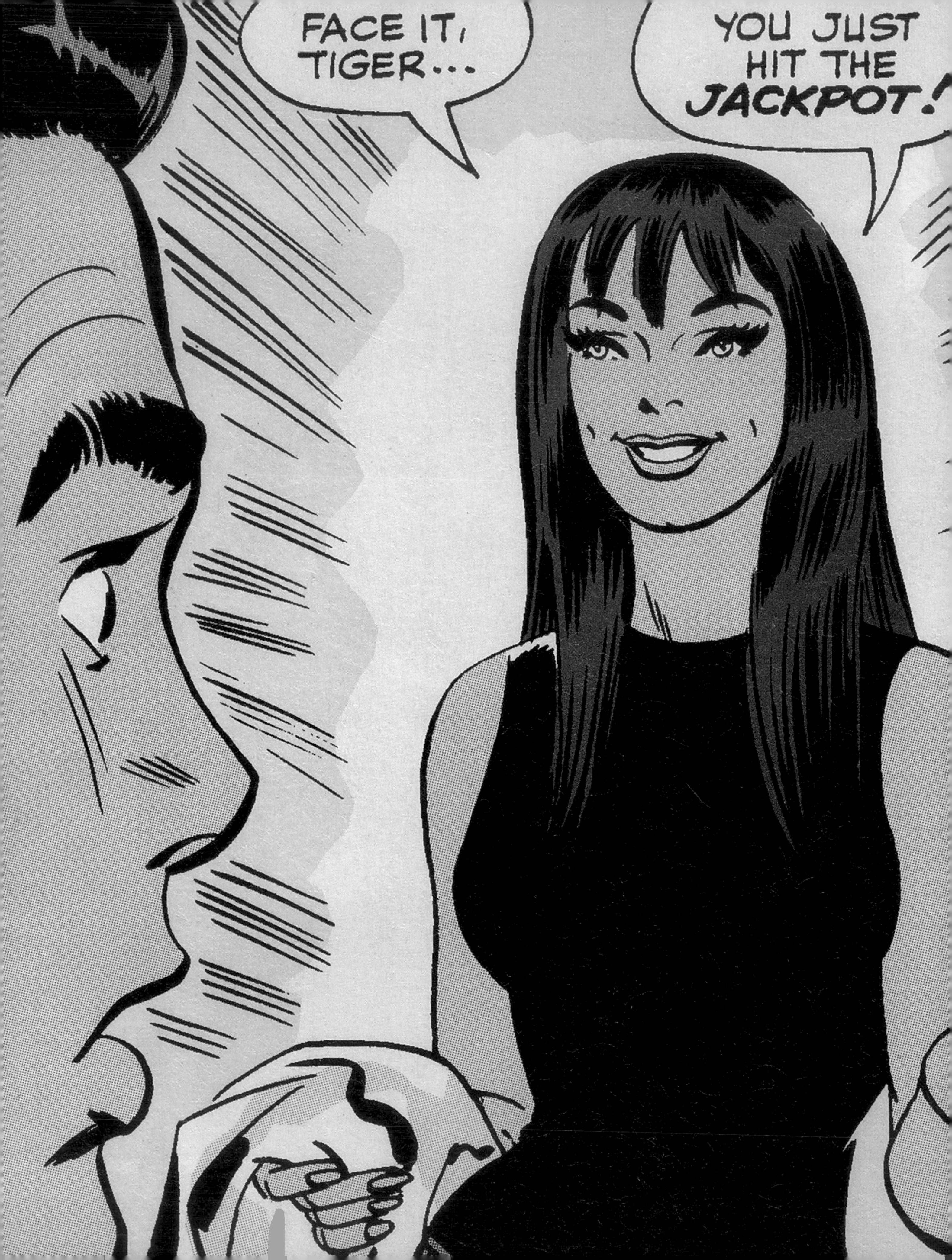
FACE IT, TIGER...
YOU JUST HIT THE JACKPOT!

"AND FOR THAT, YOU'RE GOING TO DIE!"
Spider-Man Meets the Real World

 eath had been a part of the Spider-Man legend since the web-slinger's debut, casting its shadow over the life of Peter Parker's Uncle Ben and thereby setting into motion Spider-Man's heroic obligation. When Death came knocking again at *The Amazing Spider-Man*, twice—first literally, then figuratively—in the early 1970s, it would irrevocably change the tone of superhero comic books.

The soap-opera drama that made Spider-Man so unique and so compelling in the mid 1960s often revolved around Peter Parker's love life—or lack thereof. But, eventually, Peter's "dumb luck" came up sevens and he had to choose between two of the most attractive and desirable women in the world of comic books. Peter first met Gwen Stacy when he moved on to college in 1965. She was a cool, platinum blonde (insofar as comic books could render platinum), with bangs, a black headband, and go-go boots. She was Peter's intellectual equal, but seemingly miles beyond him on the social scale. Mary Jane Watson, on the other hand, was originally set up for Peter as a blind date; he spent countless issues avoiding her, only to discover she was a bombshell ("Face it, tiger . . . you just hit the jackpot!" she famously exclaimed to him at the end of *The Amazing Spider-Man* #42). Mary Jane was a redhead, a free-swinging model and would-be actress, bursting with snappy repartee. She was "kooky"—back when that word was a signifier for the counterculture.

If they had been cast in a Hollywood movie of the 1950s, Gwen would have been played by Grace Kelly, Mary Jane by Shirley MacLaine. In their graphic incarnations, they were impeccably rendered by veteran artist John Romita, who had cut his teeth on the Marvel romance comics of the late 1950s. This only made sense, as "M.J." and "Gwennie" were the Betty and Veronica to Peter Parker's Archie Andrews.

By the beginning of 1973, Peter had more or less chosen Gwen. Stan Lee had moved off his fabled scripting chores on the title to spend time in his new role as Marvel's publisher, and Gerry

OPPOSITE: One of the sexiest panels in comic book history, thanks to John Romita; blind date Mary Jane Watson reveals herself to Peter Parker (*The Amazing Spider-Man* #42, November 1966). TOP: Death and dismay were always part of the Spider-Man soap opera (*The Amazing Spider-Man* #121, art by Gil Kane). BOTTOM: Peter Parker finds love in the arms (and lips) of Gwen Stacy (*The Amazing Spider-Man* #59).

Will it be Gwen Stacy or Mary Jane Watson? Only their hairdressers—and Stan Lee—know for sure.
OPPOSITE: The three panels from *The Amazing Spider-Man* #121 (June 1973) when comic books lost their innocence; art by Gil Kane.

Conway took over the reins. Conway was another member of the new generation of comic book writers, one of the youngest; in fact, he took on *The Amazing Spider-Man* while barely out of his teens. Conway's relative youth served him well; he was essentially the same age as Peter Parker and trying to make a go of it in Manhattan himself in the early 1970s. Conway was particularly sympathetic to Parker's various predicaments.

When Conway started on the series, there was a sense that the Spider-Man stories needed to be changed up. John Romita thought it would help if one of the characters was forced to walk the plank. Stan Lee voted for Peter's geriatric and solicitous Aunt May, but she had been on the Grim Reaper's dance card since the beginning. Aunt May's death would be sad, thought Conway; but he was going for tragic. And so, in *The Amazing Spider-Man* #121, the ground was laid for a genuine game changer in the world of comic book fantasy, amazing or otherwise.

The Green Goblin had always been one of Spider-Man's major villains, but, as the father of Peter's best friend, he was more insidiously involved in Parker's private life. Because of that connection, the Goblin learned of Spider-Man's alter ego and abducted Peter's girlfriend to exact his revenge; this impending peril was the

reason most superheroes refused to divulge their secret identities. The Goblin tossed Gwen Stacy off the tower of a Manhattan bridge; Spider-Man shot his webbing out to catch her. "Swik!" went the webbing and, in the saddest sound-effect in comic book history, "Snap!" went Gwen Stacy's neck. She was the first major ongoing character to be killed in the course of a story.

In the days before fan-based Internet websites trumpeted upcoming storylines, Gwen's death was a complete surprise; a shocker, in fact. Comic book writer Mark Waid recalls: "I was ten years old at the time and I thought of Gwen Stacy as my girlfriend. I remember where I was reading that comic and I remember walking around in a daze for the rest of the day because in comics, characters didn't die. Gwen Stacy was the one good thing in Spider-Man's life. And Gerry Conway yanked that away from him. That was devastating." Conway, who professed to be far more intrigued with the character of Mary Jane as a possible paramour for Spider-Man, viewed Gwen's death as a narrative choice with the greatest dramatic effect. "Up to that point, in a comic book, a character like Superman will catch Lois Lane, and she's safe. You always had the sense that at the end of the day, everything was going to be made right. But, when Gwen Stacy died, there was no rational reason for it other than the tragedy of life."

For Conway, Gwen's death was also a metaphor of the zeitgeist of the early 1970s. "That era was all about good people trying to do the right thing and messing up horribly. Spider-Man, trying to save the woman he loves, ends up killing her. We were in the Viet Nam War; the soldiers who went over didn't go over there to be bad guys. They went over there to try to do the right thing. In the process, they did terrible things. And that's tragic. There was a sense that the world was not a safe and nice place and comics hadn't really reflected that. But after the death of Gwen Stacy, comics started to reflect the real world."

The shadow of the real world conflict would extend further into the Spider-Man title in the form of a violent Viet Nam vet named Frank Castle. It's worth remembering that not only did the Marvel Universe revolve around New York City, but, in the early 1970s, all of the young writing talent was living there as well. During previous generations, comic book writers and artists tended to wear ties and carry briefcases and commute into town from the suburbs of Scarsdale or Mineola, but now the talent was facing the same problems as thousands of hardened New Yorkers—and those problems were plentiful. In January 1974, the *New York Times* did a survey of its citizens: 63 percent of residents said

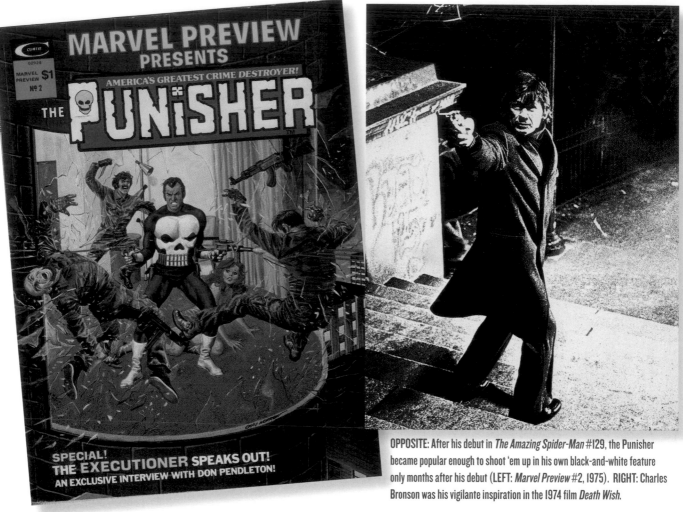

OPPOSITE: After his debut in *The Amazing Spider-Man* #129, the Punisher became popular enough to shoot 'em up in his own black-and-white feature only months after his debut (LEFT: *Marvel Preview* #2, 1975). RIGHT: Charles Bronson was his vigilante inspiration in the 1974 film *Death Wish.*

that crime was their number-one concern; 41 percent said they would never set foot in Times Square; and two out of five New Yorkers expressed no confidence that a captured criminal would ever be sent to jail. Throughout the 1970s, close to two thousand people were murdered each year in New York City alone. Clearly, in the minds of some people, something had to be done.

The idea of a comic book vigilante who would take the law into his own hands was nothing new in the Western books of the 1950s, but a costumed character with such a ruthless philosophy would seem to contradict the do-gooder ethics of the superhero universe. The Punisher made his first appearance at the beginning of 1974, in the pages of *The Amazing Spider-Man* #129, with a February cover date, the same month as the *New York Times* released its poll of the city's intimidated citizens. It was a little more than a year after Gwen Stacy's death. "Gwen Stacy set the stage and the Punisher walked onto it," said his creator, Gerry Conway. "Spider-Man as the good superhero fails to save the innocent girl.

Well, the Punisher comes along and he's the guy who is not going to fail because he is not going to play by society's rules. He's not going to wrap the villain up in webbing and put him on a ledge for the cops to come: he is going to eliminate the villain."

Although his character was originally intended as a one-shot, the Punisher character provided a full magazine of narrative artillery. A hired assassin with a death's-head emblem on his chest, the Punisher is manipulated by another villain to "take out" Spider-Man. His weapons include a lethal AK-47 and the kind of terse humorless threats mastered by Clint Eastwood in his 1971 film *Dirty Harry*. "I'm an expert at many things, murderer," he tells Spider-Man, who blames him for, among other crimes, the death of Gwen Stacy. "Your kind of scum has ruled this country too long, punk—and I'm out to put a stop to it—ANY WAY I CAN!" With a fearsome costume (although the white boots seemed both effete and impractical for someone so devoted to carnage) and a mien

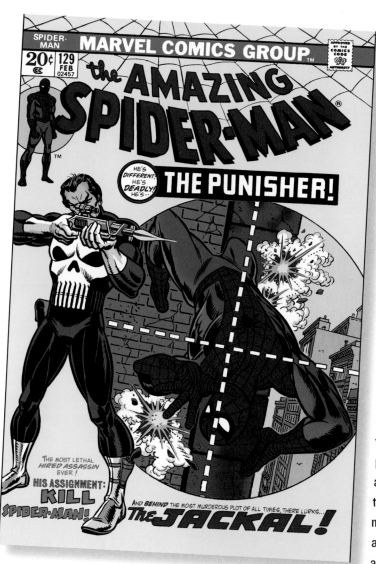

that resembled Robert Mitchum after several years of basic training, the Punisher immediately caught on with readers; his implacability mirrored their own frustrations as well as the wish fulfillment of the times.

The Punisher's path had been trod before in fiction and in the movies. Conway consciously modeled him on a men's "action adventure" character, the Executioner, a former Green Beret-turned-mercenary in a series of popular novels begun by Don Pendleton in 1969. The Executioner inspired a plethora of other paperback vigilantes and mercenaries— the Liquidator, the Death Merchant, the Destroyer— usually former battlefield vets or CIA operatives who decide to fight crime on their own merciless terms. It was a sub-genre that reached its apotheosis in 1974, when Brian Garfield's *Death Wish* was made into a frighteningly successful pro-vigilante film starring Charles Bronson.

"[The Punisher] also comes out of incredible complexity and craziness of the Nixonian period—a social breakdown of all the rules and regulations that we had all thought we were living by," said Conway. "The Punisher has a simple answer to all this: 'I'll take care of it. You know I will do it, there's not going to be anybody between me and justice.'" The character became a 1970s version of the Mike Hammer detective character that Mickey Spillane created out of the disillusioned veterans of World War II. More than a year after his debut, the Punisher was given his own backstory by Conway in another Marvel magazine, an origin that

reflects his pulp antecedents. Frank Castle is a former Marine, a Vietnam vet who takes his family on a picnic in Central Park (where, the 1974 *New York Times* poll reported, 38 percent of New Yorkers would not dare to visit alone). His wife and daughter inadvertently witness a mob hit and are rubbed out by the Mafia. Bereft with grief, Castle takes on the Mafia with a vengeance. By the mid 1980s, the Punisher was given his own title and soon became the poster boy for the "grim-and-gritty" vigilante; that title eventually begat other, more violent titles such as *Punisher War Journal* and *PunisherMAX* (with maximum violence), as well as backstories that framed his formative years in Viet Nam. Frank Castle evolved into one of Marvel's most popular characters, even though it seemed that, at the rate he was mowing down organized criminals, the Human Resources office at the Mafia would have to be working overtime.

The Punisher leapt beyond the confines of the Spider-Man book to become both a reflection and refraction of his times. As Conway states, "A character like the Punisher or like Batman is open to interpretation. The Punisher became, in effect, a wonderful Rorschach test for writers and artists over the last thirty years to comment on society, to comment on violence, to comment on the heroic ideal. He comes out of that twisted view of the Viet Nam vet—the defender of society who is also a danger to society."

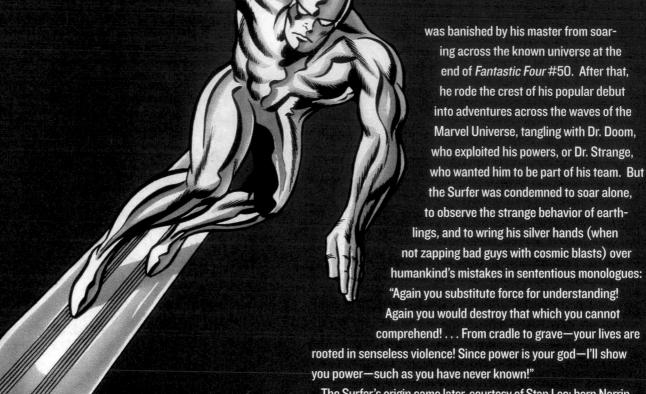

was banished by his master from soaring across the known universe at the end of *Fantastic Four* #50. After that, he rode the crest of his popular debut into adventures across the waves of the Marvel Universe, tangling with Dr. Doom, who exploited his powers, or Dr. Strange, who wanted him to be part of his team. But the Surfer was condemned to soar alone, to observe the strange behavior of earthlings, and to wring his silver hands (when not zapping bad guys with cosmic blasts) over humankind's mistakes in sententious monologues: "Again you substitute force for understanding! Again you would destroy that which you cannot comprehend! . . . From cradle to grave—your lives are rooted in senseless violence! Since power is your god—I'll show you power—such as you have never known!"

The Surfer's origin came later, courtesy of Stan Lee; born Norrin Radd on the planet Zenn-La, he lashed himself to Galactus's service in exchange for a "get-out-of-jail-free" card for his home planet. Kirby was reportedly furious, as he thought the more enigmatic the Surfer was, the better. Nevertheless, the Silver Surfer appealed to counterculture fans, eager for someone in comic books to do something other than bash out the brains of their adversaries. Musicians such as guitarist Joe Satriani and the members of Pink Floyd were inspired by the Silver Surfer, and although he never earned a successful ongoing series, that was okay: the Silver Surfer went his own way, soaring miles above quotidian concerns such as sales and popularity.

THE SILVER SURFER

First appearance: March 1966, *Fantastic Four* #48

If there were ever a case of the second banana stealing the show from the star, the debut of the Silver Surfer was it. Stan Lee and Jack Kirby had amped up their usual cosmic shenanigans in the Fantastic Four by introducing the most powerful malefactor yet contemplated in the Marvel Universe: Galactus, Devourer of Worlds. Galactus arrives for a dinner date on Earth, but he is preceded by his herald, a sleek, celestial being; the "sentinel of the spaceways" travels on a vehicle that was more likely found out in Malibu: a surfboard. Kirby created him on his own, without telling Lee first, and came up with the surfboard because, as he claimed, "I was tired of drawing spaceships." Lee christened him the "Silver Surfer," which only makes sense, as the Christ-like Surfer quickly became Marvel's resident ethical philosopher.

The Surfer betrayed Galactus by siding with humanity and

THE HAWK AND THE DOVE

First appearance: June 1968, *Showcase* #75

The quirky world of Marvel Comics subsumed most of the critical chatter in the mid 1960s, and much of the sales receipts as well. DC Comics was determined to come up with new characters who would be equally compelling and grab the attention of fans. Although they were not particularly successful in this regard, it

AND LOVED

THE MIGHTY CRUSADERS

First appearance: May 1965, *Fly-Man* #31

In a perhaps painful reminder that, in the 1960s, DC Comics and Marvel were not the only superhero games in town, the Mighty Crusaders were the last, best gasp of the publishers of Archie Comics. In the 1940s, as MLJ Publishing, the company created some viable superheroes, before Archie Andrews and his crew from Riverdale High nudged them out of their titles. Although the Fly had been buzzing around since 1959, he was renamed Fly-Man in apparent competition with Marvel's friendly neighborhood you-know-what and was joined by some other holdovers from the Archie—now, Mighty Comics—Universe: the patriotic Shield; the valiant Black Hood, who rode a robotic horse; the Comet, an alien who sported a rainbow helmet and, even worse, a moustache; and the inevitable Fly-Girl. In a poor imitation of Marvel-style bickering, the crew was unable to come up with a common moniker on which they could all agree: one of them foolishly suggested "The Fantabulous Five."

The Mighty Crusaders (yes, they finally agreed on a name) were colorful, but uninspired, although they earned a few fans before calling it quits after seven issues. The major fact that saves them from comic book oblivion? All of their adventures were written by none other than Jerry Siegel, Superman's co-creator, in his final hurrah as a comic book scripter.

wasn't for want of trying. Spider-Man's co-creator Steve Ditko had left Marvel in 1967, reportedly miffed about the lack of credit given him for co-creating the wall-crawler, and DC editor Carmine Infantino was more than happy for him to develop characters for their firm. The Hawk and the Dove was "a tale of two brothers who are a world apart—too young to fully comprehend the emotions that separate them." A clear attempt to bend the Viet Nam War into a superheroic metaphor, the Hawk and the Dove were nearly always at odds with each other in their battles against crime—one brother, Hal, used his fists and his aggression as the Hawk, while the other brother, Don, did . . . what, exactly? After three issues of terrific Ditko art (and another three drawn by Gil Kane), it finally occurred to the writers what fans already knew: a pacifist superhero, especially one who whined all the time about having to punch out the villains, was rather a non-starter. *The Hawk and the Dove* folded its wings after a half-dozen adventures; an admirable experiment in a troubled time.

DEATHLOK, THE DEMOLISHER

First appearance: August 1974, *Astonishing Tales #25*

In the 1970s, Marvel Comics unleashed a barrage of new characters, most of whom did not make it out of the decade with their own title. Deathlok was somewhat luckier than most, perhaps because he tapped into some of the anxieties and zeitgeist of the 1970s. Luther Manning was an American army colonel, critically injured following a war game in the future (!) of 1985; he awoke to find that he had been experimented upon by a covert government agency, and that he had been scientifically enhanced as a part-human, part-mechanical war machine: a cyborg. Cyborgs and bionically enhanced action heroes were to the 1970s what aliens were to the 1950s and androids were to the 1960s; the original adventures of *The Six-Million-Dollar Man* and his paramour, *The Bionic Woman*, were successful on the television screen back then. What Deathlok's creators (Doug Moench and Rich Buckler) added to the mix was the post-Watergate distrust for figures in power, plus the hairy post-apocalyptic visions of the future visited upon movie audiences in *Logan's Run* and *Rollerball*. As much of a patchwork creation of pop culture as he was a patchwork creation of the covert laboratory, Deathlok still had an engagingly dyspeptic personality, as he did his best—aided by his very own personal computer strapped to his back!—to eliminate the conspiracies of rapacious oil companies and government traitors of the future. Various versions of the Bionic Brawler survived into 21st-century storylines in the Marvel Universe.

AND VILLAINS WE LOVE TO HATE

DARKSEID

First appearance: December 1970, *Superman's Pal, Jimmy Olsen #134*

In 1970, Jack Kirby stunned the comic book world by jumping (space)ship from Marvel Comics to DC Comics. Chaffing to create ambitious projects on which he could work unfettered (by Stan Lee), Kirby was given what initially appeared to be carte blanche at DC. He planned the most ambitious project yet conceived for comics, an apocalyptic battle among a complex series of new gods that would feature dozens of original characters spread out over three new bi-monthly titles; his contract called for fifteen new pages a week, each written and drawn by Kirby—a prodigious amount, even by his voluminous standards.

In practice, the proposed galactic series turned into something more earthbound. DC forced Kirby to take on a previously published title and, supposedly to keep the publishers from firing another creative team, he took on the aimless *Superman's Pal, Jimmy Olsen* book to launch his epic. (Kirby should have sensed what was in store when DC redrew the faces of his Superman to conform them to house style.) But, throughout 1971 and 1972, Kirby kept these cosmic plates spinning, playing out his so-called "Fourth World" saga in *The Forever People, The New Gods*, and *Mr. Miracle*. It was a difficult time to launch such an ambitious series (Kirby presciently had *The Lord of the Rings* in mind), and, to be frank, Kirby's level of writing was nowhere near the incomparable imagination he brought to his art (a cryptic black superhero on skis called the Black Rider was a little too much like the Silver Surfer, but without his diverting dialogue). After more than fifty separate issues of "Fourth World" stories in various titles, the series came to a halt in 1973 before its planned apocalyptic finale.

Surviving the demise of the series itself was the indomitable Darkseid, "Ruler of Apokolips! Wielder of Holocaust! Disciple of power and death!" Or, as Jim Croce might have said, more simply: "The baddest man in the whole damn universe." Darkseid was the all-powerful ruler of a benighted planet that squared off against the enlightened world of New Genesis, and obsessed with obtaining the Anti-Life Equation so that he could bend the universe to his will. He came to represent the kind of omnipotent villain that was useful for epic mini-series and crossover dramas, so DC Comics kept him around long past the "Fourth World" series expiration date. After all, you had to admire his sense of confidence: "I am the revelation! The tiger-force at the core of all things! When you cry out in your dreams, it is Darkseid that you see!"

THE HYPNO-HUSTLER

First appearance: November 1978, *Peter Parker, the Spectacular Spider-Man* #24
Incontrovertibly, Spider-Man fought some of the greatest villains in comic-book history in his various books, including the Green Goblin, Morbius, and the Punisher. He also tangled webs with

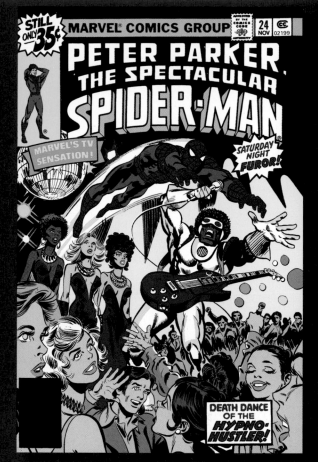

some of the lamest. For some reason, the late 1970s and early '80s provided Spidey with an unending stream of desperate adversaries, remarkable only for their contrived personas. Chief among them has to be the Hypno-Hustler, who debuted in a 1978 story promoted on the cover as "Saturday Night Furor!" The Hypno-Hustler was a misguided musician who fronted the Mercy Killers and used his enhanced goggles and guitar to mesmerize a nightclub audience and then rob them (unfortunately for him, Peter Parker was in the audience that night). The Hustler followed in the platform-soled footsteps of the Rocket-Racer, who used a scientifically enhanced skateboard to thwart Spider-Man; the Kangaroo, a high-jumping miscreant from Down Under; the Gibbon, a big monkey; and Spot—not a canine mascot, but a villain who could dive extra-dimensionally into gaping black spots.

The Hypno-Hustler had an unofficial comrade within the Marvel Universe called the Dazzler, who could transform sound into potent forces of light. Another product of the disco craze, the Dazzler was intended to be a cross-promotion between Marvel and Casablanca Records. It never quite worked out that way, but she debuted in the pages of *The Uncanny X-Men* in 1980, before getting her own title (which was a huge seller). A talented singer and dancer in "real-life," the Dazzler caught on with fans, rather improbably, and her exploits stretched into the 21st century, far outlasting the four-on-the-floor musical fad that spawned her.

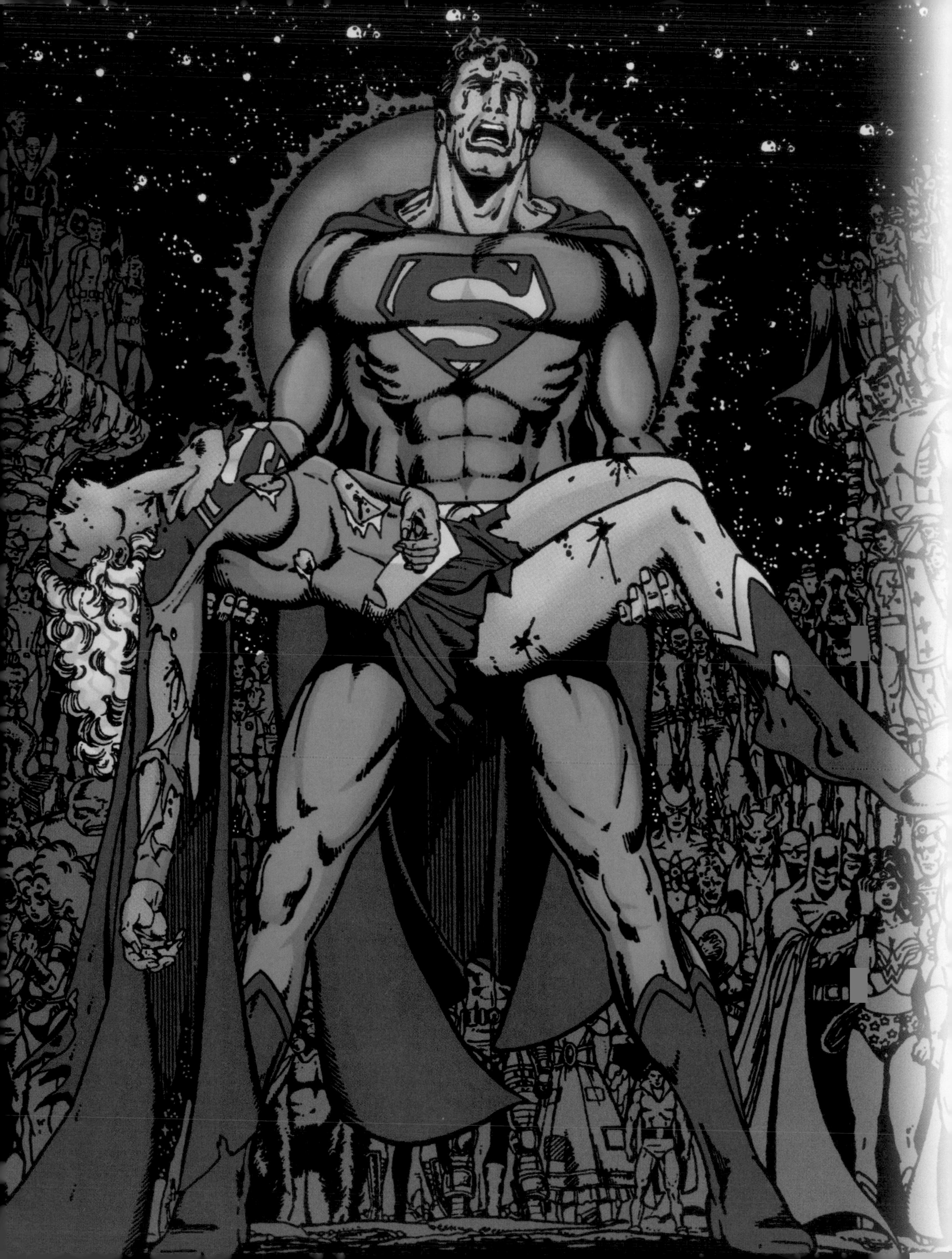

"YOU JUST NEVER KNOW WHO'S GOING TO DIE"
Crisis of Infinite Mini-Series

t Marvel Comics, they were called "True Believers"—the fans that could be counted on to follow as many adventures as possible and buy as many comic books per month as their allowance would, well, allow.

As the Reagan Administration began, it was very clear that True Believers were no longer just kids asking their parents for a quarter to buy the latest issue of *Howard the Duck*—they also included adults with discretion and discretionary incomes. They also constituted a large and increasingly powerful voting bloc called "fandom."

OPPOSITE: The death of Supergirl was a cosmos- (and continuity-) shattering event: *Crisis on Infinite Earths* #7 (October 1985). ABOVE: A Jim Steranko promotion for one of the first comic book conventions, 1968.

Fandom had existed earlier than Superman; it was Jerry Siegel who mimeographed his own fanzine back in Glenville High (among his groupies were Julie Schwartz, who would later become a powerful and influential editor at DC Comics). Comic book fans still communicated through letters and home-made magazines (such as *Alter-Ego*, begun in 1961 by Jerry Bails, and edited by the pre-professional Roy Thomas), but they rarely had an opportunity to meet, swap comics, and argue about which Spider-Man artist was better. That changed in the late 1960s, when a high-school English teacher, Phil Seuling, initiated the New York Comic Art Convention, which opened up a hotel ballroom every year (and the second Sunday of every month for smaller gatherings) for a series of panels, costume parades, and extensive buying and trading of comic books, magazines, toys, and other ephemera. This was a parallel event to the ongoing interest in science fiction—soon, Star Trek conventions were popping up across the country. By the time Marvel Comics sponsored their own three-day convention in 1975, the comic book convention had gone from a pastime to an institution. In the post-Internet days (and beyond), the comic book convention—in New York or Chicago or San Diego or your local Holiday Inn—has become an essential aspect of both fandom and the industry.

Fans were also seminal in changing the dynamic of purchasing comic books. About the same time as conventions were becoming touchstones of fandom, specialty comic book stores started opening across the country. Initially a by-product of the "head shops" that sold incense, records, and drug paraphernalia, comic book shops emerged as the major hubs of the industry. Shop owners were usually fans themselves—rather than, say, a cranky candy store owner who was always yelling at kids for reading instead of buying—and they didn't mind if customers read the comic books; they were doing so themselves. The owners also knew what readers wanted. Normally, distributors sent out a wide variety of comic books to candy stores or stationery shops, which usually returned about half their stock each month as unsold comic books, often with their covers ripped so they could not be resold. But comic book store owners could predict in advance which titles would be popular, especially if a premiere issue of some character was coming down the pike. Savvy fans-turned-businessmen, such as Phil Seuling, realized they could cut out the middleman, remove the distributors altogether, and sell comic books directly to readers.

This sensible bartering system caught on quickly; by the 1980s, the direct sales market was responsible for more than 75 percent of all comic book sales; this was a win-win, as the publishers could print runs with more precision, and the direct sales dealers got their comics at a preferential rate.

Still, sales of most comic books in the late 1970s and early 1980s were, with some exception, a fraction of what they had been in the mid 1960s—not to mention compared to sales in the 1940s. Special events soon became a clever, if overused, method of ginning up sales. Creating suspense for an upcoming premiere issue usually worked for a while—sales for *Howard the Duck* #1 were huge, but the title quacked up after a few years. The idea of an ongoing series that would hook readers sequentially began, almost by accident, when Roy Thomas created the nine-issue "Kree-Skrull War" for *The Avengers* in 1971-72. The series involved many of Marvel's most popular characters (as well as some cameos from the 1940s canon) and, when Neal Adams illustrated several of the issues, it was a high-water mark for Marvel in the 1970s.

In 1982, Marvel returned to the idea of an everybody-on-board

limited mini-series with *Contest of Champions*, but that was just a dress rehearsal for *Marvel Super Heroes Secret Wars*, a twelve-issue mini-series that stretched from May 1984 to April 1985. *Secret Wars* began as a phone call from the leading toy manufacturer, Mattel, to Jim Shooter, then editor-in-chief at Marvel Comics. Mattel wanted to launch a series of licensed Marvel action figures, but would only do so if there were some sort of marketing peg on which to hang the whole enterprise. Both companies sorted out which characters would jointly appeal to the comic book/toy market and launched the year-long series in the largest cross-promotion event in comic book history up to that point. It was also a huge hit at the cash register—it was the best-selling Marvel title of its time, although the series sold far more comic books than action figures. The series even had an ongoing legacy in the Marvel Universe, including the introduction of a new, sleek, black costume for Spider-Man (later revealed to be an amorphous alien parasite called a Symbiote, whatever that is).

If you weren't completely exhausted by *Secret Wars*, you could plunge directly into DC Comics' *Crisis on Infinite Earths*, a twelve-issue "maxi-series" that debuted the same month that Marvel's epic concluded. *Crisis on Infinite Earths* was the most ambitious series to appear up to that time, and remains one of the most seminal series in the history of comic books. The DC Comics mythology—spread out over fifty years, several galaxies, and many fictional cities—had become complex, contradictory, and clogged. Sometimes, it was so arcane (there had been different competing "Earths" since the Golden-Age Flash met the Silver-Age Flash in 1961), that it was inhibiting new buyers from parting with their dollars.

Long the brainchild of Marv Wolfman, *Crisis* came about as both an epic housecleaning fantasy and a way to make DC Comics relevant again. "If you were a fan who read Marvel, or a professional who was coming from Marvel, you knew characters had to change—or at least have the perception of change," said Wolfman. "And DC wasn't doing that. With *Crisis on Infinite Earths*, we'd actually make a major change that comics had never seen. We would call so much attention to DC that it couldn't be ignored and the readers would be intrigued."

Working with the precise, encyclopedic, detailed vision of artist George Pérez, Wolfman contrived a way to bring every DC

OPPOSITE: Editor/writer Roy Thomas brought back some neglected heroes from Timely's Golden Age for the conclusion of the Skrull vs. Kree saga (March 1972). ABOVE: The Flash makes a final sacrifice for humanity and for continuity: *Crisis on Infinite Earths* #8 (November 1985, art by George Perez).

character—hero, villain, or undecided—into his epic, which allowed him to conflate the company's various "Earths" into one manageable universe. Such an Homeric task was bound to have some repercussions; indeed, several of them influenced DC Comics for decades (and still have the power to enflame debates at panels at comic book conventions). Realizing that the profundity of Superman's mythos rested on his status as sole survivor of a dying planet, Wolfman and Co. killed off his Kryptonian cousin, Supergirl, and bumped off the Silver-Age Flash for good measure (however, he was soon replaced by his protégé, Kid Flash).

A rabid fan of comics since the 1950s, Wolfman saw *Crisis* as a tipping point, a way of admitting that the fanbase had gotten older and yet somehow needed to make room for another generation. An epilogue in the series had a deranged villain called the Psycho-Pirate expound a metaphysical view on the whole landscape of both comic books and their readers:

You see, I like to remember the past because those were better times than now. I mean, I'd rather live in the past than today, wouldn't you? I mean nothing's ever certain anymore. Nothing's ever predictable like it used to be. These days you just never know who's going to die and who's going to live.

The two major company "crossover" series in the mid 1980s were a harbinger of things to come. Annual events were now plotted by both DC and Marvel with almost numbing regularity. Sometimes the mini-series were routine and uninspired, sometimes they were astonishing and revolutionary. Two things were sure: nothing would be predictable like it used to be; and there were now plenty of citizens of "Fandom" ready—nay, eager—to argue about the consequences.

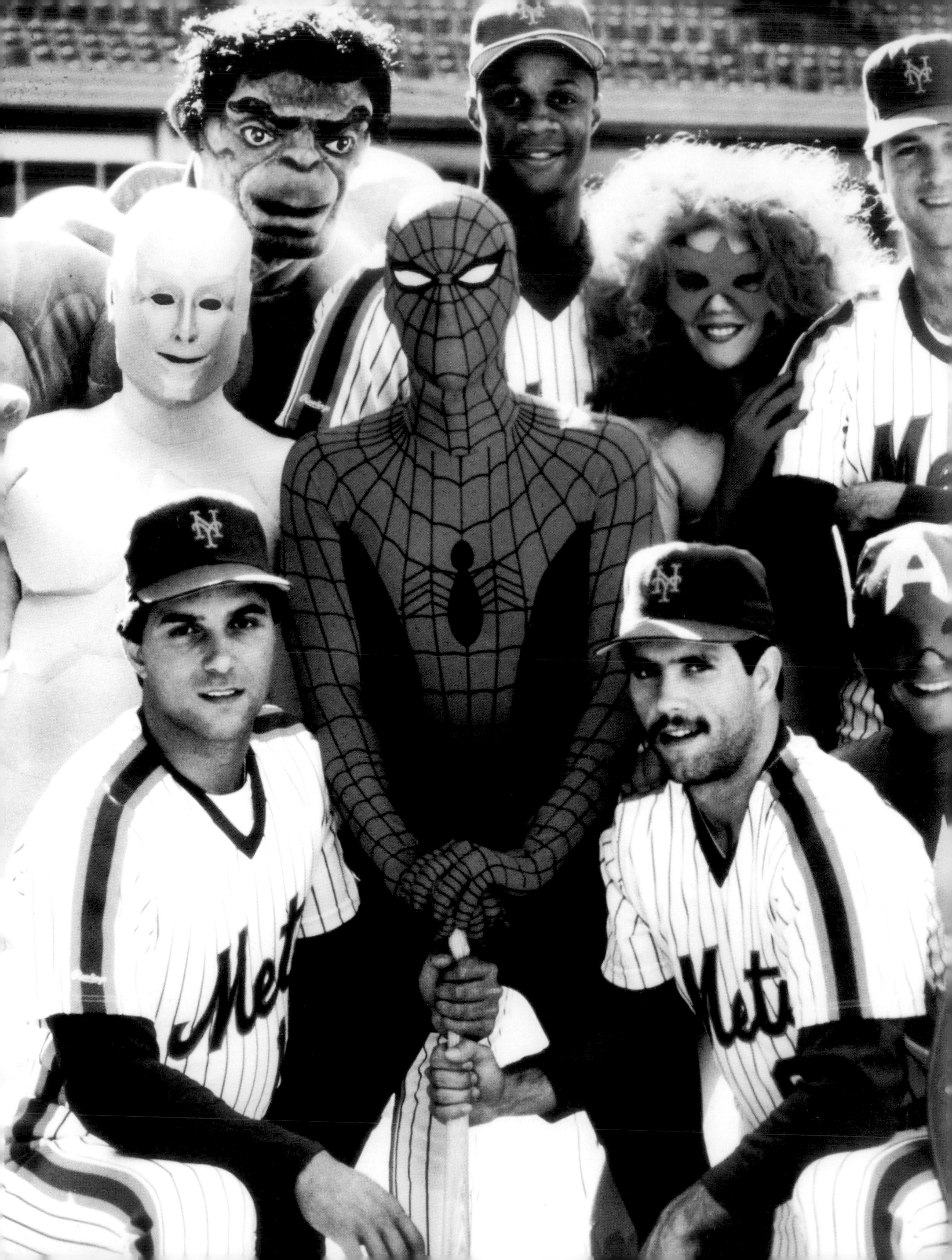

TO BE CONTINUED ...
"I Now Pronounce You Spider-Man and Wife!"

Spider-Man was conceived in 1962 as the ultimate teenager; but, in the real world, teenagers eventually grow up. And on June 5, 1987, so did Spidey.

As the 1980s began, Spider-Man had supplanted Superman as America's most popular comic book hero. He was holding down three separate comic book titles a month; he had just concluded a prime-time series and was segueing into a new animated series; and he was emblazoned on innumerable lunch boxes, toothbrushes, board games, sheets, and towels. In addition, since 1977, he had been featured in one of the few daily action comic strips to succeed in newspapers since World War II. Written by Stan Lee and illustrated by Larry Lieber, the syndicated *The Amazing Spider-Man* strip harkened back to the Holy Grail that Siegel and Shuster had sought for Superman in 1938.

Lee had a ball grabbing back the reins of the web-slinger, but as the 1980s galloped along, he decided to marry off Peter Parker to his longtime on-again, off-again girlfriend, Mary Jane Watson. "I mean, Peter Parker had been dating Mary Jane for years, he was in love with her, well, what's the next logical development?" Lee sensibly queried. There was a big glitch, however—the strip was published separately from Marvel Comics by King Features Syndicate and there was no expectation of continuity among the strip and the various comics. Marvel's current editorial staff had no plans to do anything like marrying off Peter Parker.

The Marvel editorial staff moved quickly: the countdown was to a June wedding and it was imperative that the strip and comic books intersected at the same time. (Writer David Michelinie made a quick pivot in continuity to have Peter Parker propose to Mary Jane at the end of *The Amazing Spider-Man* #290, although she took a couple of issues to accept his offer.) In a move that was a press agent's dream—and contrived to promote the wedding issue (*The Amazing Spider-Man Annual* #21) that would hit the stands the following Tuesday—the nuptials were dramatized at home plate

OPPOSITE: Spider-Man swings right up and meets the Mets: with other costumed crazies at Shea Stadium, June 5, 1987. TOP: A Marvel merchandise brochure adds a new character: Spider-Woman (1978). BOTTOM: Live from New York: one of the strangest Spider-Man team-ups ever (*Marvel Team-Up*, 1978).

at Shea Stadium, where two models would impersonate Spider-Man and M.J. in front of a crowd of 45,000 baseball fans waiting for the Mets to play the Pittsburgh Pirates.

M.J.'s dress was created by one of the hottest fashion designers in the actual business: Willi Smith, who had stunned the fashion world with his suits for the groom's party at Caroline Kennedy's wedding in 1983. Sadly, Smith, whose contemporary style was perfect for a comic book heroine—"I don't design clothes for the Queen, but for the people who wave at her as she goes by," he once said—had died of complications from AIDS weeks before the ceremony. (Lee would devote precious comic strip space to memorialize Smith's contribution.)

Still, the event was highly anticipated. The *New York Times* Style section, which covered the wedding, quoted Mary Jane as saying that the groom was nervous: "He's been pacing the ceiling for weeks." Attending the wedding were Captain America, Dr. Doom, Iceman, and the Incredible Hulk; in a felicitous bit of casting, the officiant was none other than Stan Lee: "I performed the marriage [ceremony]. It had to be legal, so, it had to be someone like me who had the authority to marry them. And all I could think of was—they had the ceremony before the game—the zillions of fans in the stands are probably thinking, 'When is the game gonna start?'"

The public-relations aspect of the Spider-Man/Mary Jane wedding was a spectacular success, picked up by major media outlets across the country, and the special issue featuring the wedding was a huge best-seller. In the real world of comics, however, there was a problem of unintended consequences. Back in 1961, Stan Lee and his collaborators had changed the whole game of comic book superheroes based on the assumption that they lived in a world that resembled ours, they had problems like ours, they could be us.

Marvel annuals were always good venues for major events: the Spider-Man/Mary Jane wedding topped them all. OPPOSITE: The magic moment: *The Amazing Spider-Man Annual #21* (1987, art by John Romita, Jr.).

Except they weren't. They were highly profitable commercial entities, too, which had developed surprisingly long lives in the marketplace. Fans had spent years following these superheroes and their supporting characters, identifying with them, growing older with them. And suddenly, the most revolutionary aspect of Stan Lee's innovation—that superheroes could appeal for the first time to older readers— became problematic for the industry that made fortunes off them. Artist Joe Quesada, who would inherit Stan's old post as editor-in-chief of Marvel Comics in 2000, framed what the Thing would call the whole "revoltin' development":

If you had been reading Spider-Man for ten years, fifteen years, this was a logical place for the character to go because you yourself had probably either gotten married or were ready for marriage. So the character was aging along with you. But, really, at the end of the day, when you have a character that has to be there for the next wave of readers, at what point do you stop? Does Peter Parker then have kids? Does he then grow old and become a grandfather? Does he then die? We really couldn't go there.

It was a dilemma that the comic book industry had made for itself out of its success, an unintended consequence of creating, cultivating, and maintaining loyal readers. For the next generation of superhero writers and artists, the choice was inevitable: they *had* to go there. And the "there" was a rarely considered, infrequently traveled territory in the world of "amazing fantasy": reality.

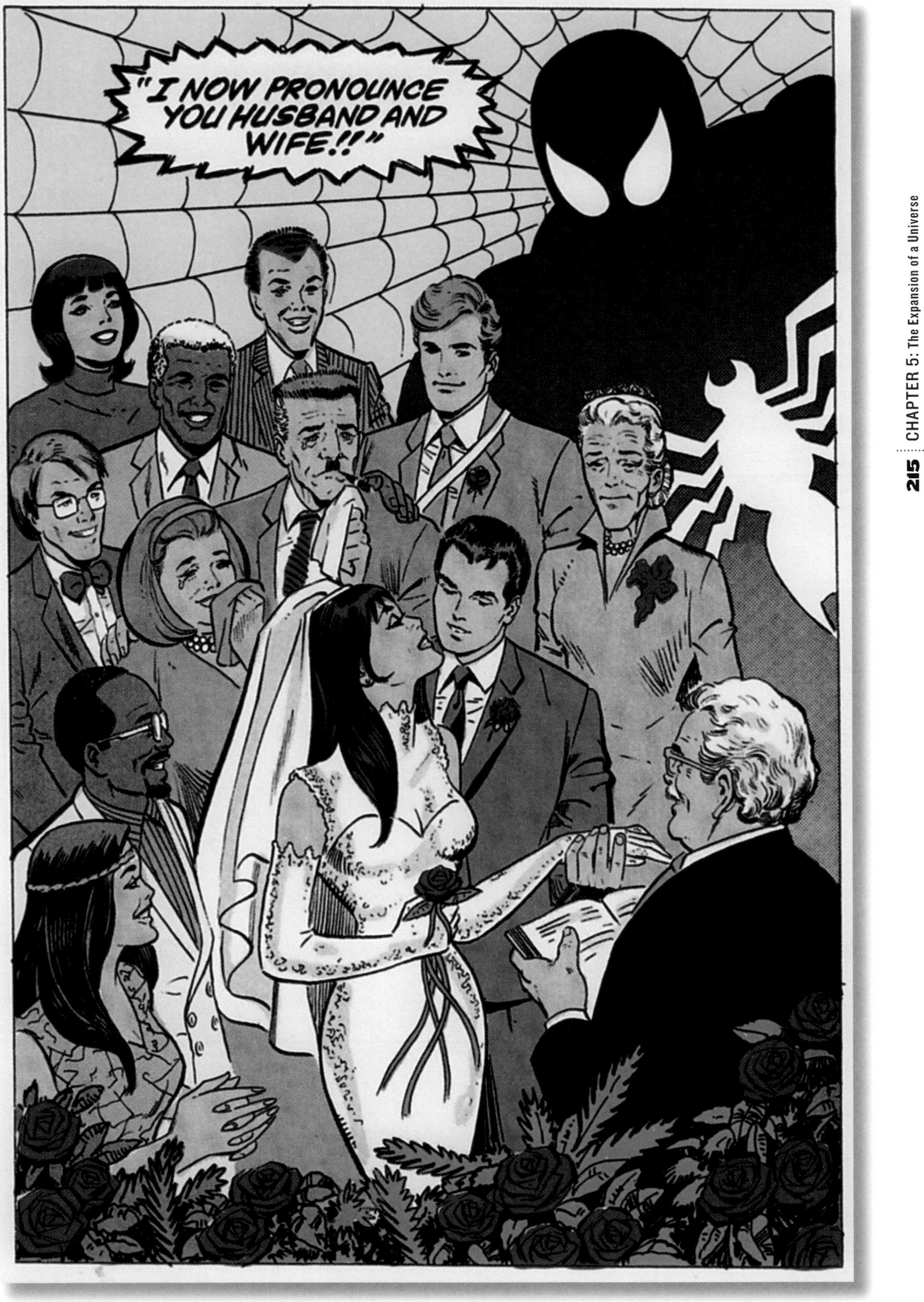
"I NOW PRONOUNCE YOU HUSBAND AND WIFE!!"

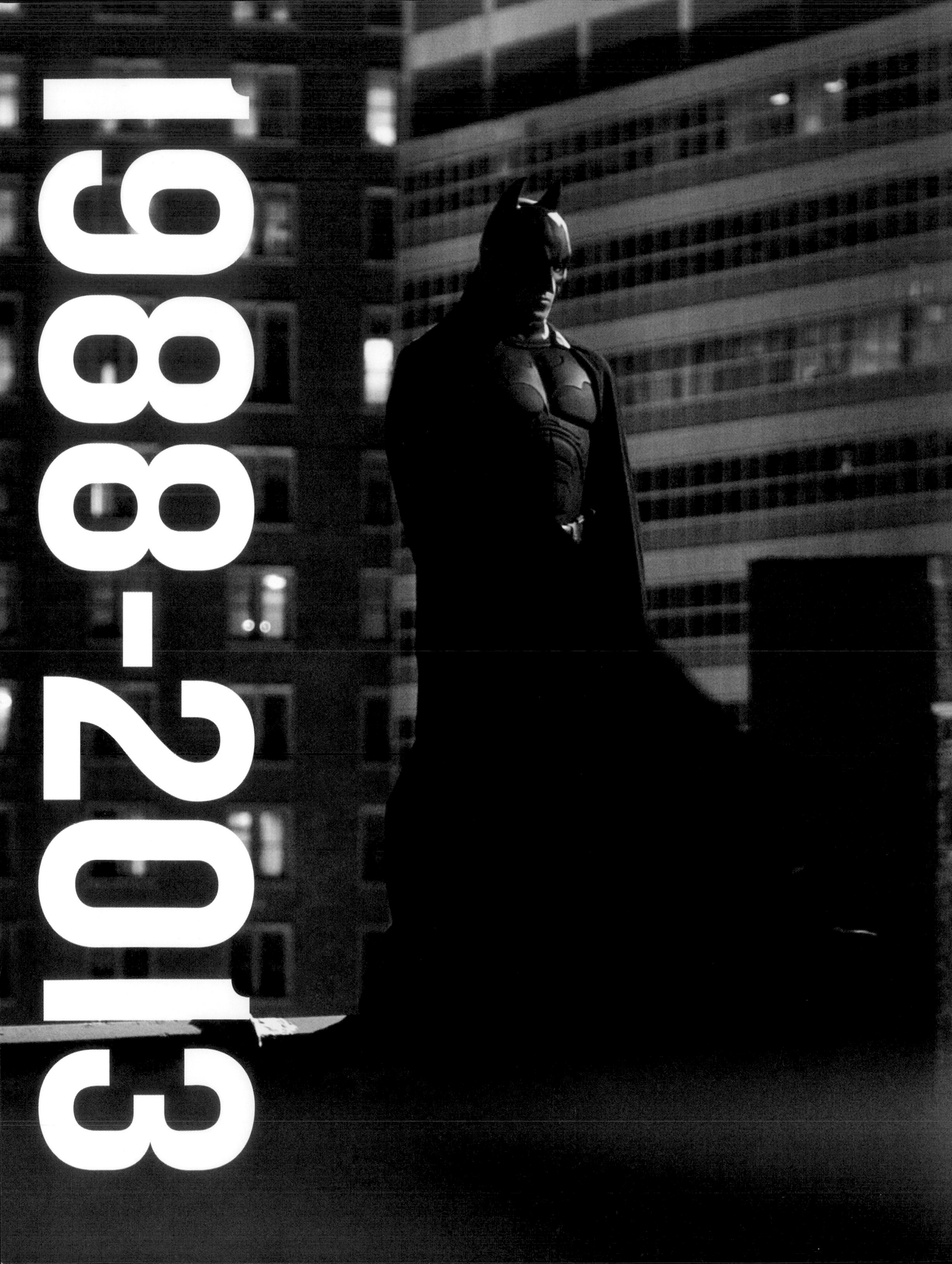
1988-2013

Part Three

A HERO ★ CAN BE ANYONE

Today . . . marks the tenth anniversary of the last recorded sighting of the Batman. Dead or retired, his fate remains unknown. Our younger viewers will not remember the Batman. A recent survey shows that most high schoolers consider him a myth."

The fatuous talking head at the beginning of Frank Miller's seminal 1986 four-issue series, *Batman: The Dark Knight Returns*, was more inaccurate than she knew. In the consciousness of most Americans, "the" Batman—the dark avenger of the late 1930s—hadn't been sighted for five decades.

When Miller's series debuted, the Batman best celebrated in popular culture was still the 1960s television Batman: brightly colored, honorable, and corny. This iteration of Batman was propagated for decades through various cartoons, endless afternoon re-runs of the ABC show, and ongoing public appearances by Adam West and Burt Ward. As writer Michael J. Uslan put it, "For twenty years, whenever anyone wrote about Batman in the press, they always attached the words: 'POW!, ZAP!,' and 'WHAM!'"

OVERLEAF: A darker Batman stands vigil over the 21st century: Christian Bale from *Batman Begins* (2004). BELOW: Neal Adams was the first artist to rehabilitate Batman to his nocturnal roots (*Batman #251*, 1973). RIGHT: Frank Miller's *The Dark Knight Returns* (1986).

The eventual rehabilitation of "the" Batman had begun discreetly—away from the view of the masses—but intently, over at DC Comics just as the 1960s were coming to an exhausted close. Denny O'Neil and Neal Adams—who teamed up so persuasively on *Green Lantern/Green Arrow*—were beginning a several-year process of returning the Caped Crusader to his nocturnal roots. Much to the relief of fans, Batman again looked like a character who could strike terror in the hearts of criminals, just the way Bruce Wayne originally planned it in 1939. For Adams, the mission was a simple one: "Every kid in America knows what Batman should be and it's not on the television show. I did the Batman that I remembered as a kid. How do you get it to be dark and gritty again? Well, you draw it better."

The world Batman inherited in 1986 had changed considerably since his primetime television heyday as well. The chaotic and refracted urban landscape that cultivated such vigilante characters as Dirty Harry and the Punisher had, in many ways, gotten worse. The Reagan Administration of the 1980s displayed more empathy for what Theodore Roosevelt called the "malefactors of great wealth" than it did for malefactors born out of poverty or neglect. "You don't have many suspects who are innocent of a crime," proclaimed Edwin Meese, Reagan's second Attorney General, while dismissing the necessity of Mirandizing suspects. The President himself—talking about the problem of the homeless, which had exploded during his tenure—was quoted on television as saying, "People who are sleeping on the grates, the homeless, are homeless by choice, you might say."

"You've got rights. Lots of rights," growled Miller's Dark Knight to some miscreant who foolishly tried to keep Batman from punching his lights out. "Sometimes I count them just to make myself feel crazy." This new Batman had been aged up to be nearly sixty years old, a barrel-chested, grizzled, self-proclaimed enforcer, covered with scar tissue and a cowl. Although frequent comic book readers might have encountered an aged Superman in an imaginary story, for example, they had never seen anything like this:

This should be agony. I should be a mass of aching muscle, unable to move. And, were I an older man,

I surely would . . . but I'm a man of thirty—of twenty again. The rain on my chest is a baptism—I'm born again . . . I smell their fear—and it is sweet.

The inspiration was personal: "I had this terrible thing happen when I was twenty-nine years old," recounted Miller. "I realized I was about to turn thirty and Batman was twenty-nine. And that meant that I'd be older than Batman. And I just couldn't stand that thought. So I had to make him older, and everything else kind of sprang from that." Miller had transformed an escapist 1940s adventure hero into an older, calloused, established figure of law and order; it might be argued that Ronald Reagan had done the same thing for himself in the 1980s.

The four Dark Knight stories (printed in sequence as high-grade comic books) gave comic readers their first real vision of dystopia in the form of a Gotham City overrun by madmen, gangbangers, mutants, and an unforgiving heat wave. The air is so thick with moral and actual corruption that Bruce Wayne is forced to come out of retirement. In the densely illustrated and prodigiously prolix series, Batman—with a new "Robin," an eager and impulsive thirteen-year-old girl—is inexorable in his pursuit of justice. Miller not only understood Batman, but thought deeply about what makes superheroes tick: "[Batman] would be the guy you'd want to have when you're threatened by a criminal, but you probably wouldn't want to have dinner with him . . . this would be a very, very strange man, and I don't think he'd be a particularly nice person to be around." Neal Adams observes, "Miller is so significant and important to Batman because he made him an elder god. He will never change. He is Batman. Until he dies, he will be Batman."

Where the comic book writers of the 1970s—Denny O'Neil, Gerry Conway—had nudged their superheroes into the worlds of the headlines, Miller swung down on a Batrope and kicked his into uncharted territory. As writer J. Michael Straczynski put it, "In a comic book world that was still pretty much limited by the Comics Code, The Dark Knight broke out most characters in ways that no one had ever dared do before. It brought an adult point of view to comics."

Miller might have rested on his laurels, but he turned again to Batman in 1987; a year after excavating the Dark Knight's omega, he decided to weave a tale about Batman's alpha. In tandem with the scrupulously uncluttered art of David Mazzucchelli, four consecutive issues of Batman (numbers 404 to 407) were devoted to the Caped Crusader's origins—or at least those origins as reconsidered by Miller and Mazzucchelli in Batman: Year One. The series was more of a police procedural than a wham-bam superhero story (reflecting, perhaps, Miller's interest in trench-coated detectives) as it covers not only Bruce Wayne's embryonic steps to becoming Batman, but the early career of Jim (later Commissioner) Gordon, Batman's uncomfortable ally on the police force. Within a year, working on his own and with Mazzucchelli, Miller officially sent TV's campy Batman down the Batpole one last time, banished to the Batcave for the foreseeable future.

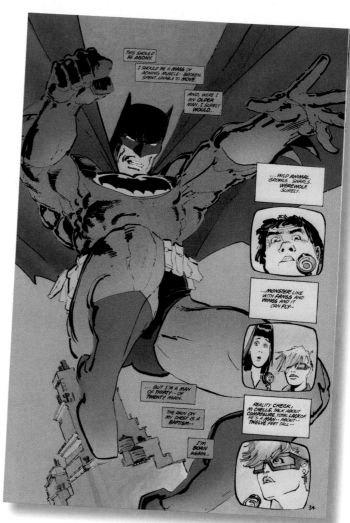

Almost incidentally, Mazzucchelli managed to reframe not only the conception of Batman, but to define the entire era in a comment he made at the back of the Batman: Year One paperback anthology, released in 2002, fifteen years after the initial series:

> With Year One, [Miller and I] sought to craft a credible Batman, grounded in a world we recognize. But did we go too far? Once a depiction veers toward realism, each new detail releases a torrent of questions that exposes the absurdity at the heart of the genre. The more "realistic" superheroes become, the less believable they are.

The wings of the Dark Knight are spread impressively wide, and that shadow extends further than that of any other hero into the consciousness of the 21st century. But the question that Mazzucchelli poses is equally penetrating and persuasive: "Did we go too far?"

CHAPTER SIX

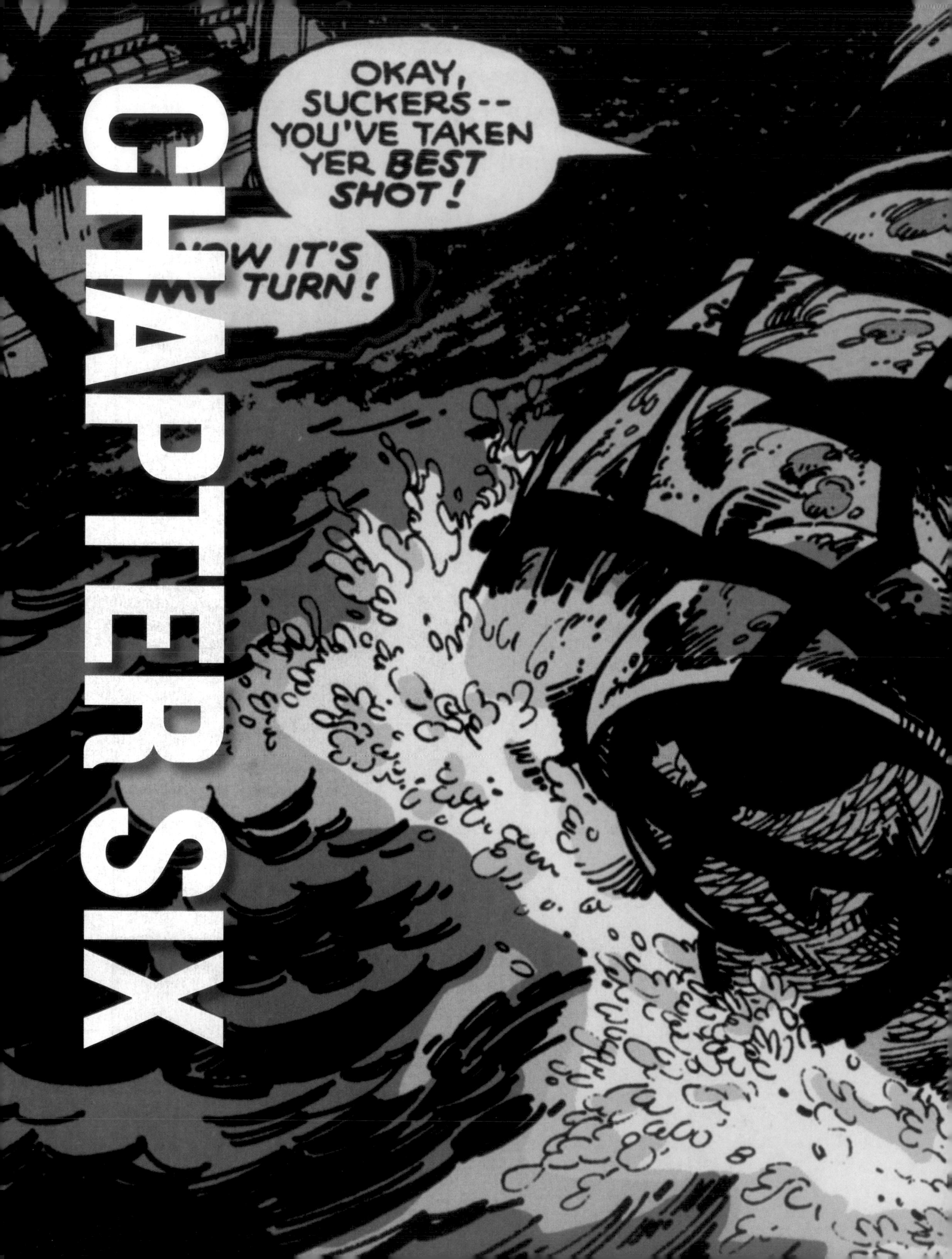
OKAY, SUCKERS-- YOU'VE TAKEN YER BEST SHOT!
NOW IT'S MY TURN!

CREATURES OF THE NIGHT
REIGN OF THE
DARK
SUPERHERO!

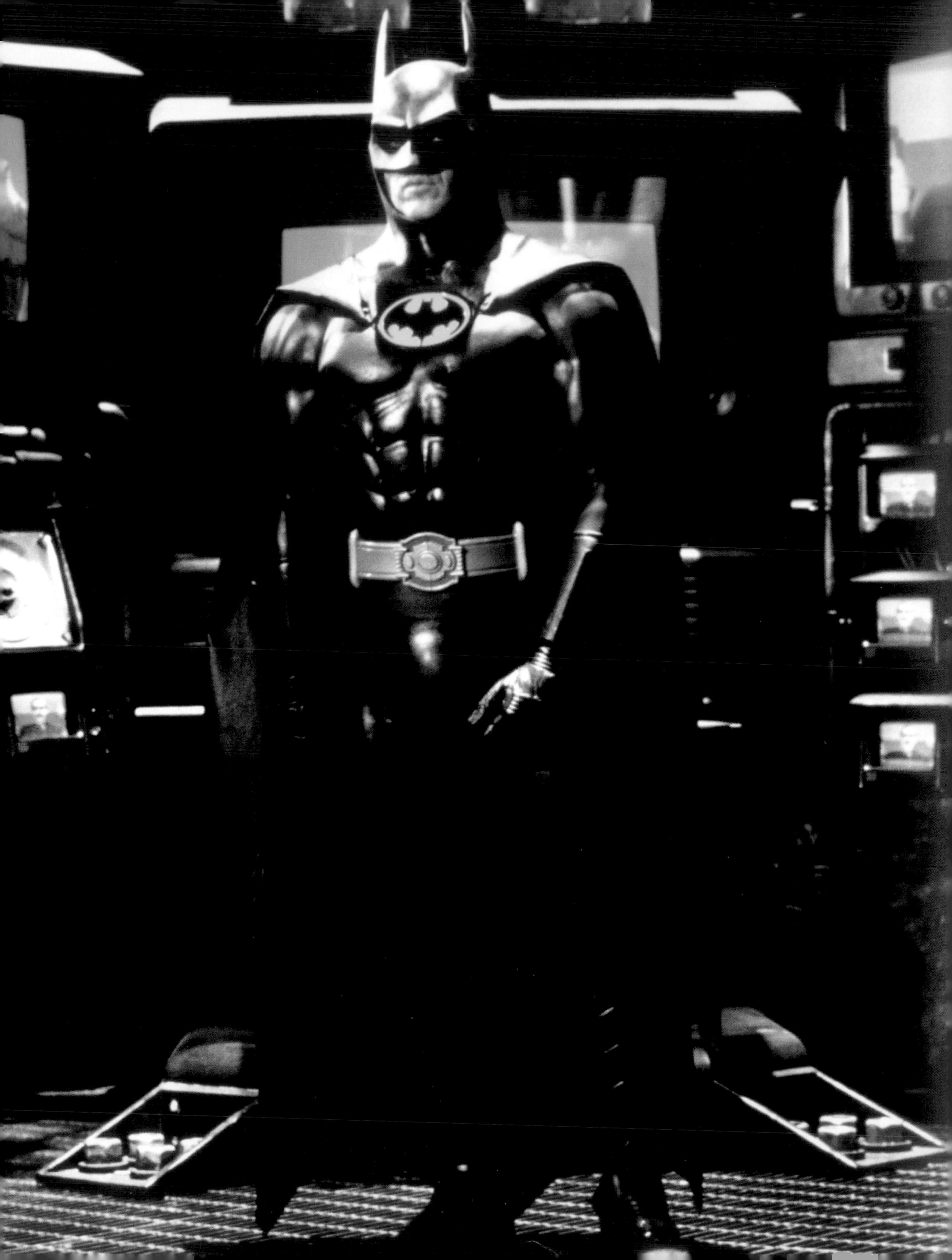

GENIES OUT OF THE BOTTLE
The Corporatization of the Comic Book Industry

Since the late days of the Depression, the comic book industry had been comprised of several immutable constants: the firms had been run by professionals who had their roots in the publishing and distribution business; the companies were based in New York; they were relatively small in nature, staffed largely by middle-aged adults who usually commuted at night to homes in the tri-state area, where they sat in armchairs and read literature other than comic books.

That would all begin to change in the early 1970s, when a new generation of comic book writers and artists entered the field, former fans who had grown up with the medium and were eager to intertwine the adventures of their favorite superheroes (or at least the superheroes they were assigned by their middle-aged editors) with the issues of their day: Denny O'Neil, Neal Adams, Gerry Conway, Len Wein, Marv Wolfman. "For a long time," said Conway, "we'd say that comics were going to be dead in ten years. By the late '70s, enough of us probably believed that that we started saying, well, maybe we better find other ways to make a living." Some of the '70s superstars (Conway, Wolfman) would follow Stan Lee's lead (once again) when he moved to Los Angeles in 1981, in his case to pursue new venues on behalf of Marvel in film and television. O'Neil and Wein would stay in comics, but expand their acumen to edit the work of newer, edgier talents.

These creators left the field to the next generation—writers and artists who had been inspired by *their* attempts to make comic books more relevant. A surprisingly large number of the next generation's most spectacular talents came from the United Kingdom, largely from the northern part of England. They included Alan Moore, Grant Morrison, Neil Gaiman, Dave McKean, Dave Gibbons, and Mark Millar, young creators who expanded into other non–comic book areas such as punk music, novels, graphic design, and the occasional dabbling in occultism.

The diverse and non-mainstream backgrounds of these U.K. artists helped to transition the increasingly dull comics of the mid

OVERLEAF: Wolverine bares his teeth in *Uncanny X-Men* #132 (April 1980), signaling the dawn of the grim-and-gritty age. OPPOSITE: Michael Keaton as Batman (1989) ushers in the bat-conquest of the media age. ABOVE: A roundup of artists and writers who either went west or expanded their horizons in the late 1970s (from top): Denny O'Neil, Jack Kirby and Neal Adams, Marv Wolfman and Len Wein, Gerry Conway.

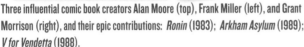

Three influential comic book creators Alan Moore (top), Frank Miller (left), and Grant Morrison (right), and their epic contributions: *Ronin* (1983); *Arkham Asylum* (1989); *V for Vendetta* (1988).

1980s and 1990s into frequently surprising departures from the norm. "It was time for us to come along. The American comic had become focused on this scorecard mentality," said Morrison. "Is the Thing stronger than the Hulk? It was a very strange time. It became almost like stamp collecting."

As different as Morrison's generation of creators was from their predecessors, the biggest change may have been in the consumer base. As comic books moved through their sixth decade, it became clear that many longtime readers weren't going anywhere—they were reading comics into their thirties and forties and they didn't want to read the same old stories where the Flash foils the Mirror Master from robbing a bank. They wanted growth and development, just as they themselves were growing and developing. "So you have this conflict between the desire of an ongoing readership and the nature of these superhero characters which is static," said Conway.

The maturing audience encouraged the new brand of creators to venture into more complex territory—much of it darker than the usual superhero fare, playing into the stereotype of the "grim-and-gritty" era. The comic book publishers, realizing that their audience was diversifying, created discrete imprints for this mature work. Vertigo Comics, an imprint marketed as "suggested for mature readers" and including well-received titles such as Gaiman's psychological fantasy series, *The Sandman* and Alan Moore's *V for Vendetta*, found a home at DC Comics. Epic Comics was Marvel Comics' repository for creator-oriented titles that explored mature storylines outside of the Marvel Universe, often without the approval of the Comics Code (Marvel followed Epic with another mature-themed imprint, MAX, in 2001). A new venue emerged for expanded, more complicated superhero-oriented tales: the graphic novel.

There had always been attempts at expanding comic book storytelling into longer, non-serial, self-contained forms—the burst of sword-and-sorcery one-offs in the early 1970s, for example—but publishers realized there was a new market for one-shot tales, as long as the characters were familiar and the printing of the books (often hardbound and softbound, concurrently) exhibited the durability of a novel, rather than the transience of a pulp comic book. One of the most successful of these early attempts was Grant Morrison and painter/illustrator Dave McKean's *Arkham*

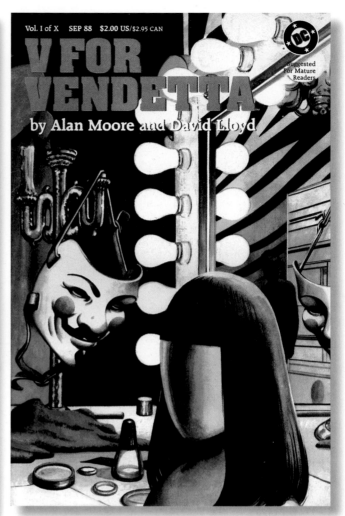

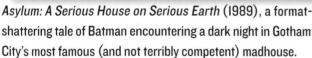

Asylum: A Serious House on Serious Earth (1989), a format-shattering tale of Batman encountering a dark night in Gotham City's most famous (and not terribly competent) madhouse.

The trade paperback was a "win-win," giving publishers another venue in which to print (and reprint and re-reprint) popular stories, while allowing literary critics to take the non-disposable publications seriously. Perhaps no other publication benefitted more than Moore's *Watchmen*, which was placed on *Time* magazine's list of "The Hundred Greatest Novels Ever" in 2005—the only comic book narrative to earn that honor—and eventually moved millions of copies. But neither *Watchmen* nor *The Dark Knight Returns* nor a host of other "graphic novels" were actually graphic novels; they were paperback (or hard-cover) compilations of material that had appeared previously in serial comic books, a distinction that was largely lost. Alan Moore personally detested the lack of clarity: "The problem is that 'graphic novel' just came to mean 'expensive comic book' and so . . . [DC or Marvel would] stick six issues of whatever worthless piece of crap they happened to be publishing lately

under a glossy cover and call it *The She-Hulk Graphic Novel*."

Be that as it may, there were vast new marketing possibilities for ancillary material. Some of this was because both DC and Marvel would be folded into larger and larger conglomerates as the 20th century drew to a close. The DC stable of characters benefitted from a well-orchestrated corporate transition when Warner Communications—which had already been instrumental in bringing Superman to the big screen through their film studio connections—merged into the mammoth corporation of Time Warner in 1990.

Since the success of the Superman film in 1978, there had been a slow, but relentless, drive to put Batman back on the screen, and Warner Bros. was the obvious studio to make it happen. One of the early producers on the project, Michael Uslan, thought it was time to break through the campy veneer that had kept Batman from the larger public he deserved. The Miller *Dark Knight* saga gave the embryonic project the credibility it needed to move forward, and in 1988 Warner Bros. hired idiosyncratic filmmaker Tim Burton to bring Batman to a new generation. According to writer Grant Morrison:

Tim Burton related Batman to things that were happening then—the fetish underground, the transgressive elements, the Gothic elements which were coming out of music as well. There was a real heavy punk element to the whole thing and Batman very quickly adapts to that; he was a black leather figure in a cave.

The rising influence of Batman conferred a new spotlight on his arch-nemesis, the Joker. Brian Bolland's deranged conception for *The Killing Joke* (1988) inspired Jack Nicholson's portrayal in *Batman* (1989).

Burton was not a comic book fan—he claimed he never knew how to follow the way the panels moved on a page—but he was inspired by another progeny of the *Dark Knight* saga, a one-off graphic novel from 1988 called *Batman: The Killing Joke*. A terrifying story of the Joker at his most disturbingly deranged, it was illustrated by Brian Bolland and written by Alan Moore. Moore and Bolland's Joker would provide the inspiration for Jack Nicholson's brilliant portrayal in the Burton film. The final result, *Batman*, released as a tentpole blockbuster in summer 1989, racked up an astounding $150,000,000 in its initial domestic release, and led to three sequels (of variable quality). Through their association with Warner Bros., DC Comics proved they could deliver first-rate films based on their signature characters.

Marvel, on the other hand, seemed to have nothing but bad luck; its parent organization was bought by Revlon founder and stock market whiz Ronald Perelman in 1989; eventually, due to some bad moves with affiliated companies, the complex corporate entity that owned Marvel Comics and its characters filed for bankruptcy. During this time, Marvel kept trying to expand its reach in various marketing fields such as action figures and video games, but the Holy Grail of a blockbuster film or two had eluded Marvel completely, despite Stan Lee's best efforts as ambassador-with-portfolio in Hollywood. Marvel sold the rights to some of its most famous characters for bargain-basement prices to independent studios on the lowest end of the food chain. Despite a much-trumpeted deal in 1990 with filmmaker James Cameron to bring Spider-Man to the screen (which never happened), Marvel was stuck with dogs so cheaply made (*The Punisher, Captain*

No supervillain could have dropped as many bombs as Marvel Comics did in their movie ventures in the early 1990s. *Captain America* (1991) went straight to video, as did *The Fantastic Four* (1994).

America) that they barely made it onto videocassettes. Most embarrassing was the 1994 version of *The Fantastic Four*, which was made (for a rumored $1.5 million) only to hold onto the screen rights: the final dismal result was never meant for commercial distribution.

Marvel would eventually find its groove in Hollywood by the 21st century, but the late 1980s represented a massive sea-change in the comic book business, a Super-genie that would be impossible to put back into a bottle—even a bottle as large as the one that holds the city of Kandor. For Gerry Conway, the corporate evolution of the industry was the biggest game-changer of all:

While we loved what we were doing in the '70s, I don't believe we thought that it mattered and certainly our publishers didn't think that it mattered. If a particular issue didn't do well, that was fine, there was next month. We didn't have this sense that careers revolved around choices that you make for this particular character a year in advance. I think that's a creative soul-killer for the business.

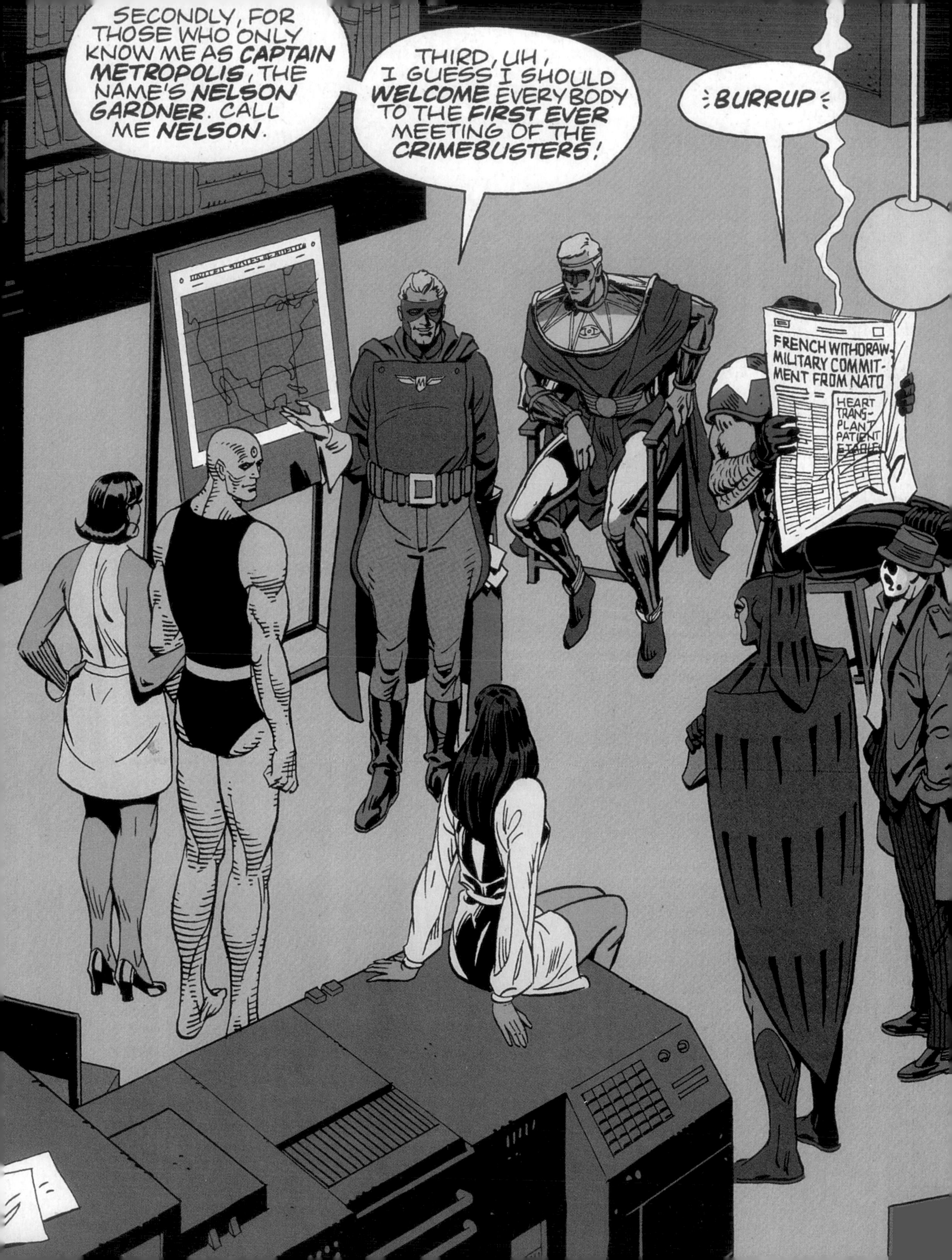
SECONDLY, FOR THOSE WHO ONLY KNOW ME AS CAPTAIN METROPOLIS, THE NAME'S NELSON GARDNER. CALL ME NELSON.
THIRD, UH, I GUESS I SHOULD WELCOME EVERYBODY TO THE FIRST EVER MEETING OF THE CRIMEBUSTERS!
BURRUP
FRENCH WITHDRAW MILITARY COMMITMENT FROM NATO
HEART TRANSPLANT PATIENT STABLE

THE SORT OF COSTUME THAT COULD REALLY MESS YOU UP
Watchmen

OPPOSITE: The first meeting of the Crimebusters—an unlikely alliance from *Watchmen* #2 (1986); text by Alan Moore, art by Dave Gibbons. LEFT: Torch-passing: Alan Moore and Jack Kirby at a 1985 comic book convention. RIGHT: DC's *Swamp Thing* deepened its roots under Moore (*Swamp Thing* #47, 1986).

The summer of 1986 may well have been the last anxiety-free period in superhero history. The final installment of *The Dark Knight Returns* would hit the stands in June, and in September the first installment of the twelve-issue limited series *Watchmen*—written by Alan Moore and illustrated by Dave Gibbons—would make its debut. Taken together, the two series would irrevocably change the conventional wisdom about superheroes. "I like to joke that when it comes to superheroes," said Frank Miller, "Alan Moore provided the autopsy and I provided the brass-band funeral."

Moore was an unconventional writer, even by comic book standards. Born in 1956 in the small English city of Northampton, where he lives to this day, Moore, by his own admission, hadn't been to a barbershop since he was a teenager. A Merlin-like figure who embraces necromancy and derides capitalism with equal fervor, Moore began his career in British comics, where his work attracted the attention of Len Wein, then an editor at DC. He engaged Moore—who continued to bang stories out at his kitchen table in Northampton—to write unpredictable spins on characters as varied as Swamp Thing and Superman. Some readers (and editors) were put off by his perspective—"I didn't realize that incest and necrophilia were still frowned on socially over here," he said—but fans sat up and took notice.

Early in 1985, Moore had a notion about an extended story that would be ignited by the death of a superhero and its reverberations through his former fellow teammates. It was important to Moore that the team be composed of heroes who had some real history behind them; luckily for him, DC Comics had recently acquired the Charlton line, which had some success with a few B-level characters in the 1960s: Captain Atom, Blue Beetle, and Steve Ditko's trenchcoated mystery man, the Question. "That'd be a good way to start a comic book: have a famous superhero found dead," said Moore. "As the mystery unraveled, we would be led deeper and deeper into the real heart of this superhero's world, and show a reality that was very different to the general public image of the superhero." Although intrigued by the possibilities of using the Charlton characters, DC editor Dick Giordano soon realized that Moore's epic vision would render these potentially lucrative

properties unusable or extinct; it was politely suggested that Moore create them out of his own considerable imagination.

Working with the precise and affectionate imagery of his fellow countryman Dave Gibbons, Moore created a credible set of 1940s heroes, called the Minutemen, and their figurative and literal descendants, the Crimebusters. (Although the series would be called *Watchmen*, no group of superheroes calling themselves the "Watchmen" ever appear.) They include Nite Owl, a nocturnal paraphernalia-riddled crimefighter redolent of Batman; and Rorschach, a trenchcoated mystery man with an ever-shifting inkblot of a face. Any readers who noticed a generational shift from the eager-beavers of the 1940s (who embodied the values of the DC characters) and the querulous do-gooders of the atomic age (Marvel Comics types) had been paying attention. What united the nearly dozen disparate characters in *Watchmen* was Moore's basic contempt for the unvarnished enthusiasm in superhero comics: "Actually, a person dressing in a mask and going around beating up criminals is a vigilante psychopath. What would that Batman-type, driven, vengeance-fueled vigilante be like in the real world? And the short answer is: a nutcase."

The complex twelve-issue story arc of *Watchmen* played out in a parallel universe to our own. In it, Richard Nixon has remained president of the United States into the 1980s and America has built a carapace of world domination, aided largely by the benign complicity of Dr. Manhattan, an atomically enhanced scientist of extraordinary powers who is, for the most part, thankfully on our side. Still, the United States and the U.S.S.R. are tied in a Gordian Knot of mutual deterrence. The death of a mercenary superhero named the Comedian—an ironical, rather than amusing, bully—sets off a chain reaction of events that involves several generations of superheroes dating back to the late 1930s. Moore's narrative, which segues in and out of time, space, and medium, comes to a climax when a lapsed superhero, hyper-brilliant megalomaniac and businessman Adrian Veidt (once known as the superhero Ozymandias), decides on his own to sever the Gordian Knot of global conflict (already coming to a head in Afghanistan) by transporting an immense mutated intelligence form to New York City. The alien form essentially explodes and kills more than three million people, providing an uneasy tabula rasa on which to build a new, coherent society.

Folded into the epic were the multiple levels of Moore's Baroque (and Mannerist) leanings— classical allusions, song lyrics, parallel texts, spurious source material—mixed in with a love for popular culture and superhero lore (a major malefactor asserts that he's smarter than "a Republic serial villain"—a reference to the

cheesy 1940s serial adventures of Captain Marvel and Co.). Gibbons' highly controlled, ordered, rectilinear panel layout not only "quoted" previous layouts from the early 1960s, but provided a contained prism through which the madness of Moore's method could be discerned, without driving the reader completely around the bend. Still, *Watchmen* was a vivid tapestry that benefited from multiple readings: "This is what I've been trying to explain to these stupid bastards for the past twenty years," wrote Moore. "[My work] was designed to exploit all the things that comic books can do and that no other medium can. I wanted to show off just what the possibilities of the comic book medium were."

The most effective and influential reading of *Watchmen* came with its gloss on the idea of fantastical characters confronting the quotidian existence of the real world: if your superhuman boyfriend teleports you through time and space, you just might get sick to your stomach and vomit; if you maintain a secret crime-cave, it might just require a lot of expensive upkeep and cleaning fees; if you gained your astonishing powers from potent radiation, you might just give your sidekick cancer. And, of course, if you were the mightiest being in the world, you might just want to control it. In a sequence of panels where an older, paunchier version of Nite Owl gives the retired superheroine Silk Spectre (whom he is awkwardly trying to seduce) a tour of his secret crime-cave, he admits:

"...BUT EVENTUALLY I REALIZED THE COMEDIAN WAS *RIGHT*: IT'S ALL CRAP DRESSED UP WITH A LOT OF *FLASH* AND *THUNDER*.

I MEAN, WHO NEEDS ALL THIS *HARD-WARE* TO CATCH *HOOKERS* AND *PURSE-SNATCHERS*? I MEAN *REALLY*?

HMM. WHAT'S *THAT*?

PROTOTYPE *EXO-SKELETON*. FIRST TIME I TRIED *MOVING* IN IT, IT BROKE MY *ARM*. NEVER AGAIN.

JESUS. THAT SOUNDS LIKE THE SORT OF COSTUME THAT COULD REALLY MESS YOU *UP*.

IS THERE ANY *OTHER* SORT?

"Here is the primary difference between the before-and-after *Watchmen* scenario," said writer J. Michael Straczynski. "Before *Watchmen*, the primary threats or darkness in comic books was about some supervillain's complicated plot to seize all the gold in the world. What *Watchmen* did was bring in the larger social elements. It spoke of the darkness inside of us, not just the external threats, and that was something that galvanized the industry." When the series was ultimately completed and eventually published in paperback, *Watchmen* became the darling of literary critics, a pop-culture manifesto that could be taken seriously. In a 2005 review in the *New York Times*, Dave Itzkoff wrote, "If we imbue our champions with the weaknesses of ordinary mortals, Moore asks, and confine them to a cosmos where good and evil are subjective notions and right never triumphs over wrong, what's the point of having heroes at all?"

Watchmen became one of the most imitated comic books of all time; one trope, about a government commission that banned superheroes, would pop up again in nearly a dozen different storylines in various comics over the years. And the book's mature themes, stark visuals, and undercurrent of nihilistic violence would feed the undercurrent of superhero comic books far into the 21st century. According to Len Wein, "*Watchmen* and *The Dark Knight Returns*

were both very violent books. They were meant to be exceptions to the rule. They weren't intended to be a blueprint for the industry to follow, they were intended to be something to show you here's what could have happened—let's not go do that. But they were hugely successful and so everybody started to do those books."

As much as Moore borrowed from the real world, the real world also tapped into *Watchmen*. In 1987, the Tower Commission Report, which investigated the Reagan Administration's questionable dealings in supplying arms to foreign radical forces, came out with a condemnation of the administration's "lax attitude" to international law: *"Quis custodiet ipsos custodes"* ran the epigraph of the report—"Who watches the Watchmen?," the same slogan that runs through the Moore/Gibbons saga.

Given the immense influence and cultural imprimatur of *Watchmen*, perhaps Frank Miller's assessment of Alan Moore's occupational status was incorrect. Perhaps Moore was not the coroner of the superhero world at all, but rather its psychotherapist: a psychotherapist who snuck away from his patients during the last two weeks in August, and hightailed it to a small city in England instead, leaving his poor, pathologically damaged superclients to fend for themselves.

OPPOSITE: The essential argument of Watchmen: superheroes are very different from you and me—and not necessarily in a good way. Nite Owl and Silk Spectre in *Watchmen* #7. LEFT: In the climax of the *Watchmen* saga (#12), Dr. Manhattan confronts the deluded Adrian Veidt, who is about to unleash cataclysm on New York City. RIGHT: Dr. Manhattan towers over his adversaries (and breaks up Dave Gibbons' controlled panel arrangement) in *Watchmen* #4.

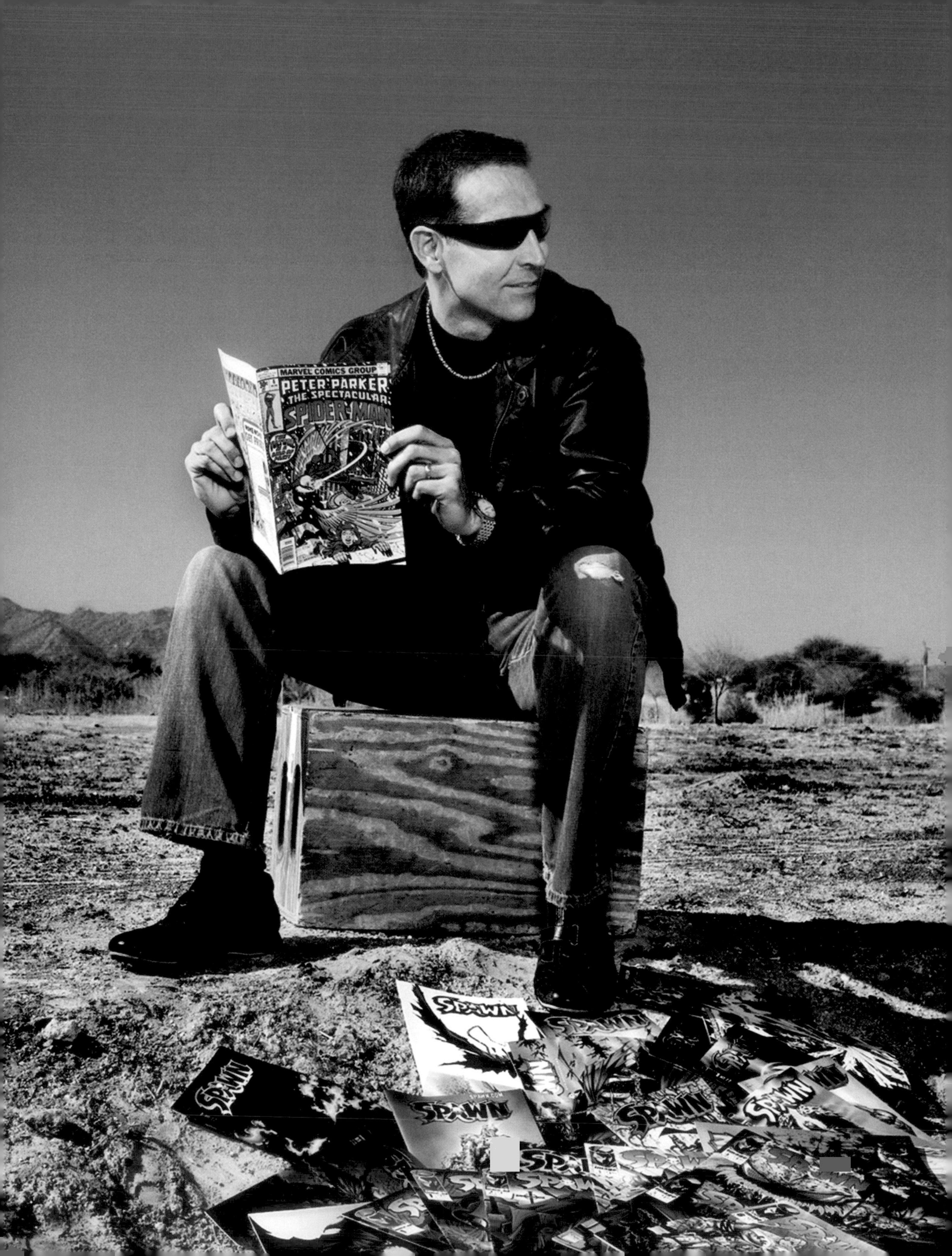
MARVEL COMICS GROUP
PETER PARKER
THE SPECTACULAR
SPIDER-MAN
SPAWN

WHEN THE BULLPEN QUITS
Image Comics

t's probably not coincidental that "▐" is the first letter in "Image Comics." When seven of the comic book industry's most popular artists stepped away from the corporate halls of Marvel and DC to form the most successful publishing consortium outside of the Big Two since the days of Captain Marvel in the 1940s, they were asserting their independence and their personal visions. Some in the comic book industry exhumed the same snarky comment bandied about when Charlie Chaplin, Mary Pickford, Douglas Fairbanks, and D.W. Griffith broke away from the Hollywood studio system to create United Artists in 1919: "The lunatics have taken over the asylum." Fans and older readers, however, were thrilled to have a new, independent company that had the motivation—and the talent—to bring another generation of characters to the super-hero universe.

The seven founders of Image —Erik Larsen, Todd McFarlane, Mark Silvestri, Jim Lee, Rob Liefeld, Jim Valentino, and Whilce Portacio—possessed powers far beyond those of mortal comic book artists; they were superhero superstars, artists who had cultivated a loyal following, with their names burnished on covers in type almost as large as the superhero logos. McFarlane's idiosyncratic and fanciful rendition of Spider-Man produced a two-million-copy seller with *Spider-Man* #1 in 1990; Liefeld's sleek, steroidal style kickstarted the four-million-copy selling *X-Force* #1 (featuring the previously dubbed New Mutants). In the big-stakes poker game of blockbuster comics, Jim Lee saw his colleagues and raised them in 1991—utilizing his skill for populating his panels with pulsating power—with *X-Men* #1, which set the record for a single title: 7.8 million copies. With such success, McFarlane, Liefeld, and Lee had everything a comic book artist could want.

Except control. Since the days of Siegel and Shuster, publishers held almost all of the cards. Although by the 1990s artists and writers were gaining some concessions from the publishers—the return of original art, a small share of royalties, top billing, and so forth—they were still confined by the fact that the superheroes

Dear Len and Ted,
I just finished reading issue #192 of Justice League of America. Stunning. This month's tale was the best of all my DCs I picked up. Centering around one member of the group (Red Tornado) and at the same time involving the other heroes was an excellent idea. Even though there were 25 pages, I thought that my reading ended too soon.
Red Tornado has fast become one of my favorite heroes. It is about time that he starts acting like the hero I know he can be.
As for the art, what can I say? Welcome back, George. Your pencils have been missed (although Buckler did a very admirable job in your absence). Besides being my favorite artist, you draw the best Red Tornado this side of the border (and the other side, too!)

Todd McFarlane
2476 Capitol Hill Cres. NW
Calgary, Alberta, Canada

(What can we say, Todd? We heartily agree!—TQF)

OPPOSITE: A man out sitting in his field: Todd McFarlane riffles through his hits. TOP AND LEFT: *Justice League of America* #192 (1981) inspired a young Canadian fan to riff on his favorite android, the Red Tornado. BOTTOM: Rob Liefeld, Stan the Man, and Todd McFarlane celebrate Marvel Comics, seemingly hours before Liefeld and McFarlane would depart.

they worked on (and adored) were owned by an increasingly bureaucratic corporate structure. An artist such as McFarlane could take a character like Spider-Man into the creative and financial stratosphere, but at the end of the day, Spidey had to swing back to corporate headquarters and report to the board of directors and their investors. As Larry Marder, Image's executive director, put it, "In the comics field you have two choices: Work on what you own. Or work on something someone else owns. Period."

The unmatched success of Jim Lee's *X-Men* #1 stretched across four variant covers (1991). OPPOSITE: The first Image Comics: Rob Liefeld's *Youngblood* (1992); McFarlane's *Spawn* #1.

By mid 1991, Liefeld and McFarlane were feeling particularly discontent with Marvel, which was putting limitations on what they could and could not draw or publish outside the company. There had been informal conversations among the duo and other artists about forming separate imprints, perhaps overseen by Malibu Comics on the West Coast. Around Christmas 1991, Liefeld, McFarlane, and Silvestri were in New York City for a highly publicized auction of original comic book art, including their own, and realized this was the moment to come together. As McFarlane, a baseball fanatic, put it, "I was always aware that they [publishers] can rotate you one at a time. You see it in sports, you can get rid of one player, they bring in another guy and eventually the franchise is okay. But, instead of us all going away one by one and doing an independent book each, why don't we do it together at the same place and leave on the same day? Make the impact." The key, according to McFarlane, was to engage Jim Lee, who was considered to be the "Golden Boy" of comics, a well-liked and amiable collaborator who had none of his colleagues' reputations

as hot-heads. Like many a superteam before them, the seven artists realized that, combined, their strengths were exponentially more powerful.

They called a meeting with the senior editorial staff at Marvel—the company where they all became celebrities—and announced, as McFarlane says, "We're leaving. We know we don't own your characters, we're not here to negotiate, we don't want anything. We're just going to tell you our reasons why we're leaving so that you may in the future do something about it so that next week you don't get another seven guys coming in the room saying they're leaving." Marvel, somewhat condescendingly, wished them the best of luck, and when the elevator opened up on the ground floor, McFarlane and Co. found themselves the co-conspirators of a new company: Image Comics. If they were daunted at the challenge of taking on two publishers who, between them, had a 95-percent market share, they didn't show it: "We weren't building a nuclear plant," said McFarlane. "We were putting ink on paper. Ink on paper; we got this thing down."

Image set up shop on the West Coast, under the initial aegis of Malibu Comics. The seven creators had their own respective studios within the publishing company, with two inviolate tenets: (1) Image would not own any creator's work; the creator would, and (2) No Image partner would interfere—creatively or financially—with any other partner's work. CNN's *Moneyline* program got ahold of the story, and after they broadcast the news that Marvel's seven top artists had bolted from the firm, Marvel's stock took a considerable hit. The program compared Image's secession to a "brain drain" and stated that the "box office" appeal of the individual artists superseded that of the Marvel characters they had been hired to illustrate. CNN predicted that readers might follow the Image artists to their new company "the way record buyers follow a rock star."

Being compared to rock stars suited the Image creators just fine, as they prepared to launch their respective titles in late spring/early summer 1992. By and large, their enormous

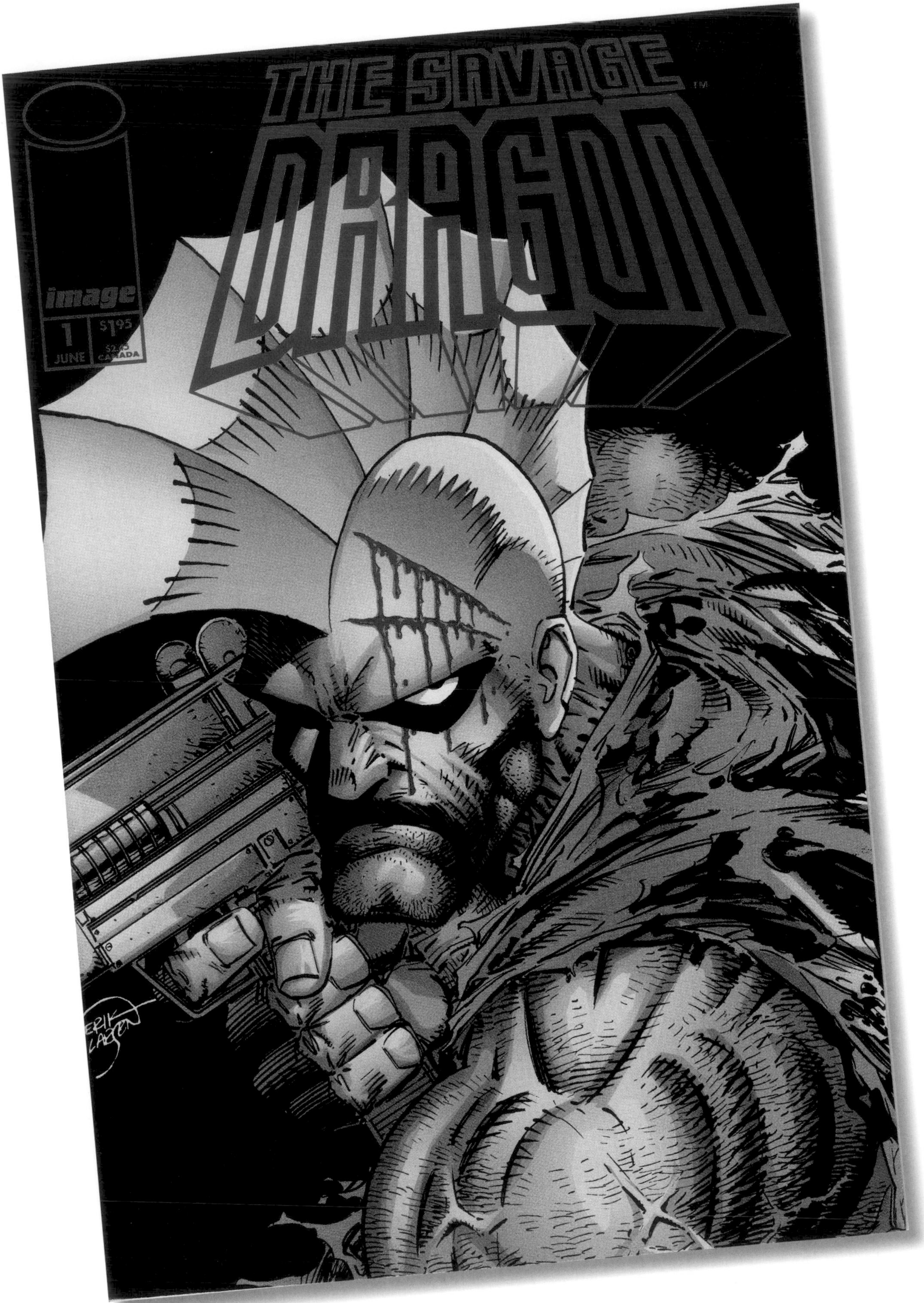
THE SAVAGE
DRAGON
TM
image
1
JUNE
$1.95
CANADA
ERIK LARSEN

OPPOSITE: Erik Larsen's *Savage Dragon* #1, the beginning of a record-breaking series. RIGHT: A new cover for a reprint of *The Walking Dead* #1, art by Charlie Adlard, from Tom Moore's original series—the title would become Image's most resilient series.

expectations were met, breaking all records for a non-DC/Marvel title: Liefeld's debut book, *Youngblood,* sold 1.5 million copies; McFarlane's *Spawn* broke that record within weeks by selling two million copies of the first issue. Lee's intergalactic, internecine *WildC.A.T.s* series would consistently top 1 million copies per issue during the first months of its run.

Inevitably, those remarkably high print runs became unsustainable. The utopian vision of Image Comics also proved difficult to sustain. Although, after its first year, Image was successful enough to break away from Malibu, some of the creators had difficulty meeting deadlines. Getting these highly anticipated books into stores became problematic, and that created an unfortunate breach of trust with loyal readers. Jim Lee would sell his Wildstorm line to DC Comics in 1998 and gradually the original seven-person partnership would splinter off. Even though the opportunity for creative freedom at Image was seductive to many outside artists, as Larry Marder put it, "They wanted the Great Power but not the Great Responsibility of owning and controlling their own intellectual property."

For some, the story of Image Comics is a paradigm of any new business model: a company founded on independence from corporate structure had better not throw out the "baby" of a well-run machine with the "bathwater" of bureaucratic interference. For others, it was significant that the creators at Image were all artists first and writers second. As Grant Morrison put it, "They'd grown up on Stan Lee and Jack Kirby, but Stan's comics were created from a literary standpoint. Image was artist-driven, so it was about sensation. I think American superhero fans [in the early 1990s] just wanted sensation and the generation of disaffected suburban kids who had grown up on wrestling and heavy metal and Goth were looking for something very cynical in the midst of plenty."

Certainly the Image heroes were grittier and overstepped the usual moral principles found in mainstream superhero comics—some of the characters wouldn't consider themselves heroes at all. The company also never bothered with any restrictions from the Comics Code Authority. Still, McFarlane's *Spawn* held on, through his and various hands, for more than 200 issues and counting. Erik Larsen's *Savage Dragon*, about an amiable hulking green powerhouse with a large dorsal fin on his head, proved popular enough to get its own animated series and extended publication into a second decade; Larsen set a record as having the longest uninterrupted tenure of artist and character in comic book history. Jim Valentino also made history with his urban vigilante, ShadowHawk, who began his crimefighting career after being intentionally infected with the HIV virus; ShadowHawk would be the first major comic book superhero to die from complications from AIDS.

More than twenty years after its inception, Image Comics is still hanging in there, with scores of different titles, including the zombie phenomenon *The Walking Dead*. Perhaps more than any one character or title, Image contributed the final breakthrough of comic book superheroes from childhood to adolescence to adulthood. As Todd McFarlane concluded:

> I had a good run on *Spider-Man* and I had a fun time with it, but when people ask me, are you ever going to do some Marvel and DC [titles]? The answer is always the same: no. Not because I think they're bad, but because it's the same answer if you ask me if I'm going back to high school. I liked high school, it was fun—but, I'm not going to do it again. It's in my past, I'm looking forward.

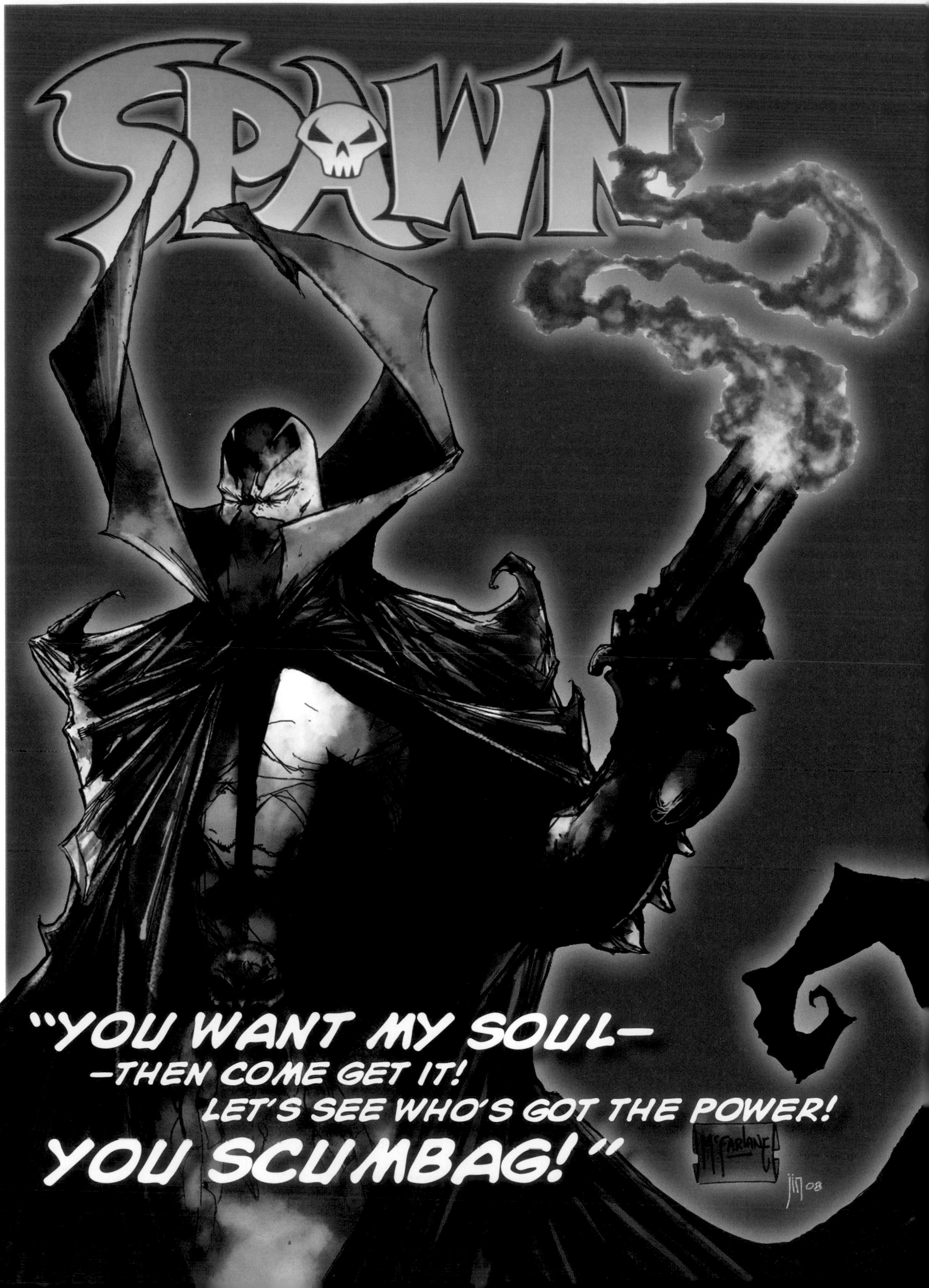
SPAWN
"YOU WANT MY SOUL—
—THEN COME GET IT!
LET'S SEE WHO'S GOT THE POWER!
YOU SCUMBAG!"

When Spawn appeared on the scene in 1992, reeking of fire and brimstone, he transformed the dreams of a sixteen-year-old comic book fan from Canada into the nightmares of the next generation.

Todd McFarlane had come up with the basic concept of Spawn when he was a high-schooler, and even designed a full costume. When it came time to create the figurehead character for his McFarlane Studio within the new Image Comics line, he pulled Spawn out of the drawer, added some fashionable spikes and chains to his look, and set forth the most popular new character of the last two decades.

McFarlane's brief tenure on *Batman* and more extended work on *Spider-Man* came in handy: Spawn had a blood-colored version of Batman's cloak, only on steroids, and his head-to-toe covering evoked Spider-Man. He was imbued with the ruthless drive for retribution so beloved of his era, additionally enshrouded by the sulfurous fumes of the underworld. In other words, to the adolescent comic readers of the 1990s, who were listening to Nine Inch Nails on their Discmans while wearing Marilyn Manson T-shirts, he was irresistible.

Spawn's origin was as carefully thought out as his costume. Al Simmons, a black covert assassin for a secret government agency, is betrayed by his boss, who puts out a contract on Simmons' life and has him killed. Simmons' lethal expertise attracts the attention of the Devil, or more accurately, one of his diabolical agents, the Malebolgia. Heartbroken at being separated from his beloved wife, Wanda, Simmons agrees to sign a pact with the Devil in order to see her one last time. But the Devil—never an advocate of fair play—sends Simmons back to earth as a Hellspawn, a hideously disfigured human in a grotesque costume, imbued with an infernal substance called necroplasm. Spawn—as he is now known—comes back to earth five years after his death, in a fetid back alley, confused and betrayed by his deal with the Devil.

> Why are you torturing me?!! What kind of sadistic pleasure are you getting from this?? You want my soul? Then come get it! Just try and get it! If you're going to screw me, I'm going to screw you! You want my soul—then come get it! Let's see who's got the power! You scumbag!

Seeking only to communicate with his wife and to protect his family, Spawn is constantly pushed by Malebolgia into committing acts of irrevocable violence. Caught in a Manichean crossfire, Spawn vainly attempts to draw upon the better angels of his increasingly demonic nature.

The fact that Spawn was not your grandfather's superhero—or maybe not even your brother's—was made abundantly clear by the fifth issue. When a convicted pedophile and serial killer procures an early release from prison, Spawn—fearing for the safety of his wife's child (fathered by his best friend in his absence, but that's another story)—tracks him down, only to find the pedophile is masquerading as an ice cream vendor. The authorities, who are investigating the pedophile on a missing child case, discover him—chained, carved up, and hanging from a rafter, with a popsicle stuck in his lifeless mouth—courtesy of Spawn's demonic retribution. "He's not like a Marvel character," said McFarlane, as if that issue's gruesome final page hadn't already proved the point. "He's not like a DC character. [In an Image book], I can do things untethered. We didn't have a comics code. I can do R-rated comic books now if I need to."

OPPOSITE: The ruthless power of Spawn. ABOVE: Early sketches of Spawn taken from McFarlane's notebooks, done during his high-school days.

Spawn operated on an almost mathematical principle of justice; because Batman, for example, refuses to kill the Joker and puts him in prison instead, each time the Joker escapes and kills ten people, the blood is on Batman's gloves. In Spawn's (and McFarlane's) consciousness, if you eliminate the villain from the get-go, you're a step ahead of the game. "He doesn't want to be the hero; he wants to lead a normal life," said McFarlane. "He has his own needs and he lets his emotions dictate his policy. That would never happen to a guy like Superman—he's too refined for that."

What Spawn lacked in refinement, he made up for in irony. The Devil had cursed him with yet another obstacle; every instance he used his superpowers, he expended a kind of reverse energy which limited his time on earth—a kind of existential library fine. Still, Spawn allotted his necroplasmic powers to impressive effect; he scrawled "I BEAT MY KIDS" all over the body of a child abuser (that didn't work out so well—it only made the abuser beat his kids more) and turned a rabid and vicious Klan leader into a black man (he was ultimately lynched by his own gang). It was also ironic to McFarlane and (some of) his readers that Spawn was both a black character and not a black character; Spawn's ravaged and decomposing skin allowed McFarlane to have a non-white hero at the center of his universe while not making it a defining aspect of his character. "I'd be [at a comic book convention] in Texas or Alabama and guys that we would call rednecks would come up and go, 'Oh, I love Spawn, he's my favorite hero!' And I'd say, 'You remember he's a black guy, right?' And they'd look at their buddy and go, 'Oh—we did forget about that.'"

The untrammeled gore and violence in Spawn's various titles (hearts were pulled out of characters' bodies as frequently as Batman tossed his batarang) helped turn him into the only character whose books sold in the millions throughout the 1990s. Comic book store owner Mike Malve would simply shrug when little kids gravitated to the racks that held *Spawn*: "You can tell an eight- or ten-year-old kid, you can't buy that, it's a little bloody—buy *Richie Rich*. But, no, they want *Spawn*. It wasn't for them, per se, but kids love *Spawn*." McFarlane managed to parlay that loyalty into a commercial empire that redressed nearly every wrong done to Siegel and Shuster. His own company, McFarlane Toys, dedicated itself to the first-rate production of detailed *Spawn* action figures, which raised the bar for the toy industry and earned millions in the process (the company diversified itself in the field and became one of the leaders in McFarlane's beloved sports collectibles). In 1997, Spawn became the first independent character to get his own eponymous feature-length film (it did not become a commercial phenomenon), which was followed up by an Emmy Award–winning HBO animated series called *Todd McFarlane's Spawn*, just in case anyone didn't know who was behind the character.

Spawn's exploits got increasingly metaphysical as the decades wore on and his readership dwindled. McFarlane's experimentation with such a relentlessly renegade character meant that there would never be the refuge of a secret identity, or allies, or secret caves, or—god forbid!—a kid sidekick; ultimately, the stories became repetitive in their unforgiving driven nature. Still, it was hard not to root for a hero who loves his wife so much that he is willing to flirt with the flames of the Devil's inferno; Spawn's eternal wrangling with Hell was, for the right kind of reader, Paradise.

FROM TOP: The demon Malebolgia from *Spawn* #3; Spawn punishes a pedophile (Spawn #5); the film incarnation from 1997.

DOOMSDAY
The Death of Superman

He had been the standard bearer of an entire industry for decades, dedicating his superhuman life and career to moving millions of copies of comic books a year. In the wake of the grim-and-gritty era, however, Superman plummeted to earth in sales, derided by certain readers as a chiseled Boy Scout, without enough psychological maladjustments to make him compelling and too downright uncomplicated to be a superstar. But, in November 1992, the Man of Steel fooled everyone. As Shakespeare says in *Macbeth*, nothing in his life became him like the leaving of it.

Ironically, in a post–Dark Knight world, Superman's ethical clarity made his stories murky and contrived. In 1986, Alan Moore had worked with Superman's longtime artist Curt Swan to create a wonderfully elegiac close-parenthesis storyline entitled, "Whatever Happened to the Man of Tomorrow?" which allowed fan favorite John Byrne to step in and reimagine Superman in *The Man of Steel*. The new title streamlined Superman's background and his powers into something more credible, if that's the word for an alien who streaks through the sky in a red cape. By 1991, Superman's adventures were unfurled in four separate DC Comics titles, but they were weighed down by an uninspired amalgam of predictable science fiction and quotidian problems in Metropolis. Still, those four titles required an annual organizational meeting of the various editors and writers who worked on the Superman universe to sort out and conform continuity. Much like the executive producers and show runners of an ongoing television series, the creative staff at DC had an ongoing investment in the property and spent hours and hours spitballing possible storylines and conflicts over the course of a year. The character of Superman continued to be the biggest challenge, according to Mike Carlin, one of the editors: "A lot of people feel that Superman deserves to be one of the better comics out there just because he was first. At the same time, they would also rather buy Lobo [an intergalactic mercenary] or X-Men, because Superman is kind of

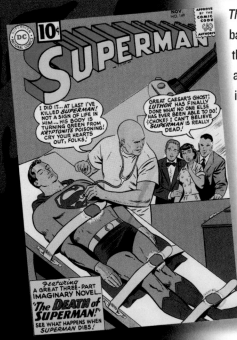

The commemorative logo for the "The Death of Superman!" (November 1992). INSET: Superman's previous death: the cover of *Superman* #149 (1961).

old-fashioned in that he doesn't like to go around killing everybody."

That year, the editors met and decided, not unreasonably, the way to change things up was to have Clark Kent and Lois Lane get married. They presented the concept to DC's then-publisher, Jenette Kahn. Unbeknownst to the editorial group, Kahn had been pitching an original Superman series to the various broadcast networks and had finally convinced ABC to pick up *Lois & Clark: The New Adventures of Superman,* which reconfigured its leading characters into a kind of screwball comedy: think of *His Girl Friday,* set at the Daily Planet. To have Clark and Lois married in the comic books would have subverted the initial bantering nature of the TV series; Kahn nixed the idea. Editor Louise Simonson recounts what happened next:

> So what that meant was, we had to go back and start over again. And we were a little disgruntled and as [Kahn] walked out the door, [editor/artist] Jerry Ordway said what he always said, which is "Let's just kill him." And instead of laughing it off, this time we said, "Yeah—yeah, let's just kill him." And it actually seemed like a good idea. I hear today from readers who say how we did it for commercial reasons. No—we did it because we were pissed.

The saga that climaxed in Superman's demise was spread out over seven separate issues of different titles, including *Justice League of America.* A relentless, powerful, spiny brute, ultimately dubbed Doomsday, breaks out of a secret lab and inexorably makes his way to Metropolis, destroying everything in its path. Superman comes to the rescue, but the creature is so powerful that he beats the Man of Steel back to the streets outside the Daily Planet, where an apocalyptic slugfest renders both adversaries wasted. "You stopped him!" exclaims Lois Lane, cradling Superman in her arms. "You saved us all! Now relax until—" But it was no use. After a harrowing battle in *Superman* #75—rendered as 24 continuous splash pages and a climactic gatefold tableau—"a Superman died."

After a several-month moratorium, the DC team spun out two more story arcs, a meditation on death and loss called "Funeral of a Friend"; then a more explosive storyline called "Reign of the Supermen!," where four different costumed adventurers arrive on the scene, each claiming to be the true heir to Superman's fame and fortune. The latter series was the most inventive of the three storylines—indeed, two of the "supermen," Steel and Superboy (reconceived as a super-clone)—became permanent fixtures of the DC landscape. At the conclusion of that saga—nearly a year after his demise—having undergone a secret Kryptonian solar regeneration at the Fortress of Solitude, Superman returned: tan, rested,

FROM FAR LEFT: Dean Cain and Teri Hatcher are *Lois and Clark* for ABC primetime television; three historic images from *Superman* #75, "Doomsday" (November 1992, art by Dan Jurgens and Brett Breeding).

245 ⋮⋮⋮ CHAPTER 6: Reign of the Dark Superhero

and ready (and with a longer haircut). No one who had ever read a comic book was surprised.

But the death of such a major figure in popular culture a year earlier had stunned the media and millions of casual followers who had no idea that death-and-resurrection was as common in superhero comic books as it was in the New Testament. While the editorial team was planning the original storyline in early 1992, word had leaked to the press. The DC public relations office literally had no clue how to handle the burgeoning interest; companies which had licensed Superman's likeness for various products were complaining and the whole enterprise seemed like bad news.

In the world of publicity, however, there is no such thing as bad news. As *Superman* #75 neared its release date of November 18, 1992, television news programs, newspapers, and magazines were heralding the death of Superman; it was front-page news, even in tabloids other than the *Daily Planet*. Aficionados of popular culture were having a field day, but that was nothing compared to an amateur investor market. DC Comics soon realized "The Death of Superman" was an unprecedented bonanza and produced several commemorative versions of the issue, particularly one sealed in a black bag that included an obituary, an armband, and other collector's items. Alerting their dealers and comic book store owners across the country of the magnitude of the event, DC shipped out nearly three million copies.

Mike Malve owned a successful comic book store in a Phoenix mall called Atomic Comics; when he showed up for work on November 18, with boxes and boxes of *Superman* #75 in the back of his van, even he was shocked:

My store was by a movie theater, and that day there was a movie that opened about Martin Luther King. There was this huge line and I was like, oh wow, they must have let kids out of school to watch this movie. And then I realized no, that's a line for my store and there were literally hundreds of people in line to get in my store. By the end of the day you were going to be sold out and so you had to put limits. So I would say look, there's a limit of two per customer and this nice old lady was arguing with me and fighting with me: "I need twelve of these because I've got twelve grandchildren that need to have the Death of Superman issue!" I tell her, ma'am, I've got a line of a hundred people here. I want to guarantee that everybody gets one. She goes, "No, I was here earlier

In spring 1993, DC Comics unveiled several superpretenders to the throne, including the Man of Steel, the Last Son of Krypton, and the Man of Tomorrow. LEFT: An in-house ad for DC underscores the historical ramifications of the issue. OPPOSITE: Comic art mirrors reality: a definitive moment of memorabilia from *Superman: The Man of Steel* #20 (1993).

than them, screw them." These are normal people talking like this.

That once-benign old lady had a point; during the previous decade, publishers had been creating collector "events"— tying premiere issue releases to major artists, while concocting variant covers, often with gimmicks such as sealed Mylar bags, or holograms, or other collector's items. When Todd McFarlane helmed *Spider-Man* #1 in 1990, the cover—of which there were several variants—unashamedly exclaimed: "1st ALL-NEW COLLECTOR'S ITEM ISSUE!" The issue sold two million copies. For veteran comics writer Marv Wolfman, the whole notion of collecting comics as a fiduciary investment is anathema

to begin with: "You should read the comic, you should want the comic because you love it and you want to read them, not put them away into plastic." Tied into these overinflated bonanzas were the occasional news stories that someone had found a copy of *Action Comics* #1 in their grandmother's attic and it would sell at auction for a fortune: in 1992, Sotheby's auctioned a pristine copy for $82,500. (In 2011, another pristine copy sold for $2.16 million.)

But even the lowliest intern at Sotheby's could have explained a simple fact to the ferocious old lady in line at the Atomic Comics store: it's all about supply and demand. In addition to its historical landmark status, *Action Comics* #1 had a print run of some 200,000 copies, of which roughly 130,000 were sold. There are only about 100 extant copies known to collectors. When three million copies of *Superman* #75 are sold (not including an additional three million reprints and trade paperback editions), a pertinent question remains: Who's going to buy them now?

Store owners such as Mike Malve saw a disturbing shift in their livelihoods, which, for most comic books store owners, had begun

with a pure love of the product: "People were buying [Superman collector's editions] ten at a time and buying them for their aunts and their uncles and their nieces and nephews and their dogs, I don't know. But nothing lasts forever. Suddenly, I started noticing we were having cases of comics that weren't selling. We were starting to become speculators." Chuck Rozanski, the owner of the Mile High Comics shop in Denver, said:

> Frankly, I view that particular marketing event as being the greatest catastrophe to strike the world of comics since the Kefauver Senate hearings. When these new comics consumers/investors tried to sell their copies of *Superman* #75 for a profit a few months later, they discovered that they could only recover their purchase price if they had a first printing, [and] their bitter disillusionment did much to cause the comics investing bubble to begin bursting.

The number of comics stores across America went from 8,000 at its height to roughly 2,000 by the end of the 1990s, which was a shame, because the local comic book store had provided an important social function for a burgeoning sub-section of the culture. Before the direct marketing phenomenon of the 1970s, new comic books could only be found in a candy store or supermarket; older copies could only be found by happenstance in cardboard

boxes in used bookstores. Sometimes, head shops would carry posters and back issues among their psychedelic paraphernalia, but the comic book store provided one-stop shopping for the fan. Usually opening early on Wednesday mornings to accommodate the customers who craved that week's new releases, comic book shops were endearingly deferential to their clientele. As the years wore on, the shops became emporiums for more than just comics: trade paperbacks, games, action figures, collectible statues, trading cards, toys, buttons, DVDs, and so on—most of which were produced in limited editions marketed specifically for collectors. More important was the camaraderie found among the boxes of dog-eared back issues: the local comic book store was a place where, as the song goes about another beloved local establishment, everybody knows your name. It was a haven for the superheroically inclined habitués. "When [our customers] took the comics home, do you think they talked to their wives about Spawn?" asked Mike Malve. "Do you think they talked to their buddies at work about—hey, what's going on in *Spider-Man*?"

The collector's movement of the early 1990s burst forth with the same kind of unexplained, remorseless energy with which Doomsday burst forth from his underground prison. The bubble exploded almost as quickly as Doomsday was vanquished. Superman, of course, survives to this day; and although the Man of Steel has had his day in our yellow sun as an icon for commercial merchandise, even he must have chafed at the idea of being reduced to a commodity.

A not-so-modest proposal from the groundbreaking *Batwoman* #17 (May 2009).

OUT OF THE BATCAVE
Gay Superheroes

The first superhero to come out: Northstar in *Alpha Flight* #106 (1992).

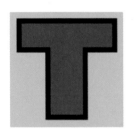

The notion espoused by Frederic Wertham in the 1950s, that Batman and Robin were in a homosexual relationship, has always been derided as "Exhibit A" when critics cite the destructive ridiculousness of Wertham's crusade against comics. But—let's be honest—hasn't this thought, however fleetingly, crossed the mind of most adults who've read their adventures?

According to Grant Morrison, such an inference "was an inevitability. You could quite easily dial up those epicene qualities of the Batman myth in an adult way—this Plutonian, lawless man who lives in a cave and recruits young boys to help him in a vague and obscure war against crime . . . yeah. But for the children who were reading those books, and even probably for the young servicemen who were reading them, it was all about adventure and there was no sexuality in those stories at all, really. Still, it is a funny perspective."

It is a perspective reinforced by essential elements in superhero mythology: guys and gals with secret identities dress up in colorful tights and capes, and step out into the night. Michael Chabon meditated on the idea in a 2008 essay in the *New Yorker* called "Second Skin": "Superheroism is a kind of transvestism; our superdrag serves at once to obscure the exterior self that no longer defines us while

betraying, with half-unconscious panache, the truth of the story we carry in our hearts, the story of our transformation, of our story's recommencement, of our rebirth into the world of adventure, of story itself." Artist Phil Jiminez sees a more direct connection to the superhero universe and gay culture:

> Certainly I've been to enough conventions to know that superhero comics have an enormously large gay fan base. I often get in trouble sometimes for saying that superheroes are essentially big drag queens. They are disguises that normal people put on to go behave outrageously: it's drag, it's costume, it's larger than life. The notion that you're a mild-mannered kid at school, but when you take off your shirt elsewhere—not literally of course—but that you reveal that you are something underneath; that's a very potent metaphor for gay kids.

In a 2010 *New York Times* story by George Gene Gustines, a book editor named Dan Avery was interviewed at "Skin Tight," a regular social event at the historic Stonewall Inn in Greenwich Village, where attendees dress up in Spandex as their favorite superheroes: "Growing up in the '80s, I guess I didn't even think gay superheroes or

LEFT: "Doc" Bruce Banner barely escapes a homosexual assault in *Hulk Magazine* #23. RIGHT: In *The Authority* #15, Apollo and the Midnighter lead a happy home life. OPPOSITE: *Astonishing X-Men* #51 featured a slightly different Marvel marriage event: the first gay wedding in mainstream comics (art by Dustin Weaver and Rachelle Rosenberg).

supporting characters were a possibility. I do remember feeling like I had two secrets I had to keep: being gay and being a comic-book fan. I'm not sure which I was more afraid of people discovering."

The emergence of the first unapologetically gay character would appear in 1992, in the pages of *Alpha Flight,* a Marvel Comics title about a Canadian superhero group with its roots appropriately in the universe of the X-Men, who, in its acceptance of outsiders, had preached tolerance for decades. However, the journey to an "out" hero was fraught with difficulty—the Comics Code had specifically proscribed depictions of homosexuality (which they initially referred to as "deviancy") until 1989—and some early attempts at showing gay characters were not always salubrious; in one infamous *Incredible Hulk* tale in 1980, the monster's alter ego, Bruce Banner, is almost sexually assaulted by two men in a Y.M.C.A. *The Alpha Flight* story, in issue #106, featured one of its leading characters, Northstar, yet another super-streaking speedster previously distinguished only by his French Canadian name, Jean-Paul Beaubier. While trying to save an AIDS-infected baby, Northstar runs afoul of a retro Canadian hero from the 1940s—Major Mapleleaf (that's his name!)—whose son has died of AIDS. Furious that his son had been marginalized, Mapleleaf takes out his frustrations on Northstar who, in the heat of battle, proclaims, "I am gay!"—which only makes Mapleleaf more furious: "By not talking about your lifestyle—by closeting yourself—you're as responsible for my son's death as the homophobic politicians who refuse to address the AIDS crisis!" A final tableau reveals a newspaper front page with the declaration of Northstar's homosexuality. If the *Alpha Flight* issue had its share of purple prose and contrived situations, well, it wasn't the first awkward "coming out"—and it wouldn't be the last.

Northstar's declaration threw open the doors of the Spandex Closet: even the *New York Times* editorial page commented on it: "Mainstream culture will one day make its peace with gay Americans. When that time comes, Northstar's revelation will be seen for what it is: a welcome indicator of social change." Other Marvel characters who followed in Northstar's fleet footsteps were Hulkling and Wiccan, two Young Avengers, who maintain a committed relationship. When two other male, somewhat mysterious, X-Forcers, Rictor and Shatterstar, sealed their relationship with mainstream comics' first gay kiss in 2006, their initial creator, Rob Liefeld, who introduced the characters in 1991, expressed his displeasure on the Internet; it did not earn him a lot of popularity. Peter David, who wrote the *X-Factor* issue that highlighted Rictor and Shatterstar's relationship, commented, "I understand that some parents have the same reaction. They were responsible for their children's appearances and, when informed of their sexual persuasion, firmly declare it's impossible, they can't be gay."

Jim Lee's Image Comics imprint, Wildstorm, ran a series called *The Authority*, a rather grimmer version of *Justice League*; its Superman/Batman avatars, the characters Apollo and the Midnighter, were not

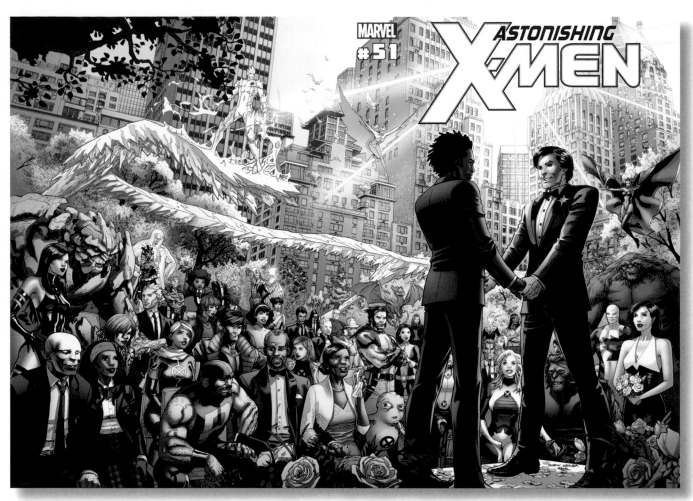

only lovers, but, in 2006, were also the first gay couple to be married in superhero comics. That year, DC reintroduced the Batwoman character as having a lesbian alter ego, Kate Kane; she would eventually enter into a relationship with Renee Montoya, a lieutenant in Gotham City's police force who would herself eventually transform into a superhero called the Question. (Batwoman proposed marriage to a different girlfriend in 2013; all of this amused fans and comic book historians who remembered the original Batwoman character who was introduced in the 1950s, ostensibly to counter perceptions about Batman and Robin's relationship.)

During the evolution of all these other relationships, Northstar had been dating a non-superhuman named Kyle throughout his various adventures (they often found it hard to date because of Northstar's crimefighting obligations). In spring 2012, Northstar proposed marriage and in issue #51 of *Astonishing X-Men*, he and Kyle were married in Central Park. Presented at the height of the presidential campaign, where gay marriage had become a contentious topic, there was inevitably some discord reflected among the wedding attendees in the comic book as well. "I'm a progressive guy, but it's a lot to take in, huh?," remarked a fellow member of Alpha Flight. But the wedding, which received massive media attention, went through without a hitch—surprising, since most weddings in the Marvel Universe involve some barrage of supervillains trying to crash the party. Northstar and Kyle rather stole the thunder that same month from DC's big news that their "Earth-Two" Green Lantern, based in the 1940s, was actually gay. By then, this earth(s)-shattering news was greeted with a collective yawn by fans: been there, done that.

"The Marvel universe and the DC universe each have about 5,000 different characters," said Jiminez. "The sheer size of those rosters creates a place for people of all stripes—but particularly gay ones—to connect, imagine, and project themselves in a world that reflects their own reality." An unfortunate reflection of that reality was the reaction of the conservative family values group One Million Moms to the marriage of Northstar and Kyle in *The Astonishing X-Men*: "Children desire to be just like superheroes," members posted on a website. "Children mimic superhero actions and even dress up in costumes to resemble these characters as much as possible. Can you imagine little boys saying, 'I want a boyfriend or husband like X-Men?'" The web post didn't make it clear whether the group objected to their little boys marrying a man or marrying a mutant.

WOLVERINE

A Frank Miller–rendered Wolverine from *Wolverine* #2. OPPOSITE: The first "snikt!" from *Giant-Size X-Men* #1 (art by Dave Cockrum). RIGHT: The feral fighter's first cover appearance in *The Incredible Hulk* #181 (art by Herb Trimpe and John Romita).

"I'M THE BEST THERE IS AT WHAT I DO. BUT WHAT I DO BEST ... ISN'T VERY NICE."

To be a popular superhero you have to have your own idiosyncratic costume, or power, or tagline. Wolverine had all those—plus his own sound effect: "Snikt!"

Fandom's favorite feral fighter debuted in the summer of 1974, when he sprang forward to sharpen his claws on the Incredible Hulk. When Wolverine was fully introduced in *The Incredible Hulk* #181, he was billed as "the World's First and Greatest Canadian Super Hero!" Whether or not North America was clamoring for a great Canadian superhero is open to conjecture, but Marvel Comics editor Roy Thomas certainly thought so and asked *Hulk* writer Len Wein to come up with a character from the Great White North. Wein was privy to conversations at Marvel about a new international version of the *X-Men* that might be coming down the pike: "I created him as a Canadian mutant, specifically so that whoever ended up with the assignment of writing the new *X-Men* book, should it ever occur, would have a Canadian mutant handy if he wanted him."

As scrappy Canadian mutants go, Wolverine proved incredibly handy—especially with the ability to have six razor-sharp adamantine claws spring out of his hands (three foot-long claws per hand, in fact). When the new X-Men title came out in 1975, Wolverine was rather casually introduced into the group; according to Wein, it was the armor-clad Russian mutant Colossus who was primed to be the featured player. But once he found his place within the X-Men, Wolverine became, fittingly, a breakout character. "He just took off like nobody's business," said Wein." Here was a character you hadn't seen much of before. Here was a hero who was a hero only by restraint. "His natural instinct was to sushi you. And he would do his best not to do that."

Wolverine's aggressive nature, his unsentimental wisecracks, his crush on teammate Jean Grey (Marvel Girl/Phoenix)—which had the potential to disrupt the X-Men—even his penchant for smoking a stinky cheroot (way back before smoking became socially incorrect) endeared him to those readers in the late 1970s and 1980s who wanted a little more spice to their action heroes. Under the literary refinement of Chris Claremont and the handsome artwork of John Byrne (who succeed Dave Cockrum on the *X-Men*), Wolverine evolved into a short, hirsute scrapper who bestrode both sides of an ethical conflict. Recalled Wein, "In one story Chris finally had him sushi somebody—some alien guard—and he killed the guy. All of a sudden, he was a bigger superstar. The second he became completely unpredictable, he became hugely fascinating to everybody."

As befitted a comic book superstar in the late 1980s and 1990s, Wolverine was spun off into several other titles, including a limited series of his own (illustrated by Frank Miller) and an extended *Wolverine* title than ran nearly 200 issues. Wolverine's tough-guy loner status allowed him to fill the boots of other figures with the same archetype; various storylines recast him either literally or figuratively as a samurai warrior or a gunslinger from the Wild West or a private investigator or a government secret agent (and secret weapon). There were several constants, however: his ongoing war with his violent nature and his amusing way with the tough-guy cliché:

> I'm an X-man. Mutants like me, band of super heroes. Good people. Idealists. Dreamers—forever looking for the best in others. With them, killing is a last resort. With me, it's second nature. I take the world as it is, an' give better than I get. Come at me with a sword. I'll meet you with a sword. You want mercy? Show a little first.

Introduced in 1974 as Canada's "Weapon X," Wolverine has always had a complicated relationship with his country of origin. How he was "abducted" by the Canadian government in the first place, what he was meant to accomplish, even when he was born—these were questions asked by Wolverine (and readers) over the course of decades. (In a 2001 mini-series, he was given a very specific family history—a cross between *Wuthering Heights* and *The Shining*.) With no other alter ego than the same simple name "Logan," Wolverine's other constant was his quest to discover who he is and (literally) what he was made of. His imperviousness made him an ideal subject for a science experiment, so Wolverine became a guinea pig for a test that grafted adamantium claws onto his skeleton (adamantium being the house impervious metal in the Marvel Universe). As his background was progressively explored in various comics, it became relatively clear that his mutant power was not his ability to retract his claws (or his astounding agility), but his ability to regenerate his body tissue and sustain any injury (within bounds) without much ado. (He also had the "power" to consume unlimited amounts of alcohol without getting drunk—a neat trick.)

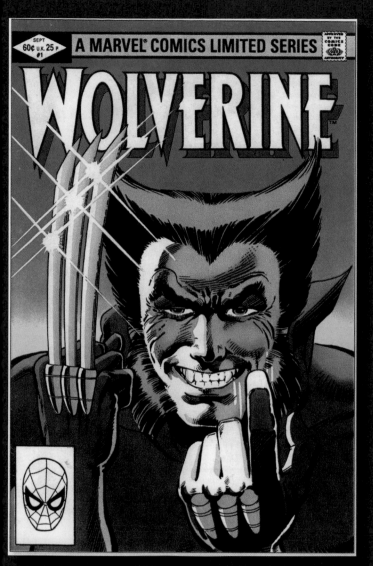

Wolverine's appeal expanded with the 2000 film *X-Men,* where he was thrillingly embodied by Australian actor Hugh Jackman. Despite their differences in height (Jackman is nearly a full foot taller than Wolverine's "official" height), Jackman has become welded to Wolverine as if he were one of his adamantine claws, playing the character in five feature-length films (two of which feature Wolverine solo) and one cameo in *X-Men: First Class* in which, upon a recruitment request from Professor X and Magneto, he tells them to "go fuck [them]selves." The Jackman/Wolverine association is the most enduring in history: no other actor has played one comic superhero in as many films.

As Chris Claremont, who knows Wolverine better than anyone—maybe even better than Wolverine knows himself—put it: "The thing for me about Wolverine is that he is a man forever in primal conflict. There is a part of him that, if you cross him, he will kill you and not even blink. But there's another part of him that is a man. And his entire life is dedicated to overcoming the monster with the man. And he can't. But because he's an X-Man, he's got to keep trying." Anyone with anger management issues could relate to Wolverine's struggles—but so could readers who were intrigued by one of the paradoxes of superhero literature: that even the toughest guy on the block cared enough to devote his life to help-

ing others. Grant Morrison saw the appeal in genre terms: "He was an outsider. The boy fans wanted to be like him because he was the cool one, the outsider, but he was a good guy with a heart of gold, and the women who read the book and the gay readers who read the book— *X-Men* was very popular with women and gay readers—they wanted to save him."

As time has gone on, Wolverine/Logan has worked with the Avengers as well as the X-Men and shows no sign of slowing down—perhaps a result of his mutant regeneration abilities. A 2011 limited series by Mark Millar and Steve McNiven called "Old Man Logan" has him living fifty years into the future, out on a farm in California, surrounded by beasties and baddies, prepared to take up the sushi-ing game once again, just an inveterate antihero with a "snikt" in his heart.

COUNTER-CLOCKWISE, FROM TOP LEFT: A Wolverine round-up: art by Frank Miller, John Buscema, Steve McNiven (for "Old Man Logan"); embodied by Hugh Jackman in *The Wolverine* (2013); and Miller again.

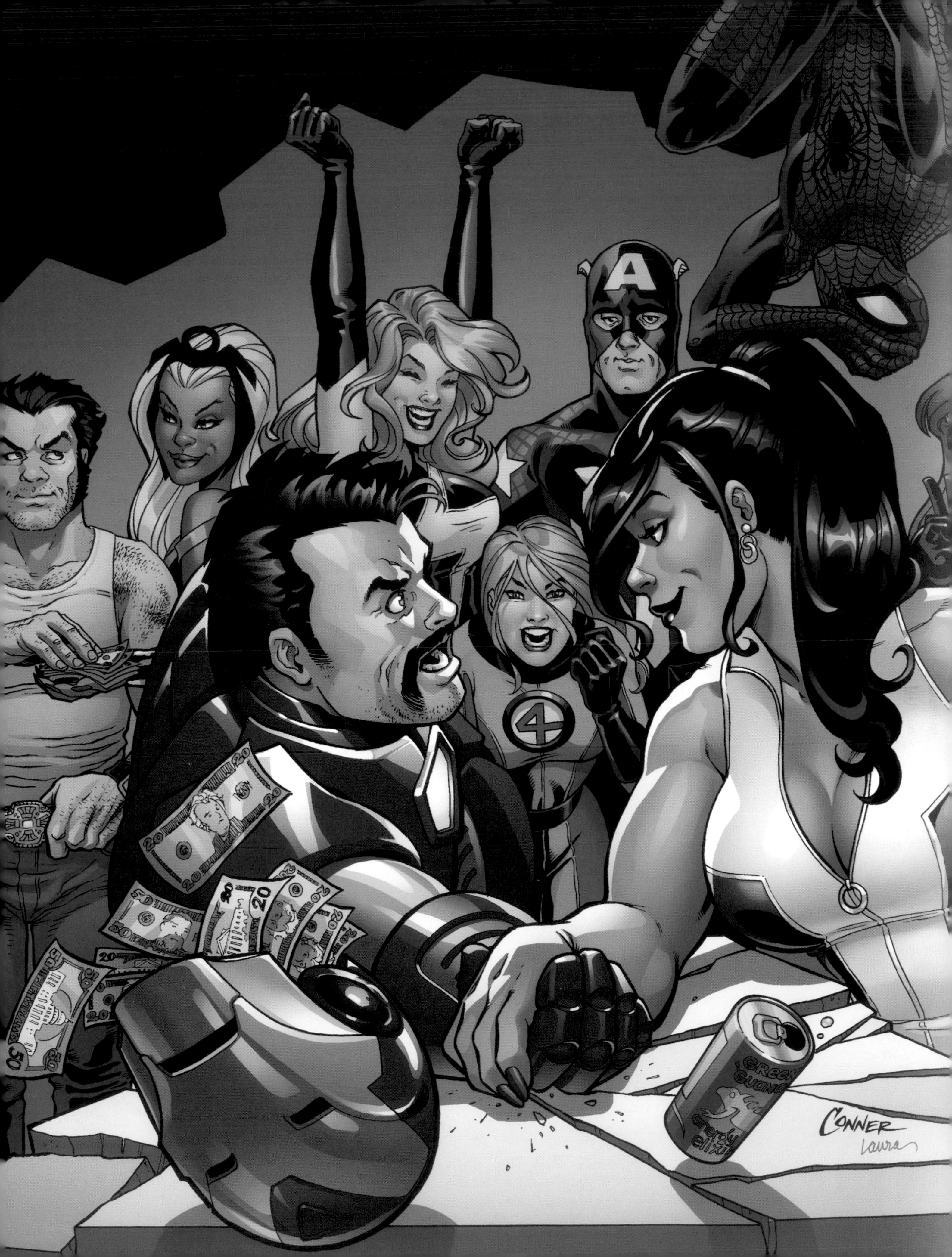
CONNER
Laura

"WOMEN IN REFRIGERATORS"
Battle of the Superheroines

That little lady sure is *tough!*" remarked a (male) bystander on the third page of Ms. Marvel's first adventure in 1977. "She makes Lynda Carter look like Olive Oyl!" That ostensibly enthusiastic statement packs much of the trials and tribulations of being a female superhero at the end of the 20th century—as well as the role of women creators, editors, and readers within the overwhelmingly boyish men's club that is the comic book universe.

Ms. Marvel was a character whose alter ego had existed in the Marvel Universe for nearly half a century. She first appeared as Major Carol Danvers in one of the last original superhero titles of the 1960s, *Marvel Super Heroes.* Danvers was a NASA security officer who tangled with a new character named Captain Marvel, a somewhat uninspired character who was actually a military officer from an alien race called the Kree named Mar-Vell. (It was important to Stan Lee, Mar-Vell's creator, and publisher Martin Goodman that the "Captain Marvel" name be wrangled from legal oblivion after the Fawcett character vanished in 1951.) In one issue, Danvers was rescued by Mar-Vell from an explosive bolt of radiation (from the Psyche-Magnitron!) expended by a Kree adversary. Unbeknownst to either of them, Carol absorbed some of the energy *through* Captain Marvel, and her human DNA was fused with Kree DNA (or the alien equivalent). She had become a sleeper superheroine.

Eight years later, Lee wanted to create a new title with a superpowered woman at the center of it and called Danvers up for active service. Along with Gerry Conway, they spliced together the "Marvel" name with the prefix that signified the women's liberation movement, giving the new character that unique mixture of trendiness and corniness which typified the Marvel Universe. Danvers was now an editor of a women's magazine (shades of Gloria Steinem, whom she resembled), published begrudgingly by none other than J. Jonah Jameson, Spider-Man's nemesis. She frequently suffered from dissociative blackouts, when she would

OPPOSITE: The Savage She-Hulk wrestles Tony Stark in *Girl Comics* #1 (art by Laura Martin and Amanda Conner). RIGHT: Ms. Marvel breaks through (cover by John Romita), and shows she can hit with the best of them (art from *Ms. Marvel* #1 by John Buscema).

turn into the feminist warrior Ms. Marvel, whose powers included superstrength, flight (courtesy of a Kree-engineered suit, with matching scarf), and a "seventh sense" that alerted her to danger.

Ms. Marvel zoomed across the Marvel Universe in her own title for several years before it was cancelled (at least she got a much sexier costume in the process), but the demise of her comic book was nothing compared to the indignities heaped upon her by editors over the next few decades. Soon after becoming a farm-team member of the Avengers, she was impregnated by one cosmic supervillain so that she might bear his child (she did, and it turned out to be the supervillain himself—don't ask). Her fellow Avengers (which included another superheroine, the Wasp) barely acknowledged that Ms. Marvel had essentially been raped; furious at their dismissive attitude, she joined the X-Men for a while, only to be transformed into an alien energy-force humanoid called Binary. That didn't do much for fans, so she was given back her normal human form and renamed Warbird, along with a diminution in her superpowers. As Warbird she rejoined the Avengers as a reliable rock 'em-sock 'em teammate, only to develop

a drinking problem as a result of feelings of inadequacy. Warbird's subsequent negligence and sloppiness in the field of battle forced Captain America to move toward court-martialing her; she quit the Avengers instead.

If Ms. Marvel's travails seemed unduly harsh and her treatment at the hands of male writers, artists, and editors seemed unnecessarily misogynistic, she wasn't alone. By 1999, the plight of superheroines in general was finally acknowledged by a fan named Gail Simone who posted a blog entitled "Women in Refrigerators." The name referred to a much-decried *Green Lantern* story from 1994 where the current iteration of the emerald ring-wielding hero came home to find his girlfriend dead, mutilated, dismembered, and crammed into a refrigerator by his current arch-nemesis. Simone simply tallied up all the superheroines (and girlfriends of superheroes) who had been "killed, maimed, or depowered" in comic books; the list was long and, taken as a whole, a condemnation of the male-dominated industry. Next to Ms. Marvel's name and list of depredations foisted upon her, Simone simply commented: "SHEESH!," employing one of Stan Lee's favorite expressions of chagrin.

The happy ending to the refrigerator story is that Simone was eventually hired as a comic book writer, first by Marvel Com-

ics, and eventually with a long-term contract at DC Comics. In 2003 she took on the only really major all-female superhero group, Birds of Prey, a snappy, aggressive team fronted by Oracle—the former Batgirl who had been rendered paraplegic by the Joker—now one of comic's most assertive and brilliant characters. Simone also became the longest-running female writer ever to render the adventures of Wonder Woman, beginning in 2007. Her point of view about superheroines (and refrigerators) was simple: "If you demolish most of the characters girls like, the girls won't read comics. That's it!"

Still, female characters continued to be demolished: in one outrageous sequence during the 2004 *Identity Crisis* series, the wife of DC's Elongated Man hero, Sue Dibny, was raped by a second-rate villain in the Justice League's headquarters and subsequently murdered. It was paradoxical that such "refrigerator" moments occurred at DC in the 1990s into the 21st century, as the company had been led by a woman since 1976. Jenette Kahn was a publishing wunderkind in her twenties, energizing a host of teenager magazines, when Warner Communications brought her on board to revitalize its superhero publications and the way they met the public. She became President of DC Comics in 1981 and steered the company through several successes, not the least of which was pioneering relationships with creators that gave them

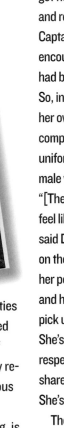

OPPOSITE: A sisterhood collapses: Carol Danvers rejects the Wasp's condescension, in *Avengers* #200, (art by George Pérez); Gail Simone was the writer for the femme fatale full house of *Birds of Prey,* including the Huntress, Catwoman, and Katana. LEFT: The infamous "woman in a refrigerator" sequence from *Green Lantern* #54 (1994). BELOW: Ms. Marvel gets a well-deserved promotion to Captain Marvel (art by Ed McGuinness).

unprecedented royalties and participation. Before Kahn stepped down in 2002, she promoted Karen Berger to become editor of DC's groundbreaking Vertigo line in 1993; Berger was generally regarded to be one of the industry's most sensitive and courageous editors; she served out her tenure until 2013.

One of Kahn's greatest achievements, by her own reckoning, is that "when I came to DC Comics we were 35 people on staff, two of whom were women—one secretary and one in production. By the time I left DC, we were 250 people of which half were women. As women got more involved in the workplace, and as creators of comic book stories, the things that perhaps were directed solely to a young male reader began to be directed also to young women as well." Kahn still realizes that comic book superheroes have traditionally had the imprimatur of a male fantasy audience and male fantasy creators: "I always said that the [male] artists drew the men they wanted to be like and the women they wanted to be with—which is why they often had pneumatic breasts."

Whether or not female superheroes will ever really share the dais with the male superheroes at the Comic Book Hall of Fame awards dinner remains to be seen. But, for what it's worth, poor Ms. Marvel's career appears to be on an upswing. Thanks to the sponsorship of Iron Man (himself a recovering alcoholic), Carol Danvers got herself straightened out, rejoined the ranks of the Avengers, and reclaimed the name of Ms. Marvel. After proving her worth to Captain America one more time (tough taskmaster, that Cap), he encouraged her to assume the mantle of the great Kree warrior (who had been killed off a few years before).

So, in 2012, Carol Danvers was given her own *Captain Marvel* book, complete with a smashing new uniform, a great haircut, and a female writer, Kelly Sue DeConnick. "[The use of 'Ms.'] made her feel like an auxiliary character," said DeConnick, who insisted on the name change. "She got her powers from Captain Marvel and he's gone. If somebody's going to pick up that mantle, it's Carol. She's knew him, she respected him, she shares his DNA. She's earned it."

The new comic was subtitled "Earth's Mightiest Mortal" in a wink to the original Captain Marvel from way back when. It was about time.

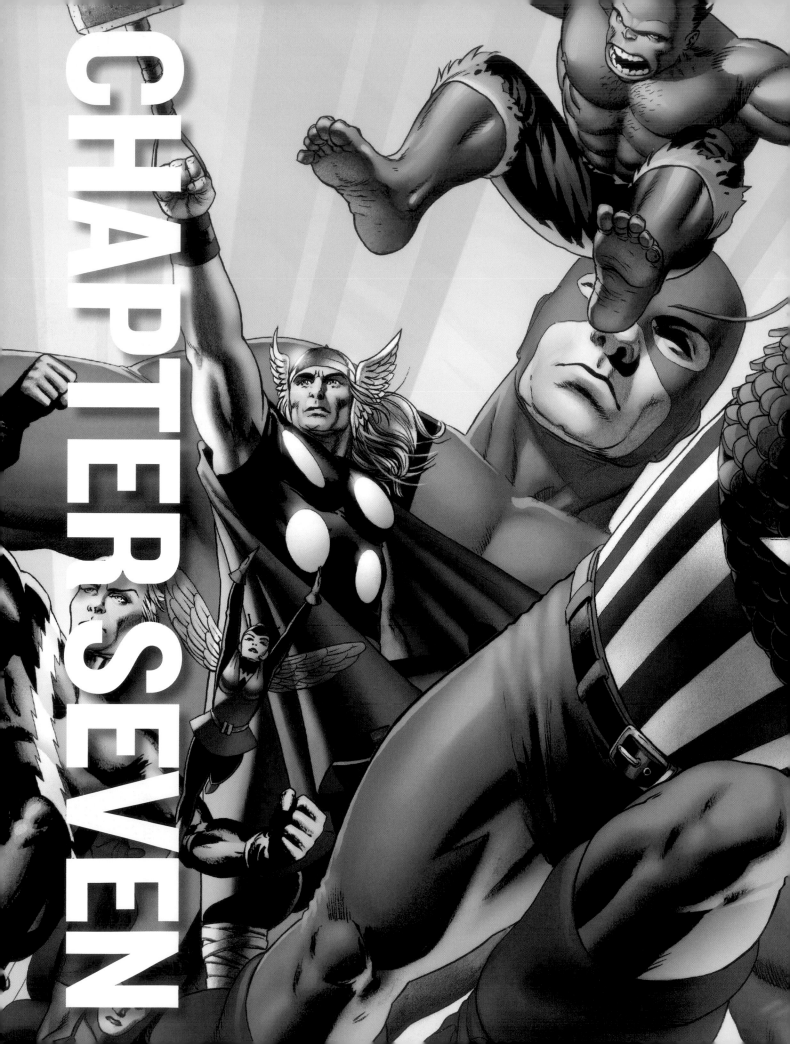

CHAPTER SEVEN

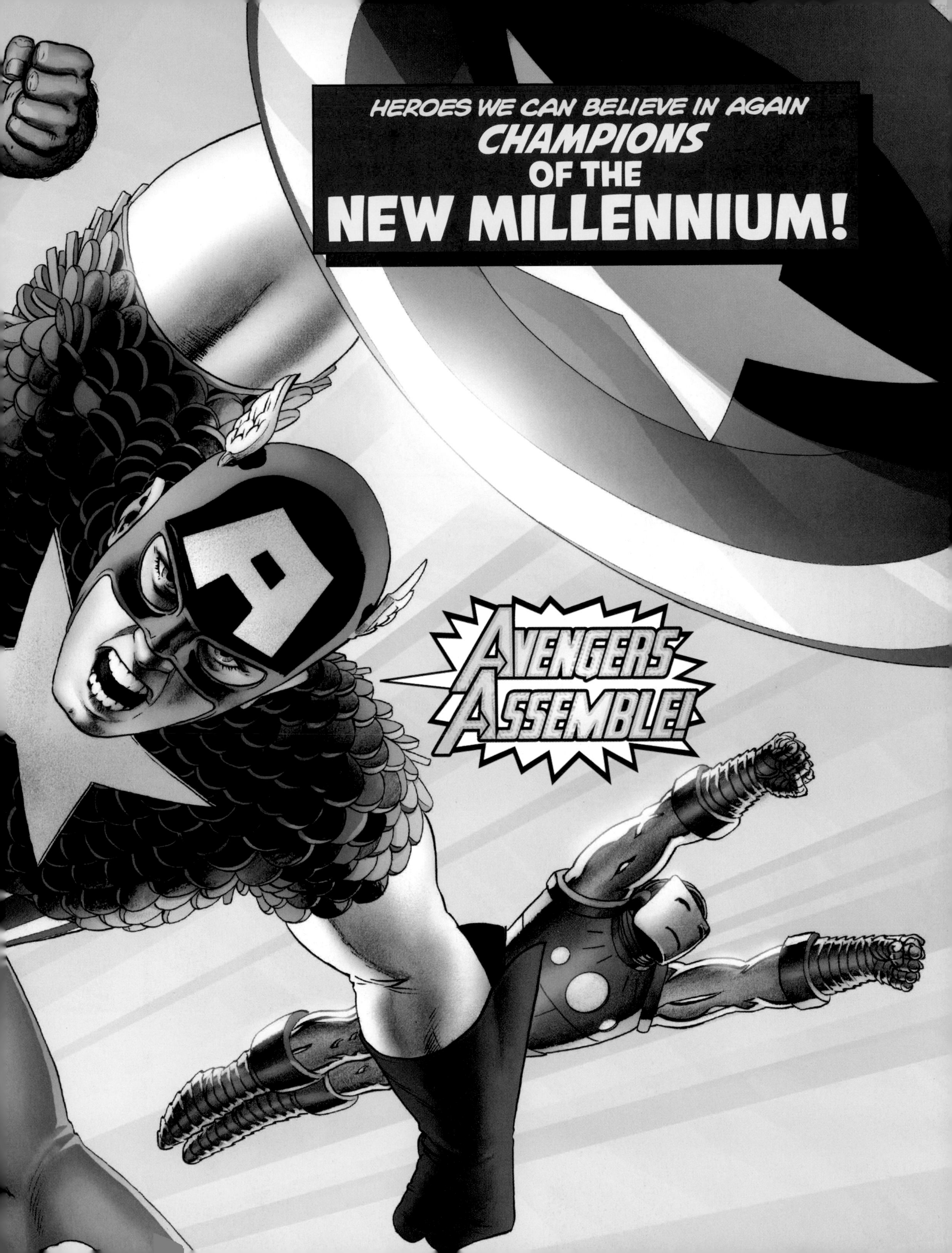
HEROES WE CAN BELIEVE IN AGAIN
CHAMPIONS
OF THE
NEW MILLENNIUM!
AVENGERS ASSEMBLE!

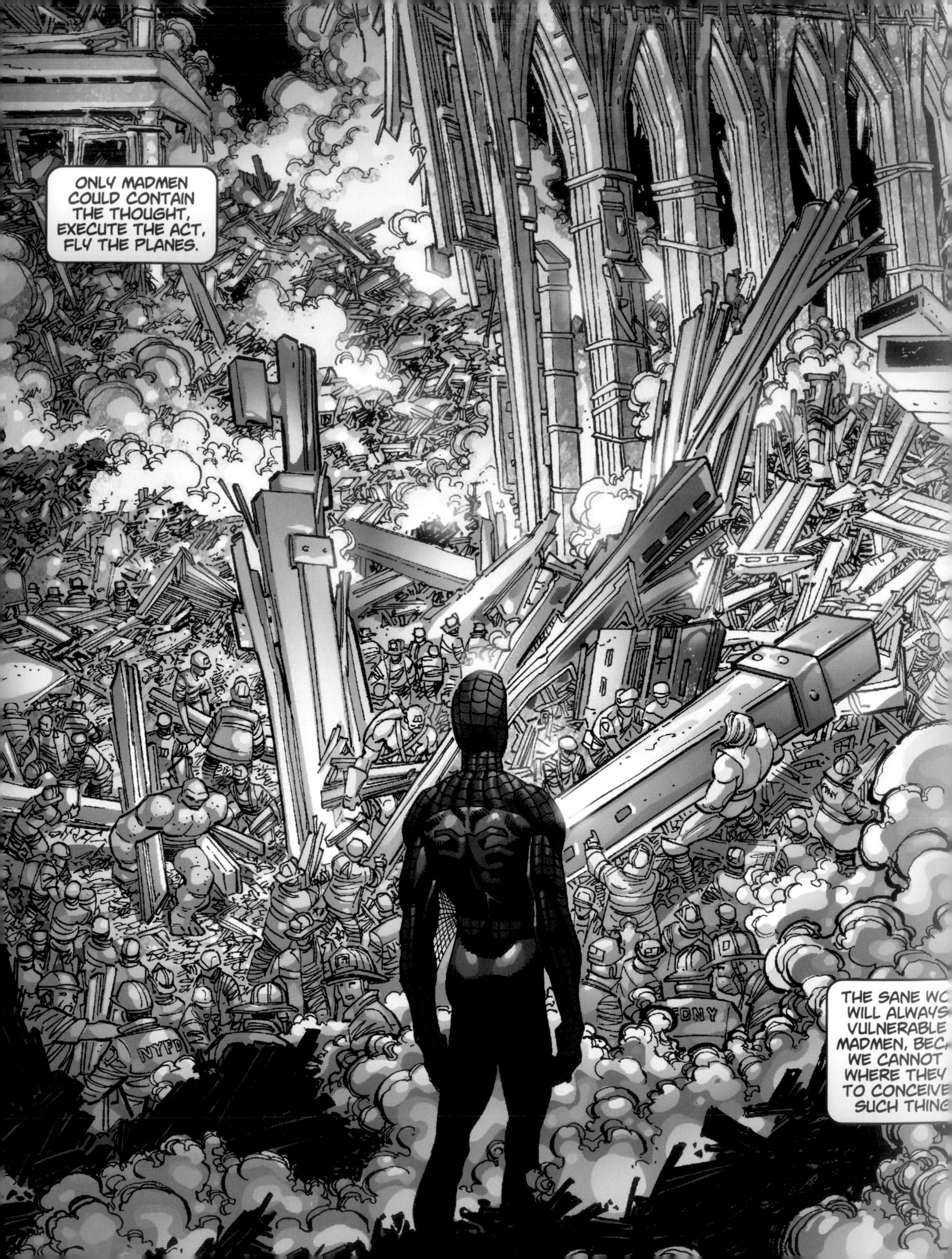

ONLY MADMEN COULD CONTAIN THE THOUGHT, EXECUTE THE ACT, FLY THE PLANES.
THE SANE WO
WILL ALWAYS
VULNERABLE
MADMEN, BEC
WE CANNOT
WHERE THEY
TO CONCEIVE
SUCH THING

"STAND TALL"
9/11 and Superheroes

OVERLEAF: From *Fallen Son* (2007, art by John Cassaday). OPPOSITE: Spider-Man views the aftermath of 9/11 in *The Amazing Spider-Man* (art by John Romita, Jr.). LEFT: Ground Zero, September 11, 2001. RIGHT: Spider-Man foils some plot against the World Trade Center in *The Amazing Spider-Man* #213, 1981.

he grim notion of Manhattan meeting an apocalyptic fate occurred in comic books as early as fall 1941 when, in retaliation against the detested surface dwellers, Namor, the Sub-Mariner, terrorized the city by unleashing a tidal wave of deadly force.

But, as comics historian Bradford Wright put it, "On September 11, 2001, the meaning of 'Look—up in the sky!' changed forever in New York City. Changed horribly. Any kid who had grown up reading comic books had seen buildings in New York destroyed over and over again in many ways, but none of that could prepare people for the reality." That morning, Marvel Comics' editor-in-chief, Joe Quesada, ran to the company's offices on Fifth Avenue to check on his staff. Amidst the terrible tragedy of the day, "it was very clear to me and to all of us at Marvel that it was something that we were going to have to address in our books. It would be callous for us not to. We were a company, a universe, that had Spider-Man swing across those towers. We're a company that had its characters fighting World War II, we're a company that had its characters experience the civil rights movement and all those things."

Quesada turned to J. Michael Straczynski, an accomplished producer and screenwriter (television's *Babylon 5*), whom he had just lured from his Hollywood career to take over as lead writer on *The Amazing Spider-Man*. Straczynski was working on location in Vancouver when Quesada asked him to consider a response to 9/11, perhaps through the perspective of Peter Parker, who was not only the torch-bearer of the Marvel label, but comics' most representative New Yorker. Straczynski told Quesada, "I don't know how to do that. I'm sure the words are in the dictionary somewhere, but which ones and what order to put them in, I have no freaking idea." Upon reflection, he reconsidered: "In this very strange prose poem meditation on the events of 9/11 in a voice and a style that I had never written in before, [the story] kind of found me. I wrote the entire thing in like 45 minutes, just in one sitting."

The Amazing Spider-Man #36 hit the stands relatively quickly, on November 15, barely two months after the events in Lower Manhattan. The artist was John Romita, Jr., one of Marvel's admired superstars and the son of the artist who had done so much to elevate Spider-Man to iconic status in the late 1960s.

The cover was entirely black, except for a white knock-out of the magazine's logo. The story's twenty-two pages were plotless, but hardly without incident, as Spider-Man surveys the scene of the tragedy, in mute bewilderment: "Some things are beyond words, beyond comprehension, beyond forgiveness," went the omniscient narration. "I wanted it to be more of a questioning," said Straczynski. "And I think by doing that, it became more long-lasting and enduring than if I just said, we're going to go get them, and march off into the horizon."

Spider-Man runs into a dust-covered couple, escaping from the debris. "Where were you? How could you let this happen?" they ask, voicing the question raised that day by people who have faith in superheroes. The wall-crawler turns away, nearly mute in his impotence, much like DC's Green Lantern who, in 1970, turned away from the elderly black man who asked a similarly rhetorical question about the efficacy of superbeings.

Later in the story, Spider-Man stands shoulder-to-shoulder with the real-life first responders, firemen, EMS workers, and policemen in the debris of the World Trade Center, although Straczynski and Romita make clear that the real heroes were the real heroes: "But with our costumes and our superpowers we are writ small by the true heroes." Spider-Man sees Captain America standing by Ground Zero, but doesn't approach him: "He's the only one who could know. Because he's been here before. I wish I had not lived to see this once. I can't imagine what it is to see this twice." Straczynski explained that "because Peter Parker is a native New Yorker I thought that his reaction would be more of a personal reaction. I didn't want to get into policies or politics or the way we might respond to this. Captain America, on the other hand, represented the larger issues at stake. I didn't want to delve too deeply in it, which is why Cap doesn't speak in the course of the book. Whereas Peter represents the people, Cap's a symbol of the country."

The creative team took some heat for a page where Marvel's most nefarious malefactors—Dr. Doom, Magneto, the Kingpin, villains who had wanted to destroy Manhattan dozens of times among them—stand amongst the rubble in contemplative silence; Dr. Doom is even glanced with a tear, streaming down between his scarred

OPPOSITE, TOP: An American hero who had seen it all: *The Amazing Spider-Man* #36; BOTTOM: Spidey watches firefighters working to find survivors in the wreckage. RIGHT: A special DC tribute to 9/11 (art by Alex Ross) referencing a comic book cover from during World War II.

face and his fiercely armored mask. "It was not Doc Doom and other villains at Ground Zero, just like it was not a young child crying for his fallen father," said Romita. "It was a representation . . . a symbol . . . a metaphor for real feelings and thoughts. To get this point across to those who don't watch Dan Rather, it was effective."

When the events of 9/11 fell upon the earth, Frank Miller was in the middle of writing and drawing a sequel to *Batman: The Dark Knight Returns* called *The Dark Knight Strikes Again*. He had just completed a sequence where a plane crashes into a Metropolis skyscraper and didn't know what to do with it:

> It was very strange to wake up in the morning and realize for the first time in my career that I didn't know what my next book was going to be, because all the plans I had seemed—well, not just trivial, but irrelevant, because these fantasies don't exist in their own little dimension. Everything is a metaphor for something that's real. This is how pop culture works—we process things and then turn them into a product that is at once more palatable, but deeply resonant.

The comic book community processed the event quickly, releasing several compilations of short meditations on 9/11, including Marvel's *Heroes* and DC's *9/11: The World's Finest Comic Books Artists and Writers*. The vignettes varied from human interest stories to superheroic meditations on retribution; proceeds from the books went to 9/11-oriented charities. But the Spider-Man issue had the most profound effect on readers; it was a best-seller and was written about in the press, nationwide. "I've heard from firemen who were there, from police officers, from reverends who used it in sermons, teachers who used it in the classroom, because kids don't watch *Nightline*. They had no way to put it in context," said Straczynski. "And it allowed them to talk about it in a different way." Quesada said, "We released the book really not caring what anybody was going to think about it, but just knowing that it was something that we had to do—and it was cathartic for us as well."

The more general effect of 9/11 on the world of superheroes is harder to quantify. Perhaps the tragedy had the inadvertent conse-

quence of steering comic book storylines out of the "grim-and-gritty" era; suddenly heroism was nothing to be ashamed of, and heroic motivations no longer needed to be imputed or psychoanalyzed into irrelevance. Certainly, there was a strange inversion of fiction and reality; the tragedy of the real events of 9/11 had only been seen before in fiction, and the power of that tragic reality had been thrust onto the broad shoulders of fictional superheroes.

Nowhere was the transformative shock of reality more apparent than in the Marvel Comics series *Civil War*. Only forty-five days after the terrorist attacks on U.S. soil, the Patriot Act was overwhelmingly, if hastily, endorsed by Congress and signed into law by President George W. Bush. The Uniting and Strengthening America by Providing Appropriate Tools Required to Intercept and Obstruct Terrorism Act of 2001 sounded like something out of a contrived Stan Lee acronym—something like the Supreme Headquarters, International Espionage, Law-enforcement Division, which was the original name for S.H.I.E.L.D., Marvel's resident superspy organization, headed by the grizzled Nick Fury.

Except the USA Patriot Act was a very real, very insidious, and very controversial piece of legislation. Intended to combat domestic terrorism by enhancing domestic security, the Patriot Act enabled law enforcement to broaden surveillance procedures, overstep previous restrictions in search and seizure, and widen

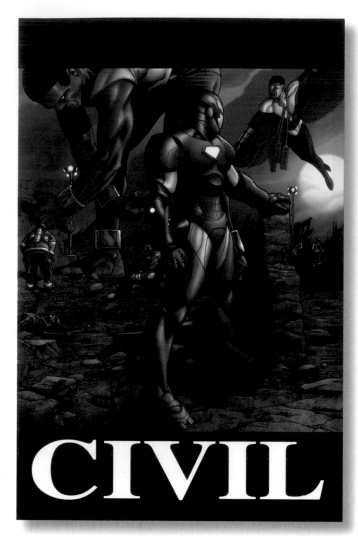

Whose side are you on? *Civil War* (2006, art by Steve McNiven).

about the Civil War, directed by Ken Burns: "Mark was fascinated by the brother versus brother [dynamic], that your house could be divided purely by ideology." The house "divided against itself" would be the Marvel House of Ideas; the ideological wedge would be the registration of superbeings with the government. The crossover event became the seven-issue *Civil War* series, which would become the nexus for a score of related spin-off stories in other books. The promotional tagline, echoing the mantra of the American labor movement, was "Whose Side Are You On?"

The sides become clearly demarcated in the first issue of *Civil War*, which hit stands in late spring 2006. A fatal cataclysm brought on by a group of inexperienced and irresponsible superheroes inflames citizens across the country: if superhumans have such extreme and lethal powers, shouldn't they be registered with the government? As Millar put it, "The civil war between the heroes is over the superhuman registration act, which mandates that anyone who puts on a costume and goes out to try and enforce the law must register with and become an agent of the federal government. It's an ideological split down the middle." On one side of the divide was Captain America—who typically would side with the federal government, but rejects the notion that heroes should surrender their liberties to a McCarthyesque decree. He winds up going underground and recruiting a corps of super-rebels, such as Daredevil and Luke Cage.

> CAPTAIN AMERICA: Masked heroes have been part of this country for as long as anyone can remember. You're asking me to arrest people who risk their lives for this country every day of the week. I think this plan will split us down the middle. I think you're going to have us at war with each other.

On the side of government security is Iron Man who, in his alter-ego as billionaire inventor Tony Stark, appreciates the functional machinery of a well-ordered state. He drafts in the scientific and technical skills of Mr. Fantastic, along with the more conservative forces of the Marvel Universe, in the hopes of creating a viable system for registering superheroes and incarcerating reprobates.

access to personal records and information—all in the service of allowing the government more influence in the comings and goings of its citizens. Civil libertarians were alarmed and outraged; more conservative denizens were relieved and supportive. For many, it was a struggle over the boundaries of law and order.

Since superheroes are in the law and order business, it was perhaps inevitable that the Patriot Act would make it into a 21st-century comic book. Multiple-issue crossover series had become increasingly prevalent in the industry; since *Crisis on Infinite Earths*, some sort of special event from both DC and Marvel, where the superstars of the respective lines would be drawn together under some contrived pretext for a multi-character slugfest of apocalyptic proportions, would appear nearly every summer. Around 2005, Marvel's editors were planning their next iteration of an annual crossover event, perhaps an epic where that selfsame S.H.I.E.L.D. might use its law enforcement skills to track down the Avengers on behalf of the U.S. government. According to writer and editor Jeph Loeb, Scottish-born writer Mark Millar was concurrently drawn into the multi-part PBS documentary

IRON MAN: We're superheroes. We tackle super-crime and we save people's lives. The only thing changing is that the kids, the amateurs, and the sociopaths are getting weeded out.

Millar didn't take sides; he preferred to set up his opposing players and get out of the way: "I think you don't want to think of your superheroes as being liberal or conservative. I think those guys should be above that."

But *Civil War* wasn't a treatise about civil discourse; at the end of the day, it was a rollicking slugfest with Iron Man and Captain America having at each other on a battleground while the other major players in the Marvel Universe were drawn into the fray. Still, it was a character-oriented saga that raised many questions about the ethos of the superhero: Why do they keep their identities secret? On whose behalf are they fighting their battles? And, finally, who asked them to show up in the first place? Millar and his artist Steve McNiven threaded those questions through the Marvel Universe. Spider-Man started on Iron Man's side and revealed his secret identity as Peter Parker at a standing-room-only news conference (giving editor J. Jonah Jameson a coronary), then switched to Captain America's camp when he thought Iron Man was in over his shelled head; the Fantastic Four were split down the middle; as non-citizens, the Black Panther and Namor, the Sub-Mariner, initially sat out the conflict; the mystic Dr. Strange went on a hunger strike.

As Grant Morrison put it, "*Civil War* starts with Captain America on the right and Iron Man on the left and, by the end, they've swapped places and now Iron Man becomes this representative of the establishment and Captain America represents old America, this kind of outlaw, liberal America refusing to bow down to the powers of the state. We'll let them fight each other and see who wins. It's a very simple way to dramatize an argument but it works really well in comics." By the end of the saga, Captain America would surrender to the government as his alter-ego, Steve Rogers (this would lead to another huge multi-story epic where he would be assassinated), and Tony Stark would become director of S.H.I.E.L.D., where he promised to safeguard his allies' secret identities. The mother of an innocent bystander killed in

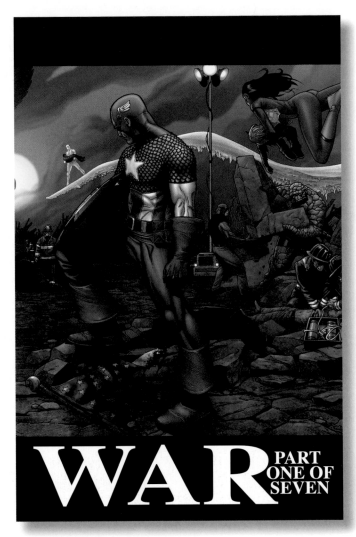

the epic's first issue gave her blessing to Stark and, in so doing, may have delivered the epitaph of the "grim-and-gritty" era: "I truly believe you've given people heroes we can believe in again." If the events of 9/II foreshadowed a change in direction for superhero comic books, *Civil War* pointed the way.

"When you work on a television show, it's going to be on a year from now; you make a movie, it's going to be out in a theater two years from now," said Jeph Loeb. "In comics, on the other hand, you start and three to six months later you're still in the middle [of the discourse]. *Civil War* was an opportunity to be able to comment on what was going on in our society in a very real-world way with larger-than-life characters."

As if to underline the profundity of Loeb's comment, it's worth recalling that the instigating incident of *Civil War* was the explosive destruction of an elementary school, instigated by the foolish move of an errant superhero, which resulted in the death of innocent children. For the comic book series, that school was set in Stamford, Connecticut—coincidentally, forty-one miles from Newtown, Connecticut, and Sandy Hook Elementary School.

THE THIRD GENERATION:

As comic book readers grew older, it was no surprise that they wanted to reach back to the comics from their childhood—a kind of serial comfort food. As the 20th century evolved into the 21st, there were many attempts at capturing the nostalgia for the late 1950s and 1960s. Nostalgia comes in many colors, and no two artists could be more different from each other than Alex Ross and Darwyn Cooke; yet no two artists

displayed as much affection for and attention toward the superheroes of their childhood. Together, as the alpha and omega of comic book illustration, they defined their own status by redefining an earlier era.

Over the course of a decade, Ross and Cooke reexamined the superheroes of the late 1950s and early 1960s from two completely complementary prisms and created two respective seminal comic book mini-series: *Marvels* (1994), a four-issue series written by Kurt Busiek and painted and illustrated by Ross, and *The New Frontier* (2004), written and illustrated by Cooke for DC Comics.

Ross desperately wanted to paint the superheroes he loved as a kid, so he enrolled at an art academy at the age of sixteen, specializing in drafting and painting. There he fell under the thrall of two classic American illustrators, Norman Rockwell and J. C. Leyendecker; by studying these two legends, Ross learned the techniques to render his beloved superheroes. He finally got the chance to put his talents to work when Kurt Busiek revisited the early days of the Marvel Universe through (literally) the lens of Phil Sheldon, a photographer for the *Daily Bugle*, who follows the escapades of superbeings (marvels, as he calls them) from the emergence of the Human Torch through the

THE RETRO ARTISTS

Are we up to the task-- are we equal to the challenge? Or must we sacrifice our future in order to enjoy the present?

That is the question of the New Frontier. That is the choice our nation must make-- between the public interest and private comfort-- between national greatness and national decline-- between the fresh air of progress and the stale, dank atmosphere of "normalcy"-- between determined dedication and creeping mediocrity.

All mankind waits upon our decision. A whole world looks to see what we will do. We cannot fail their trust, we cannot fail to try.

-John F. Kennedy

OPPOSITE: The Angel ascends to the heavens to save a mutant child on the cover of *Marvels* #2, art by Alex Ross. ABOVE: Darwyn Cooke sends DC's mightiest heroes to face the future in *The New Frontier* #4.

death of Gwen Stacy. No one had ever seen anything like Ross's hyperrealistic painting style; he often modeled his renditions on live models, action figures, and friends and neighbors. *Marvels* debuted before the widescreen adventures of most of Marvel's superheroes, so to see Spider-Man or the X-Men in full, realistic color was a breathtaking experience. The book made Ross's reputation and he remains one of comicdom's most venerated and prolific cover and poster artists.

Darwyn Cooke had been enthralled with Batman as a small child; when his mother forgot to call him in from playing in his Buffalo backyard one Thursday at 7:30 and he missed the second installment of a *Batman* episode, he stopped speaking to her for

months. Cooke entered the comics field through the world of animation, serving as a major storyboard artist on Bruce Timm's *Batman: The Animated Series*. In 2004, he took on the epic story of the "Showcase" years of the Silver Age at DC, introducing DC's new heroes in the order of when they were released—Martian Manhunter, the Flash, Green Lantern, and so on—as *The New Frontier*. Cooke's artistry called up the simple but powerful graphic pleasures of the Max Fleischer *Superman* cartoons and Jack Kirby's early 1960s explosive panels. Borrowing from John Kennedy's vision of America's future, Cooke referred to the 380 pages of *The New Frontier* as a "period piece with epic overtones and strong heroes."

"ONE MORE DAY"
Retcons and Reboots

Many of the perceived outrages in contemporary popular culture—censorship, pandering to a youth market, making movies out of inferior material, what-have-you—have existed for decades; 21st-century culture does not have the monopoly on screwing things up.

Retconning (changing the continuity of a comic book's character retroactively) and rebooting (reworking a character from scratch, or nearly from scratch) have become the twin necessary evils of the contemporary comic book world. Publishers and editors, eager to attract new readers and to inspire their current stable of writers and artists, have handed over the keys to their most valuable vehicles on frequent occasions, allowing for a plethora of variant storylines and a concordance of tweaks and changes that nearly defy coherence or clarification. Many fans, especially the newer ones, jump on board; older fans often throw up their hands or throw away their collections.

If the reappearance of Captain America in *Avengers* #4 in 1964 was comic book's first major retcon, it could be argued that the first major reboot was during the emergence of the Silver Age. What, really, was the transformation of the Golden-Age Flash into the Scarlet Speedster of 1956 other than a reboot? Granted, these were two different Flashes, but it was still a successful reinvention of the franchise. Throughout the 1960s at Marvel Comics, the character of inventor Henry "Hank" Pym ran through a walk-in-sized closetful of superhero suits during the first six years of his existence, starting out as Ant-Man, then Giant-Man, then Goliath, and finally (but not ultimately) as Yellowjacket.

Perhaps the first prominent reboot came in 1968 in the pages

OPPOSITE: In *Captain America* #14 (2006), Bucky Barnes had a hard time recalling his past lives; so did readers (art by Steve Epting). *The [New] Wonder Woman* #191 (1970) reminded readers how dramatic her renunciation was at the time.

of *Wonder Woman* #178. Writer Denny O'Neil decided to climb on the feminist bandwagon and have Wonder Woman renounce her Amazon identity and powers (not exactly her choice—the Amazons on Paradise Island decide to move on to a new dimension) in favor of plainclothes identity as Diana Prince, a humanitarian adventurer in leather pants, with a mean karate chop and an inscrutable Asian mentor. While this incarnation made Wonder Woman more hip and contemporary, it riled author Gloria Steinem, who felt that the reboot denied women, young and old, their one superpowered female role model. Steinem even put the Golden Age personae of Wonder Woman on the cover of her debut issue of *Ms.* magazine in 1972. Either Ms. Steinem or poor sales forced DC to turn the Amazon princess back to her roots by 1973.

Still, Wonder Woman's zigzagging metamorphoses proved that reboots could provide a vital shot in the arm to the right kind of character. Mid-range superheroes such as Marvel Comics' Captain Marvel and DC's Green Arrow became more interesting after being rebooted in the 1970s; and the spectacular success of the new X-Men in 1975 certainly proved the salubrious effect of a reboot. Fans mourned the eradication of a beloved figure such as the Flash in *Crisis on Infinite Earths*, but the reboot of his character in the form of his sidekick Kid Flash, now mature enough to assume his mantle, made for some compelling and complex storylines (and Barry Allen returned in Geoff Johns' *Flashpoint* epic in 2011).

Retcons are, among more loyal fans at any rate, far more controversial because they essentially tinker with (or destroy, depending on your point of view) accepted and comforting narratives. Some critics and historians point to editor Roy Thomas as the first consistent "rectonner"; Thomas's love for the heroes of the 1940s jump-started the nostalgia craze in the late 1960s when he added Golden Age characters to *The Avengers*. He also resuscitated two World War II-era superteams in the 1970s: for Marvel, the All-Winners Squad became the Invaders and, for DC, All-Star Squadron took over for the Justice Society of America.

At DC, the reverberations of *Crisis* were still being felt, a generation or two later. In the Superman universe, a 1986 retcon made Kal-El the sole survivor of Krypton's explosion (eliminating Supergirl) and had him assume his powers as an adult (eliminating Superboy). His adoptive parents, the Kents, were kept on as aging subsidiary characters (which didn't eliminate them at all). Mucking about with parents is a key device in retcons. In the Batman titles, Bruce Wayne was retconned to be younger—nine years old—when his parents were killed; and their murderer—once given the name Joe Chill and previously captured by the Caped Crusader—was now an elusive and mysterious figure. In Wonder Woman's retcon, her mother, Queen Hippolyta, was featured more prominently, her adventures during World War II were completely redacted, and she was returned more intently to her martial roots in Greek mythology; even Paradise Island was rechristened (if that's the word for a pre-Christian culture) as Themyscira (in historical reality, it was spelled "Themiscyra" and was a town, not an island).

The nature of retcons at Marvel Comics are a bit more complicated; even though the Marvel Universe is two decades younger than the DC Comics Universe, much of that mythology was more complex to begin with. The plethora of X-Men characters—so expansive and diverse in any event, especially after they started

TOP: One of comic's seminal reboots, Princess Diana must become Diana Prince in *Wonder Woman* #179 (1968, art by Mike Sekowsky). BOTTOM: The debut cover of *Ms.* magazine (1972) took Wonder Woman's role in American culture very seriously.

to have multiple adventures in outer space in the 1980s—have led to legions of esoteric retcons too encyclopedic to mention (in fact, there are encyclopedias that could rival *Burke's Peerage* which spell the whole thing out). The retcon wave engulfed poor Spider-Man in 2007 after he revealed his identity in *Civil War*. Marvel editor-in-chief Joe Quesada wanted Spider-Man to return to his bachelorhood, so a storyline entitled "One More Day" was created, where, in order to save his Aunt May from death, Spider-Man (and Mary Jane) make a deal with the devil (Mephisto, in this case) to eradicate their marriage in exchange for Aunt May's life. Boom, done. Along with this very controversial decision to wipe out any existence of Spider-Man's happily married state, the world also no longer knows his secret identity. Another retcon a few years later postulated the unhappy proposition that, in the early 1970s, Spider-Man's beloved Gwen Stacy had actually been impregnated by the Green Goblin and bore twin children a year before she was tragically murdered by the fiend. Many fans felt this added insult to injury.

As befits the granddaddy of all retconned characters, Captain America has had his share of revised continuity, although, in his case, the revisions have deepened the resonance of his legend. When he reappeared in 1964, Stan Lee simply pretended that Cap's brief 1950s entanglements with Communists didn't exist and that he had been in an icy state of suspended animation since the closing days of World War II; a nifty retcon from the 1970s conjectured that during the Cold War the missing Cap had been replaced by a B-level Timely Comics hero called the Spirit of '76—thus allowing both storylines to co-exist. Even more impressive, however, was the 2004 seven-part mini-series called *Truth: Red, White, & Black*. In this controversial saga, writer Robert Morales teamed up with artist Kyle Baker to peel back the layers that hid the secret history behind the Super-Soldier serum. They went back and merged two unfortunate chapters of American history: the infamous Tuskegee experiments begun in the 1930s, in which 400 black men with syphilis were unwittingly subjected to the various trial remedies by the U.S. Public Health service without their knowledge or consent, and the segregation of black soldiers in the U.S. Armed Forces. *Truth* spun a story set in 1940 based on a simple, but provocative, premise. As author Gary Philips articulates it:

RIGHT: Captain America was briefly called up for active duty in 1954 to fight the commies; readers hardly noticed and this issue was his last appearance until a decade later.
BELOW: From the *Truth* saga (2004): Isaiah Bradley becomes the first black *Captain America* (art by Kyle Baker).

Steve Rogers got the Super-Soldier serum injection and became Captain America. Well, what if, in fact, there had been some experimentation going on *after* that to perfect the formula, and rather than experiment on white soldiers, what if the government said, listen, we got these black soldiers here—why not experiment on them? And therein lies the truth.

A regiment of chemically enhanced black soldiers storms Hitler's fortress and liberates a concentration camp; but the formula is too unstable and one black renegade, Isaiah Bradley, who calls himself Captain America, is captured and disabled by the experience. As a bookend to the series, the Steve Rogers Captain America investigates the history of the regiment in 2004 and meets with his African American predecessor—who is now reduced to an infantilized and infirm shadow of his former self—and honors Bradley's service to his country. Although the series met with some initial outcry from various chatrooms, claiming the historical background was invented (it wasn't, and Morales backs up his facts with impressive source material), the Isaiah Bradley legend has now become an "official" part of the Captain America continuity; Bradley's grandson would even take on the mantle of another World War II superhero called the Patriot and fight evil into the 21st century.

Of course, in addition to the "inside baseball" of clever retconning, there is also the simple evolution of characters: Superman and Lois Lane got married in 1996; Batman

Cap's kid sidekick, Bucky, returns as a Soviet nemesis in *Captain America* #14 (2006).

Based on the evidence, it does seem harder to create "new stuff" in comics, and easier to go back to the "classic" heroes—all of whom are more than five decades old. Some of that, no doubt, stems from writers and artists such as Millar, who are enamored with the heroes of their childhood. Some of the apprehension toward new characters also comes from creators who are gunshy at inventing new, potentially lucrative superheroes because they are concerned that the publishers will own the characters outright. And there is a certain sense that, in the 1940s and 1960s, the original creators got it right the first time. DC editor-in-chief and writer Geoff Johns puts it this way:

> There are breakout characters that happen, but it's just harder to do because there are so many wonderful characters out there. If I'm going to create a vigilante who wants justice and revenge and he's going to build the tech to do it, well, good luck beating Batman, right? Look at Hawkeye and Green Arrow: make another costumed archer who's going to beat those two characters. It's going to be very difficult to do.

Both of the major publishers have recently come up with strategies that allow them to straddle both the world of traditional heroic narratives as well as variations on a theme. Marvel initiated the Ultimate Universe, exactly the kind of parallel universe that DC did away with in *Crisis on Infinite Earths*, but one that allowed Marvel to fast-forward some of their characters' backgrounds, so they didn't seem like yellowed remnants of the '60s generation. In the *Ultimate Spider-Man* series, for example, Peter Parker was bitten by a genetically enhanced spider, instead of a radioactive one. Furthermore, in a 2012 development in the Ultimate Universe, Peter Parker himself dies, to be replaced as Spider-Man by a half-Hispanic, half-black teenager named Miles Morales. No worries, though: Peter Parker still swings away in the regular Marvel Universe.

In a major house-cleaning, DC Comics swept through all of their titles in 2012 and rebooted them extensively as the *New 52,*

has taken several subsequent junior-varsity Robins under his wing (one, Jason Todd, was murdered by the Joker; another is actually Bruce Wayne's own son, Damian); Captain America's World War II sidekick, Bucky Barnes, emerged from the "dead"— apparently he had actually survived the war, but as a secret Soviet agent called the Winter Soldier, and was groomed to assassinate Captain America. But these alterations and evolutions beg one essential question: Why not leave well enough alone? It was a question asked of current writer superstar Mark Millar some years ago:

> I had a real moment when I was talking to Stan Lee one time. He said to me, "Why aren't you playing with your own toys, why do you have to play with my old ones?" And he didn't mean it in a mean way— you see, my ambition when I was a kid was to come in and write these characters that I loved growing up—but to keep the pop culture alive you have to be constantly creating new stuff.

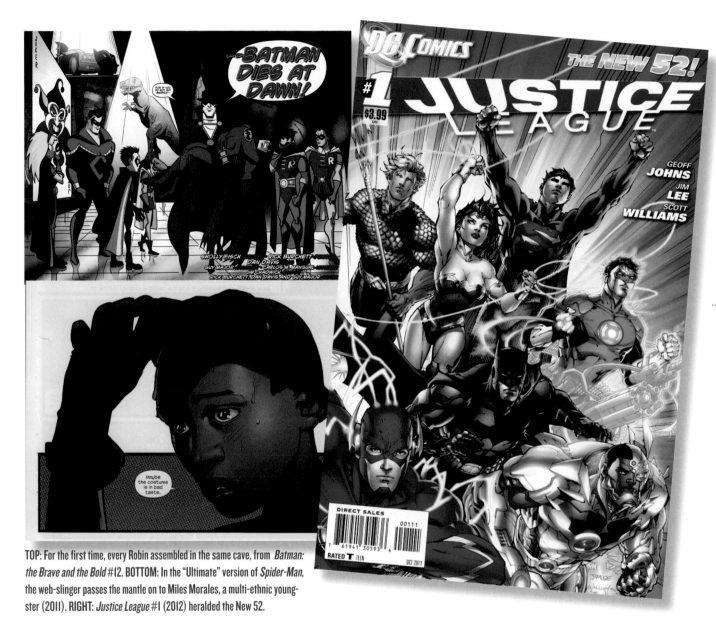

TOP: For the first time, every Robin assembled in the same cave, from *Batman: the Brave and the Bold* #12. BOTTOM: In the "Ultimate" version of *Spider-Man*, the web-slinger passes the mantle on to Miles Morales, a multi-ethnic youngster (2011). RIGHT: *Justice League* #1 (2012) heralded the New 52.

where, for example, Superman has never been married to Lois Lane and Batgirl is allowed to stalk the night again for the first time in a quarter century, never having been shot and crippled by the Joker. As if to demonstrate the cutting-edge innovation of the *New 52*, all of the DC titles were released digitally on the same day. Jim Lee, DC's co-editor, confirmed that there were many good reasons for such an extensive overhaul:

> When you're dealing with characters that have been around for seventy-plus years, there are certain barnacles that sort of accumulate on the sides of the continuity ship. And so, imagine that there are a ton of things you have to remember about who this character is and sometimes that's something that's very appealing to longtime fans, but it's also very off-putting to people that are trying to get into comics for the first time. The *New 52* gave them the opportunity to come in at the ground floor and understand who these characters are. And it also gave us a great opportunity editorially to look at all these characters and realize, hey, we have the opportunity now to strip away all the stupid stuff about the characters, keep the stuff that's really cool, and really redefine what motivates this character, what makes this character tick.

HEROES WE HAVE KNOWN AND LOVED

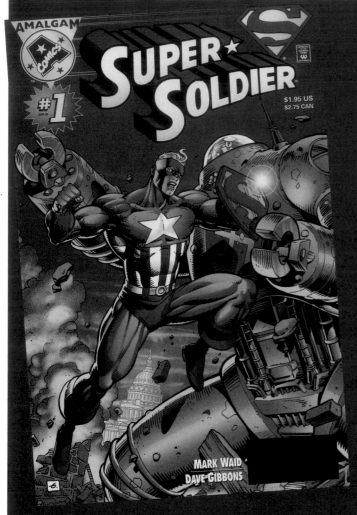

AMALGAM COMICS

SUPER ★ SOLDIER

#1

APR 96

$1.95 US
$2.75 CAN

MARK WAID
DAVE GIBBONS

SUPER-SOLDIER, MAN OF WAR

First appearance: April 1996, *Marvel Comics vs. DC* #3

For decades, comic book fans had jockeyed around the ultimate fantasy: What would happen if the Marvel heroes took on the DC heroes? In 1976, that question was finally answered, for an isolated moment at least, in the tabloid-sized, one-shot crossover book, *Superman vs. The Amazing Spider-Man: The Battle of the Century*. Apparently, in 1975, Stan Lee had been looking for a literary agent and had lunch with David Obst, the agent who represented Woodward and Bernstein. Obst queried why Superman had never fought Spider-Man and Lee countered that the legal and contractual obstacles between DC and Marvel were simply too overwhelming. Obst took the assignment upon himself as a mission; it helped that Lee and Carmine Infantino, DC's publisher,

were friendly competitors (in fact, Infantino did the cover layout).

The success of that unconventional covenant led to a few further crossover team-ups in the 1980s and early, '90s, such as Batman and the Hulk, the X-Men and the Teen Titans, and so on. In 1996, DC and Marvel decided to go all in and create a megawatt mini-series called *Marvel Comics vs. DC* (or vice versa, depending which issue one bought), where the greatest stars of each company battled it out against one other. The sales from that series opened up a door to a more imaginative idea; a year later, the companies pooled their resources to create an entire lineup of hybrid heroes under the Amalgam Comics line, in a twelve-issue series that replaced their own titles for a month.

The newly minted heroes for Amalgam were just that: an amalgamation of two complementary heroes from both publishers. Some were pretty cool (The Flash and Ghost Rider combined to become Speed Demon); some simply fessed up that one of the publishers' characters was a rip-off of the other (DC's 1940s resident magus, Dr. Fate, bonded with Marvel's 1960s mystic, Dr. Strange, to become—wait for it—Dr. Strangefate). Box-office champs Batman and Wolverine were combined to create Dark Claw, who appeared in a story about the son of a murdered millionaire who gets shipped off to Canada and gets superheroically enhanced. (A reprise of the character was even drawn in the style of the Batman animated series on television.)

The cleverest hybrid of all was concocted by industry superstars Mark Waid and Dave Gibbons: Super-Soldier. Set in the 1940s, Super-Soldier's origin begins when U.S. government scientists isolate the genes of an extinct alien and inject them as a serum into puny Clark Kent. Kent is transformed into a red-and-blue-costumed, shield-slinging warrior who works undercover for the army. Along with his trusty sidekick, photographer Jimmy Olsen, Super-Soldier sets sail for Europe, where he defends democracy against Hitler's hordes.

The Amalgam Universe (which also created a battery of fictional company histories, archival material, and letters pages) might well have been impossible to sustain, but fans could feel the pure joy surging behind the effort, however brief. Alas, as the 21st century dawned, there were fewer and fewer DC/Marvel crossovers or joint ventures. As each company was acquired by larger media

much languished in the dog pound of the DC Universe.

When Morrison took the reigns of a new Animal Man series in 1988, our hero was now married, slightly out of shape, and the slothful father of two kids in suburban San Diego. Eager to grab the lion's share of the superhero market, Animal Man tries to jumpstart his career, but discovers he is more attuned to the animal world and its dilemmas than he initially thought. During Morrison's twenty-six-issue run of *Animal Man*, Buddy became a serious advocate of animal rights and vegetarianism, and the series veered into metaphysical territory, such as the much-lauded story where Animal Man encounters a potential messiah in the form of an indestructible coyote who strongly resembles a leading Looney Tunes character. Morrison inserted his own political, societal, and literary opinions as the series grew progressively more Pirandellian: bidding farewell to his zoological hero, Morrison tells him, "Pointless violence and death is 'realistic.' Comic books are 'realistic' now . . . maybe, for once, we could try to be kind."

conglomerates, relations between the industry leaders became frostier. Another balls-out venture such as Amalgam seems as unlikely as getting Democrats and Republicans to come together and amalgamate a federal budget.

ANIMAL MAN

First appearance: September 1965,
Strange Adventures #180

"You existed long before I wrote about you—and if you're lucky, you'll still be young when I'm old or dead." Not many superheroes can boast of being directly addressed by the writer of their adventures, but in 1990, Animal Man endured this unique fate. The author was Grant Morrison, who wrote himself in as a character in issue #26, and what he said to his hero was essentially true. Animal Man first came into existence when Morrison was only five years old, in a seemingly one-shot tale in the science fiction omnibus *Strange Adventures*, entitled "I Was the Man with the Animal Powers." Buddy Baker was a stuntman who inherited an odd power while absorbing the radiation of a spaceship that crashed to earth: he could absorb the power of any animal in his vicinity. He eventually got a superhero costume and pretty

MADMAN

First appearance: October 1990, *Creatures of the Id*

As the world of comic books got crazier in the 1990s, it was only a matter of time before the heroes did, too. Perhaps no other superhero represents the anarchic world of independent comics—and their highly original takes on the superhero genre—than Michael Allred's stitched-together costumed adventurer, Madman. Originally a private investigator killed in a car accident, Madman was brought back to life by being sewn back together and reanimated by the eccentric scientist Dr. Boiffard (whose brain would eventually

grow to titanic proportions, but that's another story). Boiffard dubbed the new creature "Frank Einstein"—as a tribute to his favorite singer (Sinatra) and physicist (Albert), but any other allusion works just as well.

Madman had a swell costume (modeled on his childhood hero, Mr. Excitement), which served to cover his patchwork body, and some vague powers of agility and psychic prescience. He spent most of his time at Dark Horse Comics, where he had his own title for six years, running around in his naïve and detached way with a cadre of mad scientists, drooling aliens, humorless robots, and torpedo-breasted women. If his Ed Wood-esque (mis)adventures seemed as if they were made up as they went along, that was all part of the method behind Madman's madness. After all, any superhero who refers to his adversary, mid-combat, as "You stinky!" can't be completely crazy.

INVINCIBLE

First appearance: October 2002, *Tech Jacket* #1

Not all independent comic book superheroes were creeps or creepy. Writer Robert Kirkman spun one of the 21st century's most appealing new heroes out of the fundamental tropes that kept Superman, Spider-Man, and even Superboy fresh for decades. In a generic American town, young Mark Grayson ("Grayson"—well, there's a

throw to Robin the Boy Wonder, too) goes through the typical high school grind—falling asleep in class, mooning over a pretty redhead, working after-hours at a burger joint—only to discover one day he has assumed a host of superpowers including invulnerability and flight. It turns out that his seemingly middle-class father is actually Omni-Man, a supreme superhero from the Viltrumite race, and Mark has inherited much of his invincibility. Mark's coming of super-age, his affection for his human mother, and his complex and ultimately antagonistic relationship with his omniscient dad, was

rendered in a fresh and uplifting way by artists Cory Walker and Ryan Ottley in more than 100 issues in the Image Comics imprint Skybound.

DEADPOOL

First appearance: 1990, *New Mutants* #18

In many ways, Deadpool was a Frankenstein's monster, composed of the 1990s' most popular superhero tropes, stitched together with the kind of "you can't possibly take this seriously" thread usually found on the *Late Show with David Letterman*. Yet another government-created assassin, Deadpool, created by Rob Liefeld and Fabian Nicieza, owed his actual roots to the mutant mojo of the X-Men. Seeking a cure for cancer, Wade Wilson (ostensibly Deadpool's real name—no one really knows) volunteered for a science experiment that involved being injected with an element of Wolverine's self-healing genes; given the power of regenerating tissue, Deadpool was able to hang out his shingle as a much-desired mercenary.

Covered head-to-toe with a red-and-blue suit (not unlike Spider-Man) to disguise the corrosive cancer taking over his body, Deadpool proved to be a more-than-capable combatant, wielding a pair of samurai swords that looked as if they had been boosted from the Teenage Mutant Ninja Turtles. As if combining the characteristics of Wolverine, the Punisher, Spider-Man, and the Ninja Turtles weren't enough to ensure his popularity, Deadpool spoke in a near-Asperger's stream of consciousness, a logorrhea of pop culture references and tough-guy clichés: "Start spreading the newwwws . . ." he once crooned to a potential victim. "You're dying todayyyyy . . . because you tried to rip me off, in old New Yorrrrrk!" Under the eventual guidance of writer Joe Kelly and artist Ed McGuinness, the "Merc with a Mouth" became one of Marvel's most peripatetic, if chattiest, superstars.

AND VILLAINS WE LOVE TO HATE

THANOS

First appearance: February 1973, *Iron Man* #55

When writer/artist Jim Starlin first conceived of Marvel's baddest dude in the 1970s, he admittedly stole a page or two from Jack Kirby's Darkseid, but added a bit of Greek mythology—a concise bit: Thanos's name derived from a shorthand version of the Greek demon of death, Thanatos. Initially, Thanos was an interstellar interloper; born out of the family of Titans, he was cast out by his mother in favor of his more attractive brother. He then wielded his considerable intellect, physical strength, and cosmic powers across the galaxy, committed to the service of Up to No Good.

While other miscreants sought world domination (Dr. Doom) or universal domination (Darkseid), Thanos was a completely nihilistic narcissist, intent on destruction for its own sake. He tangled with another cosmic hero, Warlord, and facilitated the death of the Kree warrior, Captain Marvel. His main objective was to acquire the powerful "soul gems" which, when collected into the Infinity Gauntlet, gave him abilities beyond imagining. In the six-issue mini-series *The Infinity Gauntlet*, he fell in love with Death (literally) and offered her the lives of half the beings in the universe in much the same way a normal person would deliver a box of chocolates on Valentine's Day. The heroes of the Marvel Universe united against him—"Come and get me!" Thanos taunt-

ed them—and they ultimately, if temporarily, prevailed. When the "mad Titan" was revealed as the behind-the-scenes mastermind in a cameo after the final credits of the 2012 *The Avengers* film, fanboys across America shrieked in delight, eager to know what humiliations and depredations Thanos had in store for them.

BANE

First appearance: January 1993, *Batman: Vengeance of Bane* #1

Anyone who is raised in a high-security prison, isolated on an island in South America, and injected with a super-steroidal chemical, probably isn't going to grow up to work for the Peace Corps. Bane was yet another one of the highly imaginative and engaging villains to populate the Batman's rogues' gallery. While stuck in the prison of Santa Prisca (courtesy of editor Denny O'Neil), Bane was hooked up to a pump that allowed him to ingest a toxic chemical called Venom. While he developed the furthest reaches of his own intelligence, his body began a relentless mutation. Deducing Batman's identity, he escaped to Gotham City, where he released the worst miscreants of Arkham Asylum into the streets. Eventually trapping Batman in the Batcave, Bane used his brute strength to snap Batman's back; this led to the storyline of "Knightfall" in which the recovering Batman is super-ceded by a far more violent acolyte named Azrael.

While loyal comics readers knew of Bane's terribly violent nature and ruthless intelligence, viewers of the misguided 1997 film *Batman and Robin* only saw Bane as a hulking monosyllabic pro wrestler. When Christopher Nolan took over the cinematic reins of the character with *The Dark Knight Rises* in 2012, he restored Bane to the height of his homicidal dignity and gave Batman, Gotham City, and audiences around the world a terrible force with which to be reckoned.

Robert Downey, Jr., took one of Marvel's less illustrious characters and burnished him into a movie star in *Iron Man* (2008). RIGHT: Kirsten Dunst gives Tobey Maguire's Spidey the sexiest kiss in superhero movies, in *Spider-Man* (2002).

WAA-HOOOOO!
CGI Meets the Superhero

To me, the whole point of comics is a writer can sit down with a penciller and in twenty-two pages create a visual presentation that would cost Jim Cameron fifteen years and a billion dollars to figure out.

Writer Chris Claremont is correct about how much easier it is to create a comic book than a film; director James Cameron never made the Spider-Man film he announced in 1990. In the end, it took twelve more years and $139 million to bring the wall-crawler to the screen, thanks to a little magic genie called CGI.

Marvel Comics had nothing but travails in bringing their characters to the screen, and it was heartbreaking for them not to have a tentpole Spider-Man movie, while DC/Warner were cleaning up with their characters. "They didn't have the special effects that they have now," said Stan Lee. "There was no way of doing it. Today, when you see Spider-Man swinging on that web from building to building, it's fantastic. Couldn't do that twenty years ago. But it's like any movie, based on any books or anything, you have to have people who understand the story, and are able to tell it in the most interesting, believable way."

Sony Pictures found a way to make the Spider-Man story believable, hiring director Sam Raimi, actor Tobey Maguire as a sensitive but spunky Peter Parker, and bringing it all together in a 2002 movie that could finally render both the vertigo-inducing, sky-scraping-swinging world of Spider-Man and the personal trials and tribulations that toiled underneath. It didn't hurt that Spider-Man was just the hero that America needed in the aftermath of 9/11. (In fact, a summer trailer for the film in 2001 showed a helicopter full of bank robbers being stuck between the Twin Towers, courtesy of an immense spider web; it was quickly dropped from theaters and the towers themselves were digitally blurred from the background of actual location shots in the eventual release.)

Spider-Man respected the origins and background of the action hero, conveying both his derring-do and his sense of humor. When Peter Parker, exercising his newfound abilities for

the first time, attempts to shoot a web across a rooftop, he rehearses several battle cries, hoping to find one that fits: "Up, up, and away!," "Shazam!," and "Flame on!," thereby endearing himself to every comic book fan in the audience. (Eventually, "Waa-hooooo!!" seems to do the trick.) It was that rare film that satisfied both the immense fan base, while bringing in audiences that would not traditionally be lured into a summer action blockbuster featuring a guy in tights. In its initial release, *Spider-Man* earned more than six times its production costs and eventually spun two sequels and a reboot. An upside-down kiss in the rain between the mysteriously masked Spider-Man and red-headed actress Mary Jane Watson encapsulated the movie's transcendent appeal. "All of us who [worked in comics] were thought of as the types who lived in the basement with our mom," said Jeph Loeb. "Then suddenly *Spider-Man* came out and girls were going, moms were going, families were going, people were suddenly going—whoa, hang on a second. This is . . . *sexy*. Comics suddenly became sexy."

Aided by the critical and commercial success of the first two X-Men movies, which came out at roughly the same time, *Spider-Man* ushered in a string of cinematic blockbusters for the Marvel line. They had a dedicated film company, Marvel Productions, which teamed up with various studios, and under the guidance of producer/executive/president Kevin Feige, brought some highly unlikely characters to the screen, such as Iron Man, a not-quite-household-name superhero whose first two solo adventures

LEFT: The X-Men (here in *X2*, 2003) were the most popular team franchise.
RIGHT: *Daredevil*, the same year (with Ben Affleck), wasn't seen by many. BOTTOM: Heath Ledger as the psychotic Joker stole *The Dark Knight* (2008) from Christian Bale.

nonetheless brought in more than $1.2 billion at the box office. Feige, an acknowledged comic book nerd, had a particular gift for keeping fans happy while bringing in the first-weekend crowds. "I'm not sure there is a formula or a secret," he said, "but I do know that problems tend to happen when people try and re-invent the wheel. If you actually open the comics, there is a lot of depth there." Despite the occasional misfire, such as *Daredevil* and two Hulk movies (something about Ol' Greenskin allows him to smash everything except box office records), Feige's more than two dozen Marvel film projects have brought in more than $7 billion in admission tickets across the globe.

Perhaps some of the extraordinary appeal of these movies can be derived from the anxieties of the post 9/11 "new normal." Writer Grant Morrison thinks so: "Suddenly superheroes became real things that weren't completely ridiculous, and they were suddenly being explained to us in terms of how Iron Man would actually work. In the first film, there's an evenly paced half-hour of Robert Downey, Jr., banging together a suit of armor so that it's convincing to the audience." The next great superhero movie phenomenon also involved a billionaire working secretly on armored paraphernalia in a high-tech hideaway in order to bring justice to a world that desperately needed it.

When Warner Bros. decided to tackle Batman again in 2004—this time with visionary director and writer Christopher Nolan—they were, in many ways, up against the same problems they had faced sixteen years earlier when trying to create a serious Batman movie in the wake of the television series. The previous Batman film outing, *Batman and Robin* (1997), had been excoriated for its over-the-top theatrics and its disco-diva designs (especially the Bat-suits with faux nipples). So, with *Batman Begins*, the heat was on Nolan to create a serious Batman who had some resonance for 21st-century audiences; inspired by the 1978 *Superman* movie, Nolan went back to Batman's roots to explore something that, strangely enough, no *Batman* movie ever had done. "What I wanted to do," explained Nolan, "was to tell the Batman story I'd never seen, the one that the fans have been wanting to see—the story of how Bruce Wayne becomes Batman. There were also a lot of very interesting gaps in the mythology that we were able to interpret ourselves and bring in our own ideas of how Bruce Wayne and Batman would have evolved specifically."

Once again, the success of a superhero movie would depend on a balance between the director's respect for the material and the casting of the lead role. Nolan had a Bruce Wayne no one could kvetch about—the raven-haired, taciturn Christian Bale, who lost his voice three times during shooting, trying to find the pitch of the Batman's subterranean growl. The Dark Knight in *Batman Begins* (2005) was the perfect spin on the hero for his times; neither campy nor psychologically unstable, he was cruel only to be kind:

> RA'S AL GHUL: Have you finally learned to do
> what is necessary?
> BATMAN: I won't kill you, but I don't have to
> save you.

The success of *Batman Begins*—a unique and chancy reboot of a franchise, the first of its kind—surprised everyone by doubling its original investment at the box office and setting off two highly regarded sequels, also directed by Nolan: *The Dark Knight* and *The Dark Knight Rises*. Taken together, the trilogy has earned $2.5 billion, making it the most successful superhero franchise in history.

But the Dark Knight films have more to offer than box office coin. Heath Ledger became the first actor ever to win an Academy Award for a superhero film, for his twisted, original take on the Joker in *The Dark Knight*. The films also offered a prism through which audiences could view unconventional heroism in the tense times of the early 21st century. Batman's costume was composed of elements more befitting a commando or a black-ops agent than a traditional superhero, and the Gotham City under his vigilante purview was a fearsome, unstable place, where enemies could spring up out of nowhere and deliver devastating, unpredictable chaos.

In a *Rolling Stone* essay that profiled the 2012 *The Dark Knight Rises*, novelist Jonathan Lethem found the Christopher Nolan/Christian Bale team a metaphor for the time: "In any era, we get the Batman we deserve. . . . It is our belief in his great purpose that sustains him. Batman's refusal to wield a gun, the weapon that killed his parents, links him to a classic American problem, being: is the man violent enough to clear the path for civilization himself unfit to participate in civilized society? He's the manned drone of 21st-century urban warfare."

For all the dark implications of the trilogy (the three Batman movies were dark in nearly every respect), the series ended on a hopeful note, suggesting that, after nearly seventy-five years in the superhero business, Batman was inspiring enough to enflame a heroic streak in anyone's heart. Nolan's Batman was just another iteration of the most elastic crusader in comic book history—yes, including Plastic Man—a paladin of retribution who could inhabit whatever eccentricities and fears the culture could dish out, just an everyman in a black mask and cape, who devoted his existence to the enervating, but revitalizing, quest for justice:

> BATMAN: A hero can be anyone. Even a man doing
> something as simple and reassuring as putting a
> coat around a little boy's shoulders to let him know
> that the world hadn't ended.

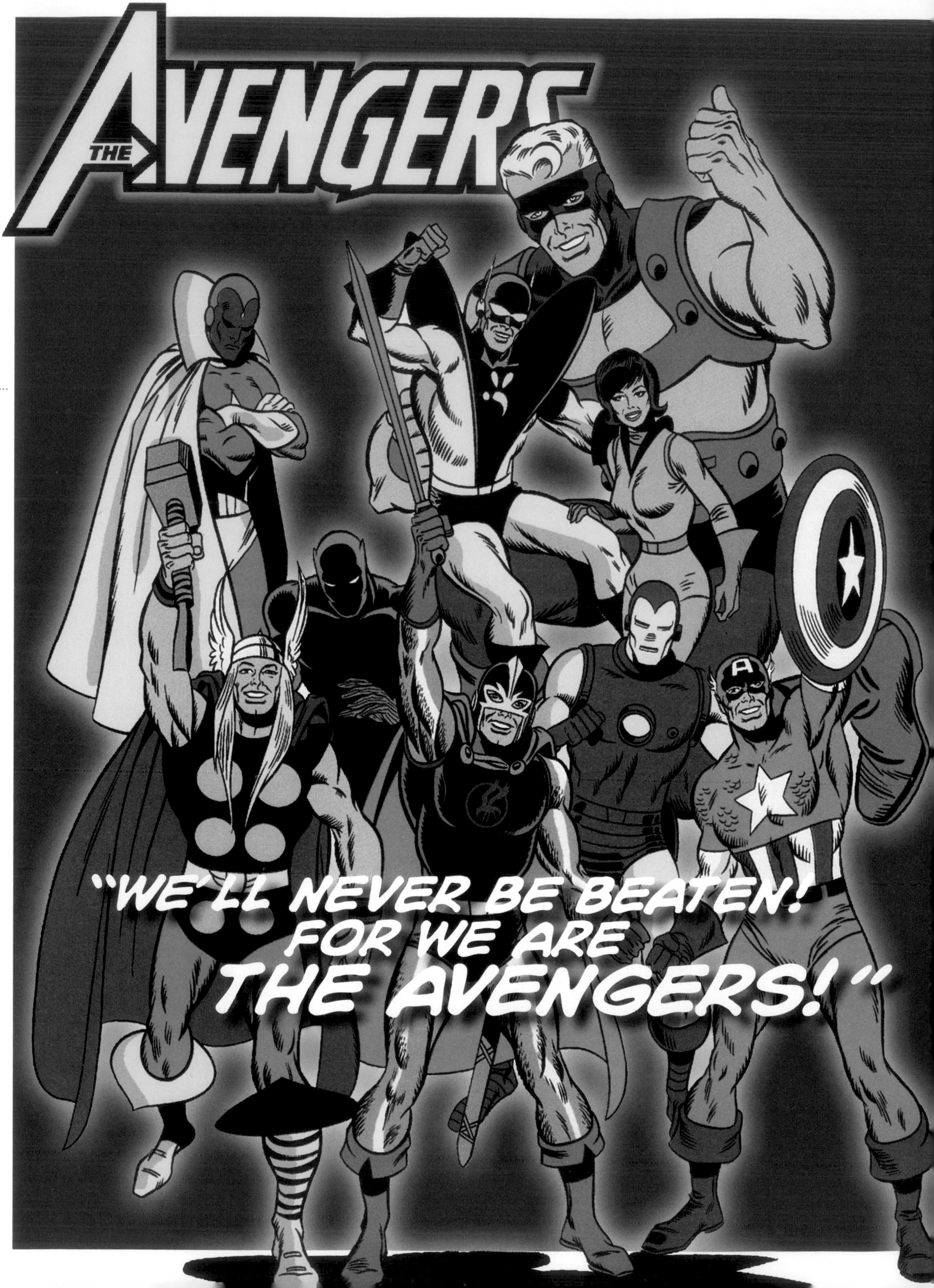
THE AVENGERS
"WE'LL NEVER BE BEATEN! FOR WE ARE THE AVENGERS!"

"And there came a day, a day unlike any other, when Earth's mightiest heroes and heroines found themselves united against a common threat. On that day, the Avengers were born—to fight the foes no single superhero could withstand!"

The Avengers have always had their headquarters in the most exclusive neighborhoods—a mansion on Fifth Avenue, and a state-of-the-art, ninety-three-story high-rise skyscraper—which is probably a good thing. Considering how much damage that they have dealt out and dealt with in their fifty-year history, you probably wouldn't want them living on your block.

When Stan Lee and Jack Kirby brought the Avengers forth on the world in the summer of 1963, they were largely borrowing from the format successfully reintroduced at DC with the Justice League of America: put all your superstars into one package. Indeed, they brought together Marvel's major unaffiliated heavy hitters: Iron Man, Thor, the Hulk, and Ant-Man and his paramour, the Wasp (the latter two were never exactly heavy-hitters in the Marvel lineup, but they were loyal; Ant-Man was also an ingenious scientist, Hank Pym, which came in handy). Why Spider-Man was never introduced into the team way back when is a bit of a mystery (he was a major draw, after all), but perhaps Lee wisely thought Spidey was not a "joiner."

ABOVE: "The Old Order Changeth!" *The Avengers* #16 set the stage for change-ups (1965).

OPPOSITE: John Buscema's vision of the Avengers in 1968.

The Avengers turned into a title that was larger than the sum of its parts when Captain America reappeared in #4 and, further, when he took over the reigns as the team's inevitable leader. By issue #16, Cap was required to become company recruiter as well when Stan Lee, mindful of the fact that Iron Man and Thor had obligations elsewhere in their own titles, cycled out his original team. The new Avengers team, still led by Captain America, was now constituted of the Scarlet Witch and her brother, the moody Quicksilver (two reformed members of the Brotherhood of Evil Mutants), and Hawkeye, a smart-ass archer with a purple costume who was also once a villain in the Marvel Universe. The fact that the new recruits were Avengers first and foremost—without solo books of their own—somehow made the group more appealing and powerful. By the end of the 1960s, the Avengers had gained the Black Panther and, under the guidance of editor/writer Roy Thomas, a brand-new character called the Vision, a synthesized android who took some of his body parts from the original Human Torch and much of his emotionless, logical mien from Mr. Spock of TV's *Star Trek*. His devotion to the team, however, made him one of the most beloved and reliable Avengers for the next four decades.

Throughout the 1970s, *The Avengers* evolved into something more exciting than a contrived team-up book; thrust by Thomas into more interplanetary sagas such as the nine-part "Kree-Skrull War" epic, the team became the go-to group in the Marvel Universe for big canvas, colorful epics—David Lean would have been a good director for their Panavision-sized exploits. *The Avengers* also contained an extra helping of Marvel-styled soap opera: Hank Pym suffers an inferiority complex, becomes a schizophrenic, and physically abuses his now-wife, the Wasp; the synthetic Vision compiles enough emotive particles to fall in love with, then propose marriage to, the Scarlet Witch, who readily accepts. The Vision/Scarlet Witch relationship would become even more complex as the years went on: he would lead a misguided attempt to take over the world's computers and, in the aftermath, be dismantled (before being restored again, of course). The Scarlet Witch would raise two children from her union with the Vision, only to discover they were only figments of her imagination, which drove her mad and caused her to wreak havoc on her teammates. It's an Avengers' world, folks!

Longtime Avengers editor Tom Brevoort wrote that the *Avengers'* appeal comes about largely because of the volunteerism of their membership: "[They are] not a family, not a persecuted minority, not grouped together by geography or gathered by the government, the Avengers are the Avengers because they want to be—because they need to be—in order to safeguard the world." Captain America, Iron Man, Thor, (usually) the Vision, and some iteration of Ant-Man and the Wasp were cornerstone members of the team throughout the end of the 20th century, but the group could also be a catchall for some of the more idiosyncratic outliers in the Marvel Universe, such as Tigra (occasionally known as Tigra, the Were-Woman); the She-Hulk (a far more articulate and attractive cousin of the Hulk); the Black Knight (a pseudo-medieval character whose Marvel Comics roots stretched back to the 1950s); and Mantis, a former Vietnamese bar-girl who was destined to give birth to the Celestial Messiah. These engaging oddballs were but a few of the dozens of Avengers members over the years.

Despite such compelling characters and storylines, *The Avengers* was not a particularly best-selling comic. Editors at Marvel Comics pondered the dilemma and, according to editor-in-chief Joe Quesada, it was Scottish-born writer Mark Millar who gave them the key to the puzzle:

> He cited going to a candy store as a kid and looking for comics. He was a DC fan at the time and he saw a *Superman* title, a *Wonder Woman* title, a *Batman* title and then all of a sudden he saw the *Justice League of America* title and he felt that that was the better place to spend his money because he could get all three in one book. So why aren't Marvel's biggest characters in the book? And he was right because as you looked at *Avengers*, it became about these sort of C- and D-level characters and every once in a while you'd sprinkle in a Captain America and a Thor and an Iron Man, but why wasn't Spider-Man in the *Avengers*? Why wasn't Wolverine in the *Avengers*? These were the characters that are prime movers in our licensing programs and on our movie slate, but yet they were nowhere

CLOCKWISE, FROM TOP LEFT: The android Vision has a teary moment in *The Avengers* #58 (1968, art by John Buscema); *Avengers Academy* #1 cover; poster art for *The Avengers* (2012); She-Hulk joins the Avengers (#221).

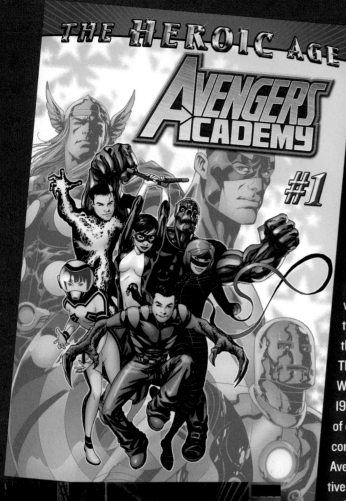

near the title that we wanted to be our number one title. So we worked out a methodology by which these characters could play all in the same sandbox—and guess what? *The Avengers* becomes our number one title.

Under the skillful pen of writer Brian Michael Bendis, the Avengers would disassemble in 2004—due to an apocalyptic meltdown by the Scarlet Witch—and regroup under a variety of successful franchises. At one point in the 1980s, a West Coast Avengers was constituted (as well as a Great Lakes Avengers, but the less said about them, the better) and had a decent run, but these new groups required a scorecard that would tax even the Vision's exceptional organization capacity. There were the New Avengers, which indeed included Spider-Man and Wolverine and were led by the same Luke Cage, Hero for Hire, from the 1970s; there were the inevitable Young Avengers, junior varsity versions of our heroes; the Mighty Avengers, a government-sponsored sub-group commandeered by Iron Man in the wake of the *Civil War* series; Dark Avengers (a disguised group of villains); Ultimate Avengers (an alternative reality where S.H.I.E.L.D. leader Nick Fury was now an African American); Secret Avengers (a black-ops version); and Avengers Academy, which recruited and trained up-and-coming Avengers—although the likelihood of Marvel running out of potential members seems highly unlikely.

Of course, the big news about the Avengers was their 2012 film debut, the result of a careful cultivation of the fan-based audience and a related slate of films that preceded it, each introducing the major characters of the Hulk, Iron Man, Thor, and Captain America. As of 2013, *Marvel's The Avengers* is the third most successful movie—of any kind or genre—in Hollywood. Director Joss Whedon painstakingly tapped into the dynamics of the team; he was strongly influenced by the early 1960s Avengers comics, of which he was a fan while growing up: "In those comics these people shouldn't be in the same room let alone on the same team—and that is the definition of family."

Whedon is on board to write and direct the highly anticipated sequel, which is due to hit movie theaters in May 2015. It may be churlish to report that a film version of the Justice League of America—the DC team that inspired the Avengers in the first place—has been stuck in development hell since 2007 with no apparent specific forward movement, so it looks like the Avengers have a long lead on the worldwide media domination front: but, heck, what's a little friendly rivalry between superteams?

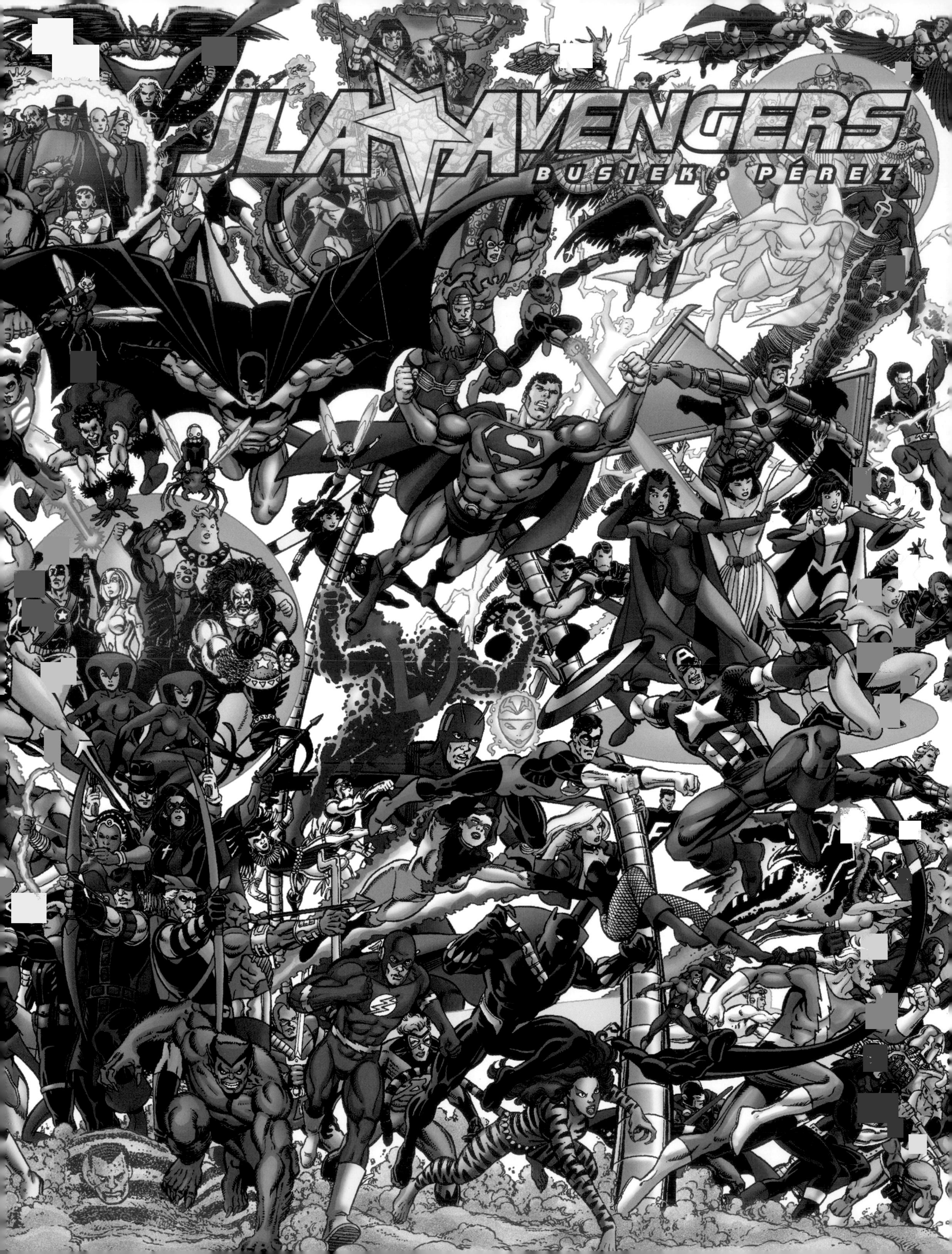
JLA AVENGERS
BUSIEK • PÉREZ

THE PULSE-POUNDING CONCLUSION!
"And So, Our Hero..."

We won," claims Marv Wolfman. He wasn't talking about a triumph by the Justice League over the Anti-Monitor or about the Avengers beating back yet another conquest by the Skrull Empire; he was talking about comic book fans:

OPPOSITE: In 2003, George Pérez contributed the most impressive crossover cover in the history of comics for *JLA/Avengers* #3. ABOVE: Batman has anchored two of the most successful video games of all time: the *Lego Batman* and *Arkham Asylum* series couldn't be more different.

> All of us who have been told that what we did was for kids or what we enjoyed was silly, or that we were geeks or dorks or whatever else—well, it turns out the whole world actually is, but it took them a while to admit it. We won because our type of fantasy is now everywhere, which means if you like superheroes, you can find it in the movies. You can find it on TV. You can find it in animation. We took our comic book readership and spread it over five other media.

It's hard to argue with a wandering Wolfman: superheroes *are* everywhere. A contributing factor to the media conquest by superheroes was two separate but equally powerful industry events in 2009: the formation of DC Entertainment within Warner Bros. and the acquisition of Marvel Entertainment by the Walt Disney Co. While DC's considerable assets were being consolidated and cross-pollinated in Burbank, over in Anaheim, Disney, which paid $4 billion for Marvel's intellectual property, found itself at a slight disadvantage, as many of the high-profile characters—Spider-Man, the X-Men—had already been optioned by several different studios. Still, the deal gave Disney a library of literally hundreds of unique and colorful characters with the potential for long-lasting franchises—and, as Stan Lee put it, "nobody knows how to play in that ballpark better than Disney."

The broad shoulders of a corporate entity allow for material to be tailored for a vastly diverse audience; there is no longer a one-size-fits-all superhero. The evolution of sophisticated video games has provided a useful example: products pitched to incipient young gamers, *Lego Batman* and *Lego Batman 2*, featuring innocent situations and simple graphics from the durable plastic block toys, have sold millions of units. In the meantime, an infinitely more mature and unsettling set of action-adventure video games based on the Arkham Asylum comic book series—*Batman: Arkham Asylum* and its sequel, *Batman: Arkham City*—has sold more than ten million units since 2009. (Parents had better not mix up *Lego Batman* with *Batman Arkham* around the PlayStation unless they want to front a hefty therapy bill for their child.) The video game, along with the embryonic digital distribution of comics, offers brand-new delivery systems for consumers of all ages, even if all the adventures of their favorite superhero can be shrunk into an app that fits snugly on your smartphone—Ant-Man himself couldn't have invented a more ingenious way to enjoy comics.

ABOVE: Inspired by comic book characters: the Batman "family" at a 2005 comics convention; and, more politically, a young man in the crowd of the Arab Spring in Cairo, 2012.

lead in years). Fifty separate titles sold more than 100,000 copies, and five sold more than 200,000—but a paradox remains: nearly all of those titles were either landmark issues—Image's *The Walking Dead* #100 sold a spectacular 353,000 copies—or part of some heavily promoted summer blockbuster series, such as *Avenger vs. X-Men*. Monthly readership of cornerstone titles—*Fantastic Four* or *Action Comics*—rarely top more than 120,000 copies, a far cry from the heyday of comic book sales.

At the movies, however, in a domain that has rendered comic book superheroes satisfactorily for only about two decades, the financial results are astronomical. In 2012 alone, superhero movies earned $3.5 billion internationally—and there's no end in sight. The standard bearer of that summer was *The Avengers*, released by Marvel Studios and Paramount Pictures. Within six months, it earned $1.5 billion worldwide, and the climax also featured the largest number of major superheroes ever assembled. On a movie screen.

In real life, comic book conventions had been assembling superheroes by the hundreds ever since the 1970s. Now, the phenomenon has reached unavoidable proportions. The San Diego International Comic-Con held every July has become the beacon of the entertainment world; Hollywood studios use the convention to offer sneak previews of their most valued products with major Hollywood stars (such as Robert Downey, Jr.) in tow, eager to spend an afternoon in a stifling, windowless room, crowded with enthusiastic fans, who are often dressed in homemade (and elaborate) costumes based on their favorite hero or heroine.

The typically three-day affairs are chock-full of events catering to every demographic and interest. There are the obligatory costume parade/competitions; panel discussions that cover manifold topics from the legal ramifications of comic books to how to break into the industry, the children's market, and the unveiling of upcoming storylines, films, and documentaries; celebrity (and pseudo-celebrity) autograph signings; "artist alleys," where leading artists will draw you an original sketch for a fee; and, at the center of it all, a vast bazaar of goods, where purveyors of fantasy push toys, collectibles, costumes, video games, weaponry, and—oh, yes—comic books. The San Diego convention attracts more than 130,000 people—as does a rival convention every fall in New

Amazing to think that, when comic books first emerged in the depths of the Depression, they were the most disposable of consumer commodities, dog-eared pulps at 10 cents a pop. In 2012, sales of comic books reached more than $318 million; the addition of trade paperbacks (graphic novels and reprints) brought the total of comic book narratives to $475 million, representing an increase of 15 percent from the previous year. A fair amount of the surge can be attributed to the interest in DC's *New 52* titles, which were introduced throughout 2011 and 2012 (it also helped DC achieve near-parity in the market share to Marvel—they each have about 37 percent of the market, the closest that DC has come to taking the

The Amazing Spider-Man #583, variant cover by Todd Nauck, released a week before the inauguration. As he campaigned for a second term in 2012, Obama was once again caught in Spidey's web.

York City—and would host even more, if the fire code regulations would permit. Nevertheless, the convention earns national television coverage, daily reports from the front in the *New York Times*, and the cover of *Entertainment Weekly*.

Five decades after they were nearly driven into the ground by a Senate subcommittee, comic books have shaken off the carapace of shame that dogged them for decades. The Comics Code Authority is defunct: Marvel Comics instituted its own ratings system in 2001; DC Comics stopped submitting their books in 2010; even that avatar of respectability, Archie Comics, bypassed the code authorities in 2012, rendering the imposition of regulations essentially irrelevant. In 2013, a researcher from the University of Illinois seems to have driven the final stake in the heart of Dr. Frederic Wertham; examining his research methods, she concluded that he may well have "manipulated, overstated, compromised, and fabricated evidence." Cold comfort to those whose careers foundered on the shoals of Wertham's campaign, but this new research into his methodology implies that his agenda drove his conclusions, rather than the other way around.

If a Senate subcommittee tarnished comic books in the mid-1950s, the executive branch gave the medium the ultimate shout-

out in 2008. Real-life presidents had appeared in comics since Franklin D. Roosevelt made a cameo in the first issue of *Captain America*, as a sponsor of the Super-Soldier project, but there had never been a President who was an outspoken fan of comic books until candidate Barack Obama stepped forward in an *Entertainment Weekly* interview in 2008. When asked about comic books (apparently, he was a collector as a kid), Obama opined:

> I was always into the Spider-Man/Batman model. The guys who have too many powers—like Superman—that always made me think they weren't really earning their superhero status. It's a little too easy. Whereas Spider-Man and Batman, they have some inner turmoil. They get knocked around a little bit.

Comic book fans around the country went berserk with the happiness of conferred recognition. Marvel Comics, seeing an opportunity, elbowed DC Comics out of the receiving line. According to Joe Quesada, "[Obama] put our name in the press and put our character's name in the press. We figured we needed to tip our hat back. It seemed to us that he was a Spider-Man kind of guy, so we put him on a special Inauguration Day cover."

Sometimes our guardian angels can arrive in the guise of devils: a stunning Alex Maleev illustration of Daredevil, the Man Without Fear (*Daredevil* #41, 1988). FOLLOWING PAGE: No sentimental conclusions for me, bub: an unpublished Wolverine illustration, courtesy of Joe Quesada.

The Amazing Spider-Man #583 featured a short introductory story that had Peter Parker covering the Inauguration of Obama in Washington and foiling a nefarious plot by the master of disguise, the Chameleon, who attempted to trade places with Obama. The Inauguration issue went into five separate printings, with variant covers, and sold more than 350,000 copies—roughly five times what a typical Spider-Man comic sold at the time. Weeks later, Newsarama.com correspondent Michael Doran questioned the potential effect of Obama's stimulus package, "but the new President has already stimulated sales in at least one American industry."

If comic books were popular with the President of the United States, comic book characters always enjoy near-universal popularity with average citizens around the world—and perhaps this has led the way for them, finally, to be accorded respect. In an interview months before he passed away, comic book legend Joe Kubert reflected, "Comic books had always been looked at as a junk medium, as stuff for kids. An adult would have been ashamed to be caught reading a comic book—that's quite different today. The utilization of superheroes in movies, and in other venues, has put the mantle of acceptance on the comic books that they have never had before." Frank Miller said that "a generation of people who read comic books have come up and taken over certain aspects of entertainment. In other words, the inmates have taken over the asylum and you're all in trouble." Trouble or no, we have become, in the words of cultural historian Bradford Wright, "a comic book nation."

Superheroes have always come to the rescue when our nation was in the direst need. They arrived on the scene during the Depression, when our nation was plunged into fear and economic chaos, and they piloted us through our most overwhelming military conflict. They returned to dispel the anxiety over the threats from our greatest rivals, found in the atmosphere of outer space and the mysteries at the heart of an atom. Superheroes shouldered the burden of living under the distress of a new not-so-normal world, encroached by the shadows of terrorism and economic collapse. They always arrive, just in the nick of time. "We want to believe in superheroes," said Geoff Johns. "And you know what? Superman will never let you down."

Superheroes are a projection of American possibility, violence, justice, risk, and aspiration. "We want to be better. We want to be stronger. We want to be more heroic. It's a craving that we all have," said Adam West, who taught a generation of kids the meaning of heroism. "And, having played a pretend superhero, I recognize it. I'm not a superhero. But I think I'm like any guy out there—it feels good to watch people do heroic things."

Whether they burst forth from an IMAX movie screen, or leap out of our video screens and computer monitors, or get rolled up and thrust into the back pocket of an eleven-year-old's dungarees, superheroes seem to have always been around, zooming through the sky, looking out for us on high. To quote another American hero, Abraham Lincoln, they are the better angels of our nature.

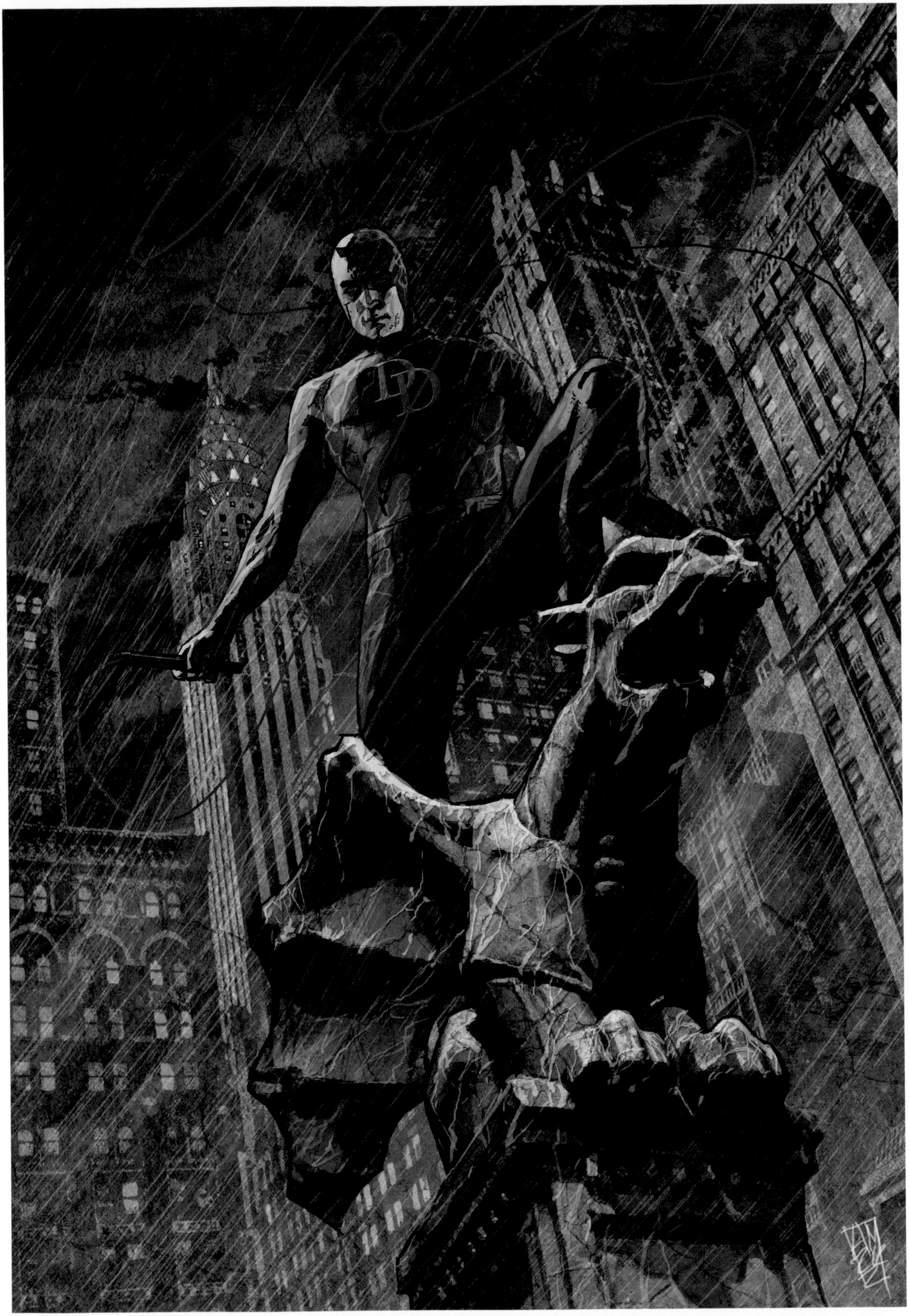

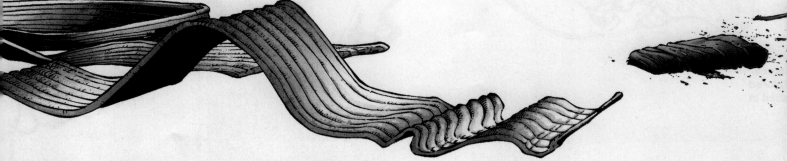

SELECTED BIBLIOGRAPHY

There was a time, hard to imagine, when there weren't any books about comic books. Two pioneers changed all that, with volumes that are still insightful and imaginative: Jules Feiffer with his *The Great Comic Book Heroes* and Jim Steranko with his two-volume (only, alas) *History of the Comics* (those covers!). Below is a very selective list of books that follow in those impressive footsteps. The many, many collected editions of various comic books are listed only if they were seminal to this book and/or have impressive introductory and historical information.

The Internet has become the logical repository of much comic book superhero lore. Two great resources are Don Markstein's Toonopedia (www.Toonopedia.com) and Dial B for Blog (www.dialbforblog.com). I'm also indebted to Roy Thomas for *Avengers* #93 (my favorite comic ever), and for his ongoing publication out of TwoMorrows Publishing in North Carolina, *Alter Ego*.

—Laurence Maslon

Amash, Jim, et al. *Carmine Infantino: Penciler, Publisher, Provocateur.* Raleigh, NC: TwoMorrows Publishing, 2010.

Andrae, Thomas. *Creators of the Superheroes.* New Castle, PA: Hermes Press, 2011.

Beaty, Bart. *Frederic Wertham and the Critique of Mass Culture.* Jackson: University Press of Mississippi, 2005.

Bell, Blake. *Fire & Water: Bill Everett, the Sub-Mariner, and the Birth of Marvel Comics.* Seattle: Fantagraphics, 2010.

Bendis, Brian, and Sara Pichelli. *Ultimate Comics: Spider-Man Vol.* I. New York: Marvel Comics, 2012.

Benton, Mike. *The Comic Book in America: An Illustrated History.* Dallas: Taylor Pub., 1993.

Bradbury, Ray (Foreword). *Comic-Con: 40 Years of Artists, Writers, Fans & Friends!* San Francisco: Chronicle Books, 2009.

Brown, Jeffrey. *Black Superheroes, Milestone Comics and Their Fans.* University Press of Mississippi, 2000.

Busiek, Kurt, and Alex Ross. *Marvels.* New York: Marvel Comics, 2009.

Campbell, Joseph. *The Hero with a Thousand Faces.* Novato, CA: New World Library, 2008.

Carlin, John. *Masters of American Comics.* New Haven, CT: Yale University Press, 2005.

Chabon, Michael. *The Amazing Adventures of Kavalier & Clay.* New York: Picador, 2000.

Claremont, Chris, et al. *Essential Wolverine.* New York: Marvel Comics, 2005.

Claremont, Chris, et al. *The Uncanny X-Men.* New York: Marvel Comics, 2009.

Conway, Gerry, et al. *Essential Ms. Marvel.* New York: Marvel Comics, 2007.

Coogan, Peter. *Superhero: The Secret Origin of a Genre.* Austin, TX: Monkey Brain Books, 2006.

Cooke, Darwyn. *DC: The New Frontier: Volume One.* New York: DC Comics, 2004.

Cooke, Darwyn. *DC: The New Frontier: Volume Two.* New York: DC Comics, 2004.

Couch, N.C. Christopher. *Jerry Robinson: Ambassador of Comics.* New York: Abrams ComicArts 2010.

Cowsill, Alan. *DC Comics: Year by Year A Visual Chronicle.* New York: DK Publishing, 2010.

Daniels, Les. *Batman: The Complete History.* San Francisco: Chronicle Books, 1999.

Daniels, Les. *Superman: The Golden Age.* San Francisco: Chronicle Books, 1999.

Daniels, Les. *DC Comics: Sixty Years of the World's Favorite Comic Book Heroes.* Boston: Bulfinch Press, 1995.

Daniels, Les. Marvel: *Five Fabulous Decades of the World's Greatest Comics.* New York: Harry N. Abrams, Inc., 1991.

Daniels, Les. *Superman: The Complete History.* San Francisco: Chronicle Books, 1998.

Daniels, Les. *Wonder Woman: The Complete History.* San Francisco: Chronicle Books, 2000.

De Haven, Tom. *Our Hero Superman on Earth.* New Haven: Yale University Press, 2010.

Eisner, Will, et al. *9-11 Artists Respond Volume I.* New York: Dark Horse, 2001.

Evanier, Mark. *Kirby: King of Comics.* New York: Harry N. Abrams, Inc., 2008.

Everett, Bill, et al, eds. *Marvel 70th Anniversary Collection.* New York: Marvel Comics, 2009.

Feiffer, Jules. *The Great Comic Book Heroes.* New York: Knopf, 1966.

Fingeroth, Danny. *Superman on the Couch: What Superheroes Really Tell Us About Ourselves and Society.* New York: Continuum, 2004.

Fox, Gardner, et al. *The Greatest Flash Stories Ever Told.* New York: DC Comics, 1991.

Gaiman, Neil, et al. *9-11 Artists Respond, Volume 2.* New York: DC Comics, 2001.

Gaiman, Neil. *Marvel 1602.* New York: Marvel Comics, 2010.

Galewitz, Herb, ed. *Celebrated Cases of Dick Tracy.* New York: Chelsea House, 1970.

Gibson, Walter Brown. *The Shadow Scrapbook.* San Diego: Harcourt, 1979.

Gilbert, James. *A Cycle of Outrage: America's Reaction to the Juvenile Delinquent in the 1950s.* New York: Oxford University Press, 1986.

Goulart, Ron. *Comic Book Culture: an Illustrated History.* Portland, OR: Collectors Press, 2000.

Greenberger, Robert. *Wonder Woman: Amazon, Hero, Icon.* New York: Universe, 2010.

Hajdu, David. *The Ten-Cent Plague: The Great Comic-Book Scare and How It Changed America.* New York: Farrar, Straus and Giroux, 2008.

Hanks, Fletcher. *I Shall Destroy All the Civilized Planets!* Seattle: Fantagraphics, 2007.

Harmon, Jim. *The Great Radio Heroes.* Doubleday, 1969.

Harvey, Robert C. *The Art of the Comic Book: An Aesthetic History.* Jackson: University Press of Mississippi, 1996.

Howe, Sean, ed. *Give Our Regards to the Atomsmashers!: Writers on Comics.* New York: Pantheon Books, 2004.

Howe, Sean. *Marvel Comics: The Untold Story.* New York: Harper, 2012.

Infantino, Carmine, and J. David Spurlock. *The Amazing World of Carmine Infantino.* Coral Gables, Florida: Vanguard Productions, 2001.

Inge, M. Thomas. *Comics as Culture.* Jackson: University Press of Mississippi, 1990.

Jones, Gerard. *Men of Tomorrow: Geeks, Gangsters and the Birth of the Comic Book.* New York: Basic Books, 2004.

Jones, Gerard and Will Jacobs. *The Comic Book Heroes.* Rocklin, CA: Prima Publishing, 1997.

Jurgens, Dan, et al. *The Death of Superman.* New York: DC Comics, 1993.

Kane, Bob, with Tom Andrae. *Batman & Me.* Forestville, CA: Eclipse Books, 1989.

Kidd, Chip, and Geoff Spear. *Shazam! The Golden Age of the World's Mightiest Mortal.* New York: Abrams ComicArts, 2010.

Kirby, Jack, et al. *Marvel Firsts: The 1970s Vol I.* New York: Marvel Comics, 2011.

Kirby, Jack. *Jack Kirby's Fourth World Omnibus: Volume One.* New York: DC Comics, 2007.

Lee, Stan, and Steve Ditko. *The Amazing Spider-Man Vol I.* New York: Marvel Comics, 2002.

Lee, Stan, and Steve Ditko. *The Amazing Spider-Man Vol 2.* New York: Marvel Comics, 2003.

Lee, Stan, and George Mair. *Excelsior!: The Amazing Life of Stan Lee.* New York: Fireside, 2002.

Lee, Stan, and Jack Kirby. *Captain America.* New York: Marvel Comics, 2011.

Lee, Stan, and Jack Kirby. *The Avengers.* New York: Marvel Comics, 2009.

Lee, Stan, and Jack Kirby. *The Fantastic Four.* New York: Marvel Comics, 2010.

Lee, Stan, and John Romita. *The Amazing Spider-Man Vol. 5*. New York: Marvel Comics, 2012.

Lee, Stan, et al. *Marvel Firsts: The 1960s*. New York: Marvel Comics, 2011.

Lee, Stan, et al. *The Amazing Spider-Man: Through the Decades*. New York: Marvel Comics, 2011.

Lobel, Michael. *Image Duplicator: Roy Lichtenstein and the Emergence of Pop Art*. New Haven: Yale University Press, 2002.

Loeb, Jeph (writer), and Tim Sale (artist). *Batman: The Long Halloween*. New York: DC Comics, 1998.

Lupoff, Dick, and Don Thompson, ed. *All in Color for a Dime*. New Rochelle: Arlington House, 1970.

Mallory, Michael. *X-Men: The Characters and Their Universe*. New York: Universe, 2008.

Marston, William Moulton, and H.G. Peter. *Wonder Woman: Archives Volume I*. New York: DC Comics, 1998.

McCarthy, David. *Pop Art*. New York: Harry N. Abrams, Inc. 2007.

McCloud, Scott. *Understanding Comics: The Invisible Art*. New York: Harper Perennial, 1993.

McFarlane, Todd, et al. *Spawn: Book 6*. Berkeley, CA: Image Comics, 1998.

McLaughlin, Jeff, ed. *Stan Lee Conversations*. Jackson: University Press of Mississippi, 2007

Millar, Mark. *Civil War: A Marvel Comics Event*. New York: Marvel Comics, 2007.

Miller, Frank. *Batman: The Dark Knight Returns*. New York: DC Comics, 1997.

Miller, Frank, and David Mazzucchelli. *Batman: Year One*. New York: DC Comics, 1997.

Miller, Frank, and Lynn Varley. Batman: *The Dark Knight Strikes Again*. New York: DC Comics, 2001.

Moore, Alan, and Dave Gibbons. *Watchmen*. New York: DC Comics, 1986.

Moore, Don, and Alex Raymond. *Flash Gordon: On the Planet Mongo*. London: Titan Books, 2012.

Morales, Kyle, and Robert Baker. *Captain America: Truth*. New York: Marvel Comics, 2003.

Morrison, Grant, and Dave McKean. *Batman: Arkham Asylum*. New York: DC Comics, 2005.

Morrison, Grant. *Supergods: What Masked Vigilantes, Miraculous Mutants, and a Sun God from Smallville Can Teach Us About Being Human*. New York: Spiegel & Grau, Random House, Inc., 2011

Nyberg, Amy Kiste. *Seal of Approval: The History of the Comics Code*. Jackson: University Press of Mississippi, 1998.

O'Neil, Dennis (Introduction). *Batman in the Seventies*. New York: DC Comics, 1999.

O'Neil, Dennis, and Neal Adams. *Green Lantern/Green Arrow*. New York: DC Comics, 2012.

O'Neil, Denny, and Mike Sekowsky. Diana Prince: *Wonder Woman*. New York: DC Comics, 2008.

Overstreet, Robert M. (Foreword). *America's 1st Patriotic Comic Book Hero: The Shield*. Mamaroneck, NY: Archie Comics, 2002.

Raphael, Jordan, and Tom Spurgeon. *Stan Lee and the Rise and Fall of the American Comic Book*. Chicago: Chicago Review Press, 2003.

Reeve, Christopher (Introduction). *Superman in the Seventies*. New York: DC Comics, 2000.

Reidelbach, Maria. *Completely MAD: A History of the Comic Book and Magazine*. Boston: Little Brown & Co, 1991.

Ro, Ronin. *Tales to Astonish: Jack Kirby, Stan Lee, and the American Comic Book Revolution*. New York: Bloomsbury Press, 2004.

Robbins, Trina. *The Great Women Superheroes*. Northampton, MA: Kitchen Sink Press, 1996.

Robinson, Jerry. *Ambassador of Comics*. New York: Harry N. Abrams, Inc., 2010.

Robison, Frank, and Lawrence Davidson. *Pulp Culture*. Portland, OR: Collectors Press, 1998.

Rondeau, James, and Sheena Wagstaff. *Roy Lichtenstein: A Retrospective*. Chicago: Art Institute of Chicago, 2012.

Ross, Alex. *Mythology*. New York: Pantheon Books, 2005.

Sadowski, Greg, ed. *Comic Book Covers of the Golden Age 1933-1945*. Seattle: Fantagraphics Books, 2011.

Sadowski, Greg, ed. *Supermen! The First Wave of Comic Book Heroes 1936-1941*. Seattle: Fantagraphics Books, 2009.

Sattler, Ian. *DC Universe: Secret Origins*. New York: DC Comics, 2012.

Savage, William W., Jr. *Comic Books and America, 1945-1954*. Norman: University of Oklahoma Press, 1990.

Schumer, Arlen. *The Silver Age of Comic Book Art*. Portland, Oregon: Collectors Press, 2003.

Siegel, Jerry, et al. *Superman in the Forties*. New York: DC Comics, 2005.

Simon, Joe. *Joe Simon: My Life in Comics*. London: Titan Books, 2011.

Simon, Joe, and Jack Kirby. *Captain America Volume I*. New York: Marvel Comics, 2005.

Simon, Joe, and Jack Kirby. *Captain America Volume 2*. New York: Marvel Comics, 2008.

Simon, Joe, with Jim Simon. *The Comic Book Makers*. Lebanon, NJ: Vanguard Productions, 2003

Simonson, Louise. *DC Comic Covergirls*. New York: Universe, 2007.

Spurlock, J. David, and Angel De La Calle. *Steranko Arte Noir*. Coral Gables, FL: Vanguard Productions, 2002.

Starlin, Jim, et al. *Infinity Gauntlet*. New York: Marvel Comics, 2011.

Steranko, Jim. *The Steranko History of the Comics, Parts One and Two*. Pennsylvania: Mediascene, 1970.

Straczynski, J. Michael. *The Amazing Spider-Man Volume 2: Revelations*. New York: Marvel Comics, 2002.

Theakston, Greg. *Jack Magic: The Life and Art of Jack Kirby*. Pure Imagination, 2011.

Thomas, John Rhett. *Marvel 70th Anniversary Collection*. New York: Marvel Publishing, 2009.

Thomas, John Rhett. *The Marvel Art of Joe Quesada*. New York: Marvel Comics, 2010.

Thomas, Roy and Stan Lee. *Stan Lee's Amazing Marvel Universe*. New York: Sterling, 2006.

Tye, Larry. *Superman: The High-Flying History of America's Most Enduring Hero*. New York: Random House, 2012.

Uslan, Michael (Introduction). *Batman in the Fifties*. New York: DC Comics, 2002.

Uslan, Michael. *The Mighty Crusaders: Origins of a Superman-Team*. Mamaroneck, NY: Archie Comics, 2003.

Waid, Mark (Introduction). *Superman in the Fifties*. New York: DC Comics, 2002.

Waid, Mark, et al. *Daredevil Vol. I*. New York: Marvel Comics, 2012.

Walker, Brian. *The Comics: A Complete Collection*. New York: Abrams ComicArts, 2011.

West, Adam. *Back to the Batcave*. New York: Berkley Books, 1994 .

Wolfman, Marv, and George Perez. *Crisis on Infinite Earths*. New York: DC Comics, 2000.

Wolfman, Marv, et al. *Marvel Firsts: The 1970s Vol. 3*. New York: Marvel Comics, 2012.

Wolfman, Marv, et al. *The Tomb of Dracula*. New York: Marvel Comics, 2010.

Wright, Bradford W. *Comic Book Nation: The Transformation of Youth Culture in America*. Baltimore: Johns Hopkins University Press, 2001.

IMAGE AND FILM CREDITS

Image Credits

Mike Allred: 277 bottom

Archie Comics: 41 top right, 67, 205 bottom

Argosy Communications: 12-13, 22 bottom

Arts Rights Services NY: 147 bottom, 148 top

Associated Press: 99 right, 170 bottom left, 224 center, 263 left, 290 bottom

Bettmann/Corbis: 24, 119, 127 bottom

Elliot Brown: 223 top

Leslie Cabarga: 59 bottom

Condé Nast: 4, 18, 21 all, 23 all

Corbis: 38

DC Comics: 9 (watermark), 26, 27, 30, 31 all, 32 all, 33 all, 34 all, 35 top, 35 bottom, 38 inset, 40 left and bottom, 42 top right, 43 all, 44 all, 45 all, 46 all, 47 all, 48 all, 49 all, 50 right, 51 top left and bottom right, 52, 54 all, 55 all, 56 , 57 left, 57 top right, 58 all, 61, 62 top left, bottom second from left, bottom right, 63 top right and bottom right, 64 bottom second from left, 65 top left and bottom right, 68 all, 69 all, 79 bottom, 80, 81 top right and left, 82, 83, 84 all, 86, 87 left, top, 88 all, 89 all, 91 all, 93 all, 94 all, 95, 101 right, 102 all, 103, 105 all, 106 all, 107 right, 109 all, 120, 121 all, 122, 123 all, 124 all, 125, 126 all, 127 top, 148 bottom left, 159 top right, 161 bottom left, 164 top right, bottom left and right, 173 top left and right, 174, 177, 178 left, 179 right, 186 bottom left, 186 top right, 205 left, 206 bottom, 208, 211 all, 218 inset and watermark, 219, 224 right, 225 all, 226 bottom, 228, 229 right, 230 all, 231 all, 232, 233 all, 235 top, middle, 243 page and inset, 244 right, 245 all, 246 all, 247, 248, 250 right, 258 right, 259 left, 265, 269, 271, 272 all, 275 right, 275 top left, 277 left, 293

DC Comics/Denis Kitchen Publishing Co.: 104 all

DC Comics/Liberty Media for Women: 272 bottom

DC Comics/Warner Bros Interactive Entertainment: 289 all

Denis Kitchen Publishing Co.: 63 bottom second from left

The Donners' Company: 193

Shel Dorf: 223 middle

EC Comics: 97 left

Jackie Estrada: 223 bottom right, 229 left

Everett Collection: 8-9, 53

Ramona Fradon: 64 bottom left

Getty Images: 8, 10, 11, 111, 194 bottom right

King Features: 14, 15 bottom, 16, 17

The Kirby Family Trust: 84 right

Kobal/Picture Desk: 192 inset, 194 bottom left, 196 left, 197 top

Erik Larsen: 238

Stan Lee: 65 bottom left, 112

Estate of Roy Lichtenstein: 147 top, 148 bottom right

Rob Liefeld: 237 top

Magazine Management Company: 161 top

Marvel Comics: 2, 36-37, 41 top left, 51 top right, 64 bottom right, 64 top, 65 bottom left, 70 right, 70 middle, 71 left, 72 all, 73 all, 74-75, 76-77, 78, 79 top, 85 bottom, 92, 97 top left, 99 left, 105 bottom right, 106 bottom right, 107 left, 114-115, 116-117, 128, 129 all, 130, 132 all, 133, 134 all, 135 all, 136, 137 all, 138 all, 139, 140 all, 141 all, 142, 143 all, 144 all, 145 all, 146 all, 150 all, 151 all, 152 all, 153 all, 154, 155, 156 right, 157, 166 bottom left, 168, 169 right, 170 bottom right, 170 top, 171, 173 bottom, 175 all, 178 right, 179, 180-181, left, 182, 183 all, 184 all, 185 all, 186 top left, 187, 188, 189 all, 190 all, 191 all, 198, 199 all, 200 all, 201 all, 202 left, 203, 204, 206 top, 207, 210, 213 all, 214, 215, 220-221, 223 bottom left, 236-237, 249, 250 left, 251,

252, 253 all, 254 all, 255 top, 256, 257 all, 258 left, 259 right, 260-261, 262, 263 right, 264 all, 266, 267, 268, 270, 273 all, 274, 275 bottom left, 276, 278 all, 279 left, 284, 285, 286 all, 286 all, 287 top, 288, 291 left

Museum of the City of New York: 10

NBC Universal, Inc./Getty Images: 166 top left

NY Daily News/Getty Images: 57 bottom right

Photofest: 6, 20 right, 59 top, 60 All, 82 inset, 108, 111 inset, 161 bottom right, 162 right, 164 top left, 192, 194 top, 196 right, 202 right, 212, 216, 222, 224 bottom left, 226 top, 227 right, 227 left, 242 bottom, 244 left, 255 bottom, 280, 281, 282 all, 287 bottom

Parallax Comic Books: 167 top left

Random House: 42 bottom

Ron Galella, Ltd./Getty Images: 235 bottom

Flip Schulke/Corbis: 169 left

Shehab in Egypt: 290 top

Martin Sheridan (*Classic Comics and Their Creators*): 29 right

Signet Books: 166 right

Joe Simon: 64 bottom right

David Spurlock: 62 bottom right

Jim Steranko: 209

Time & Life Pictures/Getty Images: 81 bottom right, 162 left, 163

Todd McFarlane Productions and Affiliate Companies: 234 (Anna Pena), 237 bottom, 240, 241 all, 242 top, 242 middle

Tribune Media Services: 25 bottom right

TV Guide Magazine: 158

United Plankton Pictures, Inc.: 167 bottom right

Warner Bros: 197 bottom

MARVEL and all other Marvel characters: ™ & © 2013 Marvel Entertainment, LLC and its subsidiaries. All Rights Reserved.

All DC Comics characters and images are ™ & © DC Comics.

TV Guide Magazine cover courtesy of TV Guide Magazine, LLC © 1966

Despite a diligent search, the authors regret that accurate source information could not be obtained for some images.

Special thanks: Nicholas Bryla, Ed Catto, Jay S. DeNatale, Eric Gimlin, Mark Halegua, "Hepcat," Matthew Thompson, Stephan West, Neil Mechem, Jeff Tingle, Derek Hoffman (The Donners' Company), Steve Asbell (20th Century Fox), Glenn Goggins, Monty Zutz, Jeff Haddad, Karl Janot, Bruce Mason, Philip Spector, Manny "Lunch" Maris, and Mark Doyle.

Film Credits

Superheroes: A Never-Ending Battle

A production of Ghost Light Films, Inc.

Directed by Michael Kantor

Written by Michael Kantor and Laurence Maslon

Produced by Michael Kantor, Sally Rosenthal

Edited by Kris Liem, Pamela Arnold

Design and Animation by Alexander Cardia

Music Direction by Christopher Rife

Associate Producer: Joe Skinner

ACKNOWLEDGMENTS

The Book

Back in the early 1970s, when I was devouring comic books and yet still ravenous for comic book history, I would have been absolutely overwhelmed and enraptured by a three-hour documentary series about superheroes, as well as a full-color illustrated history of their exploits, both on the page and behind the scenes. So, it is with the retroactive gratitude of my childhood that I extend my deepest thanks to my partner-in-crimefighting, Michael Kantor, for helming the massive *Superheroes* project in such a superduper way and for trusting me to scale buildings with him from the start; no Batrope could have a better anchor than his calm authority. Thanks also the terrific editors and staff at Ghost Light Films.

My gratitude also extends back through the decades to Steve Rotterdam and David Silberger, devoted squad members, convention-goers, and friends. Alas, one of our quartet, Michael Perillo, was not able to make it to the finish line with us, but his faith and judgment as a comrade will never be forgotten. Thanks also to Steve's partner at Bonfire Agency, Ed Catto, for being an unremitting champion of this project.

On the publishing side, our agent, Steve Ross at Abrams Agency, was unflagging in his support; always in our corner and always ready to go to bat, as it were, for us. At Crown Archetype, Mauro di Preta embraced the potential of this project, Amanda Patten thoughtfully guided the text and direction of the book, and Jessica Wallin was consistently helpful in the many moving parts of the process. Roger Gorman lent his customary taste and good humor to the design, and Karyn Gerhard came to the rescue with the strength of Wonder Woman, the tenacity of the She-Hulk, the . . . well, she knows the rest.

Lee Aaron Rosen has been a constant pillar of support, both in his enthusiasm and in his incredible work on getting the best possible illustrations for the book; thanks also to Ivan Cohen, Stephanie Bencin, Mark Waid, Jim Steranko, Brian Overton, Todd McFarlane, and J. David Spurlock for their assistance with the visuals herein. Special thanks to Karen Shatzkin & Debra Mayer for their counsel.

Invaluable support came from Fritz Brun, Jordan Gelber, Corey Stoll, Derek Wilson, Jose Maria Aguila (and the Graduate Acting Program of NYU), Jeanine Schaefer, Patrick Perkins, Martin Kurth, Matthew Stanley, the staffs of the Cooper Union Library and the Bean on First Avenue. Devoted gratitude to my father, Gerald Maslon, my stepmother, Anne Wallach Maslon, and my brother Henry for their advice, and to my mother for never once threatening to throw out my comic book collection.

Finally, infinite love for the patience and support of my own Bat-family: my wife Genevieve, for tolerating the profusion of comic books that have subsumed our Batcave, and my son, Miles, for absorbing and reflecting my own enthusiasm for the heroes of my youth, and for making Dr. Fate his favorite hero: thanks, old chum.

—Laurence Maslon

The Series

Every kid has a favorite superhero who shows up in the nick of time to save the day. *The Superheroes* documentary film series, and by extension this book, was rescued on a daily basis by a great number of superheroic people and institutions.

The series owes a monstrous debt of gratitude to Gerard "The Originator" Jones, who first suggested that I read his extraordinary book, *Men of Tomorrow*, with an eye toward creating a documentary series. Shortly thereafter, the courageous panelists and administrators of the National Endowment for the Arts and The National Endowment for the Humanities offered us much-needed grant funding. Our NEH panelists, including "Monster" Mike Frisch, served as our Justice League; David "Reassurer" Davis at Oregon Public Broadcaster cast his calm over the stormiest seas; and Larry "1040" Brown made sure all our documents were safely guarded and organized.

When Donald "The Greenlighter" Thoms and Beth "The Believer" Hoppe of PBS gave the project the thumbs-up, James "Deliverer" Guerra used his telepathic legal prowess to make the series a reality. Margie "Internationalizer" Smilow brought mighty global funding to our efforts, and Jan "The Convincer" Gura made sure that everyone in Gotham City and Metropolis knew the value of this cultural history. Beth and David Shaw, Buddy Teich, Karen Pritzker and the Seedlings Foundation, Ira and Paula Resnick, Jay Baker, and Patty Baker were the "Power Boosters" who helped to ensure the success of our enterprise.

Within our fortress of solitude at Ghost Light Films, a squadron of warriors including Eager Emily Chapman, Expert Erika Frankel, Mighty Joe Skinner, and Mustang Sally Rosenthal toiled in support of Editrix Kris Liem and Pam "The Pulverizer" Arnold. Karen "The Invoker" Shatzkin and Debra "Scrupulousity" Mayer kept everyone honest, Michelle "Keeper of Books" Jacoby was always on the lookout for villainous invoices, and Ivan "Power Daddy" Cohen brought superheroes to our office between feedings and nap times. Audrey Jensen, David Newman, and Bex Rosenblatt were the awesome "Interminables," John Vella was our "Super Super," and out in the field the tenacious teams led by Mead "Gamma Level" Hunt and Allan "Monster Green Screen" Palmer filmed all our speedy talking heads.

On the home front, Wonder Woman Kathy Landau, Rosie the Hahvahdator, the mighty Sachmio and the delicious Tootsie Girl were my Avengers. Though I was nicknamed the "Documentarian," on this epic adventure I merely served as sidekick to a superhuman force embodied in the mortal shell of Laurence "Truthman" Maslon. Larry's love of the comic book superhero informs every frame of our film and every word in this book.

—Michael Kantor

INDEX

Italics indicate illustrations.

ONLY $1.00

Enter the WONDERFUL WORLD OF AMAZING LIVE
SEA-MONKEYS.
Own a BOWLFULL OF HAPPINESS — Instant PETS!

Just ADD WATER — that's ALL! In ONE SECOND your AMAZING Sea-Monkeys actually COME TO LIFE! Yes, they hatch instantly, right before your eyes. Now, simply grow and enjoy the most adorable pets ever to bring smiles, laughter and fun into your home.

SO EAGER TO PLEASE, THEY CAN EVEN BE TRAINED

Always clowning around, these frolicsome pets swim, stunt and play games with each other. Because they are so full of tricks, you'll never tire of watching them. And raising Sea-Monkeys is so easy, even a six-year old can do so without help. Sea-Monkeys eat very little, and they keep their water so clean, they require only a minimum care although they LOVE attention. Anyone who enjoys the company of pets will ADORE Sea-Monkeys. Best of all, we even show you how to teach them to obey your commands like a pack of friendly trained seals. What a way to surprise your guests.

FREE!
1 — A ONE-YEAR SUPPLY of GROWTH FOOD
2 — LIVING PLASMA
3 — WATER PURIFIER
4 — A magnificent, fully illustrated manual of Sea-Monkey care raising, training and breeding.
5 — Our famous GROWTH GUARANTEE IN WRITING.

Transcience Corporation Dept. 38F
200 Fifth Avenue New York, New York 10010

IT SOUNDS GREAT! Please send my Sea-Monkey kit(s) and my FREE supplies and guarantee. I must be 100% satisfied or you will refund my money. I enclose $1.00 plus 30¢ shipping charges for each kit.

Send _____ kit(s) ☐ Cash ☐ Check ☐ Money Order
(No C.O.D.'s Please) Total amount enclosed $ _____
Name ....
Address ....
City .... State .... Zip ....
☐ SUPER-RUSH ORDERS (50¢ extra)

AMAZING
X-RAY VISION
INSTANTLY!

A HILARIOUS LAUGHINGLY FUNNY ILLUSION!

$1.

...e through **fingers** - through skin - see yolk of egg ... see lead in pencil. Many, many, amazing, astounding, ...usory X-Ray views yours to see ALWAYS- -when YOU ...ar Slimline X-Ray Specs. Bring them to parties, for ...I FUN - - GUARANTEED - - They give you a 3 ...mensional X-Ray Vision - - the Instant you put them ... When you look at your friends you'll "see" the ...st (blushingly funny) amazing things! Full Instruc-...ns Of How To Enjoy Them To The Fullest! Last For ...ars - - Harmless - - Requires No Electricity - - Or ...tteries - - Comes Complete - - Permanently Focused -...othing Else to Buy - - Send $1. plus 25¢ for postage ...d handling - - Money Back If Not 100% Satisfied.

SLIMLINE COMPANY
Dept. 248   P.O. Box 90
5 Market Street   Newark, New Jersey

SLIMLINE COMPANY, Dept. 248
285 Market Street, Newark, New Jersey

I enclose $1 plus 25¢ for postage and handling
(Total ($1.25) send me the Slimline X-RAY SPECS.
My money will be refunded in full if I am not 100% Satisfied.

Send me. . . . . sets at $1.25 per set.
Total enclosed is $. . . . .
My money will be refunded in full if I am not 100% Satisfied.

Name . . . .
Address . . . .
City & State . . . .

HIGH SCHOOL

741.5
MAS

Maslon, Laurence,
author.

Superheroes!

DIPLOMA

THROUGH HOME STUDY
PREPARE FOR GED OR COLLEGE ENTRANCE
United Schools and Services
401 N. Interurban   Richardson, Texas 75080

**Texts Purchased By: Departments of
Education • Private Schools • Colleges**

Mail This Coupon NOW   For Persons 16 or Over

UNITED SCHOOLS AND SERVICES   Dept. M106
Box 1088, Richardson, Texas 75080

Please Rush FREE Information about High School.

Name _____ NOV 15 2013 ___ Age ___
Address _____ Apt. ___
City / _____
State / Zip _____

No Salesman Will Call

JACK POT BANK

2⁹⁵

Fun Bank For
The Family

It works like a ...
pull the ... the real ... because ... so good for ... 95 plus
HONOR HOUSE Dept 77JF55   LYNBROOK, NY 11563

Take In Up To
$750.00 Per Week!

CUSTOMIZE
AUTO / VAN INTERIORS

UPHOLSTER ANY VEHICLE - START WITH YOUR OWN
CAR OR VAN! A business so big growing so fast you
need an appointment in most auto trim shops! Send
for FREE MASTER PLAN, ILLUSTRATED BOOKLET on
learning auto upholstery and interior
customizing in your spare hours. No
experience needed. VET APPROVED
AUTO UPHOLSTERY INSTITUTE, Dept ATB
1205 W Barkley, Orange, CA 92668

FREE BOOKLET!

U.S. COIN-FILLED BARR

We bought ... barrel from old time collector ... and can't spare mont ... cataloging and pricing ... thousands coins ... s ... out they go ... mixed '... bag' style. You'll find old-type nickels, din ... early Linco

COINS FROM 1880's
to WORLD WAR 2

Sample Sack $
of 25 only ...
Bag of 100—$18

5

& Indians, etc. 32 page catalog
cluded with order, otherwise 50¢.

CENTRE COIN CO., BOX 1
Dept. MA Sherman Oaks, Calif. 91413

COMICS!
Complete Marvel, DC, & Golden A
Send 25¢ for Giant Catalog & Buying
If you're selling only — send 10¢ for separate Buying
DAVID BELMONT 55 Greenaway Rd. Roch. NY 1

Send 75¢ for your Giant Catalog to GRAND BOOK, INC., DEPT. M, 659 GRAND ST., BROOKLYN, N.Y. 11211.
We have more than a ½ million comics from all publishers in stock. To sell comics, send a list of
titles, numbers, and conditions with a self addressed stamped return envelope for a reply.

Design...
Make - Repair JEWELRY
Train at home   in Spare Time

Make real money plus all the jewelry you can wear. Send for
FREE "Career Kit". No obligation. No salesman will call.

NAME _____ AGE ___
ADDRESS _____
CITY _____ STATE ___ ZIP ___

Careers by Home Study • JEWELRY DESIGN CENTER,
4401 Birch, Dept. RJ086, Newport Beach, CA 92663

---

25 LIVE SEAHORSES 2.98

Kit has two mated pairs of freshly caught sea horses,
including ONE PREGNANT MALE, who will give birth
to as many as 25 babies. Marine salt, food and instruc-
tions included plus a live marine snail. ABOVE KIT
WITH CUSTOM AQUARIUM, SEA HORSE TREE,
SEASHELLS, CORAL AND SILICA SAND $5.98
LARGE DELUXE AQUARIUM AND ALL ABOVE
ACCESSORIES WITH 5 MATED PAIRS OF SEA HORSES
(2 PREGNANT MALES—OVER 50 SEA HORSES) $10.95

All kits sent ppd. Via Air Mail Live Delivery Guaranteed.
Sea Horses, Dep MC 976, Box 342096, Coral Gables, FL 33134

POEMS

See how your words can be turned into a song,
recorded, phonograph records made. Send your
poems or songs for prompt FREE information.
CROWN MUSIC CO.
1270 Broadway Studio 11 New York 1

KARATE

JUDO - SAVATE
JIU-JITSU

THE GREATEST SELF-
DEFENSE SYSTEM
KNOWN TO MAN!

FREE!

Learn-At-Home-Course
reveals hundreds of deadly self-
defense secrets which will enable you to protect yourself from
any attacker! Easy to learn!
FREE COLORFUL BROCHURE
Send 25¢ to cover postage and handling costs.

Send to: UNIVERSAL, Dept. P
BOX-39303 DETROIT, MICHIGAN 48239

Send now for our latest selling list of Marvel and DC Comics
RICHARD ALF, BOX 20622-MC, SAN DIEGO, CA 92120
or visit our store, 1733 University Av., S.D. (714) 291-1515

FAST TRACK TO A COOL JOB...
as a MOTORCYCLE
MECHANIC...

Train at home

GOOD PAY! ACTION CAREER! No need
to quit school or job. Experts
teach you step by step. Prepare
for good job or your own repair
shop. Special Cycle Tools and Test
Instruments Included. Send name,
address, age for FREE "Career Facts."

NORTH AMERICAN SCHOOL OF MOTORCYCLE REPAIR
4500 Campus Dr., Dept. RJ-086, Newport Beach, Calif. 92663

COMIC BOOKS!
Thousands of old comic books for sale: TIME
MARVELS, D.C., FAWCETT, CHARLTON, etc.
Send $1 for big new list! Comics also BOL
BUYING LIST, $1. PROMPT SERVICE!
F. L. BUZA, 5206 FULLER, SCHOFIELD, WIS.

FREE COMIC CATALO
Discount Comics
Box 164-F, Santee, CA 9207

WOW   WOW
FREE

GENUINE, RARE
Original Hot Rod Decals
— Thousands of Uses —

Actual decals for a '32 Deuce Coupe!
You'll receive free over 100 different.
Use on your bike, model car, van,
plane, or on glass, painted surfaces,
metal, plastic, etc. Hurry, yours free
while supplies last! Just send 50¢ in
coin for postage and handling along
with your name and address to:
DECAL OFFER
Box 3085 Centerline, Mich. 48015

Man-Eating SHARKS TEETH
That are over 50 Million years old

Enjoy the thrill of carrying a pair
of genuine prehistoric fossilized
man-eating shark's teeth. Over 50
million years old and in perfect
condition. Some believe they bring
good luck. Excellent for science
projects, collections, souvenirs.
Guaranteed
to be genuine man-eating sharks teeth and over
50 million years old. Teeth from 2 species with
historical story, only $1.95. 5 teeth for $3.95.
Send cash, check or money order and we send
postpaid. Rush order, supply limited.

SHARKS TEETH, Dept. 176
P.O. Box 4471, Miami, Florida 33014

Giant Comic List . . . Send 50 cents
Huge Magazine List . . . Send $1.00
World's largest pulp mag. list $1.00
Our 9 specialized lists. $3.00
(E.C., Timley, Fawcett, Disney, etc.)
All above, only $4.50
All above, plus 5 old comics
    only $5.00